Karen Donovan

v. Goliath

Karen Donovan is a former editor and reporter at the *National Law Journal*. Her work has appeared in *Wired*, *BusinessWeek*, and *The New York Times*. Formerly a practicing attorney, she has also been a Knight-Bagehot Fellow in Economics and Business Journalism at Columbia University's Graduate School of Journalism. She lives in Brooklyn, New York.

v. Goliath

v. *Goliath*

THE TRIALS OF DAVID BOIES

Karen Donovan

VINTAGE BOOKS
A DIVISION OF RANDOM HOUSE, INC.
NEW YORK

FIRST VINTAGE BOOKS EDITION, JANUARY 2007

Copyright © 2005 by Karen Donovan

The Library of Congress has cataloged the Pantheon edition as follows:
Donovan, Karen, [date]
v. Goliath : the trials of David Boies / Karen Donovan.
p.   cm.
Includes index.
1. Trials—United States.   2. Boies, David.   I. Title.
KF220.D48 2005
340'.091—dc22
[B]   2004053447

Vintage ISBN: 978-0-375-72655-2

Author photograph © Sigrid Estrada
Book design by Soonyoung Kwon

www.vintagebooks.com

For my parents

The practice of law has always appealed to the spectacular in life.

—Clarence Darrow

Contents

Prologue

The idea for this book began during my time as a reporter at the *National Law Journal,* which sent me to cover what was then known as the Trial of the Century—the trial of the government's antitrust charges against the Microsoft Corporation, the greatest success story of modern American capitalism. There, I got to know David Boies well and came to see him as the quintessential trial lawyer for a generation that does not exalt legends or firebrands, but embraces the charismatic and conversational. Boies possessed those qualities in abundance, without apparent effort, at every turn at the Microsoft trial, both in the courtroom and before the television cameras. Everyone was drawn to him. He was the Un-Lawyer, an appealing figure at a time when the legal profession consistently runs a close second to journalism as the most reviled sector of our society.

I first met Boies in 1997, and by then I had been a legal journalist for ten years. The occasion was his departure from Cravath, Swaine & Moore, one of the most prestigious law firms in the country, longtime counsel to such blue-chip companies as Time Warner Inc., CBS, and Big Blue itself, IBM. Boies had decided—it seemed on a dime—to leave Cravath after thirty years of practicing there because his client, George Steinbrenner, the irascible owner of the New York Yankees, had a lawsuit that Cravath found in conflict with Time Warner's interests. The Yankees suit had put the name of David Boies back on the front pages of newspapers. He was the greatest trial lawyer of his generation, everyone said, everyone knew, but he hadn't seen much action lately.

I arrived at Boies's corner office on the forty-eighth floor of the Cravath tower and was greeted by Linda Carlsen, his secretary of many years. (She left the firm to join Boies's fledgling practice six months later.) Linda, I would come to learn, has no time to waste on small talk and is extremely protective of Boies. And like Boies, famous for his uniform of cheap blue suits from Sears, she didn't look like she belonged at a tony white-shoe law firm. That day, she was wearing a crocheted vest that reminded me of the ones I used to wear as a kid in the 1970s. Boies was running late. She sent me into his office, where Evan Chesler, a Cravath partner who was sent by the firm's brass to watch sentinel over the interview, was waiting.

What struck me first was the wall. A huge wall was covered with pictures of Boies with his children—he has six in all, from three marriages—dressed in jeans, driving a Jeep, looking boyish. There were several bottles of red wine on the windowsill, and a box of Cheez-Its on his desk. These were part of the Boies lore: he loves expensive wines and carb snacks.

In a moment, Boies bounced in with a big "Hi!" and took off his blue jacket. He wasn't cautious. He was completely indifferent to the fact that someone was monitoring our conversation. When I asked him whether his jacket came from Sears, he laughed. No, he said, he bought it at Macy's while on the road. He was charming and casual, and he took all of my questions without a flinch. (Later, the editors noted something stunning about the transcript of the Q&A: Boies spoke in perfect paragraphs.)

As luck would have it—and Boies is blessed with an embarrassment of riches when it comes to luck—the government hired him to help craft its case against Microsoft shortly after Boies opened his own law firm. During the Microsoft trial, I broached the idea of a book with Boies, trailing him as he built his practice while litigating the government's case. The book evolved into much more than that, for Boies, who has a knack for knowing exactly what to do when he arrives on center stage, has in a short time established himself as the lawyer to hire for the most important cases in any legal arena.

Boies allowed me to travel with him to report this book, giving me access to the lawyers at his firm, even allowing me to attend its annual "retreats," and to his family life. He cooperated with me, but this was to be my book, and he has his. During the course of my reporting, Boies signed a contract with Talk/Miramax Books to pen his own memoirs. In October 2004, as this book was going to press, Boies published his memoirs, *Courting Justice: From NY Yankees v. Major League Baseball to Bush v. Gore 1997–2000*. In its pages, I saw many of the talents that were on display during my travels with him—his ability to simplify the complex, and the clocklike precision with which he ticks off the several most important principles at play as a lawyer prepares for a trial or the negotiation of a big settlement. The victories are noble, but there is one valiant loss as Boies presents his casebook; the view from my perspective was often far more complicated and controversial.

PART I

Youth, Cravath, and a
New Firm Called Boies & Schiller

ONE

"Once it's over, it's over."

10:25 a.m., December 10, 2000, Westchester County Airport

"Well, I have twenty-four hours," David Boies said, finally settling into his seat in the Learjet that was idling on the tarmac.

The statement begged for a question, and I obliged. "To do what?" I asked from the seat across from him. "To learn the constitutional law," Boies replied matter-of-factly, his steely blue eyes staring ahead.

On this morning, Day 33 of the postelection fight between Vice President Al Gore and George W. Bush, we were headed toward Washington, D.C., for the final court appointment that would decide who won the presidency in 2000. Each of the previous thirty-two days had presented a roller-coaster ride, swinging wildly often by the hour, for the opponents, and for the nation, which woke up the morning of November 7 to discover that the presidential race was too close to call. The state of Florida hung in the balance, with Gore pressing for recounts of the ballots and Bush opposing him at every turn.

As Boies boarded the plane, I mentioned that I had caught part of his ABC appearance on *This Week with Sam Donaldson and Cokie Roberts* before leaving my Brooklyn apartment. He told me that was one of four Sunday shows he had taped, beginning at six-thirty that morning.

Boies pulled out the draft of a legal brief that was due at four o'clock that afternoon at the U.S. Supreme Court; the case was scheduled for argument at eleven a.m. the next day. In all likelihood, the argument would be Gore's last chance to gain the White House.

By ten-thirty, we were airborne. As Boies began to mark up the faxed pages in his hand, I noted the time that the draft brief had arrived at his home in Armonk—9:59 a.m. He must have grabbed it just before leaving, along with the box of sourdough pretzels and blue duffel bag (which contained another box of pretzels in addition to a cheap blue suit, a blue striped shirt, and a blue knit tie).

On this ride, I wouldn't have the opportunity to ask many questions. But I didn't need much explanation. It was clear that Boies would be arguing for Gore the next morning instead of Laurence Tribe, the Harvard Law School professor considered one of the country's most renowned constitutional scholars. Over the course of the Bush/Gore fight, Tribe had argued twice against the Republican claim that the Florida recounts violated the Constitution, on one of those occasions at the U.S. Supreme Court. Nominally, Boies was the Gore team's man in the Florida courts. But of course he was much more than that—he was their hero.

So it seemed clear to me that Boies would take center stage for the final act, even though he had told reporters gathered for a hastily convened Saturday-afternoon press conference in Tallahassee the day before that he was "going home" to Armonk. The U.S. Supreme Court, in a bitter 5–4 split between the justices, had just voted to halt manual recounts across Florida and to hear Bush's case on Monday. Boies's work in the case was ostensibly finished.

On the plane ride home to Armonk that Saturday, I had asked Boies whether he wanted to argue the case. "You always want to do an interesting case like that," he said, but added: "I would frankly rather not do it, given Larry's prior involvement. Larry will do a fine job." If asked, he said, he would advise the Gore team to stick with Tribe. "There's no reason to replace him, and if they were to ask me to do it, that's what I'd tell them."

Still, as we parted company at the Westchester airport in the chilly December wind, he told me to call him later that night—and later that night I got a brief message to meet him the next morning back at the Westchester private-plane terminal.

Now, as we taxied down the runway, I took a stab at asking why we were headed to D.C. after all. Did he suggest that Tribe do the argument? "Yeah, I did suggest that," he said. And what did they say in response? "That they wanted me to do it," he said. Did they say anything else? "Nope."

The conversation was not untypical. Boies was loquacious before the TV cameras, holding forth like Abe Lincoln, point by point, in perfect paragraphs, on his reasons why it was important to "count every vote." But he was often taciturn in private. He would offer me only a word or two when I became the least bit inquisitive. Boies was concentrating on the brief, and on the twenty-four hours he had to learn the constitutional law.

I had been this route before with Boies. In late August 2000, the federal appeals court in San Francisco set a schedule for oral arguments that would determine the fate of his client, Napster, the Internet company under assault by the entire record industry for allowing users to copy music for free online. The date for the Napster argument was October 2, 2000. "Oh, I have another argument scheduled for that day!" Boies enthused to me over his cell phone one day in late August, as he was headed by car to meet his law school friend Jimmy Miller for a weekend of gambling in Atlantic City.

Boies seemed thrilled by the Houdini-like prospect of flying from one federal court to another, all in a day. As the date approached, the Pasadena court alleviated some of the difficulty (and the drama?) by providing a video hookup at the San Francisco courthouse where the Napster case would be argued. That allowed Boies to address the judges in Pasadena, then take the elevator upstairs to appear before more cameras at the eleven a.m. arguments in the Napster case, an event that would be broadcast live over the Internet and the cable channels. I ventured to ask him why he had not tried to reschedule the Pasadena case. He told me he didn't like to ask courts to do that sort of thing.

The weekend prior to the arguments, Boies prepared for both cases in a windowless conference room at Fenwick & West, the law firm that Napster had first hired for its defense and that had played second fiddle since the company hired Boies. Sometime after seven o'clock that Sunday night, Laurence Pulgram, one of Fenwick's lead lawyers on the case, poked his head in to ask how things were going and say good night. "What's your first line?" Pulgram asked, more than a little hesitant. Boies, who doesn't rehearse or "moot" his arguments even with his closest partners, put Pulgram off. "Oh, I don't know," he demurred. "But there's still time," he said with a little laugh.

Boies thrives on tackling insuperable odds, making it look easy, traveling light. He keeps counsel with no one, as far as I can tell. Associates and partners working with him pull cases, draft memos, and answer his questions, but they rarely have a clue about what arguments he will present to a court until they, with the rest of us, watch him at the podium for the main event.

"You don't understand," his assistant Patrick Dennis once told me, when I was trying to track Boies down as he shuttled from D.C. to New York and back in a single day. "David Boies is Superman."

Now, as the taxi made its way from Reagan National Airport to the Watergate Hotel on December 10, about a day before the presidential election would be argued, I asked Boies about the logistics of the task ahead of him in the case of *Bush v. Gore*.

In every case, it is Boies's custom to read all the relevant legal decisions. Every single one. And usually, there is a point in any argument when he will reference a passage in a case and offer the court the exact location on the given page where they might find it. How many cases will you have to read? "Well, I don't know. I don't know," he said. He was yawning again. He was clearly tired.

Boies disappeared into the Watergate, to locate the suite occupied by the man he had ousted, Laurence Tribe, and begin preparing for the arguments. Warren Christopher, the former secretary of state tapped by the Gore campaign for the postelection fight, announced on CNN that Gore had made the call to replace Tribe with Boies because the issues before the Supreme Court were so factually entwined with what happened before the Florida courts. No one—not Christopher, nor the reporters, who called in for a backgrounder with the Gore team later that day— paused to question the choice. When the news went out that Boies would argue Gore's final Supreme Court appeal, no one stopped to consider the obvious—Gore's last-minute choice of Boies over Tribe. It was a monumentally bad idea. That Boies jumped at the chance to do it was beyond hubris.

5:30 p.m., December 13, 2000, Albany International Airport

The U.S. Supreme Court issued the decision in Bush's favor at ten p.m. on December 12. By then, Boies was already back at home in Armonk. The next morning, after one last conference call with Gore and his legal team— the call in which they made the final decision to concede the election to Bush—Boies headed for Albany on the Learjet, back to business as usual.

At midday, Boies had arrived in Albany in relative anonymity, but by the dinner hour, when we headed home, camera crews and reporters from the local network affiliates had the Albany airport staked out, waiting to get reaction from Boies about the fateful Supreme Court decision. Boies greeted them, saying that the highest court in the land had spoken, that we all must accept that, whether we agreed with the decision or not. How were the vice president's spirits? Boies didn't want to comment on that. The vice president would address the American people that night, he said. And, yes, Boies believed that the American people would come together to support President Bush. We had all learned a great civics lesson, he said; votes are important, every vote should count. "I think this country is strong enough. People will rise above this. I believe that people will unite," he said.

Who could argue with any of that? The man had perfect pitch.

It was time to go, time to get into the plane. Boies stopped to sign an autograph on a businessman's card. The man said his wife was a fan. "You did a really great job, though, you really did. To go to the U.S. Supreme Court with no notes. Five justices against you." Thanking the man and signing the card, Boies said, "You don't have time to look at notes, even if you take them up."

On the way back to Westchester, I asked about Boies's own spirits. "Oh, my spirits are fine." He shrugged. "You'd always rather win than lose. But once it's over, it's over."

Midafternoon, Sunday, December 17, 2000, Grand Floridian Resort, Orlando, Florida

Disney World was the Learjet's final destination in the week that began with the presidency on the line. This trip had been on Boies's calendar for some time. Each year, in mid-December, Boies slated a weekend for the annual retreat of his law firm, Boies, Schiller & Flexner. The retreat was probably the only tradition in the firm's short history. Mainly, it was a chance for the lawyers' families to mingle, throw a party, and brag about the firm's successes in the last year.

When Boies opened his law firm in September 1997, along with his first partner, Jonathan Schiller, there were ten lawyers. By December 2000, there were one hundred, mostly centered in New York and D.C., but also scattered in tiny offices elsewhere, like Hanover, New Hampshire, and Hollywood, Florida. The lawyers barely knew each other.

"David never gives a speech" at the retreats, Patrick Dennis said. This didn't surprise me. There was no need. The firm revolved around him. When Boies opened the floor to questions from associates on Sunday morning, the retreat's last day, there were only a few brave souls who took him up on the offer.

Throughout the weekend, tourists in the Grand Floridian's lobby often recognized Boies as he passed, and stopped to say what a wonderful job he had done for Gore. Schiller toasted Boies at the firm's dinner dance, saying, "I want to thank David Boies for everything he has done for this firm and for our country." But throughout the weekend, Boies barely spoke of Gore. It was part of his grace.

By the pool at the Grand Floridian, Boies lounged on a chaise, weirdly soaking up the sun in his trademark blue polyester suit, masked behind his sunglasses. A Learjet was waiting to take Boies and his law partner, Robert Silver, back to Armonk that night. The plane would fly through a storm that had canceled or rerouted the commercial flights for that day. The private flight would allow Boies to make a crucial appearance the next day before the judge overseeing Boies's class action against Sotheby's and Christie's auction houses, a case where Boies stood to make a $26 million fee. Boies had brought to the swimming pool a transcript of Linda Wachner's deposition in Calvin Klein's case against her. At the pool, Boies held the transcript but didn't look at it. Instead, he closed his eyes and lounged on the chaise, chatting with Silver, who had long been part of Boies's inner circle.

Boies enjoyed sparring with Silver, a genuine child prodigy who had a master's degree from Yale by the age of nineteen. Boies used Silver as a sounding board, quizzing him with Socratic questions before important legal arguments. By the swimming pool, the two men wondered aloud how much the firm would grow by the next year. A number came up—140 lawyers—and Boies suggested that he would take "either side" of the bet. Silver didn't take a side; he wanted to know whether that was what Boies wanted. If Boies wanted the firm to grow that much, Silver said he would do whatever he could to achieve that. But then the subject was dropped, and Silver lost his chance at the case of wine that was on the table in the bet.

The conversation moved on to the subject of law firm management, a topic in which Boies seemed decidedly disinterested. The firm of Boies, Schiller & Flexner seemed to have no management, aside from the three men who were its name partners. Silver suggested an executive committee to review the delicate topic of compensation. Boies casually asked Silver to prove how it would work. Boies had already maddened Silver by telling him that he, the founder of the firm, wouldn't sit on such a committee alongside Silver.

Silver's voice was rising. He tended to get emotional. There was something childlike about Silver, a teddy bear of a man with a penchant for expensive shirts and Marlboro Reds. His worries were always on the surface; in that, he was the perfect foil to Boies. Silver wondered which block of partners would vote with him on the executive committee that he was envisioning. Boies was, as usual, blasé about the subject of law firm management.

"You never have to fight with anyone!" Silver finally fumed to Boies. "Tell that to Justice Scalia!" Boies laughed in response, for a moment opening one eye as he lounged on the chaise. But Silver had a point: there was no fighting with David Boies. He always got what he wanted.

TWO

A Ticket for Speeding

David Boies was always tempting fate—and making it look easy when he beat the odds.

When he was going to high school in southern California, he says, he wasn't sure whether he would go to college. He was having too much fun, playing bridge for money and working on a construction crew for $3.50 to $4 an hour. That was a lot of money in 1959. Boies sometimes cut class to work with the crew.

Early in his senior year, he took the National Merit Scholarship exam, given to the school's junior and senior classes, a total of about six hundred students. There were three finalists: one of them was the girl with the highest grades, and the two others were Boies and Ronald Davies. Both Boies's and Davies's fathers worked for the Fullerton school system. "There was a nontrivial rumor that our fathers must have gotten us copies of the tests because it was so counterintuitive that the two of us did so well," Boies told me. He obviously took some satisfaction in the story.

David Boies was born on March 11, 1941, in Sycamore, Illinois, farmland about sixty miles northwest of Chicago. Boies's parents were born there, and their parents had been born there too. The Boies family had been in the rural Illinois farming community since the 1880s. Boies's great-grandfather, a true Republican, was editor of the Sycamore newspaper. Life there hasn't changed much since then. Nearby Marengo's population in 2001 was about 6,300 people. In 1998, when the Boies clan last gathered for a family reunion, the same popcorn stand patronized by their parents was still open for business.

Boies grew up in Marengo, a farming community of about 2,500 people, where his father, David, taught high school history. His mother, Barbara, also a schoolteacher, stayed at home to take care of the children. She would eventually have five: after David, she had another son, Stephen, in 1943, a daughter Barbara was born in 1947, a son Richard in 1951, and a daughter Catherine in 1960.

Money was tight. Their father always had a second job, working evenings and weekends, to supplement his teaching income. He worked at Sears, Roebuck, sold real estate, and drove a Helms truck. When the elder Boies got home, he would offer his children a treat—their pick of desserts from the truck's panels. While the family was still living in Illinois, the elder Boies took his sons David and Stephen to the occasional Cubs game in Chicago. Even then, David was a fan of the New York Yankees—the Yankees were always champions. When David and Stephen went to the movies, their parents would give them a quarter each. The movie cost nine cents, a drink was five cents; candy was another five cents. The boys brought the remaining six cents back home to their parents. When Barbara Boies gave her sons a piece of fruit, one of them would cut the fruit in half, and the other would choose which half he'd take.

Most children learn the value of competition through the neighborhood stickball game or at school. Boies learned it at home. On Saturday nights, the Boieses would have bridge parties. David would often play his mother's hand when she got up to serve the food. The family played all sorts of other games—hearts, Michigan rummy, Chinese checkers, Monopoly, Clue, and charades. "We played these games to win," says Stephen Boies, who has a PhD in psychology from the University of Oregon and is a research analyst at IBM. "But you know, it was more the fun of winning rather than the shame of losing."

David Boies remembers it another way: "I have a pretty good card sense," he says, a glint in his eye. "My siblings are smarter than I am, but I am a better card player."

Richard Boies, who is ten years younger than David, has a very different memory. His older brothers thrived on the tremendous competitiveness of these games, and young Rick resented it. He came to despise the game of bridge. "They would pull us into that mentality that we would just have to win. And I was always on the losing end," says Richard, who realized early on that there was no way he could beat his much older brothers at games.

The extreme competitiveness worked its way into their games of charades, in which the men played against the women. The game was scored by counting the seconds it took each side to guess the mimed subject. The side with the least time on the clock at the end of the game won. Neither side trusted the other to keep score. Each had its own clock, and had to agree on the time expended. But nobody, in any of these games, lost sight of the fact that someone was going to win, and someone was going to lose.

According to Richard's wry memories, the Boies family could turn just about any activity into a competition. Sunday dinner was a ritual. A favorite Sunday dinner was Beef Olives—with no olives—a dish made of slices of roast beef rolled up with salt, pepper, and breadcrumbs and held together by toothpicks, covered with gravy, and cooked slowly in the oven. At the end of the meal, the family would go around the table and count the number of toothpicks left on each plate to see who had eaten the most. Young Rick also saw the slicing of the fruit—one sibling with the knife and the other with the choice—as a kind of competition. There was an ongoing exchange between his brothers over the contents of their fruit cocktail. One liked cherries, the other grapes, and they would trade. A cherry was worth two grapes.

In the summer after Boies finished seventh grade, he recalls that his father piled his wife and four children into the family station wagon and headed for California. He had spent some time at a San Diego military base during World War II and thought it was wonderful. The elder Boies did not have a teaching job lined up in California when the family drove across the country that June. But it was the land of opportunity in the 1950s. "It was an adventure," Boies recalls of the trip. "How much of an adventure, I don't think any of us knew."

Boies Senior landed a job teaching high school history in Lynwood, and the family moved to Compton. The family moved again, to suburban Fullerton in Orange County, at a time when the place actually had orange groves. It was so near Anaheim, and Disneyland, that they could hear the fireworks go off at nine o'clock every summer night.

Boies Junior made his first appearance in court as a teenager—to contest a speeding ticket. "He decided to fight it; he was *determined* to fight it," recalls Boies's high school girlfriend, Caryl Elwell, who became his wife while she was a junior at Fullerton Union High School. Did Boies win? "I don't think so; I think they fined him anyway," she told me.

Boies says he challenged the speeding ticket based on California law, which at that time provided that the speed limit was what was "reasonable and proper under the circumstances," regardless of the speed posted on the freeway. Boies's version is that when the cops pulled him over, he was driving five or ten miles over the limit. They also issued a ticket for another infraction, maybe a broken taillight. He went to court and won the challenge to the speeding ticket, but got fined for the other infraction—his first split decision.

But Boies's high school buddies, who were on hand for that first courtroom appearance, have a different memory. Gordon Christopherson accompanied Boies to the San Clemente courtroom where a justice of the peace heard the case. "Did he tell you about his first loss?" Christopherson snorted when I phoned him. Christopherson remembers that Boies had been clocked driving 105 miles an hour in a 55-mile-an-hour zone. The old geezer who presided over the case was not amused by hearing Boies's "reasonable and proper" challenge, Christopherson says.

Two other high school friends surprised Boies by cutting classes that day and appearing at the courthouse. Just before Boies's case, the justice of the peace heard another. The defendant was apparently a golfing buddy of the judge, and the two joked about golf. "David was prepared in his grand debating style to offer a defense," Robert Carter recalls, but the judge was rude to Boies. "He was nasty," Carter says. It seemed unfair to Carter, especially after the judge's joking from the bench with his golf buddy. The episode triggered a rare moment for Boies's friends: they watched him lose control. "Dave got emotionally upset, a little bit," says Carter. "And the judge just told him to compose himself in his court."

The judge told Boies to get out of his courtroom or he would hold him in contempt, and imposed a $100 fine, a big sum in the late 1950s. Christopherson says he dragged Boies out of the courtroom, as he was vowing an appeal. On the drive home, Boies complained about the horrible way he was being treated by the American judicial system. Never mind that he had, in fact, been speeding. "That detail just seemed to be lost on him," Christopherson said, laughing.

When the Boieses moved to Fullerton, David, as the eldest child, got his own room, a den off the living room with sliding glass doors. One day, young Rick ventured into his older brother's room. The ice cream truck was in the neighborhood, Rick had no change, and he knew that his brother kept a stash of change in one of his desk drawers. Rick sneaked in and took some dimes for himself and his friends.

Hours later, his older brother called him into the bedroom. Young Rick was panic-stricken. David said he didn't mind that Rick had taken the change, he just wanted to know if he had done it. Young Rick thought his older brother must be psychic. But Boies always left the drawers of his desk slightly open, a detail lost on Rick when he closed the drawer after he took the dimes. "That was one of my most vivid and early memories of David," Richard recalls. He felt as though his big brother trusted him as a partner, letting him in on his secret drawer trick.

All of the Boies children recall their childhood as an idyllic time. To an uncanny degree, they have the same memories, tell the same stories. They are fond of saying that their parents, despite their modest means, did an exceptional job of raising "five only children," five children who all thought they were special in their own way. But David Boies was clearly more special than the rest. Richard has a vivid memory of the first time the Boies family had a color television in the house. His father rented one because David was appearing in a televised high school debate.

Boies seemed to fall casually into debating. He began at the Franklin S. Whaley Junior High School in Compton, California, with the topic "What America means to me, or something like that," he remembers. The people running the tournament came into history class to recruit students. Boies signed up. "I didn't know anything about it," Boies told me.

When Boies got to the tournament, all the other contestants were memorizing written speeches. Boies hadn't written a word. "I had sort of thought about the topic but I hadn't written anything. I didn't know that you wrote out speeches."

The speech was supposed to last five minutes. Boies spoke for only four, which cost him a lot of points. "But even so I took second place," he said. "They took off a third of my points or something."

Debating came naturally to Boies. At Fullerton Union High School, he joined the debating team and took "speech and debate" as an elective. His high school debate teacher and coach, Duane Johnson, was Boies's greatest booster.

The Fullerton debating team picked a subject each year. One year the topic was foreign aid. Another it was whether the United States should adopt the British educational system. Robert Ball, Boies's debating partner at Fullerton, remembers that Boies would read every magazine article on a topic. Stephen remembers his brother working extremely hard on the debating team. David started out with file folders that contained eight-by-five-inch index cards with dense notes printed on them. The eight-by-five cards gradually shrank to four-by-six cards, with fewer notes. Then to three-by-five cards with even fewer.

Boies took the rebuttals. Ball always spoke first, and Boies responded to the other side's arguments. Ball says, "He was good at hearing the other arguments. He would remember them all and then go through it point by point." In the debating tournaments, Boies's favorite event was impromptu speaking. The debater would be handed a slip of paper with the topic on it. He was allowed thirty to ninety seconds to prepare his argument—essentially the amount of time it took to walk to the podium.

Ball says he and Boies won almost all the time. For the debates they lost, Ball blames himself. "I cost us a few debates because I had a hot temper. I lost my cool," he says. "Boies never did anything like that."

William M. Bush, another member of the debate team, who still lives in Fullerton, was featured in an article in the *Orange County Register* in December 2000, at the height of Boies mania. "While the rest of us were shuffling our note cards trying to decide how to formulate a response, Dave would stand there without any note cards and start debating," Bush told the *Register*. "He was as polished then as he is now. In fact, when I see him on TV, it's déjà vu—particularly with the mannerisms and the voice."

Boies and Ball traveled together for tournaments. They once spent the week at the University of Redlands for a series of speeches and debates. When Boies ran for class president in his junior year at Fullerton, Ball was his campaign manager. (Boies lost.)

Boies's high school guidance counselor, Luis Armijo, told me that the young Boies could not resist pranks—especially with his poker-playing buddies. One of the poker buddies, Robert Gosney, who became an assistant district attorney in Los Angeles, says the games were a standing Saturday event. They usually lasted all night, and the winner bought breakfast. "It was a tough game," says Gosney, who started playing poker for baseball cards at age eleven. Gosney remembers Boies as a "very conservative" player who rarely ever bluffed, while Gosney and Gordon Christopherson, another regular, bluffed every other hand.

Gosney used to watch Boies read, moving his finger quickly down the middle of each page. He thought Boies must have taken a speed-reading course, and had no idea that it was just the opposite. Boies did not learn to read until the end of third grade. The first books he read—perks from his paper route—were comics like *Spider-Man* and *Captain Marvel*. "The great thing is that comic books have few words, short sentences, and the pictures help you figure out what the words mean," Boies told me. In rural Illinois in the 1940s, no one had heard of dyslexia, and his parents were not wringing their hands about their son's inability to read. "Nobody was that upset about it. It was no big deal. Some people read slower than others," he said.

Once, Gosney was in deep trouble with one of his courses. The grade depended on a term paper, and Gosney hadn't done it. Boies offered to write the paper overnight for $50. The next day, he presented Gosney with the term paper, complete with footnotes and a cover page. There had been no time to do real research. "He made it all up," Gosney says. "He was a machine."

Christopherson regaled me with what he called the poker gang's "reigning thing." They set off cherry bombs made with explosives smuggled across the border from Mexico. Carter, who didn't play poker with the gang, joined in for some of these antics. "We were kids in high school, and in those days cherry bombs were not really illegal," Carter says. One night, the local police finally stopped them. The boys denied throwing cherry bombs, but when the police asked them to open the car door, a cherry bomb fell to the pavement. The cops didn't charge them, or even call their parents, but just told the boys to stop. "We lied to the police, but they gave us a break anyway," Carter says.

When Boies was a senior, he won a scholarship to Antioch College in Los Angeles. His classmates remember it as the most prestigious scholarship offered to the class of 1959. Boies had also been accepted at Stanford. But he was playing cards for money—he and his mother had been playing bridge in tournaments and winning. He was also playing in the American Contract Bridge League, whose members would pay for the chance to play someone they knew to be good and thought could be beaten in order to rack up masterpoints for the honor titles awarded by the league. Boies thought it was too good to be true—he was getting *paid* for playing cards. Even so, Boies says he would probably still have gone to Antioch, had he not gotten married.

Caryl Elwell met Boies when she was barely fifteen; they were on the debate team together. To Pauline Rickett, who won a bunch of debating competitions with her partner, Bill Bush, Elwell seemed like a "debate groupie," and "was just gaga about David." Gosney recalls that Caryl followed Boies around. Caryl and David got married in Mexico on April 20, 1959. The first time they tried to cross the border, Elwell says, police in Tijuana stopped them. They got through a different border crossing at Tacali. Their parents thought they had gone to a high school dance. They returned to their separate homes, and didn't tell their parents of the marriage until that summer. Caryl said her parents were "shocked" when she told them. Caryl came from one of the more well-to-do families in Fullerton.

Boies recalls the events more casually. He and Caryl ran off and got married, he said. He had just turned eighteen; she was sixteen. Her parents reacted "about how you would expect," he said, with a laugh. Caryl gave birth to David III the next March. Boies was still playing cards and working construction when his wife discovered she was pregnant. "And this really free spirit, fun-loving, irresponsible girl, within sixty days, turns into a responsible human being. Begins to say things like, 'You really ought to get a serious job, don't you think you ought to go back to school, what are you going to do with the rest of your life?' " Boies laughs.

Boies took a job as a bookkeeper at the United California Bank. At eighteen, he was too young to be a teller. The American Bankers Association had an annual speaking contest, which Boies entered and won. Shortly after that, he rang up the University of Redlands and talked with the debating coach. The college offered him a full scholarship with room and board.

It wasn't long before Boies realized that Redlands was "really easy." In his first semester, Boies took courses for the standard sixteen units of credit.

Since each unit represented an hour of classroom time, that amounted to just sixteen hours a week. He was accustomed to working forty-five.

Redlands was a tiny place, then part of the American Baptist Convention. Bible classes were mandatory. There were only 350 or so students in Boies's class. In history and world civilization that first semester, there were weekly in-class quizzes. The other freshmen weren't paying much attention to them, but Boies quickly figured out two things: it was easy to impress professors with knowledge of a single obscure fact, and cumulatively, these weekly quizzes were worth as much toward the final grade as a midterm.

Through a friend at Redlands, Boies took a job teaching journalism at the Patton State Hospital for the criminally insane, overseeing an inmate-run weekly newspaper. He was also president of the Young Republicans Club. (These were California Republicans; Boies's successor was Sam Brown, who went on to campaign for George McGovern and head the Peace Corps under President Jimmy Carter.) Boies stayed home afternoons to take care of David III, while Caryl worked the three-p.m.-to-midnight shift at the phone company. He still remembers the cost of student housing: $28 a month, with a $2 fee for the refrigerator. Caryl would often come home from work to find Boies and his friends in a game of Risk or cards.

At the end of his first semester at Redlands—when most other students were settling into four years of study—Boies decided to take the Law School Admissions Test. He took the LSAT because he saw a sign posted in one of the hallways of Redlands. "Do you want to be a lawyer? Take the LSAT," it said. At the time, some law schools would admit students who had completed only three years of college—a prospect that appealed to him. And Boies seemed to think that he could complete the three years of college credit in record time. One of the schools offering admission with just three years of college credit was Northwestern University School of Law, which recruited him.

When did Boies decide he wanted to become a lawyer? It depends on whom you ask. Boies says he thought about the law during high school. The *Perry Mason* television series and books inspired him. Caryl, however, who always wanted to be a lawyer, says Boies didn't think about it until she suggested it. Boies's father swore that his son wanted to be an antitrust lawyer from the time that he was a wee tot. Boies says he wasn't sure whether he wanted to be a history teacher or a lawyer. After that first semester, he loaded up on courses and blew through three years' worth of credits in just two years at Redlands.

"I was probably the only person at Redlands who ever stayed there two calendar years and was Phi Beta Kappa," Boies says. Redlands did not have a Phi Beta Kappa chapter until 1977, but Boies was elected as an alumni member to the Redlands chapter in April 1993, though Redlands refused to issue him a degree, and Boies received his college diploma from Northwestern. Redlands awarded him an honorary doctor of laws in 2000.

Boies went to Northwestern at the urging of one of its alumni, Harold Shapiro, a Chicago lawyer who also taught at Northwestern and recruited promising students. On a trip to California, Shapiro stopped at Redlands. The law advisor there happened to be one of Shapiro's former professors. Of Boies, he told Shapiro: "I want you to meet this kid, he's really extraordinary." Shapiro recalls that Boies more than measured up to the advanced billing. Shapiro told me, "He was just smarter than hell!" Shapiro returned to Northwestern and pressed the administration to admit Boies and award him the prestigious Hardy Scholarship. (Boies had scored a 683 out of 800 points on the LSAT, a high score, but hardly perfect.)

In August 1962, Boies and his wife packed their Fiat and made the forty-hour trek to Chicago with David Boies III and their daughter, Caryl, who was six months old.

At Northwestern, Boies almost immediately stood out as the most brilliant student in the class. But Boies still needed to earn a living, and worked as a night auditor at a local hotel while his fellow students were studying court decisions. He claims to have read the decisions while in class, moments before being called upon to answer the professor's questions. Law school wasn't hard, Boies recalls. A coterie of students followed Boies when he talked with his professors after class.

Before the school year was out, Caryl got into the Fiat and left with young David III and Caryl. When I asked Boies about the end of his first marriage, he told me simply that "it didn't work out." Caryl headed for Carson City, Nevada, where she got a divorce. "It just wasn't working for me," she told me. When she and I met for breakfast one morning at the Waldorf-Astoria Hotel in Manhattan—she had come to New York for Boies's sixtieth-birthday party at the Rainbow Room, atop Rockefeller Center—she described that year in Chicago as "very traumatic."

In 1963, when Caryl Boies obtained her divorce, "no-fault" divorce was unheard of, even in the divorce mecca of Nevada, which allowed a person to file for divorce after establishing a residency there of only six weeks. Caryl's grounds for divorce were "extreme cruelty, primarily mental in nature." Boies consented to default in the matter, and so he did not appear at the brief hearing in Carson City in September 1963. At the hearing, in order to establish the grounds for divorce, Caryl answered several questions posed by her attorney: "Is it a correct statement to state that during your married life the defendant has had an extremely violent temper, that during many times he would disappear from the home for days at a time, not telling you where he was or when he was coming home; is that correct?" Caryl answered yes. "Is it also correct that he was likely to show up all the way from eleven o'clock at night to four o'clock in the morning and become extremely angry if you didn't have a hot cooked meal prepared for him?" Caryl answered yes again. In the hearing, she said this conduct had gone on for all of their married life.

In the property settlement, Caryl kept the Fiat and took $900 of the couple's $1,400 in savings. Boies kept one hundred shares in a mutual fund worth about $1,000. He assumed $2,500 in debt because it was agreed that the majority of those debts were his, and kept the furnishings in the Chicago apartment that Caryl had left. The agreement specified that Caryl "will not seek and husband will not be liable for the payment to wife of any alimony or child support whatsoever." But it did allow that Caryl could go to court to ask for a "reasonable sum" for the support of the children if she found herself unable to provide for them. The couple agreed that Boies would have the children for the summers and that they would rotate visitation at holidays.

At our breakfast, Caryl described Boies as superlative. "Of course, he was superior, pretty much how he is now—bright, focused, very competitive." She ran through a list of Boies's high school and college friends for me. She mentioned in passing a woman named Joan Harvey, a fellow student at Redlands, to whom Boies—who was then about twenty-two years old—was engaged for a time. She did not say what was clear—he left people quite easily, it seemed.

In Boies's second year at Northwestern, he dazzled professors in the classroom, and pursued one of their wives outside it. In the first semester, Boies had been a student in Jeffrey Fillman's class in corporation law. Boies got an 87. At Northwestern, a grade of 85 or above represented "work of the highest distinction." The next semester, Boies went after Fillman's wife. When I tracked Fillman down at his home in Charlestown, Massachusetts, where he is retired, he had remarried and been widowed. His first words about David Boies were: "The brightest student I ever had; the smartest student I ever had in corporations law." Judith Daynard, Fillman's wife, entered law school on a lark. She had been a Spanish teacher, but when the couple moved from the East Coast to Chicago, she took a job as a secretary to the youngest associate at the law firm of Baker & McKenzie, and quickly discovered that the practice of law "was not rocket science." On a Thursday, she decided she might go to law school, and she took the LSAT the next Saturday. "And that's about the amount of effort that I was willing to put into it," she said. Like Boies, she was fiercely smart; achievements came easily to her.

Northwestern relaxed its policies to allow Daynard to attend the law school, even though she was the spouse of a professor. Judith told me that she "didn't love" law school, but that she did well. In her second year, she became associate editor of the *Law Review* and Boies became editor in chief. Until then, Judith barely knew David. "Nobody knew him well; he was married the first year, and God knows, they had no money. He came after me, what can I tell you?" Judith told me matter-of-factly, all those years later. "This was your basic affair." For their first date, David took Judith to a duplicate bridge tournament at a hotel on the north side of Chicago. Judith was unfamiliar with the rules. Five or six times, fellow players screamed "Director!" to call attention to her infractions. "I barely got out alive," Judith recalled. All the while, Boies was concentrating on winning. "But he is a very tense player. He is actually working out what the cards are that people have in their hands."

How did Fillman find out about the affair? "Well, I'm not stupid," he said. "The *Law Review* office was I think right on top of my office." Fillman paused a moment and then added: "I don't know how I got aware of it, but it became obvious. Everybody knew Kennedy was screwing around. Everybody knew about Bill Clinton."

Fillman went off to stew and failed to get his grades in on time, and the dean became alarmed, according to a Northwestern colleague, Victor Rosenblum. The faculty decided to rid itself of any trace of the sordid incident by asking Boies, Daynard, and Fillman to go. "All three were encouraged to complete their careers elsewhere," Rosenblum told me.

Judith Boies says Fillman was "deeply offended" when he discovered the affair, and made it a matter of school policy. She says, "The school, only reluctantly, decided it was their moral duty to get rid of us. [Boies] was, after all, the seducer." In fact, she suggested, the affair might have remained just that, if Fillman had not pressed the issue. "Were it not for good old Jeff, David and I might not have gotten married."

Fillman disagrees with Judith's account. He says neither he nor the other young professors on the faculty who were his friends had that kind of power. He maintains that Judith chose to head back to New York, where she grew up, and that Boies chose to follow her. When Fillman read Ken Auletta's book on the Microsoft trial, *World War 3.0*, which quoted a close friend of Boies's saying that he "got kicked out of Northwestern Law School," Fillman was amused. "I thought that might be part of a David Boies myth." Fillman stayed on for a year at Northwestern, then got a job at Cardozo Law School in New York City.

Judith recalls the episode as "lurid and unpleasant," and chalks it up to a time in her life "when danger and excitement seemed interesting to me." Boies, meanwhile, has no such regrets. When I asked Boies about the affair, he made the most of my struggle to bring up this awkward topic: "See, you didn't ask me what students I was close with in my second year," he remarked with a devilish grin. "Well, there was Judith Daynard. She's the one who comes to mind."

Boies allows that "Judy and I were probably not as discreet as we might have been." As their relationship became increasingly obvious on the tight-knit campus, the dean called Boies into his office. "And he was perfectly friendly, but he said that, obviously, this is complicated for the school and embarrassing to Judy's husband to be confronted with the two of us over the academic year. He asked whether there was any other school that I would like to go to." Boies told him that he thought Yale was a fine school and would like to go there.

I asked Boies whether this period was an uncomfortable time. He shrugged it off. "No," he responded. "I was twenty-four years old. How uncomfortable can you be at twenty-four?"

Yale Law School professor Louis Pollak was sitting in his faculty office in the summer of 1964 when he got a most unusual call from John Kaplan of Northwestern. Kaplan told Pollak that he had a "very, very remarkable student" who had completed two years of law school and wished to transfer in his third year. "I didn't know much, but I knew that that didn't fit our ordinary rule," Pollak told me. Then Pollak heard the reason, which nearly knocked him out of his chair. "The student in question was having an affair with the wife of a faculty member, and it was the feeling of the faculty that it would be a good thing if the student went elsewhere," Pollak recalled.

Boies's application to Yale Law School was dated June 22, 1964. His "personal statement," the essay that law schools require of applicants, was at once brilliant and eerily detached. The application asked, "Why do you wish to study law?" Boies's response must have taken the the the Yale academics' breath away. His three-paragraph answer began with canny simplicity. "First, I wish to be a lawyer, and the study of law is of course an essential means to this end."

Boies explained that he believed the law to be the "perfect vocation" because of the challenges it posed. His articulation of those challenges showed unusual sophistication. "More than ever rules of law delimit and direct the actions of individuals, businesses, even nations," he wrote. "Without passing a value judgment on this expansion of the rule of law, it seems sufficient to note that such expansion can not help but be filled with opportunities for personal and public service." He cited some examples: "Modern law affirmatively delimits, to name but a few examples, what an author can publish, what an architect may build, what treatments a physician may prescribe, what partners a lover may pursue, what customers a merchant must serve, what prices a seller may not offer, as well as who owns Blackacre."

Boies ended his essay by explaining that it was "essential" that every citizen in a democracy "make themselves aware of their existing rights and duties, but also of such alternative rights and duties by which action they may establish or to which their inaction may condemn them." As Boies wrote this statement, the civil rights movement was brewing. It was as muted a call to action as one could imagine. As I read the document now, it seems to reflect an astonishing understanding of where the law was heading.

"This was a person of unusual originality," says Guido Calabresi, a member of the admissions committee at the time and now a federal appeals court judge. He was struck by "the fact that a kid from really no particular background just could have so much spark."

Yale agreed to accept him. But, of course, it wasn't that simple. The school did not accept credit for more than one year of work at another law school and required that the last two years of law school be completed at Yale. "He was stunningly good; he had fantastic grades and was obviously excellent. The problem was that we have this rule, and so he really wasn't eligible for transferring," Calabresi told me. But Calabresi came up with a way around the rule. The school would admit Boies into the four-year graduate program in economics, a subject in which he had expressed an interest. The Yale brass quickly accepted this solution.

The records show that Professor Kaplan repeatedly pressed Yale about Boies's application. On July 15, barely three weeks after Boies submitted his application, Kaplan called Jack Tate, associate dean for admissions at Yale. By then, Boies's transfer to Yale was all but done. A day later, Tate wrote a memo to the Yale file about Kaplan's call and the acceptance of Boies's application. Unable to reach Kaplan by telephone with the official news, Tate sent him a telegram on July 16.

There is nothing in Boies's file at Yale referring to the delicate matter of the affair, the catalyst for the transfer. Tate's note to the file states simply: "After some discussion we agreed that we could treat this case as unusual and allow the boy to enter as a third year student in the Four Year Program." The Northwestern professors who recommended him to Yale vaguely hinted at the soap opera. Calling Boies "a gem," Professor Rosenblum noted that "personal considerations have been allowed to intrude upon his career." Boies viewed transferring to Yale "as a means of enhancing his professional goals while minimizing—if not eliminating—his personal problem." Kaplan's letter of recommendation was positively fawning. Boies was first in a class of 129 at Northwestern, and Kaplan pointed out that he was first "by a huge margin." Boies so towered over his Northwestern classmates that, in Kaplan's opinion, he had not fully applied himself. "Finally, the energy possessed by Mr. Boies is truly remarkable. Despite the demands upon his time and effort he has had ample energy left over for numerous extra curricular affairs."

Boies graduated from Yale two years later, second in his class. At Yale, very few fellow students knew him well. "David arrived at Yale Law School with an air of romantic mystery about him; there were rumors of some romantic engagement that led to this transfer," said Walter Dellinger, who was also one of the top three Yale graduates in 1966. To all but the few faculty members who handled his application, the details of the romantic liaison remained a secret. Professor Pollak could not resist telling his wife about it, and she was so intrigued that she asked him to point Boies out at a Yale function. She was surprised to find that he looked like a solid midwesterner, "foot-shuffling and corn-fed, hardly a smooth-talking lothario." Judith never went up to New Haven to visit him, and he came to Manhattan rather than stay at Yale on the weekends. A Barnard graduate, class of '59, Judith decided to finish her legal education at Columbia. She graduated in 1965.

Boies was a distant character at Yale, even to those who worked with him as lawyers after graduation. "The more I think about David, the less I know about David," says Dellinger, upon whose recommendation Boies was hired to represent Gore after the 2000 election. In class, Dellinger recalls, Boies spoke only when called upon. "The first time I heard him speak in class, my ears perked up," Dellinger said. "I thought, this is a formidable intellect." Tony Clappes, who would later work closely with Boies on the IBM cases, was at Yale with him but didn't know him well. Clappes does have a clear memory of the antitrust course that he took with Professor Robert Bork, the scholar whose 1978 book, *The Antitrust Paradox,* turned traditional thinking about the subject on its head. "Boies was frankly second only to Bork in that class in terms of moving along the discussions of antitrust law."

"I played a lot of bridge," Boies says of his Yale days. He discovered a permanent bridge game in one of the undergraduate dorm rooms, where students had given up their residences and moved in with friends in service of the card game. "You could go there almost any time of the day or night and there was almost always somebody there, and you could sit around until a seat opened up," Boies told me. How long did it take him to find the rolling bridge game? "Not long," he said.

David and Judith got married in March 1966, at the home of his parents in Fullerton.

Most of the big law firms courted Boies. One offer came from the Los Angeles powerhouse Gibson, Dunn & Crutcher, where Boies had spent the summer of 1965 as a summer associate. But Judith did not want to move away from New York, so he settled on Cravath, Swaine & Moore, the most prestigious firm on Wall Street, and the firm that set the standard for modern corporate practice. It was the obvious choice: Cravath was simply the best.

THREE

The Cravath System

David Boies officially began his career as a lawyer in May 1966, on the Monday after his last law school exam. The common practice of law students, then and now, is to spend the summer after graduation from law school immersed in studying for the bar exam, which is given toward the end of each summer, and then begin work in the fall. But Boies began at Cravath as soon as he could. Why? "Because I was going to make money, and they weren't going to pay me until I started." Boies didn't need to study; he needed the money.

Boies's starting annual salary at Cravath of $9,000 equaled his father's gross income from teaching and odd jobs during Boies's last year at Yale, according to Boies's applications for financial aid. Money was always an issue for Boies. He had attended the University of Redlands on a full-tuition scholarship. At Northwestern, he received a $2,000 scholarship in his first year, and $2,075 for the second year, which more than covered the $1,200 tuition. He worked as a summer associate for $350 a month after his first year, and for $450 a month after his second year. He also worked twenty to thirty hours a week as a research associate in a law firm during his first three semesters at Northwestern. The law firm paid him a rate of $2 an hour, a detail he still remembers.

Yale had also given Boies financial aid, with a $500 grant and a $2,000 loan. In his final year, he got a $1,000 grant and a $1,500 loan to cover the $725 annual tuition and his expenses. Those applications said he received no funds for his education from his parents, who were supporting three young children still at home. Times were so tough that Boies got an emergency cash advance of $200 toward the loan that Yale offered him in January 1965.

By the time I began reporting on him in the late 1990s, it was part of the lore surrounding David Boies that he had flirted with academia early in his career, that he planned to become a professor rather than seek a partnership at Cravath. Boies told me, "I thought I was going to teach and thought it would be good to get a couple of years experience in New York because I was going to teach in New York generally."

But that is not how those who knew Boies as a budding young lawyer remember him. Judith Boies never believed it. When I saw her at her law office at Fifth Avenue and Fifty-seventh Street, Judith Boies (who still uses the Boies name professionally, though she has remarried) paused when I asked her about her former husband's professorial aspirations. Like David Boies, Judith is fiercely intelligent. Unlike him, she is reflective and forthright.

So was her former husband really serious about becoming a professor? "The thing that makes me wonder about it is that David always knew he was going to make a lot of money," Judith says. Even as a young Cravath associate, when Boies had no money at all, he would incur large debts, buying her jewelry that he couldn't afford at Tiffany's—on her charge account, no less! "He explained to me that he was going to have a lot of money someday. And he was going to even it out by spending regardless of whether he had it." It was a philosophy that Boies had thought out carefully, and it amused Judith.

In his first year at Cravath, Boies earned a master's degree, an LLM, in trade regulation from New York University Law School, and began teaching as an adjunct professor the next year. He and Judith lived at 110 Bleecker Street in Greenwich Village, in NYU housing. Paul Verkuil, who got to know Boies at Cravath and went on to be a lifelong friend, believes that Boies did intend to become an academic. "We were both interested in the academic side of things," says Verkuil, who spent most of his career as a law professor and dean. Verkuil thought that Boies never made the move "because he couldn't afford it." By the early 1970s, Boies had four children from two failed marriages to support. But his other colleagues at Cravath never thought that Boies wanted anything other than what they were all vying for—the gold ring of a Cravath partnership. "I never got the sense that he was seriously interested in being an academic. I think he was determined to succeed. He was very focused," says Jay Gerber, who arrived at Cravath in 1965, a year ahead of Boies. Gerber suspected that Boies thought his teaching gig at NYU, aside from the housing perks, "added a certain luster to his career."

Judith Boies looks back on that time with some amusement. "I think NYU thought he was teaching full-time and Cravath thought he was working there full-time," she said. "David always likes running two or three things at once." Boies himself said that practicing law "wasn't that hard." He noticed that his colleagues would spend weeks or a month on a brief that could be written in a few days "if you just sat down and wrote." Other associates spent a lot of time walking around the office, talking to each other, putting in face time.

Boies wasn't much interested in putting in face time. In fact, in the summer of 1967, his second summer after having joining Cravath, he took the entire summer off. But it wasn't a routine holiday. Cravath had a program in which it offered to match time an attorney spent on vacation doing public interest work. That year, Boies was owed four weeks of vacation, and he told the firm that he would take all four weeks to work on civil rights cases in Mississippi, with the firm matching it, giving him eight weeks there to work on voter registration cases and defend civil rights workers who got arrested. Boies had his first "Gotcha" moment in the courtroom that summer, when he traveled from Jackson up to Lexington to represent two workers from the Student Nonviolent Coordinating Committee, known as SNCC. SNCC grew out of student sit-ins that began at a Woolworth's counter in Greensboro, North Carolina, and was the most active civil rights organization in Mississippi at that time. Boies defended two black SNCC workers who had been stopped for not having Mississippi driver's licenses, and who eventually faced charges for resisting arrest and disorderly conduct. The workers had apparently been mistreated, and Boies cross-examined the arresting police officer. "I think he was not used to being cross-examined," Boies recalled. "I think he got mad." The judge allowed the examination to continue. The officer was "partly nervous and partly angry," and in the end he walked off the witness stand. But before he did, Boies told me, the officer said, "I don't have to sit here and take this from this Yankee nigger lover." Judith went with him to Jackson, and they lived in a group house in the black section of town. Once a week, the Boieses got dressed up and went across town to a duplicate bridge club to play the game with southern ladies and gentlemen, "these absolutely charming people, who were probably defendants in some of the suits we were bringing," Judith recalls.

Cravath had Democratic leanings, so Boies's sabbatical—while brazen for a first-year associate—was supported by most of the Cravath brass. The Boieses were hardly revolutionaries. In many ways, Judith and David were a typical young, ambitious couple. Judith's father was a tailor, and Boies— whose off-the-rack blue polyester suits would become part of his legend later in life—wore custom-made, silk-lined suits. They attended the ballet and opera regularly. Judith developed an interest in collecting wine, an interest Boies did not initially share. At their dinner parties, Boies often kept a half-gallon bottle of Diet Pepsi by his feet. It was not until 1969 or 1970, after a dinner at a French restaurant in Westchester with Thomas Barr, the Cravath partner who became his fiercest champion, and his wife, where the couples enjoyed a 1959 Margaux, that Boies decided that wine was an interest worth pursuing.

Boies and Barr had first met, not in the hallways of Cravath, but on the Stanford campus. In February 1968, Stanford Law School invited Boies out to visit, to interest him in joining the faculty. Judith, who was then more than eight months pregnant, joined Boies for the trip. Judging by the couple's behavior, Boies never really seriously considered joining the Stanford faculty. "We drove them crazy," Judith said. Boies was unavailable to meet the other members of the Stanford law faculty because he and his wife were engaged in some highly competitive Ping-Pong games. While Boies was at Stanford, Barr happened to be on the campus, recruiting potential associates. At thirty-seven, Barr was one of Cravath's youngest litigation partners, and was poised to embark on the case that would mark a generation. Over thirteen years, the case would refine and redefine the workaholic ethic set by firm founder Paul Cravath; it would be remembered as the most difficult, the most time-consuming, the most expensive, and the most frustrating battle of the lives of many who worked on it—the case of *United States v. IBM, Inc.*

"I didn't really know David," Barr said, recalling their meeting at Stanford. Under the Cravath system, associates work solely for one partner for a year, and then move on to work for another. But by the time of their encounter, Boies had already impressed the Cravath litigator to whom he was assigned. "He was just so alert, so energetic, and so brilliant," Allen Maulsby recalls. Boies had already done some work for another Cravath partner on IBM matters when he bumped into Barr at Stanford. The government's investigation of IBM was headed inevitably toward the filing of a complaint accusing the computer giant of illegal monopolization and seeking a breakup of the company. Barr asked Boies if he would like to work with him on IBM. "He said fine, and away we went."

Boies quickly became Barr's protégé. By the time the government filed suit in January 1969, Boies had a leg up on the case. "He became the person who was most knowledgeable about the case and thus became a very valuable person," says Jay Gerber, who worked closely with Boies during the early years of the IBM litigation. "He was the guy you had to go to to find things out, and everyone really needed him." Boies assumed this role after his fellow Cravath associate Frederick A. O. Schwarz Jr., whose family owned the Fifth Avenue toy store, left the case. Nicholas deB Katzenbach, who was IBM's general counsel during the litigation, recalls that Boies became Barr's "controller": "Barr entrusted him with a lot." Gerber recalls chatting with Boies about which partner had the most influence within the Cravath structure—classic associate chatter at any big law firm. At the time, that partner was Barr. "Barr made it abundantly clear that the IBM case was going to be the most important case in the office, which it was, not just because of the bills, but because of the consequences," Gerber told me. Of Boies, Gerber said: "He's a bright guy; he figured out the politics."

IBM was willing to stop at nothing and spare no expense to win, and that philosophy meshed perfectly—and, over time, absurdly—with the rigors of the "Cravath system." The Cravath system began with the philosophy and principles of the imperious and dictatorial Paul D. Cravath, the firm's leader from 1906 to his death in 1940. The Cravath system still remains gospel to the lawyers who practice there, who believe it is part of what separates them from other white-shoe law firms on Wall Street.

When Cravath left his own practice in 1899 to join the firm, it was the custom of law firms to hire law students and associates who were akin to apprentices; they received no salaries, but made their living by developing business for themselves and paid for their desk room by assisting in office business. "Cravath could not tolerate the inefficiency and divided loyalty implicit in such an arrangement," according to Robert D. Swaine's 1948 history, *The Cravath Firm,* a three-volume set published privately. When Cravath arrived, he abolished the study of law within the office, and began paying even the greenest associates. In fact, he insisted that the firm select the best graduates from Ivy League law schools—"A-men," in the parlance of Swaine's book—and train them according to Cravath's methods. The firm made it clear what was expected in return. In 1904, Joseph P. Cotton Jr., a 1900 Harvard Law School graduate to whom Cravath delegated management details, wrote to a new recruit: "The time of your coming I leave to you. The sooner it is the better we like it, but as you know we do not want anyone who is not in good shape, and I warn you that you won't get too many long vacations while you are with us."

In practice, Paul Cravath's ethic meant that associates had to work with him late in the evenings, since his days were filled with client and partner meetings, followed by social events. Associates left their sessions with him past midnight, with instructions to return to the office with an answer to a question or a new draft of a document by eight o'clock the next morning. By the mid-1960s, when Boies arrived at the firm, the work ethic was so engrained in the Cravath system that no words were required. Associates left briefly at five o'clock for dinner near the firm's offices at One Chase Plaza and then returned, staying until well into the night, every night.

Barr had spent two years in the marines, handling more than thirty court-martials, before entering Yale Law School in 1955, and applied military discipline to the IBM case. The legal team working on IBM moved from Cravath's headquarters on Wall Street to White Plains, first occupying a house owned by IBM on Red Oak Lane and then moving into an IBM office building. Barr kept a poster in his office that said, "I just want a few good fighting men," and worked just as relentlessly as the associates, which meant seven-day weeks for years on end.

IBM's fight against monopoly claims quickly became a war on many fronts. The company faced a barrage of lawsuits from competitors, and several enormously complicated cases were concluded long before the government's case against IBM finally went to trial. The first of the private cases went to trial in Arizona in the late spring and early summer of 1972. Two leasing subsidiaries of Greyhound Computer Corporation accused IBM of monopolizing the market for leased computers by manipulating the difference between its lease and purchase prices. The case resulted in a stunning victory for IBM and, according to some at Cravath, solidified the relationship between Barr and Boies, leading to a partnership for Boies late in 1972. "Boies just never slept; he slept at his desk," said one Cravath lawyer.

A year later, IBM suffered a devastating loss in the next case to go to trial, when a Tulsa, Oklahoma, judge awarded $350 million in damages to Telex, the manufacturer of equipment that plugged into IBM's giant mainframe computers. While IBM eventually won the Telex case on appeal in 1975, the whopping damage award inspired a raft of copycat "plug-in" lawsuits, and they led the government to add the Telex charges to its complaint. Meanwhile, Greyhound appealed its loss. The cases required Cravath to maintain a tortuous juggling act—making sure that its arguments before one court would not harm its case in another—all the while keeping its main sights on its endgame with the federal government, which began in earnest in 1975, when *U.S. v. IBM* finally went to trial before Judge David Edelstein in Manhattan.

Barr had intended to be lead trial counsel for every case in the maw of the IBM litigation, but circumstances in early 1976 made that impossible. Telex had spawned three California lawsuits by plug-in manufacturers, and in February of that year, Judge Ray McNichols of Los Angeles, who was handling two of the three suits, surprised everyone by setting an October 1976 trial date for a case brought by a company called California Computer Products Inc. A series of complications followed that would lead to an unlikely opportunity for David Boies in what became known as the CalComp case: IBM had hired the Los Angeles law firm of O'Melveny & Myers to coordinate the California cases, but O'Melveny decided that handling the trial would represent a conflict of interest because the firm had done some corporate work for CalComp. One solution—that Katzenbach oversee the glacial proceedings in the government case while Barr litigated the CalComp case in California—was rejected out of hand by Judge Edelstein, who had by all accounts formed an immediate and lasting disdain for Barr, Cravath, and IBM. In the end, the government case was paramount, and Barr knew he had to stay in New York. That left Boies with the Cal-Comp case, since he had the most comprehensive knowledge of the cases. "David was the best choice available at the time," says Barr. "I mean, we didn't have many choices."

Boies had about as much trial experience as any young partner at the firm—which is to say, none. That, too, was part of the Cravath system. "At the outset of their practice Cravath men are not thrown into deep water and told to swim; rather, they are taken into shallow water and carefully taught strokes," according to Swaine's book. In practice, that meant that Boies never played much of a role on his feet in the courtroom in the Greyhound or Telex cases. (His own first memory of a courtroom victory—his grilling of the Mississippi police officer—did not count at a corporate law firm like Cravath.) "His inexperience did worry me," Katzenbach recalls. "I was frightened to death, despite David's talent." Katzenbach convinced Jack Brown, a seasoned trial lawyer and a friend, to take the unlikely role of sitting second chair to a thirty-five-year-old handling his first jury case, with $350 million in damages on the line for IBM. O'Melveny's cocounsel, another experienced trial lawyer, Stuart Kadison, from Los Angeles, also took a back seat.

Boies was literally on the other side of the world when he received word that he would be responsible for the CalComp trial. By early 1976, Boies had somehow extracted himself from the grind of the IBM work and had begun representing other clients. He had just completed an arbitration in Bombay when the CalComp crisis erupted. Boies was traveling with his son David III. By now, Boies had divorced for the second time; David and Judith split up in the summer of 1971, when their twin sons, Christopher and Jonathan, born in March 1968, were still just toddlers. It marked the second time in less than a decade that Boies had parted company with a spouse and left behind two very young children.

When Boies divorced his first wife, Caryl, a decade earlier, he seemed not to look back. On his Yale Law School financial aid applications, Boies answered "no" to the question of whether he had any dependents. Boies was mostly absent from the young lives of David III and Caryl (known as Cary within the family), who was just an infant when the marriage ended. In fact, Cary's earliest memory of her father is a jar of pennies that sat on the hutch of the kitchen in Auburn, a town near Sacramento where her mother and her new husband had settled. The pennies waited there so there would be money for poker when her father visited. While Judith and David Boies lived near one another in Manhattan, the twins didn't see much of their father growing up. Christopher recalls that Boies made an effort to see the twins on the weekends at his Scarsdale home, but even that was impacted by his frenetic schedule. On those weekends, Boies and the twins would go to Nathan's in Yonkers and eat hot dogs, or play video games and miniature golf. Or they would head to Rye to an old-fashioned amusement park with a turn-of-the century roller coaster. When the kids brought their friends along, they all played football on Boies's lawn. "Dad was a very good host to children's friends," Jonathan said. "He'd like to have fun and be the fun guy."

Weekends with Dad changed dramatically with the arrival of David III from California. Boies had an understanding with Caryl that he would be allowed to have custody of David III during his high school years—his way, it seemed, of making up for lost time. When the time came, Caryl resisted it. "If it had been totally up to me, he would not have gone," she told me. But David III went to Westchester after all.

Paul Verkuil told me, "When he got off the plane, he was a kid with scruffy clothes, you know, totally out of his element. I think David always felt a little guilty because he left those kids out there. His first wife never progressed along the lines of David." Judith Boies recalls David III being awed by the sight of the Scarsdale High School building. "I remember him saying, 'Oh my God, it looks like Notre Dame.' " Academics did not come up when David III recalled his high school years to me. "I had a lot of freedom," he said, readily admitting to being a fairly wild teenager.

Jonathan sensed a "whiff of resentment" in his older siblings, who had barely known their father as small children and now saw their younger brothers living the kind of life that a rising star at Cravath could afford. "I hated him," Jonathan says of David III, who was eight years senior to the twins and very tough. David III got into a fair number of fights and car wrecks. "They knew me on a first-name basis at the White Plains emergency room," David III said, laughing. His father never reproached him.

"Part of it is he realized what a horrible example he was," David III said. When David III was fourteen or fifteen, Boies owned a supercharged red Trans Am, a car with a 6.6.-liter, 400-horsepower engine. Boies would arrive home from a day at Cravath and say, "Let's see if we can red-line the Trans Am," meaning that Boies wanted to run the car up to seventy miles an hour in a matter of seconds, on Park Road in Scarsdale. David III eventually totaled the Trans Am, smashing it into a tree one day while he was driving it by himself. He didn't yet have his license. Boies bought another Trans Am, this time a blue one.

Father and son lived like bachelors, according to Judith. She called the Scarsdale house "a pigsty." On one visit, she discovered that sculptures she had bought for Boies on a trip to Africa following their separation were sitting in a closet. She also found her expensive Le Creuset pot in the kitchen sink, encrusted with popcorn, one of the staples of Boies's diet. When she looked at Boies in horror, he told her, "That's my popcorn pot!" Judith told him she would buy him a popcorn maker and left with the Creuset pot and the sculptures. For a time, while the Scarsdale house was being renovated, Boies and son lived at the Ryetown Hilton, and it didn't seem to faze either one of them.

Boies had, by now, established himself as a mostly absent but fun-when-around parent with both sets of children. Jonathan says that one of his first memories of his father is the day, perhaps in first grade, when Boies took him out of school so Jonathan and his friends could go to the Central Park Zoo. They went sledding afterward. "It was like Dad's first sign that he would break the rules to win our affection. It seemed like a big deal at the time," Jonathan said.

Long vacations together would eventually become a fixture for Boies and his children, often by Jeep traveling across the country. In 1975, when Boies got the call for the CalComp trial, he was on one of these trips, an exotic one. He and his son had been traveling for a couple of weeks in Thailand, Singapore, and Hong Kong. They finally landed in Tokyo, and when they checked into their hotel, an urgent cable was waiting, asking Boies to call New York, and soon he was off to Los Angeles. To help Boies, Barr agreed to release senior associate Ronald Rolfe, known for his round-the-clock work habits, from the government case to Boies.

The opposing sides in the CalComp case had been fighting bitterly about scheduling of the case until Boies arrived on the scene. One of his first moves showed an intuition about judges: Judge McNichols suspected that IBM was doing everything in its power to delay the case, which, of course, it was. Boies, in his first appearance before McNichols, said he would accept whatever trial date the judge wished to impose, so long as the judge refused to grant any extensions. There were two big companies involved, Boies told the judge, adding that he did not want to demand that his team miss vacations and time with their families only to have Cal-Comp's lawyer ask for an extension. Boies impressed the judge with this first flourish of commitment. McNichols held the parties to a firm trial date. As the case headed toward trial, Boies complained to friends about the short time he had to prepare but displayed no nerves about the task ahead of him. He could instill fear in his underlings without uttering a word. "He was omnipotent among the Cravath folks," recalls one lawyer who worked on the case. "He could raise his eyebrows and they would quake." There was no affection lost between Boies and the firms forced to play second fiddle to the lawyer trying his first jury case. One of those lawyers described Boies as the enfant terrible of the CalComp case: "A number of us just tried to keep our distance from him; he was a difficult person. He was just very petulant and difficult." Boies likely did not care what his colleagues thought of him. Paul Verkuil recalls, "He used to say, 'I don't have to be nice to people, I'm a litigator.' "

IBM lavished many extravagances on the Cravath team. Within the firm, the lawyers assigned to IBM were considered a breed apart: IBM arranged for them to rent luxury estates with pools in Westchester or nearby Connecticut for the summer months and sent associates on tropical vacations. In California, Boies rented a house in Los Angeles. Owned by the silent-screen star Billie Dove, it stood next door to the house owned by the actor Eddie Albert. Boies and Verkuil were working on a law school textbook on antitrust, and they finished it by the pool of Boies's rented house, under the avocado trees. IBM made sure that a secretary was available to Boies twenty-four hours a day.

IBM had also hired a jury consultant, Donald Vinson, who put together a panel of jurors that mirrored the people sitting in the jury box before Judge McNichols. Those involved in the case believe it was the first use of a shadow jury, and Boies pored over their daily impressions, which often revealed confusions that the actual jurors might be having about the complicated antitrust issues on trial. The novel tactic eventually made the IBM executives back in White Plains nervous, and the shadow jury was dropped midway through the case.

In Boies's opening to the jury, he pulled off his first "Gotcha" stunt, by assembling some of the other items that CalComp had manufactured during the time that IBM had allegedly wronged it in the marketplace. The counsel table was lined with, among other things, nightlights shaped like the Disney character Mickey Mouse, to make the point that CalComp was busy with frivolous products while IBM was engaged in the pursuit of technical excellence. According to Katzenbach, Boies phoned Barr several times a day to get advice on how to present the case. Rolfe would meet with Boies at six o'clock each morning for a couple of hours to prepare him for the cross-examination of witnesses.

The method of cross that Thomas Barr taught his associates demanded months of tedious work. Cravath used cross books for the examination of each witness, compiled faithfully by hapless young associates; these books contained every statement the witness had ever made or written, every written communication the witness had ever made or received, and sections for every issue in the trial, regardless of whether the witness had anything relevant to say on the topic. The books required updating each night as the witness testified. Barr drilled a single principle into his charges about cross-examination: Never decide what your next question will be until the witness has finished his answer. "The important thing is that your preparation is so thorough, so complete, so a part of you can listen to what's going on in the courtroom—to the answers that you are getting, to the objections from opposing counsel, to the rulings from the judge—that you can continue to readjust what you are going to ask, based on the answer to the last question," Barr told me. Many young lawyers, intent on asking the list of questions they have prepared, had trouble with this concept—but not Boies. Boies was a natural at cross, and possessed a gift that Barr did not have: a nearly photographic memory, which he employed to great effect at the trial. Innocently, Boies would begin a question with the preface that he believed the witness had said such and such that morning. The opposing side would invariably object, asking the court reporter to read back the transcript of what the witness had said, which was always exactly as Boies had stated it. Each exchange planted a seed with the jury that he had been forthright with them and the other side had not.

Boies particularly flustered CalComp's chief executive officer, Lester Kilpatrick, who had testified that CalComp had been doing just fine in the marketplace, making products that plugged into IBM's mainframe computers, "and then competition raised its ugly head." IBM, like every big successful company facing allegations of antitrust violations, asserted the defense that its accusers simply couldn't take the competition. And the antitrust laws are meant to preserve competition—the competition that Kilpatrick said "raised its ugly head"—not to favor one competitor over another.

Boies bore down on Kilpatrick's quote, and it appeared many times in the voluminous motion Cravath handed Judge McNichols on the morning of February 11, 1977, after CalComp finished presenting its case. The motion asked McNichols to direct a verdict for IBM. Such a motion effectively takes the case away from a jury: to find for IBM, Judge McNichols needed to find that the case, as presented by the plaintiffs' lawyers, was so weak that a jury could not possibly find in CalComp's favor. Defendants often file motions for directed verdicts, but judges rarely grant them, because they are reluctant to take cases away from a jury. But Barr and the team from Cravath poured unlimited resources into their motions for directed verdicts in the IBM cases. Barr had gotten a directed verdict for IBM in the Greyhound case. The Cravath brief in the CalComp case was voluminous, 102 pages in all, and had been prepared by a team of lawyers separate from those working on the daily trial preparation, the usual Cravath practice. Judge McNichols heard the opposing arguments on the directed verdict on the morning of February 11, and then adjourned the trial for lunch. The next phase was to be IBM's defense, but during the lunch break, McNichols appeared from his chambers and, according to Katzenbach, told Boies, "If I were you, David, I wouldn't work too hard." By then, McNichols had clearly formed an affection for Boies, and his questions from the bench suggested that he would rule against CalComp.

When the judge returned from lunch and read from his decision granting a directed verdict for IBM, it stunned the courtroom. Barr's victory in the Greyhound case had been stunning, but this directed verdict, won by a neophyte named David Boies, was spectacular. IBM held a grand party at the Beverly Wilshire Hotel, where the company's chairman, Frank Cary, presented Boies with a helmet that had been worn by General Patton and played the theme from the movie starring George C. Scott.

Boies had won his first jury trial—but, more important, it was the Cravath system that won the CalComp case. Boies was brilliant, but there was no magic in the inevitable march of IBM toward victory. While Boies does not discuss the case in these terms, Barr makes no bones about it. "Very few lawyers prepare as thoroughly and as carefully as we do. And there's one very good reason for that—our clients can afford it," Barr said. "There was nothing, almost nothing, that IBM wouldn't have done to beat those cases." In an April 1982 article in his magazine the *American Lawyer,* legal journalist Steven Brill calculated the costs of the IBM litigation: Cravath billed $10–15 million a year for the services of the twenty-five to thirty lawyers they devoted full-time to IBM for the thirteen years of the case.

IBM used more than one hundred of its own executives to transmit their expertise to the Cravath team. The effort approached the surreal during the government's trial against IBM, which devolved into a bizarre exercise in sheer boredom shortly after it began. Judge Edelstein—who was charged with rendering a decision in the nonjury case—would often leave the bench for the entire day, as government lawyers read the transcripts of depositions into the record, while court officers puffed on their cigarettes. Edelstein would return to the bench at the end of the day to adjourn the session. For Cravath, it remained a military pursuit supported by the firm's legendary cross books.

The process achieved a height—or nadir—during Boies's marathon cross-examination of the economist Alan McAdams, the government's last witness and the person meant to sum up the Justice Department's claims. Boies was fresh from his triumph in the CalComp case.

McAdams was on the witness stand for seventy-six days. The first thirty-eight days comprised his direct testimony for the government, but much of that time was spent on voir dire, which allows opposing counsel to question a witness during his direct questioning if the witness asserts a particular expertise.

According to McAdams, "Cravath did everything they did to slow down the case and take it off into tangents." At one point, Boies quizzed McAdams for four days on a one-page document. The thirty-eight days that Boies kept McAdams on cross-examination were exactly equal to the time he had spent on direct. Even IBM thought it was excessive. "It began to be silly after a while," says Katzenbach. Boies was particularly obsessive. "David could have gone on for months."

In 1977, as the government finished presenting its evidence against IBM and the company began its defense, Boies chose to leave Cravath and join the staff of Senator Edward Kennedy in Washington for two years. IBM was still mired in its antitrust woes, but Katzenbach couldn't blame Boies for leaving. "The government case looked like a life sentence anyhow," said Katzenbach. "David had done his stint."

Boies's departure for Kennedy's office seemed a natural move within Cravath, which as a firm favored liberal Democratic politics. In fact, Boies's mentor, Tom Barr, had taken time off from Cravath in 1968 to serve on a committee investigating the causes and prevention of violence after the death of Robert F. Kennedy.

Boies began as chief counsel for the Senate antitrust subcommittee, handpicked for the assignment by his friend Stephen Breyer, who had a legendary reputation on Capitol Hill for his work for Kennedy. When Breyer left to teach at Harvard's Kennedy School of Government, Boies's antitrust expertise and work on the IBM case made him seem a natural candidate, but he didn't fare well at brokering political alliances. "He's an independent cowboy; he's a world unto himself," recalls one of his colleagues from Kennedy's staff. Boies was not good at building consensus, and had no interest in being a good administrator. While he was brilliant at preparing Kennedy for the questioning of witnesses, Boies had no intuition for politics.

Kennedy introduced a bill intended to reverse a 1977 U.S. Supreme Court ruling called *Illinois Brick*, which prevented consumers from suing big manufacturers for such antitrust violations as price-fixing because they were "indirect purchasers." The Kennedy bill would have revived consumer class actions against monopolists. Senator Joseph R. Biden Jr. was the pivotal vote on the bill, and his counsel, Mark Gitenstein, warned Boies that he could not count on Biden's vote. Even so, when Biden voted against the bill, "Boies went nuts," Gitenstein recalls. "He was stunned and was very angry." Kennedy and Biden had a very contentious relationship, and Biden was unpredictable on commercial issues generally, but "Boies had no sense of that," Gitenstein said. Boies had taken Biden's vote for granted, and that assumption cost him dearly.

Boies spent two years with Kennedy, his second as chief counsel of the Judiciary Committee, and returned to Cravath in July 1979, but not to the IBM case, which was still grinding along before Judge Edelstein. The Cravath system carried on until 1982, when William Baxter, President Reagan's antitrust chief at the Justice Department, called the case to a halt. Baxter dismissed the IBM case on the same day that he brought monopoly charges against telecom giant AT&T. By then, Boies was barely involved in the IBM case.

FOUR

The Seed of the Myth

Ronald Rolfe's voice boomed from the other end of the line. I had called him to ask whether he would sit for an interview about his former partner. Rolfe's reaction was explosive. "No, no, no!" he repeated. Rolfe seemed exasperated, and he told me he was simply tired of reading "myths" about David Boies. Rolfe's main issue—in fact the main issue for many Cravath partners—concerned the central myth of Boies's participation in the IBM case. Story after story described him as the company's lead lawyer and the mastermind of its successful defense. This simply was not true, and it drove the Cravath lawyers absolutely crazy.

This myth was repeated endlessly in media coverage of the Microsoft trial. The firm's partners kept silent, but they were clearly keeping score. The dike broke when Joseph Nocera cited the myth in his widely read diary of the trial in *Fortune* magazine, calling Boies IBM's "chief litigator in its

13-year fight with the government" in his diary entry for the January 11, 1999, issue. Samuel Butler, who had recently stepped down as Cravath's chairman, took the time to write a three-page letter to Nocera. "This mistake has appeared repeatedly in the media during the last six months," Butler noted. "While the firm has been ignoring it, I would like to now point out this error because of the firm's close relationship with Time Inc. [*Fortune*'s parent] over the past 75 years and our knowledge of its desire for accurate reporting."

Butler's letter detailed at length the genesis of the IBM litigation in 1969, and the choice of Tom Barr to lead it, and pointed out that Boies was then a "two and one-half year associate and would not become a partner for another four years." Butler allowed that Boies's win in the CalComp case had been "a brilliant victory for David," but added that Boies would "readily concede that he followed the strategy established by Tom. In the main show, the Government case, Tom did most of the important trial work with lots of help from many others, both at IBM and Cravath, including David." Butler also chose to point out Boies's two-year hiatus both from the firm and the IBM case to serve as counsel to the Senate Judiciary Committee. Butler ended by citing the plaque IBM sent Cravath to commemorate their victory. The only Cravath lawyer named on the plaque was Thomas Barr. Butler enclosed a copy of the plaque with his letter. "I hope this will clarify the facts as to who was in charge of the IBM case at Cravath," Butler signed off.

The lengthy letter, and the attached plaque copy was evidence of something much deeper than a request for a correction. The Boies myth was one the firm had lived with, endured, and suffered silently, for many years. Stoic corporate citizens that they were, they chose the path of dignified silence. But their resentment and annoyance ran deep, and if triggered, a Samuel Butler or a Ronald Rolfe would let it rip. The myth of David Boies, I believe, goes a long way toward explaining why many of Boies's former partners declined to speak with me about the lawyer they practiced with for thirty years. They had lived with the myth long enough, perhaps too long.

The myth began when Boies was chosen to defend one of the country's most powerful media companies, CBS Inc., against libel claims brought by General William C. Westmoreland in 1982. A ninety-minute CBS documentary called *The Uncounted Enemy: A Vietnam Deception* claimed that Westmoreland had led a conspiracy to suppress estimates of the enemy's military strength, all the while encouraging President Lyndon Johnson to escalate the war because victory was at hand, and ultimately leaving America unprepared for a dramatic turning point in the war, the Tet offensive of January 1968. Westmoreland's $120 million lawsuit created breathtaking media fascination, testing the press's sacred constitutional protections under the First Amendment while promising to put the most unpopular war in U.S. history on trial in a courtroom. CNN, then in its infancy, was so interested in the case that it made a motion to get its cameras into the courtroom. It failed, but CNN camera crews waited on the courthouse steps each day. Reporters covered the trial daily, obsessively. Eventually, six books were published evaluating the documentary and the lawsuit it spawned. The trial of Westmoreland against CBS—then known as the "Tiffany network"—its star broadcaster, Mike Wallace, and George Crile, the CBS producer mainly responsible for the documentary, would become the paradigm for modern litigation, where spinning of the media outside the courtroom is as important as the proceedings before the judge or jury. And at this spin, Boies proved himself a master with no equals.

CBS was very much on the defensive by the time Westmoreland filed his lawsuit in the federal district court in Gainesville, South Carolina, on September 13, 1982. When *The Uncounted Enemy* aired on a Saturday night in January 1982, Mike Wallace intoned, "Tonight we're going to present evidence of what we have come to believe was a conscious effort—indeed, a conspiracy at the highest levels of military intelligence." Wallace introduced Sam Adams, a former CIA analyst, who explained that he believed there was something "terribly wrong" with estimates in the fall of 1966, at a time when there was growing optimism that we would win the war, based on Westmoreland's statistics. Wallace's first questions to Westmoreland on the broadcast concerned the general's unusual trip from Vietnam to Washington in April 1967, when he was summoned by President Johnson, amid angry street protests, to reassure the American public that we were in fact winning the war. When Wallace asked Westmoreland whether the president was "a difficult man to feed bad news about the war," Westmoreland responded, "Well, Mike, you know as well as I do that people in senior positions love good news." And Westmoreland had good news that day; the enemy strength had leveled off at 285,000 men.

Westmoreland admitted that the CIA thought the military was underestimating the enemy strength, but he dismissed the agency as "very remote." Westmoreland called his own intelligence chief, General Joseph

McChristian, "a superb intelligence officer." Then Wallace informed the listeners what the general "failed to tell us in our interview." When Westmoreland returned to Vietnam from Washington, Wallace said, he was briefed on a report from McChristian that pointed to a "dramatic increase"—something like 200,000 more Vietcong than previously estimated. On camera, McChristian said the numbers "disturbed" the general because they would "create a political bombshell" if sent back to Washington. Now on the defensive, Westmoreland told Wallace that he had rejected McChristian's figures because they were "specious."

"Consider Westmoreland's dilemma," Wallace asked the television audience. "If he accepted his intelligence chief's findings, he would have to take bad news to the president. If he didn't, well, there was only General McChristian to deal with." Wallace intoned ominously that McChristian was transferred out of Vietnam shortly after Westmoreland "suppressed" his report. In the summer of 1967, Westmoreland cut an entire category of the Vietcong, the "self-defense militia," from the enemy strengths—a force of 70,000 men—to keep the totals under 300,000. Wallace pressed Westmoreland on whether those forces were dropped "based on political considerations." Westmoreland said, "No, decidedly not. That—that—" and then Wallace cut him off, confronting him with a cable he had written in August 1967, in which he had said those forces "must be removed or the newsmen will immediately seize upon the point that the enemy force had increased." Wallace laid out the final act of the alleged conspiracy: a conference in Langley, Virginia, between the military and the CIA, which was then pushing for higher estimates, where Westmoreland ordered his subordinates to stick to an "arbitrary ceiling" of 300,000 men. Colonel Gains Hawkins, a colorful figure who rounded out the main characters on the documentary, was one of Westmoreland's delegates at Langley. He said the figures were "crap," and Adams, his CIA counterpart at Langley, recalled that Hawkins "looked sick, looked like he didn't believe what he was saying."

In all, eight people were interviewed on air to support Adams's thesis, while one person appeared for twenty seconds to defend the general's views. By the end of the program, Westmoreland was licking his lips, the broadcast having made him an apparent liar and the architect of a Watergate-style conspiracy during the Vietnam War. The ratings that week ranked *Uncounted Enemy* in seventy-second place—*last* place—on a night when ABC ran *Love Boat* and *Fantasy Island*. But the broadcast struck a chord where it mattered. That Sunday, the *New York Times* ran an editorial complimenting the program for showing that "Lyndon Johnson himself was victimized by mendacious intelligence."

Four months later, *TV Guide* published an article that portrayed the broadcast as a shoddy piece of attack journalism at its worst. The nine-page article, "Anatomy of a Smear: How CBS Broke the Rules and 'Got' Gen. Westmoreland," was unusual for *TV Guide*. The writers of the article, Sally Bedell (who later joined the *New York Times*) and Don Kowet, had gotten access to the uncut interview transcripts and the so-called Blue Sheet for the broadcast, a document that producers prepare to pitch their ideas. The article they produced left the broadcast without credibility. While CBS and Wallace presented the show as groundbreaking, the controversy over possible falsification of enemy numbers in Vietnam had been public for more than a decade, largely due to the obsession of Adams, the CIA analyst whose charges appear uncontested on the broadcast. Adams had written an article, "Vietnam Cover-Up: Playing War with Numbers," for *Harper's* magazine, where his editor for the piece was George Crile. CBS paid Adams a $25,000 consulting fee, a fact it failed to mention on camera, coached him extensively before his interview, and lobbed him softball questions. Bedell and Kowet identified eleven major problems with the broadcast, from showing sympathetic witnesses the statements of other witnesses on film while never offering the targets of the conspiracy charge the opportunity to hear their accusers, to misrepresenting the accounts of some witnesses while completely ignoring others.

The president of CBS News, Van Gordon Sauter, was acutely embarrassed, and commissioned an internal investigation of the broadcast by Burton Benjamin, a veteran newsman who was among the network's elder statesmen. Sauter's intent was to keep Benjamin's actual report confidential. When Benjamin completed his investigation in July, Sauter released only an eight-page memo to the news division and to the clamoring press. Sauter announced that CBS supported the "substance" of the broadcast, but found that the use of the word "conspiracy" was "inappropriate," confirmed five violations of CBS guidelines in the making of the documentary, and accepted that it had flaws.

George Vradenburg III, CBS's general counsel, took one look at the lawsuit that Westmoreland filed in September and concluded, "it was going to go to trial. We wouldn't be able to dismiss it on First Amendment grounds," a profound statement of just how worried the network was. General Westmoreland was a "public figure" who faced almost insurmountable hurdles in pursuing libel claims under the standard set by the U.S. Supreme Court's historic 1964 ruling in *New York Times v. Sullivan*. That case would require the general to prove that not only had CBS got it wrong in the documentary, but that it acted with "actual malice," which the Sullivan case defined as "reckless disregard" for the truth. Vradenburg believed that Westmoreland's complaint would get past a motion to dismiss, because there were enough allegations to suggest actual malice. "But more important, I thought one of our best defenses was going to be to discover what was really going on inside the military and the CIA with respect to counting enemy force strength," Vradenburg told me. With the reputation of CBS News on the line, Vradenburg believed that the network needed to establish the truth of the broadcast, even though the law under *Sullivan* did not require that. He said, "You had to win by proving that in fact your broadcast was well founded. And therefore you had to defend the journalism as well as the law. We were in a public battle as well as a legal battle."

CBS needed to be rescued; it needed a man with a red cape.

Vradenburg and Boies, as young Cravath associates, had worked together on the IBM litigation. On the surface Vradenburg, tall and aristocratic, had little in common with Boies, the brilliant maverick. After Vradenburg left Cravath in 1980 to join CBS as its associate general counsel, the first major litigation to come across his desk was a suit by CNN, against the Reagan administration and the three major networks, claiming that CNN was being illegally excluded from the White House media pool. Vradenburg hired Boies to represent CBS. When the Reagan administration decided to exclude all TV cameras from the White House until the dispute was resolved, Boies went after the White House itself, obtaining an injunction against the rule on constitutional grounds. The case was eventually settled, and CNN joined the White House pool.

The choice of Boies for the defense in the Westmoreland case was not immediately popular, Vradenburg recalls. Shortly after he told Sauter, the CBS News president, that Boies would handle the case, Vradenburg got an "apoplectic" phone call from Mike Wallace. "He said, 'What the hell are you doing hiring this guy?'" Vradenburg recalls that Wallace, whose reputation was on the line in the lawsuit, did not know who Boies was, and wanted the network to hire Floyd Abrams, the renowned First Amendment specialist.

At a meeting with the CBS brass in Sauter's office, Boies argued that CBS should make a motion to the South Carolina judge before whom the complaint was pending to move the case to the Southern District of New York, where CBS was sure to find a more sympathetic jury pool. But the other lawyers in the room, some from CBS's in-house staff, and a posse of others, among them defamation specialists, thought the motion was a loser. Westmoreland, as a libel plaintiff, had an almost absolute right to bring suit in his home state of South Carolina. The motion would succeed only in offending the South Carolina judge with whom CBS would be living for a long time to come. Vradenburg went around the conference table and took a poll, which confirmed that most people were either neutral or negative about Boies's proposal. Then he got to Wallace, who by then had come to know and trust Boies's talents. Wallace declared that Boies was their lawyer and that they ought to take his advice. Once Wallace had spoken, Vradenburg polled the table again, and suddenly everyone agreed with Boies's position. "Mike Wallace was my biggest supporter," Boies told me—several times.

Westmoreland was represented by the Capital Legal Foundation, a conservative Washington, D.C., "public policy" firm that described itself as having a "free market bias." They agreed to take the general's case—and fund it—after several prestigious lawyers advised him against bringing the suit. Capital Legal's president, Dan Burt, a tax specialist who had never tried a case before a jury, would be Westmoreland's lead lawyer against David Boies and the Cravath firm.

Westmoreland's lawyers had filed the complaint, not in Charleston, where the general lived, but more than two hundred miles away, in Greenville, in Spartanburg County, where the general had grown up. In Boies's brief to transfer the case from Greenville to New York, his opening shot was that the CBS local affiliate had preempted *The Uncounted Enemy* to air a local basketball game. When Boies recalled his argument for me years later, he relished the moment when he had presented what he called an "atmospheric" point, that Westmoreland was scheduled to officiate as the grand marshal of the Greenville Veteran's Day parade that year. Boies argued that the general traveled to New York as often as he did to Greenville. The documents, the witnesses, the broadcast itself were all in New York. Boies told the judge there was just one reason that Westmoreland wanted his case tried in Greenville: he could get a favorable jury there.

Dan Burt regretted his decision to file in Greenville. Burt later said, "I had a feeling in my gut it wasn't right." Boies got the case moved to New York, and the victory was crucial, not only because it gave CBS a jury pool where it would have a "fairer shot," but also because it made CBS more comfortable about resisting Burt's demands for an early settlement.

In the eighteen months leading up to the trial, Burt had the advantage both in court and with the press, and he became CBS's worst nightmare. Peter J. Boyer, in his 1988 book on the decline of CBS News, *Who Killed CBS?*, noted that *Uncounted Enemy* produced a public relations nightmare, but that "the really scary part didn't begin until Dan Burt entered the picture." Burt laced his conversations with reporters with expletives, and referred to himself as "a short, foul-mouthed Jew from the streets." He had opened a tax practice in Marblehead, Massachusetts, five years after graduating from Yale Law School in 1975, and within a few years, he bragged to reporters, the business had made him a millionaire. Burt's first conversation with Richard M. Clurman, a *Time* magazine veteran media columnist who wrote about the trial, was a screed: "You wouldn't believe how those CBS motherfuckers and those other shitheads lie. I'm just a little Jew but if they'll do it to Westmoreland, you can imagine who they'll do it to next." Invectives like this suggest that Burt was a caricature of the in-your-face lawyer, but in his public and television appearances he was passionate about his belief in the general's cause and very effective. Even now, Vradenburg admits: "He did a very good job for an amateur."

Burt's greatest moment—and CBS's worst black eye before the trial— came when the presiding judge, U.S. District Judge Pierre Leval, ordered the network to turn over the full text of Burt Benjamin's investigation into *TV Guide*'s allegations. Boies and his team fought relentlessly to keep the Benjamin report from Burt, arguing that the document was protected from discovery by the privilege of "self-evaluative analysis." In April 1983, when the Benjamin report was finally released, it triggered another cycle of damaging stories. "We are about to see the dismantling of a major news network," Burt said, according to *USA Today*. Though Burt later denied ever saying that, it was a great sound bite, and was repeated again and again in news accounts of the episode. CBS was still reeling from the revelations of the Benjamin report—fifty-nine pages of detailed criticisms—when Burt leaked another explosive charge to the *New York Times*. He accused CBS of secretly taping an off-the-record interview with former secretary of defense Robert McNamara, and then destroying the tapes. Following that accusation, George Crile searched his files and discovered the McNamara tape—which had not, in fact, been destroyed—and those of several other former high-ranking United States officials, all of whom had been taped without their permission, a practice forbidden not only at CBS but throughout the media business. The fiasco ended in Crile's suspension.

In September 1983, the case was given a full-dress treatment by the *American Lawyer*. The first of Connie Bruck's four articles on the Westmoreland case was a knockdown piece attacking the decisions that led to the Benjamin investigation and the ultimate release of the Benjamin report. "This is one lawsuit that never should have been," she wrote. She laid the blame on Vradenburg, concluding that the case was "fueled, if not created" by mistakes that he, Sauter, and Benjamin had made. Boies suffered some minor abrasions in the piece. He implied that he would have represented Westmoreland had the general come calling. "I'd take a plaintiff's libel case without a moment's hesitation. I'm in no way ideological about this—I just want to win my case." Boies was, perhaps, too frank with Bruck: she wrote that he told her he wished that a lawyer, rather than a journalist like Benjamin, had been the author of the report. This would have rendered it more likely to be protected by the attorney-client privilege and also would have been "more sensible." Boies later wrote a letter to Bruck, calling the quote "completely inaccurate" and rising to Benjamin's defense.

Bruck's article contains one astoundingly astute, crystalline observation about David Boies: "Boies is in the peculiarly lucky position of a lawyer whose case is perceived to be a real loser but who, when the decision comes in from the judge (in summary judgment) or the jury, will look like a magic maker."

The trial of *Westmoreland v. CBS* held out the tantalizing prospect of revealing the secret history of the Vietnam War to a press corps still convinced that government officials had lied to the public about the debacle. Boies seized the opportunity to make himself available to the press, and in so doing violated an unspoken rule that prevailed at Cravath and every other corporate law firm on Wall Street. Boies drew the press in with his open manner, his charm, and his insatiable desire to engage with them about the pressing issues in the case. He was dogged by reporters who trailed after him as he walked the blocks from the downtown courthouse to Cravath's offices. At that time, the standard response of a lawyer representing a corporate giant like CBS when approached by the media was "no comment," and Boies's unconventional approach was frowned upon within Cravath. "You keep your head down and your mouth shut and you do your job," one Cravath partner told me. Thomas Barr stuck to this traditional path in defending *Time* in another extraordinary libel suit by the Israeli defense minister Ariel Sharon. The Sharon and Westmoreland cases went to trial at the same time and in the same courthouse, but Boies was much more open to the press and got all the front-page coverage. "It was frowned upon within Cravath; nobody sent him out to the woodshed, but it is frowned upon," the Cravath partner told me.

Frowned upon? This was an extraordinary understatement—and classically courteous, in the Cravath tradition. "The ethic in those days was that you stayed away from the press," said Jay Gerber. "You were supposed to decline comment unless your client *expressly* told you to do it, which rarely happened. It was very strongly imbued in all of us." Whether Boies had the go-ahead to speak with the press as freely as he did during the Westmoreland case is doubtful. William Duker, a young Cravath associate assigned to Boies during the Westmoreland period, remembers that Boies was often at odds with John Scanlon, the public relations specialist that CBS had hired. And Vradenburg was circumspect on the topic when I interviewed him. "We tended, at least at the outset, to take the traditional view that we don't talk about matters in litigation," he said. "Boies counseled against that, and urged us to speak our mind, and eventually we did and eventually spoke as much as Burt did."

Boies took what his good friend Steven Brill, founder of the glossy monthly magazine the *American Lawyer*, calls a Chauncey Gardiner approach to dealing with the media. "It seems like he's really naive. 'Well, this reporter asked me a question so I guess I'll give them a truthful answer. A reporter calls me on the telephone, the polite thing to do is to return the phone call. A reporter wants to come see me, the polite thing to do is to set up an appointment. I'm not doing anything unusual, am I? I'm just dealing with people like they're people.' On one level, there's nothing special about this. But an element of it is extremely shrewd. Because it really works, and it really works in a field where no one else does it."

The Cravath team rereported the broadcast to prepare what became known as CBS's "truth defense," with the crucial difference that the legal system afforded them the power of subpoena. In the course of discovery,

Boies deposed not only McNamara, who was forced to break his vow of silence on the Vietnam War, but also former secretary of state Dean Rusk. At the outset of Rusk's deposition, Rusk announced that he would comply with the order to videotape only if Boies was videotaped too, a process Boies apparently enjoyed. McNamara, who was extremely careful and had a photographic memory, matched wits with Boies. At McNamara's deposition, there were CIA agents present, looking out for potential national security issues that might arise. For a legal assignment, it was most unusual. "We re-created the war," says William Duker.

Boies had at his disposal the Cravath system, which typically would have assigned layers of partners, junior partners, senior associates, and a small army of others to the effort. Instead Boies relied on the sweat labor of four young Cravath associates, none of whom was more than five years out of law school. They worked seven-day weeks, around the clock, for more than two years, and were alternately exhilarated, inspired, and driven crazy by their boss. "We were as wet behind the ears as you could find at Cravath," recalls Duker, who of the four associates has kept in closest contact with Boies. "And we had enormous responsibility, which is not the typical thing that happened back then at Cravath. And, I think, as a consequence the level of commitment was enormous, largely inspired by David's genius. I mean everybody wanted to be compatible with that level of ability."

The team functioned like a mini law firm within Cravath. Boies made no use of Cravath's elaborate back-office support system. He held the four associates and the few paralegals working with them accountable for every aspect of the case, down to the messengering of papers across town. "That's the way David minimized mistakes," Duker says. "He knew exactly what everyone was doing, and didn't want to have the responsibilities spread beyond that small group." They lived in fear of him. On the eve of the trial, Boies delivered a lecture to his team: "I could get three trained chimpanzees to do what you guys are going to do. But the reason I have associates is because you won't make any mistakes at all."

The case was called to trial on October 11, 1984. Once the jurors were seated, Judge Leval urged them to put aside their personal feelings about the war in Vietnam. But Boies was intent on re-creating the war to appeal to the liberal sentiments of a New York jury, and his first coup occurred in his opening statement. Because Burt's presentation took up most of the day, Boies had only an hour to begin his argument. As he drew to a close, Boies said that, at the time of the Tet offensive, the "junior senator from New York was asking the same questions that CBS would raise in its documentary." His statement had all the makings of a Boies moment, deceptively low-key yet heading toward high drama. The junior senator to whom Boies referred was the late Robert Kennedy, and Boies was about to play a tape of Kennedy delivering an emotional and eloquent speech on the steps of Capitol Hill.

Judge Leval hastily called the lawyers to a sidebar. After a lengthy argument, Leval decided the Kennedy tape was part of the background CBS relied upon and therefore was relevant to the network's state of mind on the key issue of "actual malice." Boies got to play an excerpt from the fifteen-minute videotape of Kennedy, whose haunting image captured the promise of a generation, and the first day of the Westmoreland trial ended on that note. "It was a dramatic moment!" Boies recalled with glee. "Here was one of the most electric speakers in the country." On the tape, the junior senator from New York intoned that what the American people were being told about the enemy in Vietnam was a lie.

While Boies may recall the Kennedy moment with relish, his Westmoreland opening was not universally considered a blockbuster. Observers in the press declared the opening statements a draw. And the Kennedy moment seemed to have no impact at all on at least one member of the jury, M. Patricia Roth, an art teacher from Westchester County who kept a diary during the trial that became a book called *The Juror and the General.* Early in her diary, Roth was unimpressed by both lawyers. "I find it rather puzzling that a case of such supposed magnitude is to be fought by two lawyers who seem to have such little courtroom experience," she wrote.

John Scanlon, CBS's PR specialist, had set up an elaborate system in an office near the courthouse manned by two assistants, who frantically copied and distributed key documents to the press. CBS lavished particular attention on Myron Farber, the *New York Times* reporter covering the case, making sure that each night a messenger hand-delivered the first official transcripts of the proceedings to the *Times*. The network was constantly wringing its hands over Farber's coverage—Farber left court early to file his stories, and CBS believed he was not paying enough attention to Boies's zingers on cross, which tended to happen, as if on cue, toward the end of the day.

While the reporters soaked up the benefits of CBS's well-oiled, spare-no-expense PR campaign, Boies took pains to present a very different picture of the network to the jury. There were several television sets in the courtroom, in constant use for presentation of portions of the broadcasts and of the outtakes that never made it into the documentary. Boies insisted on loading the tapes into the videotape machines himself. As he was fiddling with the machinery on the opening day, he told the jurors, "My client is the expert in this, I am not." Duker said, "I think it was important for him, at the very beginning, to dispel the notion that he was some slick Wall Street lawyer." Flanked by a handful of fresh-faced twentysomething lawyers, the image had the desired effect. "There is an electric youthfulness surrounding the defendants," juror Roth wrote in her diary. "Even their counsel is youthful—it occurred to me that this is not a trial of *Westmoreland v. CBS* but a trial of Old-Time Military Thinking and Youthful Idealism."

And there were the blue suits. Boies wore his cheap navy polyester suit from Sears, a blue-striped shirt, and a navy knit tie to court each day. By the Westmoreland trial, he knew the impact this habit could have on a jury. Boies had worn the same uniform for the *CalComp* trial. After the judge took the case away from the jury and ruled for IBM, the legal team interviewed the jurors and discovered that Boies's style of dress had intrigued them. Clappes, the in-house IBM lawyer, recalled, "It had the effect of making him more interesting to them." The jurors in the Westmoreland case were no different: Roth's book reveals that the jurors made bets about whether he would ever change his outfit. At one point early in the trial, Roth noted in her diary, "I believe he may be consciously trying to avoid looking slick." But as she became more dazzled by Boies's command of the cross-examinations, Roth wrote, "I don't think that David Boies ever goes to sleep. I am certain that he only owns blue suits, blue ties, and blue and white shirts, so that he can get dressed in the dark. Maybe he's colorblind and his wife only lets him out of the house in monochrome. Anyhow, he certainly does his homework."

Boies also insisted on passing out documents to the jury himself. One of the baby lawyers at his side would pass him a document, and Boies would smile at the jury. Then he'd turn around, his face transmogrified with rigid intensity, and bark a command to one of the petrified young Cravath lawyers. "Everything for David had to be perfect," Duker recalled. "He was obsessed with the copies of the documents. Less than perfection was not tolerated." The associates were there to serve his needs, but in the end, Boies, like a mathematician or an artist, worked alone. As the trial wore on, Boies often took off to Atlantic City for a weekend of gambling, unreachable. Among the Boies legends that emerged from the Westmoreland case was his preparing for the trial while at the U.S. Open Tennis Championships, sending for associates by car with piles of depositions for him to read. Duker, for one, got to stay to watch the tennis.

Dan Burt, the tax lawyer trying his first jury case, had the far tougher burden of proof. Burt had to establish not only that the broadcast's assertions that Westmoreland's military command "systematically blocked" figures on higher enemy strength and ordered an "arbitrary ceiling" were false but also that CBS acted with "actual malice." In theory, CBS had a much lesser burden, but Boies's "truth defense"—in which he and his team undertook to rereport and establish that the assertions of the broadcast were true—made his job more difficult in practice. The strategy also meant that the trial would revisit the conduct of the war itself, as well as reexamine how the broadcast was produced.

The predator in Boies emerged as he took on Burt's sixth witness, General Phillip Buford Davidson, a much-decorated West Pointer and a potentially devastating witness against CBS. He had taken over as Westmoreland's intelligence chief in the spring of 1967, when CBS alleged that the conspiracy to keep a ceiling on the enemy strength began. CBS had not interviewed Davidson for the broadcast; on air, Wallace described Davidson as a "very, very sick man." Davidson had, in fact, fully recovered from cancer surgery at the time CBS claimed he was at death's door. The Benjamin report established that Crile, the CBS producer, had been sloppy about Davidson. He left the task of contacting Davidson to his secretary, and she had no luck, but never tried to reach him at his home in the evenings.

In his direct testimony, Davidson had told the jurors that his telephone number had been listed since 1974, and though he did travel three times in 1981 during the period when CBS tried to reach him, his teenage daughters were at home to answer the phone. Burt gilded the damning facts against CBS with broad questions about Davidson's patriotism, in the end asking whether Westmoreland had ever asked him to "fake intelligence." Davidson responded with a booming, "No!" It was drama, but Boies trumped it.

When he began his cross, he whipped out one of the cables that became an explosive piece of evidence, for both the jury and the press. Davidson had sent the cable from Saigon to Washington, D.C., where Westmoreland's delegates were preparing for their meeting with the CIA, at the very time when, according to the CBS broadcast, Westmoreland instructed them to stick to the arbitrary ceiling of 300,000 in enemy strength. "Would you read from the cable, please, General?" Boies asked, his manner, as ever, courteous.

And so the general read from the cable he had written in Saigon seventeen years earlier: "Further consideration reveals the total unacceptability of including the strength of the self-defense forces and the secret self-defense forces in any strength figure to be released to the press. The figure of about 420,000, which includes all forces including SD and SSD, has already surfaced out here. This figure has stunned the embassy and this headquarters and has resulted in a scream of protests and denials." Boies interrupted to ask whether Davidson recalled what he was referring to by a scream of protests and denials. Davidson said he did not. "Please continue," Boies said. The next sentence from the cable directly implicated Westmoreland: "In view of this reaction and in view of General Westmoreland's conversations, all of which you have heard, I am sure that this headquarters will not accept a figure in excess of the current strength figure carried by the press." Boies asked Davidson what "conversations" with Westmoreland he had been referring to in the cable. "I cannot recall, Mr. Boies," Davidson answered. "Can you recall any of them?" Boies asked. "No."

In that instant, the courteous Boies turned savage. He pressed Davidson to admit that Westmoreland's lawyers had shown him the cable at least six months before he took the stand, and that he had discussed it with them at length, suggesting that Davidson's total lack of recall on the cable was less than honest. As the day wore on, Davidson experienced a complete failure of memory. At the end of the cross-examination, Boies had both destroyed the decorated general's credibility and gotten a sizzling document about the secret history of the Vietnam War—one that portrayed a military cynically obsessed with how it was being portrayed in the press—in front of the media covering the trial.

The Davidson cross was merely a warm-up for Boies's relentless, sweat-drenched questioning of General George Godding, the man who headed up Westmoreland's delegation at the fateful Langley conference where Westmoreland allegedly ordered the "arbitrary ceiling." CBS looked bad for not reaching Davidson for the broadcast, but its handling of God-ding was much worse. He had been interviewed four or five times, but never on camera. On air, Mike Wallace made the unequivocal charge that the head of the military delegation at the Langley conference "told us that General Westmoreland had, in fact, personally instructed him not to allow the total to go over 300,000." A moment later, the broadcast cut to an interview with Colonel James Hamscher, leaving the impression that he had been the head of the Langley delegation.

When Godding, who had retired as a two-star general, took the witness stand, he described his military career, how he had landed on D day in 1944 in Europe, how a mortar shell had hit him as he came across Omaha Beach. He was every bit the general. Under direct examination, Godding forcefully testified that "there was no ceiling placed on us," and that the figures he carried to the Langley conference were "our best estimates from intelligence sources."

At his pretrial deposition, Godding had repeatedly said that the enemy numbers he took to the Langley conference came from what was known as the May order of battle. This could not possibly be true, because the May numbers included the irregulars—the SD and SSD forces—which by August had been eliminated. When Godding testified at the trial, he said that the May numbers were presented only as the "previous estimate" at the Langley conference, and said the numbers he took to Langley were the "revised" estimate. It was as muted an admission of a mistake that a witness could possible make.

Boies pounced on this testimony as he rose for the cross. "When you gave the answers that you did at your deposition, you understood that you were under oath, did you not, *sir*?" Boies asked Godding, employing his tactic of using the honorific "sir" as if it were a slur, implying that the witness didn't really deserve to be called that. "And you said that *every* time it came up in the deposition, correct, *sir*?" Godding finally had to admit, "I was in error on that."

Boies pressed Godding about whether he knew "at the time of his deposition" of General McChristian's estimates on enemy strengths, the numbers that had been "suppressed" according to the broadcast. Godding tried to explain that Westmoreland's lawyers had sent him documents in recent months that refreshed his memory. After some more badgering, Boies produced and read from the damning deposition, when Godding had testified,

"I do not remember anything, any estimates that pushed up the irregulars significantly." On the witness stand now, Godding was more circumspect, saying that he was aware of the studies, but "did not remember specifically the results." Shortly after that, Boies asked Judge Leval whether it would be a convenient time to break the proceedings for the day.

What did all of this prove? All these years later, I stared at the transcript to try to understand it. Boies relished Godding's repeated mistake at deposition—that he took the May order of battle, the numbers that still included the SD and SSD forces, to the Langley conference. Was it just an error, the product of a failed memory? It didn't matter. Reporters on the scene noted that jurors who had been dozing off suddenly woke up, and others started writing on their notepads. In the heat of the afternoon's questioning, the press and jury picked up only on the atmospherics that Boies had created. "It turned out to be the most exciting afternoon so far," juror Roth wrote in her diary.

Boies returned the next Monday for what would prove to be the most brutal session thus far in the trial. Godding, like the other military officials who came to testify, intoned the mantra that their intelligence estimates were completely unaffected by politics or by how the enemy numbers would play in the press. Boies set a trap for Godding on this subject with a few innocuous questions just before the lunch break: he asked Godding whether he understood the purpose of the Langley conference was to arrive at the "very best intelligence estimate that they could"; the general, of course, said yes. But after lunch, Boies bullied Godding relentlessly, whipping out yet another declassified cable that pricked up the ears of the press. Godding had not been the recipient of this particular message, which was sent in July 1967 by George Carver, the CIA's chief of Vietnamese affairs, to CIA director Richard Helms, referring to the numbers dilemma. The cable described the "chief problem" as a "political and presentational one"—in other words, the kind of cynical purpose that Westmoreland's lawyers sought to avoid at the trial. Arguably, the cable was irrelevant: Godding had never received it. But Boies used it to put Godding off guard, to great effect, and its juicy contents—candid moments between CIA agents—were duly noted by the press.

By the day's end, Godding crumbled. He had been the recipient of Davidson's "screams of protest and denial" cable, in which Davidson warned that headquarters would not accept enemy strengths higher than those already "carried by the press." And Boies got Godding to admit—contrary to his deposition, in which he had steadfastly maintained that public relations issues had no impact on the enemy estimates—that he was aware of public relations concerns at the Langley conference after all. In the end, Godding testified that he was ordered to "present and defend" an estimate of 297,000 at Langley. This was something quite different from saying there was an "arbitrary ceiling" imposed by Westmoreland, but that nuance was lost on everyone. As the day ended, Boies baited Godding yet again, asking the general what percentage of the irregulars carried arms, and Godding said around 10 percent. When Boies pressed him on his basis for that observation, Godding said he drew on his perceptions in the European war. At this, Godding was finished: Boies had turned him into an old geezer, probably lying, who failed to grasp the new enemy that America faced in its first guerilla conflict. Boies lingered on the point. Incredulous, Boies asked, "Are you saying that you based your observations on what you saw in the *European war,* sir?"

Boies was taking control of the trial, as the book published by juror Roth notes. Her diary entry for October 29, 1984, read: "Boies was ruthless today. As the courtroom scene has unfolded, he has, too. He is relaxed. He is in his element. He is sharp, confident and is calling the shots. Every moment had become almost purposeful. . . . It is exciting to see this mild, mannered, conservative boy flapping his wings." In the gallery, reporters covering the trial took to quietly humming the theme to the movie *Jaws* when Boies rose to begin his cross-examinations.

Burt's case had a lackluster feel until November 15, when the white-haired, seventy-year-old General William Childs Westmoreland took the stand. Fittingly, the general had recently returned from a Veterans Day trip to Washington, D.C., for the dedication of the new Vietnam Veterans Memorial, where he had been greeted by the cheers of supporters and by organized demonstrations backing his cause. When Westmoreland took the stand for four days of direct testimony, he seized control of the trial. Ramrod straight, he was a very striking man. He *looked* credible, and he grew larger than life on the witness stand, supported by his younger, spirited wife, Katherine "Kitsy" Westmoreland, who tended to her needlepoint during the trial and doted on reporters like a caring mother. He bore no resemblance to the shifty image presented by CBS in the documentary. He even had an answer to his licking his lips during the broadcast: he explained that his wife had suggested that he use "this wax stuff" to prevent dry lips, and Kitsy later identified the stuff as Chapstick. Over fierce objections from Boies, the general was allowed to testify about what he said to Mike Wallace after the cameras stopped rolling. "I said I was deceived as to the nature of the interview and I said, 'I have been rattlesnaked.' "

Boies has maintained many times that the Westmoreland cross-examination was the most difficult of his life. "His direct testimony was moving," Boies told me, more moving than the trial transcript could possibly reveal. At one point in his direct examination, Westmoreland pulled from his breast pocket a card that he distributed to his officers. On it was a fifteen-point code of conduct, a list of homilies. When Burt told him that he would have to mark the document in evidence, Westmoreland pleaded that it was his only copy, and Burt hammed it up by telling the general that he would put "a very little tag" on it. The first point on the card read, "Make the welfare of your men your prime concern with special attention to mess, mail and medical care." The second, "Give priority to matters of intelligence, counterintelligence and timely and accurate reporting." An article by Eleanor Randolph, the reporter covering the trial for the *Washington Post*, described the scene as "a moment that would have warmed Perry Mason's heart." And even now, it is one of the moments that lingers in Boies's mind. "It was a dramatic direct examination; he was sympathetic, he was attractive."

The general's direct testimony ended with a review of the pain he had suffered after the broadcast aired; the calls he received from fifty friends, the astonishment of his children, the letters he received and threw away because they made him so angry. Burt read at length from a searing letter from a Houston woman: "You played God with those lives and to this day American parents are still grieving. . . . After seeing that show on TV I hope the American people never give you another moment's peace." The last exhibit, a devastating cartoon entitled "Body Count" that the general received in the mail, depicted him holding a machine gun over the bodies of three dead soldiers, identified on their bodies as Duty, Honor, and Country. "It was the most humiliating experience," Westmoreland said. Burt's final question: "General Westmoreland, while you were in uniform, did you ever lie to one of your superior officers?" He replied, "Never!" As he left the stand, reporters noted that his wife was quietly weeping.

For Boies, manipulating the general would require a delicate approach.

Beyond Westmoreland's stature, there was the problem of his testimony itself: the crux of his direct testimony was that he took the guerilla forces out—an act that CBS called a conspiracy to "suppress" certain categories of the enemy—because he believed they didn't amount to a military threat. In a trial about numbers, his testimony focused on his opinions and conclusions about the rising number of guerrillas, rather than the fact of them. "It didn't have the hard edge that allows you to confront it with objective facts," Boies said. "It wasn't 'The light was red or green,' it was 'I believe this.' "

When Boies rose to cross-examine Westmoreland, it was already midafternoon on November 20. Judge Leval had called a ten-minute recess after the general's emotional last words on direct. Boies had about an hour and a half to begin his questioning—and to give reporters in the gallery a headline for the next day's papers.

Boies began by confronting Westmoreland with his testimony—both at his deposition and at trial—that he could not recall discussing enemy strength estimates with President Johnson. This testimony went to the heart of what was in dispute. Burt, on the eve of trial, had whittled his libel case down to just one charge in the CBS broadcast: that Westmoreland had lied to his superiors, including the president. Boies directed Westmoreland to his deposition, where the general had stated, "I don't precisely recall talking to him with respect to specifics." The general knew, by now, of official notes on his meetings with Johnson—they had already been introduced at the trial—and he had admitted that "the configuration of the enemy" came up. "Well, it was a little bit more than just that, was it not, sir?" Boies shot back. "You discussed actual numbers of the enemy with the president, did you not?" Westmoreland stuck to his guns. "Frankly, I don't remember being that specific, no," he said. Boies produced notes of Westmoreland's April 1967 meeting with the president, when he was summoned to Washington from Vietnam. These notes put the enemy strength at 285,000, and, more important, asserted that "we reached the crossover point," meaning that the enemy was losing forces faster than it could put them back on the battlefield. "Do you see that, sir?" Boies asked. Still, the general couldn't recall. "Do you have any reason to doubt the accuracy of these notes?" Boies demanded. "I have no reason to doubt or not doubt the accuracy," the general replied.

It was possible that the general simply failed to remember. But over the course of the short time remaining in the afternoon, Boies set up the general with a series of questions that put his failure of memory in a sinister light. Boies began with broad questions that would cause the general to defend himself firmly—to stake out a position that Boies would later use against him. Did the general, when he gave the president a figure of 285,000 in enemy strength in April 1967, suggest "that the figure was inaccurate in any way?" Certainly not! The general told Boies it was "the best estimate that my intelligence people had." Then Boies employed one of his standard tactics, taking the exact words from the witness's answer. "And you presented it to him as the best estimate that your intelligence people had, correct, sir?" The general said yes. Again, Boies asked the question. It was "the very best that you could, correct, sir?"

With that locked down, Boies moved on to an intelligence report from a February 1967 conference in Honolulu. On direct, Westmoreland had testified confidently about this report, calling the conference a chance for the military command to coordinate intelligence so they "would be playing off the same sheet of music." Now Boies read from a portion of the report: "Preliminary indications point to a sharp increase in the number of irregulars to be carried out in the order of battle." Suddenly, it seemed that the numbers presented to Johnson months later may not have been the "very best" after all. With great fury, Boies built to a crescendo, peppering his questions with references to the fact that "the entire intelligence community was focused on this" so that they could, in the general's own words, be "playing off the same sheet of music." Finally, Burt registered some objections.

Time was running out on the day's session, but Boies squeezed in a question about the draft cable with which McChristian presented Westmoreland in May 1967—the cable with increased guerilla strengths, the cable that, according to the broadcast, Westmoreland "suppressed" because it would have been a "political bombshell," and thus launched the conspiracy. Did Westmoreland recall if McChristian referred back to the February conference while they discussed the May cable? "I don't recall," the general said. With the dramatic thread pulled, Boies asked Judge Leval if it was a convenient time to break for the day, leaving the press and the jury hungering for the general to answer more questions about the notorious cable.

Westmoreland, a veteran of three wars, came to court the next morning steeled for combat with Boies. That day, the testy remarks tended to come from Boies, whose relentless questions seemed to offer the general straight lines for him to retort with whimsical banter that left the courtroom in stitches. Boies bullied the general about his habit, at the trial, of referring to the "order of battle," with the preface "so-called." Boies began: "When you say the so-called order of battle, it was so-called by MACV, correct, sir?" The general could only agree. "And you were the commander of MACV, correct, sir?" The general shot back, "Mr. Boies, you know that." And Boies rejoined, "Yes, I do know that, what I am wondering is whether you forget it, *sir*. You were the commander in 1965 and 19—" Burt, who behaved like a potted plant for most of Boies's cross-examinations, finally registered an objection. Judge Leval scolded Boies as if he were a misbehaving child. "Mr. Boies, Mr. Boies, Mr. Boies, is there a question to the witness? Question, *please*," instructing the jurors to "disregard the argumentative passage."

Boies began the day by confronting the general with his own diary notes from the war, which made no reference to any May meeting with McChristian to discuss the draft cable on increased guerrilla strengths. Westmoreland insisted that he had not mentioned the meeting in his diary because it was so "inconsequential." He said he dictated things that he thought were important. Boies then snickered that the general's notes mentioned his arranging for his surgeon to see a visiting congressional aide who had a head cold. This should have been a "Gotcha" moment, but the general mused, "I may have. That would cover a human interest item."

As the day wore on, Boies attempted to trip Westmoreland up on a semantic technicality. In his direct testimony, the general admitted that if he had sent the cable it would have created bad publicity, but he insisted that he had never called it a "political bombshell"; "Bombshell," he said, "is not part of my lexicon." Boies reminded him of this as he whipped out excerpts from the general's deposition, in which Westmoreland had said the draft cable "would have been a real bombshell" had it been sent. The general took the opportunity to ham it up. "Bombshell had been thrown around so much, and I heard it so much during the some fourteen days of depositions with you, Mr. Boies, that you just thrust it right into my lexicon," he said, to guffaws in the courtroom.

Boies demanded that the general look over the pages of the deposition to find where he had thrust the term into the general's vocabulary. Judge Leval interjected, incredulous: "*Over 1642 pages?*" Boies made the lawyerly point that Westmoreland never sought to correct him at the deposition, when he supposedly thrust the phrase into the general's lexicon. "I should have done it," the general replied. "If I thought this was going to be a big issue in this case, I sure as hell would have done it!" Another punch line at Boies's expense.

Though Westmoreland admitted that he routinely deferred to his intelligence chiefs, Boies's efforts to suggest something nefarious in the failure to sign off on the McChristian cable only put Westmoreland in high dudgeon. "What he believed was one thing; what I believed was another. And I happened to have the responsibility. I was the commander."

The day ended with one last laugh for the general, when Boies pulled out Westmoreland's own autobiography, *A Soldier Reports,* for cross-examination over whether he was merely disappointed or "extremely" disappointed when Johnson decided to scale back his troops. The general said he wouldn't say "extremely." Out came his own book. "If I said it in the book, that's one thing," the general cracked. All these years later, even on the dry pages of the transcript, the general's grin jumps out.

Given the general's age and back problems, the parties had agreed that his time on the stand would be limited to four hours each day. At the end of this session, reporters showed Boies a wire story that quoted the president of CBS News predicting the network would lose at trial but win on appeal. The comments were featured prominently in news stories, just as the trial broke for the Thanksgiving holiday. As Connie Bruck of the *American Lawyer* said in the second part of her series, Boies reacted with the same winking frankness that has since become his staple in media portraits of him. Boies "gave a crooked grin and slumped to the floor," she wrote.

Westmoreland may have won the first full day of his cross-examination, when Boies the craven, nitpicking lawyer fussed over words like "bombshell" and "extremely." But the general's strength—the righteousness with which he defended his judgments during the war—turned into a weakness as Boies continued to question him for two more days. It started with a chart.

The bar chart presented three years of enemy strength—1965, 1966, and 1967—and showed that the enemy's strength was 285,000 in the third quarter of 1966, and had dropped to 242,000 by the third quarter of 1967. The first witness to stand up for the general at the trial, Walt Rostow, Johnson's national security advisor, said the change reflected the exclusion of the SD and SSD forces, and that President Johnson was well aware of that fact.

But Westmoreland testified that neither Rostow nor Boies understood the chart as he did, turning imperious and in the process contradicting his own lead witness. Boies played up the point: "So what you're saying is that both Dr. Rostow and I don't understand the chart?" The general insisted that the self-defense forces had been taken out for *all three* years on the chart through a "retrospective analysis." But Boies showed the general another chart—the military's monthly intelligence report for August 1966—which put the enemy strength at 282,452, a number that very closely corresponded to the 285,000 figure presented to Johnson, the figure that supposedly had *taken out* the SD forces. Boies pulled that chart out, and asked if he could pass it around to the jury. This was a patent inconsistency, and Boies wanted the jury to see it in print.

Meanwhile, the general offered an explanation as to how the different numbers could make sense, digging himself into a hole. He claimed that in the latter part of 1967, a new category of enemy called "administrative forces" came into being, and that these forces were added to the chart for *all three* years. Desperate, Burt sputtered a "Time, please?," trying to get Westmoreland off the stand. But Boies turned the vise. He wanted to be clear—this chart that did not include the self-defense units but, according to the general, did include a category called administrative forces "*just happened* to come out at 285,000?"

"That was strictly coincidental," the general said. "*Strictly coincidental?*" Boies said, now incredulous. He then turned to the bench and told Judge Leval that this was the time the parties had agreed to break for the day.

Boies kept the general on the witness stand for another three days, during which time Westmoreland did not regain the confidence that had given him the upper hand earlier. Boies drew no grand admissions of guilt from the general, but continued to bait him with small inconsistencies that often produced high drama in the press simply because the questions invoked larger-than-life images from the war.

One typical exchange was over whether Westmoreland misled Washington about there being a "light at the end of the tunnel." This phrase, probably the most memorable of the war, conjured the hypocrisy perpetrated on the public about what was really happening in Vietnam. Westmoreland had the misfortune of using the expression in a cable that landed as evidence in a trial conducted by David Boies, who took several opportunities to pass out copies of it to the jurors during the course of his cross-examination. In it, the general summarized a trip to Washington in November 1967, when he asked Johnson for more troops. "We are grinding down the enemy," the cable read. "The concept is compatible with the evolution of the war since our initial commitment and portrays to the American people some 'light at the end of the tunnel.' "

Westmoreland testified that he had never used the expression. Out came the excerpts from Westmoreland's deposition. Boies asked him to turn to page 604 of the deposition, at which the general had stated, "I never had quite that of op, quite that degree of optimism." Boies had arrived at his "Gotcha" moment and relishes this exchange with the general even now. "Oh, he was just devastated," Boies told me. "Because he had staked his position on it; he had overstated. He had said, 'No, no, never, never,' and then he was confronted with his own words." To understand the impact of this moment from the words on the transcript, all these years later, was impossible. Westmoreland had only referred, in quotes, to a phrase coined by someone else, and he pointed that out to Boies from the witness stand. It seemed that Boies had merely trapped the general in another bit of semantics. But Boies's atmospherics over the "light at the end of the tunnel" dominated the newspaper accounts of the session the next day. Juror Roth, in her diary, recognized that the phrase was not important, but wondered why the general kept quibbling with Boies. "Westy didn't learn," she wrote.

One of the myths that grew, over the years, was that Westmoreland surrendered after Boies cross-examined him. But it was not Boies's grilling that rendered the case hopeless. It was Westmoreland's own lawyer who destroyed the general's case. When producer George Crile came to the stand as a hostile witness, Burt kept him there for seven straight days, and squandered thirty precious hours of the time limit set by Judge Leval, all the while gaining nothing from Crile to help his case. Burt simply had none of the skills required to question a hostile witness, never confronting Crile with excerpts from his deposition, but repeatedly asking him "why" he had made certain decisions about the broadcast. Crile answered these open-ended questions with long speeches justifying his course of conduct. David Dorsen, an experienced trial lawyer who served as Burt's cocounsel, called Crile's testimony "a true disaster." Burt, he said, "didn't have the foggiest idea of what to do."

Boies dealt with Burt as he did many of his adversaries: he befriended him. As the trial wore on, Boies and Burt chatted endlessly, and Boies certainly spoke more often with Burt than he did with his Cravath associates.

Did David Boies snooker Burt into his course of folly with Crile? "In retrospect, that was the product of the Boies strategy," Dorsen told me. By the time of Crile's testimony, Burt had stopped talking to Dorsen, and was seeking advice from two jury consultants on the team, and, much more weirdly, from his adversary Boies. At one point, when Boies was preparing Mike Wallace for the witness stand in Wallace's apartment, a phone call came in. It was from Burt, asking whether Boies thought he should continue the pursuit of Crile on the witness stand. Boies told him to keep going.

When I asked Boies about it, he casually offered, "What I said to him, on more than one occasion, including some call when I was actually preparing Mike, was that if you take on the lead defendant at a trial, you've got to either succeed or your whole case is in jeopardy. You can't try to kill him and fail. And I believe that, I believe that's true." It sounded quite logical and sincere.

At one point, Judge Leval brought the lawyers up for a sidebar conference and asked Burt whether he "still felt in control of his time budget." Burt announced that he would drop two hostile witnesses—one of them being Mike Wallace, who was overwrought at the prospect of taking the stand. When Burt finished questioning Crile, he had only twenty hours left to finish up his last witness and cross-examine all of CBS's witnesses. It was, therefore, almost cruel when Boies pulled a stunt he still relishes today: Boies called Crile back to the stand as part of CBS's defense, and after Boies finished his questions, he took the opportunity for one of the mini summations that Judge Leval had offered to each side. Addressing the jury, Boies challenged Burt to ask Crile, point by point, whether he had a basis for believing that the assertions about Westmoreland in the broadcast were true. Burt scurried to the sidebar, where he asked Leval for an instruction that Boies's challenge was improper. Leval told Burt that he saw nothing "wrong" with Boies's tactic, but he threw Burt a bone. He instructed the jurors, "Mr. Burt is entitled to conduct his case as he sees fit and he is not under any obligation to ask questions that are suggested or challenged by Mr. Boies." After questioning Crile just briefly, Burt made his own mini summation to the jury: "I'd ask you to remember, we have all been here a long time, and we are not fighting over nothing," he said.

Boies's unusual relationship with his opposing counsel became one feature in a series of articles about the Westmoreland and Sharon libel trials in the *New Yorker* by Renata Adler. Adler's articles were an indictment of what she saw as arrogant journalism that led to the libel claims, of the aggressive defense that Cravath mounted for media giants CBS and Time. Adler viewed the thesis of *Uncounted Enemy* categorically as "preposterous." She described Boies as "a particularly aggressive litigator even within Cravath," whose ambition at the trial was "nothing less than to rewrite in court the whole history of the war to conform with what the broadcast said." She maintained that the "unusual and developing relationship" between Burt and Boies would "eventually determine the actual outcome of the trial." It surfaced when Burt launched his lengthy hostile questioning of Crile. "Burt began, increasingly, to glance not toward Judge Leval, but toward Boies, as though in anticipation of a reaction from opposing counsel rather than of a ruling by the judge."

Cravath sent out the team of Boies's associates to research a document sent to the *New Yorker,* attacking Adler's articles as "plainly false, gross misrepresentations and distortions of the record." That Cravath would go to such extremes was natural. More spooky was Boies's reaction to Adler's observations when I spoke to him about it those many years later. "I was certainly young enough, at that point, to think it was fun to have a piece in a major publication like the *New Yorker* crediting me with the power to cloud men's minds," he told me icily, staring straight ahead at nothing. "But I think it was a little overboard," he added for measure. After all these years, Adler's articles still galled him.

The Westmoreland case came to a sudden halt in February 1985, when the general and CBS settled. Conventional wisdom had it that Westmoreland capitulated after five months of trial when CBS put on two members of Westmoreland's military command who gave blockbuster performances on the witness stand.

Renata Adler took a different view, suggesting that the first two military officials to testify for Boies—the witnesses who set up the general's fall—were not star witnesses at all. She had a point. One of those officials was General McChristian, the man who drafted the cable that Westmoreland never sent. McChristian testified for CBS reluctantly, only after he had given affidavits supporting the general's case. On the broadcast, it had been McChristian who recalled that Westmoreland saw the draft cable as a "political bombshell"—words that McChristian testified as "burned" into his memory when Boies questioned him on direct examination. But out-takes from the broadcast revealed that McChristian had told Crile he could not recall the precise words that Westmoreland had used, and McChristian had told one of the reporters from *TV Guide* that he "absolutely" was not asked to suppress information on enemy strengths. On cross, McChristian explained his discrepancy away by offering that there was a difference between talking to a journalist and answering questions under oath. (At the sidebar, Judge Leval said that David Dorsen, who had taken over for Burt in the cross-examinations, had "brought out that he lied.") The next day, the judge complimented Dorsen's cross-examination, calling it a shame that the *Times* chose to print only what occurred before three p.m. each day.

Colonel Gains Hawkins, the most anticipated witness to testify in CBS's defense, followed McChristian. Hawkins called the enemy figures "crap," in a context that made it seem as if he was referring to the figures presented at the Langley conference when Westmoreland ordered the arbitrary ceiling. Forcefully and emotionally, Hawkins took responsibility for his actions, saying "If it was immoral or illegal or reprehensible, the fault is here." The trouble was that the outtakes revealed that Hawkins was referring to *other* figures when he used the word "crap." They also showed that Hawkins repeatedly refused to confirm the 300,000 ceiling, saying, "I'm not familiar with that instruction" when asked a direct question about it. Hawkins told Crile he had "no specific instructions," except to defend the figures at Langley—"Defend them, which I did." But Hawkins became a staunch defender of the broadcast after the *TV Guide* article appeared, and even attempted to convince Benjamin that there was, indeed, a ceiling during his internal investigation.

Lawyers from CBS had traveled to Hawkins's home in Mississippi to prepare him fifteen times: Boies himself, while on a Jeep trip with his children, spent a day with the colonel. Hawkins was willing to vow to a ceiling, but Boies had to ask some roundabout questions to get that testimony. Typical was this exchange: "Did you have an understanding" about limits on enemy strength? to which Hawkins boldly responded, "That there was a ceiling of 300,000 and we could not exceed that ceiling." This testimony was circular: Boies never questioned Hawkins about where or from whom he got his "understanding" on the ceiling. Because Boies failed to question Hawkins on the basis for his conclusion, there was, in the legal jargon, "no foundation" for it. Over the course of the afternoon, Dorsen objected repeatedly as Boies continued to dance and Hawkins continued to testify about his "understanding," and Leval called the lawyers up for sidebars several times. Leval warned Boies, calling the testimony "highly prejudicial unless his understanding was based on communications from upstairs." Distinctly absent from the questions was the conduct of Hawkins's superiors—ultimately Westmoreland—which led him to conclude there was a ceiling. Finally, Leval lost patience with Boies. "You have approached the examination of this witness backwards in several instances," he told Boies, warning that "there are serious problems" with this sort of questioning.

All of this was out of the earshot of the press and the jury, and Hawkins charmed both audiences with his folksy manner. He often had the courtroom in stitches. When Leval interrupted a rambling answer, Hawkins apologized. "I am wrapped up in the subject. If you would tap me on the shoulder, I will shut up when you say so." The news accounts of Hawkins's appearance on the witness stand uniformly pointed out that he looked like Yoda, the adorable and wise alien hero from *Return of the Jedi*, which was then playing in cinemas. "He was the witness who was going to make or break CBS's case," juror Roth wrote in her diary. When Hawkins, in a whisper, confessed that he had ordered his men to lower their enemy strength estimates, his eyes watered, and Roth too began to cry. "In the distance I could hear Boies's voice trying to stay unemotional," she wrote. Boies ended the day in high melodrama, asking Hawkins whether he was "absolutely" certain that the charges he had made were true. Yes, he was. Did Hawkins have any animus toward Westmoreland or the army? "No, sir!" he boomed. "I carried out these orders as a loyal officer in the United States army, sir." Boies had no more questions, and Hawkins's passion inevitably made it into the accounts of the day's proceedings.

The next morning, Dorsen came to the courthouse demanding a conference in Judge Leval's chambers before the courtroom proceedings began. Dorsen had a copy of the *New York Times*, which, like every other paper, quoted from Hawkins's wrenching last words from the witness stand, without noting that a motion to strike them had been sustained by the judge. Dorsen was just getting started. He also had a list of the questions that had no legal foundation. Dorsen wanted Leval to instruct the jury that all of it was stricken from the record, but more troubling for Boies was that Leval was still bothered by the manner of Boies's questioning. Leval wondered aloud whether Boies proceeded in that fashion "because you were worried that his memory might be so spotty or might go in and out, so that you wouldn't get the answers that you needed." Boies took a cocky approach. He accused Dorsen of trying to confuse the jury about testimony that "he obviously finds, and I think properly finds, harmful to his case." But the judge saw through it; he even offered Boies examples of the proper questions he could have posed. He suggested that Boies might have planned the whole thing—getting a broad conclusion from Hawkins, putting Dorsen "unfairly" in the position of having to object, which only called attention "in a particularly dramatic way" to the laying of the foundation after Hawkins made his broad conclusions. That left poor Dorsen in the position of "poking his chin out to get it bashed" by objecting at all. There it was: another Boies trial trick.

Boies started to talk about the "amount of foundation" the court would feel comfortable with. Leval cut him off. There was no foundation at all! But Leval, ever judicious, was at odds about how to fix the problem. He told Dorsen that he would grant his instruction on striking the testimony, but if he did that, Leval had to in all fairness allow Boies to question Hawkins further. Dorsen decided to proceed with his cross-examination. After that, Leval would reconsider the instruction. Once court began, Hawkins hammed it up on cross, but also exhibited some gaping failures of memory. He was on the witness stand for a few hours on the morning of Wednesday, February 13. His questioning was brief, to allow another witness with scheduling problems to take the stand.

Dorsen planned to grill Hawkins further when the colonel returned to the stand the following Monday. But the following Monday never came. The case settled on Sunday, February 17.

That day, lawyers from the Cravath team were preparing Wallace to take the stand for the defense when Boies and Vradenburg came in and told him it was over. "I can't remember seeing Mike more relieved," Duker recalled. The general got no money, and the network did not take back a word of the broadcast. The parties issued a joint statement; CBS said it never intended to assert that the general was "unpatriotic or disloyal in performing his duties as he saw them," and the general said he respected "the rights of journalists to examine the complex issues of Vietnam."

Both sides held press conferences at New York hotels to spin the deal. Looking ashen but standing tall, Westmoreland told reporters that he had come to court to defend his honor and—implausibly—that he achieved that with the joint statement. "Now I'm going to try to fade away," he said. The general's pain was obvious. The CBS press conference, on the other hand, had the air of a celebration. Wallace declared it a great day for journalism and CBS. Boies was as light on his feet as ever. Deflecting reporters' questions on why the network offered an olive branch to the general, he flashed a boyish grin and said, "When a plaintiff wants to drop a lawsuit without money or apology, I think you ought to let him."

The network declared victory, but the journalists on the scene didn't buy that. "This was not CBS's finest hour," the *Times*'s Farber told me. Gerald McElvey, the reporter covering the trial for New York's *Newsday*, recalls it as a "spin" that CBS pushed on reporters at the time of the settlement, calling it "ungracious" and "typical of TV arrogance." But years later, McElvey heaps praise on Boies: "He loved it; he was good at it; he was just a dynamic combination. It's a very rare combination. He is gracious. He is not patronizing. And he does all of this effortlessly." And Boies was, of course, "always available" to the media. In McElvey's view, Boies "didn't work" the media, "he was just there."

The jury's verdict was, in fact, far from certain. Juror Roth told Mike Wallace that she thought the broadcast was absolutely true. The jury was leaning toward CBS by a narrow margin, according to *Time*'s Clurman, who interviewed them for his book. But four jury members were undecided; they expected deliberations to last for weeks, and intended to reexamine many exhibits. The jury foreman said it could have easily gone either way. But they all loved Boies. "They were all beguiled by Boies's informal competence and humor, unimpressed by Burt's earnestness and put off by his obvious inexperience," Clurman wrote. "For his handling of the case, Boies was the only undisputed winner on either side."

The nuances of the compromise between CBS and the general have been lost with the passage of time. No one would remember that CBS did *not*, at least by a jury's verdict, establish the "truth" of the broadcast. No one would remember that Boies had been tremendously lucky in the adversary he faced for the trial that would establish him as a mythic figure. By the time of the Microsoft trial, when the myth was reborn, reporters regularly shorthanded the Westmoreland case by calling it a victory for Boies, in which the general raised the white flag after being devastated on cross-examination.

FIVE

"Everyone recognized that the time had come for him to go."

David Boies's victory for CBS in the Westmoreland case occurred at the moment when the Cult of the Corporate Lawyer was beginning to emerge. The man who created this infatuation, or at least stoked it into a frenzy, was Steven Brill, who founded the *American Lawyer*, a glossy magazine that was colossal in length and width, in 1979, at the age of twenty-nine. With a staff of young, ambitious Ivy Leaguers, Brill intended to shine a spotlight on shrouded legal institutions like Cravath—particularly on how they made their money. Firms such as Cravath suddenly lost their invisibility, a prospect that instilled fear but also the potential for glory. Now the behind-the-scenes workings of Wall Street law firms seemed intriguing and fascinating, if not downright sexy.

The *New York Times* caught the bug. In June 1986, the *Times Magazine* ran a ten-thousand-word cover story, just as Boies and a team from

Cravath were in the midst of preparing an appeal on behalf of Texaco in which the megacorporation's very life hung in the balance. A Texas jury had awarded a $10.5 billion judgment—the largest civil damages award in history—to Pennzoil, after finding that Texaco had illegally induced the Getty Corporation to break its deal to sell most of its assets to Pennzoil. Texaco had the right to appeal, but the state of Texas had unusual rules, which required Texaco to put up a bond during the appeal for the full amount of the judgment—$10.5 billion, an impossible amount.

Boies came to the rescue by rushing into federal court in White Plains, New York, where Texaco is based, seeking and receiving an injunction against the enforcement of the bond. Pennzoil appealed, and during that appeal Cary Reich, the reporter who wrote the *Times Magazine* piece, arrived on the scene. "It is early Saturday afternoon, but at the lower Manhattan headquarters of Cravath, Swaine & Moore, it could just as well be Monday," was the first line of Reich's article.

After presenting the image of bleary-eyed lawyers in open-necked shirts seated around tables covered with xeroxes of past cases and empty Diet Pepsi cans, Reich introduced his subject: "At the center of the table, calmly munching a fistful of pretzels, is the man who is clearly the group's leader." That would be David Boies, who had allowed Reich to trail him for a solid month. "He permitted this reporter a degree of access to his day-to-day activities that is virtually unprecedented in this normally secretive profession," Reich wrote.

When the article appeared, the *Times Magazine*'s cover bore a portrait of Boies, staring coolly at the camera from his office at Cravath. At great length, the story profiled Boies: his stellar record, his quirky work habits, his photographic memory, his cheap suits, his demand that champagne be chilled properly, alongside the breathless account of his quest to save Texaco from a corporate death spiral. Reich did not judge the behavior that had caused Texaco to be found guilty by a Texas jury, and he spent little time pondering the substantive issues at play in Boies's heroic bid to save the corporate giant—such as the fact that there was absolutely no case law to support Boies's rush into federal court in the first place. The cover headline read: "The Litigator: David Boies, the Wall Street Lawyer Everyone Wants."

The publication of the story shocked Boies's fellow Cravath partners. "Everyone was stunned," says one Cravath lawyer. Boies's partners believed the *Times* reporter was working on an article about the great institution of Cravath, and would feature Boies's work on the Texaco case as one of "the custodians of a great franchise," one Cravath partner said. "Somewhere along the way, David decided that there was an intrinsic value in being a celebrity."

The adulation kept piling up. In March 1986, the *American Lawyer*, which was forever picking winners and losers at the bar, ran a feature called "The Next Establishment," in which the magazine picked the twenty-seven "future leaders" of the nation's major law firms. Boies, then forty-five, was *Am Law*'s choice as the future leader of Cravath. *Am Law*'s fixation on winners and losers resulted in another roundup in the magazine's first issue of 1987. Both Boies and his wife, Mary, got awards in the coverage. The magazine gave Boies himself the "Bruce Springsteen Media Darling Award." The item mentioned the "fawning" *Times Magazine* cover story, along with Boies's membership in *Am Law*'s own "All-Stars of the 90s." It noted, in typically snarky fashion, that Boies, like the Boss, "is good at what he does, but the deification may have gotten out of hand." Mary got the "Best Legal Analysis Award," based on the quote that she gave to the *Times Magazine* reporter on why her husband should have taken on the Westmoreland case with no prior First Amendment experience. She had said, "It's a very short amendment; he will learn it."

Brill met Boies early on, when he was reporting a Cravath story for the magazine. Brill found Boies to be a "breath of fresh air." Brill remembers even then that Boies was "walking an interesting line." He was revered by and close to "some of the stiffest and most curmudgeonly" of Cravath's partners, chief among them Thomas Barr.

Boies and Brill had mutual friends in the Democratic Party, lived near each other in the horsey hills of Bedford, and spent Thanksgivings at each other's houses. Each year, Boies held an Easter egg hunt at his estate for their families, hiding a real silver Kennedy half dollar in one of the eggs. Cravath partners widely believed that Boies began leaking information to Brill for *Am Law*'s annual survey of partnership profits at the large law firms, since they soon noticed the figures on Cravath becoming more accurate. But the glowing treatment that Boies received in *Am Law*'s pages came from something much less direct, and more insidious, than a quid pro quo between buddies. Boies's personality, his easy intelligence and guaranteed success, meshed with the brash image of *Am Law* and its founder. They were of a piece.

Over the years, Boies received overtures from several big New York law firms. Among them were Skadden, Arps, Slate, Meagher & Flom, the prototype of the 1980s deal-making firm, and Weil, Gotshal & Manges, which was not exactly a white-shoe firm, but one aggressive in its payment of "rainmaker" lawyers. Weil Gotshal senior partner Ira Millstein, an antitrust lawyer and Manhattan socialite, courted Boies vigorously. These firms offered Boies the prospect of even bigger money than he was making at Cravath.

But Boies never made a move, and that was probably wise. The 1980s established that a law firm was a business like any other. A whole new consulting field emerged, led by management guru Bradford Hildebrandt, to teach lawyers how to hew to the bottom line. But Cravath ignored the trend. Then as now, the firm held itself out as a partnership with a pure democracy: every partner's vote counted equally, regardless of whether one was a "rainmaker" or not. An Old World system of seniority ruled, down to the last detail: when one partner vacated a corner office, the lawyer next in line to him, strictly according to seniority, was entitled to the prestigious real estate.

The outward stuffiness belied the sometimes idiosyncratic nature of the lawyers who practiced there. The firm prided itself on awarding partnerships based solely on talent and achievement. This was, in fact, part of the Cravath system as articulated in Robert Swaine's *The Cravath Firm,* which notes that advancement at Cravath "arises out of competence in doing law work, as contrasted with family or social connections." In the late 1800s, that was a radical notion. The two firms that Cravath's lawyers believed were on a par with it—Davis, Polk & Wardwell and Sullivan & Cromwell—had in their early histories hired only lawyers with an aristocratic lineage. The Davis of Davis Polk was John Davis, a former ambassador to the Court of St. James's, who was backgammon partner to Jack Morgan as well as the chief Morgan lawyer and ran on the Democratic ticket for president in 1924. Sullivan & Cromwell counted among its deceased partners John Foster Dulles, Eisenhower's secretary of state, and Harlan Fiske Stone, a chief justice of the U.S. Supreme Court. Eventually birth came to matter much less. In fact, by the 1990s, Sullivan & Cromwell had as its chairman Ricardo A. Mestres Jr., a Hispanic lawyer, albeit via Phillips Exeter, Princeton, and Harvard Law School. The ethos of Paul Cravath—that family or social connections would play no role in advancement—was so deeply engrained in Cravath's lawyers that, even as of the late 1990s, they lauded it as something that distinguished their firm from its few peers. Cravath partners liked to point out that their colleagues came from simple roots. Barr, for instance, grew up in a middle-class home in Kansas City—a fact that was pointed out to me by several members of the firm. But there was, in my experience as a legal reporter, something different about the lawyers from Cravath. Their belief in Cravath as a meritocracy was so ingrained that they were, in fact, a pretty tolerant bunch. Partners at Cravath didn't question their fellow men if they appeared a bit disheveled or eccentric. "They point out some of the weirdoes who've become partners because their work was just so damn good," one third-year associate told Steven Brill in an *Am Law* article on Cravath that appeared in March 1983. The work was all that mattered; that was what every Cravath partner believed. "Cravath is supposed to have a lot of individualists; they're not supposed to be cookie-cutter people. I mean, one guy ended up in a motel in the Bronx," Brill told me, referring to a Cravath partner who became notorious in death when he was found murdered in a Bronx motel room that rented its rooms by the hour. He had been stabbed by a young black man from whom he had solicited sex. Cravath, Brill told me, was the "only place that would have taken someone like David, for sure."

Boies, too, agreed with this. "Cravath institutionally was primarily a meritocracy where, if you were a good lawyer, they were prepared to accept all sorts of behavior that was different from the norm." Boies also agreed that Cravath was the only large firm at which he could have remained for such a long time. "I think there are some large firms that I would have found also to be tolerant. But there are certainly not a lot of large firms that I would have lasted in."

Cravath's partners did not question each other. It was part and parcel of the vaunted freedom imparted to each partner by the pure democracy. But as the years went by, Boies's lavish expenses became a topic of endless speculation among some of his partners. Boies always had a limousine and driver. He chartered private jets. He had lavish dinners at places like Lutèce and La Caravelle, the quaint midtown French establishment whose staff still addressed Boies as "Mr. Mumm's" until it closed in July 2004. Speculation centered on Boies's assistant, Michael Peyton. Some partners suspected that it was Peyton's job to figure out which clients would get charged for

Boies's various expenses. Another saw Peyton's role as screening out the most lavish expenses to make sure that the clients would *not* get charged. "No one banged through expenses like David," says one former colleague.

How much time Boies actually spent in the office was anyone's guess. His friend Vradenburg, an admirer, says, "David was a wild duck; he did not fly in formation." By the time Vradenburg arrived at CBS and hired Boies as his lawyer, he knew the drill: Boies's secretary kept a short list of clients whose calls Boies would return, wherever he happened to be, whether on a gambling junket in Atlantic City or a Jeep trip with his children. Even for his most important clients, Boies was almost impossible to reach. "Work travels to David, David doesn't travel to work," Vradenburg says, with mischief in his eyes.

"There was always a lot of mystery," says Cravath partner Francis Barron, who worked as one of Boies's associates. "David would disappear for long periods of time and then reappear. It was kind of scary."

The Cravath partners put up with Boies's behavior for several reasons. First, the partners were "just not a confrontational group of people," says one of his former colleagues. But overwhelmingly, Boies benefited from the abiding loyalty and protection of his mentor, Thomas Barr. "Barr defended him every step of the way," according to one of Boies's former partners. Barr referred to Boies as the greatest litigator of his generation. "It was very difficult to get beyond Tom Barr." That Barr was so steadfast was odd, given that Barr, the squeaky-clean marine from Missouri, had little in common with Boies, whose rumored sexual dalliances titillated his fellow partners. "Barr would brush it off," says another Cravath partner.

How much work Boies actually put in for Cravath's stable of corporate clients is another matter for speculation. At the time of the Microsoft trial, when *New Yorker* writer Ken Auletta was reporting his book *World War 3.0*, Sam Butler, then Cravath's managing partner, talked to Auletta about Boies. "After the Westmoreland case, for the next ten years, David didn't do a lot of mainstream Cravath work," he told Auletta. "He worked mostly on his own clients." Butler estimated that Boies was in the office about a third of the time from 1992 to 1997, when he left.

Butler refused to be interviewed for this book, but Boies was glad to talk to me about Butler. "Sam was concerned about, threatened by, unhappy with me, for decades," Boies told me on a plane ride to Washington, D.C., in September 2000. He was headed to a meeting with Capitol

Hill staffers to persuade them that Napster's online music service did not violate copyright laws. At the time, Boies's new law firm was involved in a nasty fight with lawyers from Cravath. Boies's firm had touted a $40 million arbitration award it won for Worldspan, a worldwide system for reserving airline tickets, against another reservation system called Abacus, finding that Abacus, which had contracts with Worldspan, was secretly negotiating with a competitor and in the process disclosed Worldspan's trade secrets. Abacus was represented by Cravath, and the Cravath lawyers were livid when they discovered that Boies's firm had distributed copies of the entire, lengthy judgment to members of the press (including myself, at the *National Law Journal*). Cravath claimed the papers were sealed, and its lawyers stormed into court seeking a motion for contempt against Worldspan.

This was only the latest episode in the catfight that Butler has pursued against Boies in print for a long time. In April 1998, when the *American Lawyer* ran a glowing feature about Boies and his then new law firm, it was early in Worldspan's lawsuit against Abacus, and an Atlanta judge had denied Worldspan's motion for a preliminary injunction against Abacus to stop its allegedly illegal practices. A cheeky sidebar called "Boies v. Cravath: Round One" summed up this early skirmish. Three Cravath partners pointed out that the judge had denied Worldspan's motion. But Butler, who was still Cravath's chairman, tallied the score. "So far, it's Cravath one; Boies & Schiller, zero." Though the Atlanta judge stopped short of granting the injunction, his three-page order contained some pretty damning references to Abacus. He said the evidence in the case showed "numerous, egregious breaches" of contract by Abacus, and that the defendant "without question" and "with great secrecy" used Worldspan's confidential information. It didn't take much for Boies to deflect Butler's declaration of a win. In his breezy fashion, he brushed it off. "If anybody at Cravath tells you that they enjoy having their client found by a court at the beginning of a major arbitration to have egregiously and secretly violated their contract, I think they're funning you," Boies told the *American Lawyer*.

In 1986, when the *Times Magazine* published its Boies cover story, Butler had said, "David is kind of the eccentric genius here," a comment that many at Cravath—Boies included—took as a subtle dig. "The thing I never understood was why he felt intent on being in competition with me," Boies said. "He was considerably older than I was. He was a partner at the firm when I joined the firm. When I was a young partner, he was the presiding partner of the firm. He was in the corporate department. I was in litigation." Boies saw Butler's early scorekeeping in the Worldspan case as an attempt "to personalize this into some great competition between Boies and Cravath." And Butler, in Boies's mind, had to go out on a limb to do it. "It's not his case. He had nothing to do with it. So he sort of rushes out to say, at the end of the first inning, we're ahead one to nothing."

Boies dated Butler's antipathy to 1967, when he took the summer off to do civil rights work in Mississippi. "The view of Sam and some of the other partners was that this really wasn't the kind of work they had in mind" when they set up their matching program, Boies told me. "He probably takes himself a lot more seriously than I take either him or me." Butler took an Old World view of the practice of law, and of the relationship between Cravath's partners and their associates. Boies said he himself approached things differently.

The notion that Butler had dated the timing of Boies's disappearance from the firm's work to the Westmoreland case particularly galled Boies. Butler had overstated, for in the late 1980s and early 1990s, Boies handled one of Cravath's largest cases, defending Westinghouse against claims of corruption brought by the government of the Philippines. The lawsuit alleged that Westinghouse had funneled about $20 million in bribes to former dictator Ferdinand Marcos in exchange for a contract to build a $2.1 billion nuclear power plant. For Cravath, the Westinghouse work was a matter of historical pride: Paul Cravath himself had represented George Westinghouse, rescuing the Westinghouse Electric Company from a financial crisis in 1907. Westinghouse remained a client of the firm for many years, although eventually Cravath lost the business to other firms. When Boies returned to Cravath from his stint at Senator Kennedy's office in 1979, Butler arranged a luncheon between Westinghouse general counsel Robert Pugliese and Boies. With a lawsuit stemming from the alleged bribes on the horizon, Westinghouse turned to Cravath and Boies. The company asked Jonathan Schiller, the head of a Washington, D.C., boutique law firm that had previously represented Westinghouse in the scandal, to come to Manhattan to brief Boies. Instead, Boies asked Schiller if he would be his cocounsel; Schiller was delighted.

Smoking-gun documents found in the discovery—such as a handwritten Westinghouse memo that referred to Herminio Desini, the Marcos buddy hired by Westinghouse as its "special sales representative," as the "front man for Marcos"—made settlement almost inevitable. The documents showed that Westinghouse and its engineering consultant described Disini variously as a "bagman" or "bagperson." One telex read, "Herman, the contact, while boarding helicopter, assures us the fix is in."

Once again, Boies pulled a rabbit out of the hat with a verdict for the defense. Mark Augenblick, the lawyer for the Philippine government, spent most of the opening day of the trial on the fifteen hot documents in his case. Boies was to present his opening the next morning. But with ten minutes left on the clock, he asked the jury to "indulge him," because there were "two or three points that I simply do not want to let rest overnight." Whereupon Boies painted Augenblick as offering only half-truths about the documents. "There is nothing illegal about hiring a special sales agent, a lobbyist, to go lobby President Marcos," Boies told the jurors. "It may not be the best way in the world to run a country. I don't happen to think it is, but however it operated, there is nothing illegal about that."

The jurors were out for five days, and they gave everyone a start when they asked the judge whether their decision had to be unanimous. Augenblick believes, from their questions, that they wanted to render a split decision, which the judge said was not permissible. "You read these documents, and you say, How did David pull this off?" Augenblick asks. Even today, Augenblick marvels at the magic of David Boies. "Because I don't think he'll ever say his people didn't do it; he'll say we didn't prove it." Boies, he said, took a very damaging set of facts for his client and "put the best spin on it possible in the context of an American jury trial." Boies portrayed for them a foreign country whose ruler at the time was engaged in immoral and corrupt conduct—a factor that he somehow persuaded the jury should block the current Philippine government from holding Westinghouse accountable for its dealings with Marcos.

The Philippine case established a tight bond between Boies and Schiller, although the other Cravath lawyers who worked on the case viewed Schiller with disdain. "Jonathan was very sycophantic to David during most of that trial; it didn't wear as well with the rest of the team," says Cravath partner Richard Clary.

Sam Butler may have overstated Boies's detachment, but there is no question that Boies disengaged from the core business of Cravath's corporate clients in his last years there. Even his closest friends acknowledge this fact. "I don't think they thought he was working hard enough to bring in clients," says Paul Verkuil. "I think David had gotten a little bit bored with the practice," Cravath partner Francis Barron says of Boies's last years at the firm. Barron was the source of an oft-told Boies legend, which appeared in the 1986 *Times Magazine* piece and has been repeated many times since, for it distills both Boies's photographic memory and the fear that Boies provoked in his younger colleagues. Barron told the story to me as well. Barron says that as a young associate he saw his career flash before his eyes as he rode with Boies toward an argument at the federal appeals court in lower Manhattan. Boies had Barron meet him at the CBS headquarters, known as "Blackrock," where Boies had had a meeting that morning. Barron did not have the chance to talk with him about the case until they got into the cab heading downtown. Boies instructed him to tell him what the case was about, and to be very careful, because he would repeat exactly those facts to the court. Misspeaking to Boies, Barron told me, was "like a mortal sin" among Cravath associates. "It was unforgivable to tell him something that was not true," Barron said. Boies simply would not tolerate mistakes. Part of it, Barron told me, was that Boies didn't do much of the reading himself. "He relied on people working for him to gather the information," Barron says. "I felt as if his eyes could burn through your head."

Barron and Boies remain friends. "I got the impression in the last couple of years that David might have sort of been looking for a reason to leave but—I mean, he didn't want to on his own initiative—leave the firm. That's a very hard thing for David to do. He's an intensely loyal person. His way of dealing with that was to kind of push the envelope of, you know, how far can a Cravath partner push the vaunted sort of freedom that Cravath partners are given." Barron says that Boies did not work on Cravath's main clients in his last few years at the firm because "he really wasn't interested"; he wanted to take clients that were not in the mainstream.

Among the clients that Boies took on, to the dismay of his Cravath partners, was Bruce Winston, the high-flying heir to the Harry Winston diamond dynasty, who was embroiled in a Byzantine and messy estate fight with his Harvard-educated brother, Ronald. "It was not a productive case for the firm," Paul Verkuil said.

Worse yet was the case of Amy Habie, a divorcée from Boca Raton, Florida, whom Boies represented as a favor to his old law school friend

Jimmy Miller. Boies began to represent Habie in 1992, in her international battle to regain custody of her children from her ex-husband, a Guatemalan textile baron. Boies's various cases on behalf of Habie—including one involving a lawn-care business in which Boies himself was an investor—racked up $4 million in "pro bono" time. And there was the case that Boies brought on behalf of the stonemason who worked on Boies's pool at his Armonk home. The case stemming from the stonemason's failed real estate deal on Shelter Island was not as big a sinkhole of attorney time as the Habie morass; it ate up about half a million dollars in lawyers' time, but as a pro bono matter it seemed even more ludicrous.

Then there was Boies's habit of enlisting his wife, Mary, as cocounsel, which galled his fellow partners even more when she filed a lawsuit against the pharmaceutical industry, including Cravath client Bristol-Myers Squibb, a move that angered Butler and had the rest of the legal community gossiping that the couple was cashing in on both sides of the legal aisle in the same case. And there was his habit of outsourcing the paralegal work—usually a profit center at a place like Cravath—to a woman named Ellen Brockman, a former Cravath paralegal who worked closely with Boies on the Westmoreland case and had opened her own paralegal firm.

In addition, Boies was eager to take on contingency fee cases, lawsuits of the type that Cravath institutionally, if not viscerally, opposed. Barr also wanted to partake of the big bucks he saw the plaintiffs' lawyers making. In 1990, Barr convinced his Cravath partners, against their better judgment, to engage in a contingency fee agreement of sorts, when the federal government hired Barr and Boies to pursue claims against junk bond king Michael Milken, the most notorious crook of the 1980s boom, and his bankrupt firm, Drexel Burnham Lambert. People like Milken and his partners, all of whom were sued individually in the course of the litigation, represent the bulk of a big law firm's client base. Many of Drexel's alumni emerged from the wreckage to form their own firms or land elsewhere on Wall Street, and they did not forget having been sued personally by Cravath. One lawyer called the case "one of the biggest disasters in Cravath history," one that cost the firm tens of millions of dollars in potential business. Many of the partners argued strongly against taking the case, but Barr gave an impassioned speech arguing that the firm owed it to the government to take it on as a public service.

The contract between Cravath and the Federal Deposit Insurance Corporation, the agency pursuing the claims against Milken, had a performance incentive: Barr and Boies would charge the government just $300 an hour for their services, but their rate would go up to $600 an hour if they collected $200 million or more in judgments or settlements. Similar increases applied to the fees charged by everyone else on the Cravath team, from the partners down to the paralegals.

The deal became public in April 1991, only after the *New York Times* made a request under the Freedom of Information Act. "The fee arrangement . . . is potentially the most lucrative ever between the Government and a law firm," wrote the *Times*'s Stephen Labaton. Labaton's scoop created quite a stir in the bar and on Capitol Hill. Some members of Congress criticized the situation as a waste of federal tax dollars and a "sweetheart" deal for Cravath. The case came to a swift conclusion in 1992, when there was a global settlement of all civil cases pending against Milken and Drexel: the $1.3 billion deal gave $500 million to the government, leaving $800 million for private plaintiffs and the army of attorneys representing them. The payment to the government represented just a quarter of the $2 billion in damages that Barr and Boies alleged in the complaint they filed on behalf of the government, and an even smaller fraction of the $6.8 billion in damages they sought under the civil racketeering law known as RICO. Still, Cravath had met its "success" threshold. The contingency kicked in, the firm received about $40 million in fees, and, once again, Cravath's unusual deal with the government came under fire on Capitol Hill. "This legal gravy train is what gives the legal profession a black eye and brings disillusionment and bewilderment to the taxpayer," Senator David Pryor, an Arkansas Democrat, told the *Washington Post*. That fall, the government conducted a preliminary audit of Cravath's bills, sampling three months' worth, and found $379,000 in improper fees and $165,000 in improper overhead expenses. One enterprising Cravath lawyer had billed twenty-six hours in one day. The Cravath lawyers billed for first-class airline travel for associates, something forbidden under the contract; billed for more than $3,000 in improper expenses for routine commuting in New York; charged about $600 for a New York lawyer to spend two nights at Manhattan's Helmsley Palace; and charged another $1,400 for a weekend hotel stay when no work for the government was even billed. Both Barr and Boies brushed off the audit. "The result we obtained has been recognized by everyone to be an extraordinarily good result," Boies told the *Washington*

Post. "If the government can get the same result from people who don't work all night and who stay in inexpensive hotels, then that's what the government ought to do."

The government's case against Milken, in the minds of Cravath partners, had at least the patina of legitimacy. But in 1993, to the chagrin of his Cravath partners, Boies hooked up with none other than Joseph Jamail on a plaintiff's antitrust case. Jamail was the smooth-talking Texas trial lawyer who had won the $11 billion verdict against Texaco. Granted, Cravath had not represented Texaco at the trial, but the firm—Boies, no less!—was Texaco's lawyer on appeal. The firm already had a palpable disdain for contingency work, but Boies's joining forces with Jamail amounted to disrespect of Cravath. Boies and Jamail teamed up to represent Continental and Northwest Airlines, which accused American Airlines of violating the antitrust laws. The trial ended in a loss for Boies and Jamail; the jury rendered a verdict for the defense after less than three hours of deliberation.

At the trial, Boies complained to one of his cocounsel, Parker Folse III, of Susman Godfrey, that Cravath's compensation system was holding him back. Folse says, "I remember him talking about the fact that partners at Cravath really got paid in lockstep based on seniority, and so despite the fact that he was bringing in an awful lot of money he wasn't making appreciably more than people who were bringing in a fraction of that."

Under the firm's compensation system, a partner of seventeen years made three times as much as a new partner. Increases topped out at seventeen years, after which all partners received the same pay. That was the deal, and the democracy of the partnership rendered the situation permanent, even if a "rainmaker" like Boies didn't like it. The irony, of course, was that Boies's partners did not consider him a rainmaker at all, when he left Cravath in May 1997 rather than give up a case against one of Cravath's most important clients, Time Warner.

On May 13, 1997, sportswriter Murray Chass of the *New York Times* broke the story that a lawsuit by Yankees owner George Steinbrenner against Major League Baseball was about to suffer a setback, owing to a potential conflict of interest for Cravath, the law firm representing him. The suit challenged MLB's centralized agreement governing sponsorship and licensing of merchandise with team logos, like T-shirts and jackets. The thirty MLB teams shared equally in the revenue generated, and Steinbrenner thought the Yankees should get more because merchandise from the most successful baseball club in history was such a big seller. The club had struck a ten-year, $95 million sponsorship agreement with Adidas in March 1997, and when MLB tried to block the sales of these items, the Yankees and Adidas sued.

The lawsuit charged MLB, and baseball's twenty-nine other ball clubs, with a "concerted effort" to "combine and conspire together to restrain competition" in the licensing of baseball club trademarks, and accused the defendants of implementing a "cartel" for the licensing of club trademarks. There was, on the face of it, an enormous problem with these allegations: Major League Baseball has enjoyed an exemption from the antitrust laws since a 1922 U.S. Supreme Court ruling. The complaint shrugged off this hurdle in a paragraph, stating that the defendants' actions were "unrelated to, and outside of the reasonable scope of, any exemption the business of baseball may have from the antitrust laws." In Chass's *Times* story, an anonymous lawyer involved with baseball called the ninety-one-page complaint "exquisitely pleaded." In any lawsuit, the complaint is the first shot filed by the plaintiff: these documents often "plead" the bare bones necessary to allege a claim. But Boies's style is to offer a compelling narrative in his complaints. His complaint began: "The New York Yankees are, and have long been, the most successful baseball club in history. . . . At least since the Yankees purchased Babe Ruth from the Boston Red Sox in January 1920, many clubs have expressed envy and enmity toward the Yankees. . . . This action arises out of a concerted effort by defendants to combine and conspire together to restrain competition in the businesses of the licensing of Club trademarks . . . and to misappropriate rights and revenues belonging to the Yankees and Adidas."

The suit against Major League Baseball was an audacious move—completely in character for Steinbrenner, and one designed by Boies. Boies again teamed up with Schiller, who represented Adidas in the lawsuit. The complaint was filed in a Tampa federal district court on May 6, 1997, and sued the Atlanta Braves, along with every other team in MLB. The Braves were owned by Ted Turner; by virtue of Turner Broadcasting's merger with Time Warner, the team was a subsidiary of Time Warner. And Time Warner was one of Cravath's most important clients.

Was Boies's representation of the Yankees a conflict of interest? Lawyers and ethicists could split hairs on the issue—and in the days following the filing of the suit, they did just that. Technically, it was probably not a conflict, but it didn't matter. A powerful indication of how little it mattered lay in the on-the-record statement that Butler gave to Chass for his scoop on the client-conflict problem, laying the blame for the firm's embarrassment at Boies's door. "I don't think anybody thought there was an idea that there would be a lawsuit against the Braves. That developed at the last minute and I think it was an oversight on the part of Mr. Boies."

An oversight on the part of Mr. Boies. The average reader of the *Times* probably did not grasp the significance of that bland statement. But within the culture of Cravath—a firm where the partners by tradition followed their colleagues to the grave, attending the funerals of their deceased colleagues en masse, side by side, performing the "Cravath Walk"—Butler's subtle remark was tantamount to a public disinheritance.

Schiller immediately knew the significance of what Butler had said. William Isaacson, then one of Schiller's associates, recalls that "Schiller came in one day and said 'David is leaving Cravath.'" Isaacson asked whether Schiller was kidding, and whether he had spoken with Boies. Schiller said he didn't need to, and he read the apparently innocuous quote to Isaacson.

"Sam was absolutely determined to get rid of David before all of this," one of Boies's former partners told me. "This was the final straw." Boies had failed to file a new business memo—a document that lawyers at big firms know as a "conflicts sheet"—when he filed the lawsuit against MLB and all of its teams. The firm was aware that he represented George Steinbrenner, but had no knowledge of the massive complaint. Cravath only learned of the Yankees lawsuit when Time Warner CEO Gerald Levin called. Levin spoke either to Robert Joffee, the partner who oversaw Time Warner's business, or to Butler directly. At any rate, when Butler found out, he was irate. "Everyone recognized that the time had come for him to go," one lawyer from Cravath told me.

Boies talked with Steve Brill, who told him, "This isn't about the Yankees; it's not about the Yankees." Boies agreed. Brill gave his friend a piece of advice about law firm economics: "I said, listen, you should have done this a long time ago." He told Boies that he shouldn't worry about the details; that Boies could make much more money than his $2.1 million partnership draw at Cravath if he struck out on his own. If he put up $100,000 to $150,000 of his own cash, he would make that investment back in no time.

Boies phoned his wife, Mary, and told her that he was seriously considering leaving Cravath. He asked her what she thought. Mary told him that whatever he thought, she thought. What she was really thinking, she told me later, was that he should not leave. Less than a day later, he rang her to say that he had left. Stunned, Mary said she thought he was just thinking about the move. Boies replied, "Now I've thought about it, and now I've left, and remember, you agree with that."

Butler sent an internal memo on May 14 to all of Cravath's employees, announcing, "David Boies has decided, after long thought and discussion with other partners at the Firm, to retire today from the Firm to devote himself to the areas of legal practice that he finds most challenging. He expects in the future to represent substantially more plaintiffs than he is able to do as a Cravath partner because of the inherent conflicts that develop with Cravath's clients and the nature of its large case practice. . . . I and the entire Firm are disappointed at David's decision to retire but respect his reasons." Butler went on to note that the firm was "delighted" that Boies had agreed to continue to work with Cravath on some cases, citing current litigation involving DuPont and Westinghouse. "I know that you will all join me and the other partners in wishing David great success with his new practice," Butler signed off.

Boies's departure from Cravath was front-page news in the *New York Times* on May 15, 1997. Brill, as if on cue, made the obligatory baseball analogy when contacted by the *Times*. "In the legal industry, it's like it's 1956 and Mickey Mantle is suddenly a free agent," said Brill, who was identified by the paper as the publisher of the *American Lawyer* and founder of Court TV. "This is a terrible loss for Cravath," he continued. Later Brill would joke with Boies that he wanted a check for his services. "I remember calling David and saying, 'You know, that's worth a lot of fucking money. I mean I want my check right now. Getting an ad on the front page of the *New York Times*.' But it was a true quote," Brill told me.

The *Wall Street Journal* also called Boies's departure a "rare loss" and a "blow" to Cravath as it prepared for a change in leadership. The article said Boies was "at one time considered a potential successor" to Butler but that he had taken himself out of the running. The pronouncements of the *Journal,* mandatory reading for Cravath's clients, mattered to the firm's partners, and several of them were determined to counter the notion that Boies's headline-making departure was such a blow after all. A week after

Boies's resignation, the *Journal* ran a long feature on the cover of its Marketplace section, entitled "Some at Cravath Don't Lament Boies's Departure," in which anonymous partners complained about Boies's work with Jamail on the Continental Airlines case, and, once again, Butler publicly criticized Boies, revealing for the first time Boies's pro bono representation of Amy Habie. "We represent plenty of people pro bono—in discrimination cases and death-penalty cases, for example—but wives of Guatemalan tycoons are not exactly what we have in mind," Butler told the *Journal*. He also faulted Boies for the latest revelations about the Habie mess. About two weeks before Boies resigned, Butler had received an anonymous fax of depositions from a lawsuit involving Habie's landscaping business, which Boies took on for her, also on a pro bono basis. The testimony showed that Boies had invested $100,000 in Habie's business. Boies hadn't bothered to file a new business memo for this lawsuit, but the slip was potentially more serious than the Yankees case, because Boies also failed to get the required permission to represent a company in which he had a significant ownership stake—definitely not acceptable according to the rules set down by Paul Cravath. Butler called it "an example of David marching to his own drummer." Even so, some partners believed Boies's departure would be a loss, despite his lack of productivity in recent years. "I was sad to see him go," one partner told me. When he asked Boies if Boies was sure he wanted to resign, Boies told him, "You know, it's time. I kind of have one career left in me."

The resignation was documented in an agreement negotiated between Boies and Butler. It entitled Boies to benefits of between 15 to 25 percent of his salary when he retired permanently. Boies signed the document in the same matter-of-fact way he had resigned his partnership. That day, he was defending a deposition for the wife of one of his favored associates, Philip Korologos, who would eventually join Boies's new law firm. Boies had agreed to represent her as a favor in a malpractice case stemming from the death of her father. During the deposition, Boies had taken off his sneakers, as he often does when he arrives somewhere and knows he will be staying for a while. In his stockinged feet, he took a break from the deposition, walked into the hallway at Cravath, signed the agreement, and returned to continue the deposition. And that was it.

SIX

The Tribe

About two weeks after Boies's departure from Cravath, Steve Brill arranged for him to meet with Steven Susman, the Houston litigator whose firm had worked with Boies on the Continental case. Susman, a Harvard Law School graduate, divided his practice between plaintiffs and defense work.

Brill thought that a firm led by Boies and Susman could be a winning combination. The three men met for dinner in Manhattan, at a restaurant on the Upper East Side called Butterfield 81. Things were going well, Brill thought, until the subject of the firm's name came up. Susman insisted that the firm be named Susman & Boies. "Are you out of your fucking mind?" Brill burst out at Susman. Brill told Susman that—no offense—Boies was "instantly" a "bigger name" than he was. The conversation went downhill from there. Susman countered: he said Boies didn't know how to run a law firm. Brill started to get angry, and told Susman that he would regret this, he'd become like the guy who didn't join the Beatles. Boies was sinking into his chair; Brill's wife, Cynthia, herself a lawyer, was enjoying the melee. Brill later told his friend that the outcome was for the best; Susman clearly had too big an ego to work well with Boies. Susman could get confrontational, and Boies wasn't confrontational. The partnership wouldn't have been worth it, Brill said. "It really would have worked if Susman were a different guy, and now Susman must be killing himself. David has gotten every case he would love to have."

Susman's memory of the conversation is different. He says the talks broke down, not over the firm name, but because Boies didn't want to jeopardize his lucrative corporate work, for which he billed on an hourly basis. "I wanted to be a real plaintiffs' lawyer, representing people on a contingency fee basis," Susman says. "My motto is the less you work, the more you make." But Boies had a different approach. "My impression was that David was high maintenance. He had a lot of lawyers around him. He needed a lot of help."

Boies also considered joining the law firm of Milberg, Weiss, Bershad, Hynes & Lerach in Manhattan. In legal circles, a move from the illustrious ranks of Cravath to Milberg Weiss was tantamount to joining a pool of sharks. Milberg Weiss was known as the largest and most powerful purveyor of the "strike suit," the class action filed against companies in the wake of bad financial news, alleging securities fraud on behalf of shareholders and designed to elicit a quickie settlement and send the lawyers home with a healthy fee. In 1995, the high-technology and accounting firms that considered Milberg Weiss and other firms like it to be extortionists took advantage of the "Republican Revolution" then raging in Congress, and pushed for passage of a law called the Securities Litigation Reform Act, aimed at shutting Milberg Weiss down. The firm simply found ways around the new law. The top partners at Milberg Weiss made as much as $19 million in a very good year, and about $12 million on average, amounts they were forced to admit during a 1999 trial over their tactics.

On the day of his departure from Cravath, Boies was already beginning to assemble a coterie of loyalists to work with him. On the morning of May 14, Robert Silver got a call from Boies, asking him if he would join him in a new law practice. Silver said he would be honored. Silver had worked as an associate at Cravath in the mid-1980s, after graduating from Yale Law School and clerking for a federal appeals court judge on the Second Circuit.

Silver was known as one of Cravath's most scholarly associates. The litigators at Cravath believed that every once in a while the cases required "brain surgery," and they viewed the bookish Silver in this light. Silver worked closely with Boies on the Texaco case; in fact, Cravath's Frank Barron recalls it was Silver who came up with the idea of relying on a case that became central to Texaco's attempts to avoid the $11 billion bond that hung over its head in the state of Texas. Silver was considered quirky even within Cravath's laissez-faire environment. He left Cravath after several years to take a fellowship at Yale Law School. He never returned to Cravath, but opened his own firm on Madison Avenue. Silver remained extremely close to Boies, and often landed as Boies's cocounsel in Cravath's cases. Over time, Silver became much more than Boies's colleague; he hung out with Boies's children, got to know Jimmy Miller, Boies's law school friend and most devoted acolyte, and became part of the Boies family. Silver was the first lawyer to join Boies's new venture. At that moment, there was no real office, and Silver remained at Madison Avenue. At first, Boies did not officially hang out a new shingle. He crashed at his wife's law offices in Bedford for a while, apparently driving everyone mad by overloading the fax machine and the phones. The arrangement didn't last long.

Boies needed another name to start the new firm and settled eventually on Schiller, his cocounsel in the Yankees case. Schiller, a 1973 graduate of Columbia Law School, had carved out a niche for himself specializing in international arbitration as a partner at the Washington, D.C., office of Kaye Scholer, a large New York law firm. Tall and blond, Schiller had been a serious college athlete on Columbia University's basketball team, and had played in the NCAA championships. He was a presence in the D.C. bar, and was known as a decent litigator.

Their planning was minimal. In the garden of Boies's Armonk home one afternoon that August, Schiller sketched out the proposed budget for the firm from some handwritten notes. Their start-up investment was $800,000. (The firm had not earned back this investment when Boies agreed that December to become the Justice Department's special trial counsel in its antitrust suit against Microsoft.) The law firm of Boies & Schiller opened for business in September 1997, with ten lawyers. The firm's partners included Silver; William Isaacson, who had been Schiller's associate; Andrew Hayes, a former Cravath associate who was studying at Harvard's Kennedy School of Government; and Stephen Neuwirth, who had spent a summer at Cravath as Frank Barron's associate but prided himself on his relatively minor connection to Cravath. Neuwirth had his own impressive résumé; he had worked in the White House counsel's office during the Clinton administration.

There was one person in Boies's inner circle opposed to the new firm, the most important person in his life: his wife, Mary.

David Boies met Mary McInnis in 1977, when he took the leave from his partnership at Cravath for the job with Senator Kennedy. At twenty-six, Mary was ten years younger than Boies. She was then a recent graduate from the University of Washington School of Law. Her father was a military man, and the family had moved from base to base during her childhood—she had attended five different high schools. Mary started college at Berkeley at a time when the students were rioting over the Vietnam War, married one of her professors, and moved with him when he took a job in Seattle. By the end of law school, Mary's marriage was over. Since she was one of the top graduates, she was awarded a fellowship on the Senate Commerce Committee. By the time she met Boies, Mary had moved into a job at the White House, working for President Jimmy Carter's domestic policy advisor.

Theirs was a love affair built on the fight over airline deregulation. Mary Boies told me, "You take your romance where you can find it." Airline deregulation was on President Carter's agenda. The Carter administration had a bill it wanted to pass, and Senator Kennedy had another one, which pushed the move toward deregulation more aggressively than Carter's.

Mary had been dealing with a Kennedy staffer named Phil Bakes, who called her one day to tell her that he was leaving Kennedy's office. Mary believed this would be a disaster for airline deregulation, but Bates assured her otherwise. He told he that a guy from New York was replacing him. "I'll never forget his words," Mary told me. Bates told her, "You'll love him." Mary groaned when she heard the particulars: he was a partner at Cravath and had been defending IBM.

"The first time I met him I was instantly moon-eyed," Mary says. "But I was also determined not to let him know that." Boies had a reputation. She had been warned, by Bates and others, who told her that "women were always throwing themselves at him and he was quite a man about town." Boies had a live-in girlfriend back in New York, where he returned for the weekends.

David and Mary had their first date on January 13, 1978. They met at a restaurant called Il Gardino, and Mary was an hour late. By the time she arrived, a plate in front of Boies was mounded with the insides of bread. (Boies had torn off the crusts and devoured them in his usual fashion.) They spent the entire dinner talking about the IBM antitrust cases. Boies regaled his date with his antics before the jury of his opening for CalComp. "And I was fascinated, the odd thing was I really was fascinated," Mary told me.

David and Mary began seeing each other regularly, while his live-in girlfriend waited in New York. They became an item. A gossip column in the *Washington Star* referred to them as Romeo and Juliet, but suggested that Juliet didn't know that Romeo was married. Mary called David in a fit. When he told her that he wasn't married, she said she didn't believe him and hung up.

Mary learned early in the airline deregulation fight how to negotiate with Boies. "It's either surrender early, or just hang in there," she says. "If you try to debate with him, you will probably lose." But personally Mary could not say no to David Boies. They were married in 1982 at the Bedford Presbyterian Church, not far from the large property that Boies had purchased the year before as a weekend retreat.

Mary had competition for Boies's affection. Jonathan Boies recalls that his father came close to marrying a woman named Thora Easton, an employee from IBM whom his former Cravath colleagues refer to as one of the "Boies acolytes." According to Jonathan, "You couldn't have cut it any closer."

Boies had landed with the right woman. During the time I spent with him, he was always on the cell phone to Mary, giving her advice on her cases and, as she listened attentively, telling her of the latest client demand or court deadline he had to meet. They had two children together; Mary Regency and Alexander. He called her "sweetheart," and always signed off their conversations that way. As Jonathan aptly put it, "His ship is definitely tied to hers." Mary Boies, who loved him, immediately recognized something that some of his future partners would discover: Boies would always finish first. "You know, when we compete together it's usually a race for second place, and I'm usually occupying that spot," she told me. "But that's okay, I like that; I like living with somebody who's very smart."

Mary adored David Boies; she doted on him; she worried about him when he was overworked, massaged his neck, and preened about him to the press. It was Mary who told me what is known in the Boies family as the Cadillac story. The story concerns Boies and his father, a person whom all of Boies's wives described as the sweetest man they ever met. As a teenager, according to the story, Boies was walking in the woods with his father one day, and asked him if he was happy being a teacher. The elder Boies told his son that he was happy, but he would probably never have a Cadillac. Boies bought his father a Cadillac soon after he attained his partnership at Cravath, and his father ordered a vanity license plate that read "FROMJR." When that car died, Boies bought his father a new Cadillac, and his father ordered a new plate with the same inscription. "It was cute," Mary told me. It was also great press. In fact, you could not ask for a better spokeswoman than Mary Boies—she was a professional, having spent several years in the communications department at Boies's client, CBS. And Mary did everything for Boies.

Mary told me she opposed the idea of the new firm of Boies & Schiller because she thought her husband "would get buried in management aggravation." Boies had no clue what it meant to practice law at a start-up. "This all happened very fast," Mary said, recalling the whirlwind days surrounding her husband's departure from Cravath. Mary had indeed told her husband that she thought whatever he thought about his possible departure, but when he told her he had done it—and that she should remember she had said she agreed with that—she thought it was a "disaster." Mary could not imagine Boies divorced from the elaborate and intricate services that Cravath provided to its partners. "He had never bothered with the details that can grind you down," Mary told me. "He could pick up the phone at any time of the day or night—and I've seen him do this at eleven o'clock on a Sunday night and say to the operator, 'Get me dictation.' And he would dictate for twenty minutes. He would hang up the phone, and an hour and a half later, a package would arrive at the apartment, which was what he had just dictated."

But Mary may have had other reservations. Boies's son Jonathan was the most blunt: "She was afraid that the firm was going to end up with a bunch of hapless misfits who Dad would take care of."

Boies tended to collect people, most often those people who trailed after or clung to him. "The way that someone became a friend of David's was that they kept after him and kept asking him," his former wife Judith told me. The resulting cast of characters was an odd lot, ranging from the brilliant but wonky Silver to Jimmy Miller, the former Northwestern Law student. Judith insisted that Boies and Miller had not been friends in law school, and that Miller only sought Boies out after graduation, upon the death of a colleague. Miller quickly came to worship Boies as if he were a god. He showed up to watch him perform his pyrotechnics during the Westmoreland case, and the idolatry continued. As Boies's new law firm took on class action cases, Miller became the unlikely divorce specialist amid a roster of plaintiff's trial lawyers, leading up megacases such as ones against the nation's vitamin manufacturers and HMOs. It would be difficult to assess what the group had in common, aside from Boies. But once they found themselves in Boies's inner circle, they were part of the tribe, and Boies was true to them. "Once you are a member of the tribe, you basically can't get thrown out," says Cravath's Frank Barron.

I met Jonathan Schiller one night in the middle of the Microsoft trial, in mid-January 1999. Boies, by then, was eviscerating Microsoft's witnesses during the day, and often spending the nights in an afterlife, tending to his nascent law practice, often meeting with his new partner. Boies, Schiller, and I met for drinks at a swank D.C. establishment called 701, a vaulted white amphitheater of a place. That evening, Boies and Schiller were set to have one of their regular dinners, and over the course of the night, they reviewed their cases and discussed such practical matters as where they might locate their D.C. offices. Boies was first to arrive, and ordered his then standard drink, vodka and grapefruit juice, also known as a greyhound, in a tall glass. The wait staff at 701 had trouble with the tall glass part, and the drink went back. Recently divorced, Schiller was very much a man about town. He arrived at 701 wearing a black leather jacket, an unconstructed beige silk shirt, and a striking chenille scarf, and started to quiz me on my book and where he and the firm fit in. Boies made it seem as if press coverage arrived effortlessly at his doorstep, but Schiller wore his outsize ego on his very chic sleeves.

After drinks, we got into Schiller's gold Lexus and headed for dinner. On the way, Schiller pointed out possible locations for the firm's offices. Boies seemed only vaguely interested; he never paid much attention to his physical surroundings.

That night, we had dinner at The Prime Rib, an old-fashioned power haunt where tall blondes lingered at the bar and gentlemen waiters shuffled about in white jackets over a carpet with a leopard-skin print. The atmosphere of the place was decidedly retro; it took diners back to a time when dry martinis and red meat and sexy women were all just enjoyed without guilt. It was also a place where Boies was known by name, where the staff knew exactly how Boies wanted his favored foods to be served, including incredibly greasy potato skins. As we checked our coats, a maître d' delicately informed Schiller that ties were required in the dining room and presented him with a tacky one. Boies, in his blue suit, blue knit tie, and black Reebok sneakers, was perfectly fine. The two talked shop all night, interrupted constantly by Boies's cell phone.

The Armonk office, the headquarters of Boies & Schiller, was in a squat building in a nondescript office park off the highway near IBM's worldwide headquarters and, more important, only a short drive from Boies's house. The office was in a perpetual state of disarray, its hallways piled high with boxes of case files. Aside from framed newspaper and magazine clippings on the walls, there was no attempt at design. Boies's own office—because he was never there—was occupied by an associate and a paralegal.

The young firm functioned in a state of chaos, primarily because clients wanted Boies himself to handle the pivotal events of every case. Stephen Neuwirth brought a case for Unisys to the firm, but the company wanted Boies as its lead courtroom lawyer to defend $100 million in fraud claims brought by a Czech bank. As the case headed toward a trial scheduled for January 1999, that prospect became increasingly problematic as the Microsoft trial dragged on. Boies's underlings drafted a motion asking for a continuance; they pleaded that the company would agree to begin its trial the day after the Microsoft trial ended. The other side was furious. They had legitimate reasons for opposing a postponement: they had planned to fly half of the bank's executives from the Czech Republic as witnesses.

On a Tuesday in late December 1998, the Boies firm got a call from the Philadelphia judge overseeing the case, requesting oral argument on their motion for the next day. At the time, Boies was in Cancun, in the middle of the vacation that his family and Jimmy Miller's took each year after the Christmas holiday.

Unisys sent its corporate jet to Cancun to pick Boies up that night, so that he could be in court the next morning. Eric J. Brenner, a young associate, was dispatched to brief Boies on the plane ride from Cancun to Philadelphia. One of Jonathan Boies's friends at the firm sped Brenner by BMW from the Armonk office to Brenner's apartment in Manhattan to pick up a suit for court, and took him on to the Trenton airport. Brenner had with him a binder of materials that the firm had furiously put together so he could brief Boies.

In Philadelphia, the hearing dragged on for three hours, during which time it became apparent that the judge would rule for the postponement, and against Gadsby & Hannah, the Boston law firm representing the Czech bank. As the senior Gadsby lawyer stood to address the court, his junior partner sat at the counsel table, slouched in his chair, his face reddening. He was the lawyer responsible for the logistics, responsible for getting the witnesses and documents across an ocean. Finally, he interrupted his partner's argument and burst out, pointing to Boies, "Your honor, it's not fair! It's just not fair! This man is not God! He may be close, but he is not God!"

But it seemed Boies *was* God. Working for Boies & Schiller offered the prospect of touching the messiah of the trial bar. That was part of its appeal, part of what drew young lawyers like Brenner to leave their jobs at large firms in Manhattan to join Boies & Schiller and commute to a shabby building in Armonk.

Brenner was one of the first associates to join Boies & Schiller. Cravath was not considered a hot place to go as a litigator when Brenner was attending law school at New York University in the mid-1990s. Brenner didn't even know who David Boies was during law school. The celebrity lawyer every student longed to emulate then was Arthur Liman, lead counsel for the U.S. Senate in the Iran-Contra hearings and the subject of a profile in *Vanity Fair*. When Brenner graduated in 1996, he became an associate at Liman's law firm, Paul, Weiss, Rifkind, Wharton & Garrison. When Brenner got a call from a headhunter in 1998, he was about to hang up the phone when he heard the name David Boies. A week earlier, the *Wall Street Journal* had run a feature on Boies, and Brenner was intrigued.

Brenner had one condition before he took the job at Boies & Schiller: he wanted to meet with David Boies himself.

Brenner did meet with Boies, not at the super-lawyer's Armonk office, where he rarely touched down, but in a "war room" in midtown Manhattan. Brenner made the plunge, switching jobs without taking even a day off—an early sign that he would fit in well at the firm—and on his first day flew to Washington with Boies and Neuwirth for a preliminary meeting on the Unisys case.

But Brenner's hiring was downright formal compared with the manner in which most of the first lawyers arrived at Boies & Schiller. Take Robin Henry, the only female partner in the early days of the firm. She knew a great deal about the complicated world of derivatives. Henry lived in Armonk, had a young daughter, and was simply getting tired of her commute to downtown Manhattan.

Henry met with Boies as most people do, which is to say on the fly. She says, "It was the wildest interview I've ever been on in my life." Henry accompanied Boies to an enormous Christmas gala in downtown Manhattan in December 1997. She hung out at the party while Boies mingled. The two talked on the car ride home to Armonk. "It would be crazy for you not to come to our firm," Boies told her. "You can pick up your dry cleaning at lunch." Henry, when I spoke with her in late 2001, had yet to pick up her dry cleaning at lunch, and by then she knew Boies well enough to understand that he never focused on everyday matters like dry cleaning anyway. "It's such a bizarre concept, coming from him," she said.

To survive at the firm as an associate, you had to be willing to put up with the constant chaos. Some lawyers fled within a week. Boies refused to hire a human resources manager and was not willing to consider the basic human needs of those under him. Associates were expected to bill between 2,800 to 3,200 hours a year, a level only one or two of the hundreds of associates at the large Wall Street firms reach. "The partners—they are all, like, oblivious," one associate told me. That much could be said of just about any big firm in Manhattan, but at Boies's firm, where lawyers fixed their own computers while tending to their legal practice, there was something else to contend with: "Everyone else worships David," this associate said. Boies believed that the partners put in charge of the various offices could deal with management issues in their spare time. But those partners preferred to spend their time working on cases. "It's one of the costs of the ethic of the firm, which is 'Bill, bill, bill,' " an associate said. Boies's attitude was Darwinian; he figured that those who could handle it would stay.

There was one associate he wished he could have taken with him when he left Cravath, Boies told me. That was Philip Korologos. Korologos, the son of one of the most influential lobbyists in Washington, grew up spending Saturday afternoons with his father at the White House. As a child, he had met Kissinger and Nixon. Early in his career at Cravath, after graduating from the University of Virginia Law School in 1991, Korologos was assigned to Boies as a litigation associate, and Boies put him to work on the morass of litigation in Amy Habie's fight against her ex-husband. "I was the Habie lawyer at Cravath for a good two or three years," Korologos told me. "Much to the chagrin of many," he quickly added. Korologos managed to juggle the Habie case with important corporate cases for Cravath, and after a few years with Boies he was rotated to work for another partner. Korologos came very close to making partner at Cravath—several of the firm's brass described him to me as a "solid citizen." When he did not, a Cravath lawyer tipped Boies off and he made Korologos an offer. Boies made Korologos the managing partner of the firm's Armonk office, even though that seemed to grate against Silver's nerves. Silver was much closer to Boies in the tribal sense.

Yet Boies's problem was that the firm was terribly short of bodies to do the work that kept streaming in. The firm was looking for associates with credentials like those of Edward Normand, Phi Beta Kappa, editor in chief of the *University of Pennsylvania Law Review*, who had two federal clerkships under his belt. While a student at the College of William and Mary, Normand had taught tennis to Paul Verkuil's son Gibson. Verkuil considered himself Normand's mentor. Normand was about to take a job as an associate at a large Manhattan law firm when Verkuil convinced him that joining Boies's firm would be a much more exciting opportunity.

Normand had a sardonic take on what it meant to work at David Boies's law firm. When Normand and a team of lawyers were about to leave for Houston for a meet-and-greet gathering on a new case, Normand summed up the purpose of the trip for his colleagues: "I think this is purely to say 'Hi y'all, we're your attorneys, we're helping you. We know David.' " Everyone laughed.

While associates like Brenner and Normand rolled with the chaos, Clayton Marsh decided it was not for him. In May 2000, Marsh had been working for more than two years at Cravath, putting in brutal hours, when he placed a call to Philippe Selendy, a former Cravath associate who had jumped to Boies's firm when he didn't make partner at Cravath.

Selendy told Marsh he found the work exhilarating, and said that Marsh should give him a call if he was interested. But Selendy didn't wait for a call. That weekend, he called Marsh and arranged for him to take a tour of the Armonk offices the next Tuesday. But the firm couldn't wait until Tuesday. Selendy called Marsh again on Monday to ask Marsh if he could run across town to meet with Boies. Marsh was in the middle of a hair-raising day at Cravath, but disappeared for two hours to meet with Boies.

"I was totally taken in by him," Marsh recalls. Boies offered Marsh a job on the spot, and Marsh took it. "I really thought it would be a great adventure. I realized it would be risky. But it turned out to be too risky."

Marsh discovered the firm was far from a well-oiled machine. There were crazy days when he found himself taking a deposition and fixing his computer at the same time. "Boies is not a guy who has ever been dependent on a system; he can't even fathom basic human needs because he's in such a different world," says Marsh.

When Marsh left in February 2001, he had a final conversation with Boies. Marsh told him, "There's a level of chaos here that I just can't get comfortable with." Boies responded, "It's in that level of chaos that I find my opportunities." Boies told Marsh he hoped that the firm would find some middle ground.

Beyond the chaos, there were mysteries and absurdities. Boies surrounded himself with very few people—what one associate called "a mini internal cocoon"—and others suspected that Boies wanted only a certain few to have information about billing and finances. Jodie Egelhoff, the person responsible for getting out the monthly bills to clients, was Jonathan Boies's fiancée.

Jonathan was one of the firm's four associates when it was founded in September 1997. As the firm grew and lured associates away from the big Manhattan firms, Jonathan became the subject of endless snickering by the other associates. He breezed in and out of the office without a care, while they were expected to put in grueling hours. As of the time that this book went to press, Jonathan had not yet passed the bar examination. His mother, Judith, told me that Jonathan "has been waiting for as long as I can remember for the skies to open up and tell him what he wants to do when he grows up."

While Jonathan was growing up, Boies was ever the absent parent. One memory stands out in Jonathan's high school years, when he was playing in a varsity baseball game. Boies had promised his son that he would come to the game. By the end of the sixth inning—near the end, according to the rules of high school baseball, which is played in seven innings—Jonathan had all but concluded that his father was not going to show. In the seventh inning, Jonathan, about to bat, saw a limousine snake its way along the driveway of the baseball field. Just as Boies got out of the limo, Jonathan hit the ball. "It was only a triple, but . . . ," Jonathan told me, trailing off.

"I don't know what place that has, but I guess it speaks to his timing." Jonathan, like his brother David III, lived with his father for a time while in high school. Jonathan was sixteen when he moved to his father's apartment on Park Avenue, not far from the apartment where his mother, a successful matrimonial lawyer, lived. Jonathan did it for the freedom from his more disciplined mother. "There was not the same level of oversight," Jonathan told me, laughing.

Jonathan had been diffident about the future ever since he was a teenager. He attended the Ethical Culture Fieldston School, an upscale prep school in Riverdale. While his Fieldston classmates were being counseled with their applications to Ivy League colleges, Jonathan wasn't interested. "I just had no vision of college," Jonathan says, and he added he couldn't remember his parents taking the time to frame one for him. "I can't remember one conversation with either one of my parents about what to expect from college, or, you know, what to even think about after high school." Jonathan landed at Boies's alma mater, the University of Redlands, where David III had also gone. It was the only college that Jonathan applied to. He studied philosophy and political science. His first job after graduation was in Hollywood, working in television commercials. He stayed in Los Angeles for several years, hanging out on the beach at Marina Del Rey, and, for a time, running an import-export business with one of his friends.

When Jonathan decided he wanted to go to law school at Tulane, Boies told him that he would not pay the tuition for the first year. "I don't know what to say about this," Jonathan told me. "But it was definitely the case that he for one reason or another thought that I didn't have a good enough reason, or thought I wasn't properly motivated." If Jonathan made it through the first year, Boies promised him that he would pay the tuition back. Jonathan made it through, and when he finished at Tulane he began working at his father's firm, though many of the other hardworking associates complained to me that they didn't see him do much work.

It was hard for associates to avoid the fact that, in many ways, Boies treated the firm as "his own personal fiefdom," as one former associate called it. Within a few short years, three of Boies's four adult children—Cary, Christopher, and Jonathan—had joined the firm.

The first of his children to go to law school was his daughter, Cary. She was the only one to choose law school directly out of college, and was quick to correct me when I suggested her father might have had any influence on her decision. "Well, I wasn't around Boies that much," Cary pointed out. There was the example of her mother—the fan of Perry Mason novels who prodded her then husband to be a lawyer—and who was running a restaurant, the Country Kitchen, when Cary was growing up. (Cary worked at the restaurant as a waitress.) Cary's mother had always wanted to be a lawyer and eventually attended Empire State Law School in northern California with financial assistance from Boies. Cary went to Tulane Law School, where Boies's old friend Verkuil was dean at the time. (Her older brother, David III, tried his hand at real estate in Los Angeles when he graduated from the University of Redlands in 1982, but eventually went to law school, he said, inspired by the example of his younger sister, and enrolled in the law school of the College of William and Mary, where Boies's friend Verkuil was then president, graduating in 1991.) Cary was an active member of the tribe; for a time, she worked at Mary Boies's law firm, and she kept in close contact with Jimmy Miller's family.

In October 1997, a month after Boies opened his new firm, Cary took a trip to Florida that was part business, part pleasure. She wanted to spend some time with the Millers and visit Disney World, and had planned not to call her father, who was also in Florida at that time, preparing for a trial in the mess of lawsuits that the Habie case had spawned. Cary feared her father would ask her to come to the office to help him—which, of course, is exactly what happened when she called. Cary agreed to help her father with this Habie trial, which was set to begin in the spring of 1998 in Miami. Boies left in the middle of the trial—he was scheduled to try another case in New York—and while he was waiting to catch a plane, he asked his daughter if she would join his firm as "of counsel" and see how things worked out. Cary worked out of office space in Hollywood, Florida, that Boies shared with Jimmy Miller's law firm. This was the tribe at its core. Under a deal with Boies, she would become a partner once she settled a pending class action, in which she represented bank tellers for denied overtime wages due them under the Fair Labor Standards Act. (In her law practice, she identified with her modest roots more than her father had.) Cary settled the case and became a partner in October 2000.

A third Boies child eventually joined the fold, but it took some persuading from Boies for Christopher, arguably the most driven, most ambitious, and most like his father, a Yale Law School graduate, to join the fold. Christopher, like his father, is dyslexic. "It was clear that something was wrong," Christopher told me of his childhood difficulties in reading. He took a battery of tests, and the experts concluded that Christopher would probably never go to college; if he did, he would need a tutor. At this point, Christopher's well-heeled, divorced parents said, "Bullshit." Christopher had a tutor, Miss Lubo, every afternoon for years on end, and graduated at the top of his high school class.

Christopher spent a lot of his spare time as a child trying to catch up with his father. "If I had a vacation, like a school vacation or a long weekend or something, rather than staying at home I would call my father and say, 'I've got some time off,' and basically sort of latch on to wherever he was going. Whatever city, whatever country, whatever," Christopher told me. "At some point, pretty young, I think it became somewhat clear that in order to spend more time with him, you know, the most efficient, effective way to do that was going to be to travel with him." Once, at the end of high school or the beginning of college, he had a five-day vacation. He met his father in New York and they flew to Chicago on the first day. On the second day, they went to Arizona. The third day, they flew to California to visit with David Sr., Christopher's grandfather. The fourth day, they flew back to New York and caught a plane to London. They came back to New York the next day. Christopher was a fly on the wall while his father conducted meetings with clients. "It was always very interesting. I would sort of sit back in the corner and take it all in," he says.

Christopher interviewed at Harvard when he was applying to college, and a refreshingly honest recruiter told him that, while he probably would excel at Harvard, his scores on the college admissions tests would inevitably keep him from gaining acceptance there. Christopher landed at Hamilton College and graduated summa cum laude in 1990. At the time, the country was in the throes of a recession. His mother, Judith, recalls that he wanted badly to enter the business world, not to become a lawyer. Christopher got a job at a Boston consulting firm, but lost it within six months in a massive layoff. Only then did Christopher consider going to law school and following his father's path.

Christopher entered Yale Law School in the fall of 1991, thinking he would become a litigator in the family tradition. But he discovered that he preferred corporate work and landed at Sullivan & Cromwell. Christopher learned of his father's hasty departure from Cravath in the newspapers, along with the rest of the world. At the time, Christopher had been toying with the idea of leaving the practice of law for investment banking, and made the jump, joining CS First Boston.

Boies made the case for his son to join his budding law practice while they were on the beach, on one of their annual Christmas sojourns with the Millers. "We sort of joked about, wouldn't it be fun to sort of have a nice family practice," Christopher recalls. But Christopher described the potential move to me as if it were a formal business decision; he weighed the odds, just as his father would have. "The opportunity cost for me leaving was huge. I spent a lot of time thinking about this." Christopher wanted to practice corporate law—a field that requires armies of lawyers to grind out regulatory filings and assess the tax implications of big deals—and his father's practice was a litigation boutique. In the end, Christopher took his father up on his offer; he joined Boies Schiller in October 1998, heading up the unlikely "corporate group" of the firm, which, by December 2001, consisted of himself and three associates, one of them his brother Jonathan.

Boies paid a price for surrounding himself with his children in his law practice. There were those at the firm who looked at the Boies children and saw rampant nepotism. "To me, it's a red flag," said one lawyer, who left a prestigious firm to become an associate at Boies's firm but stayed only a few months. The firm had pitched itself as working toward building an institution, but what this lawyer saw was a firm that was working "to build a platform for David Boies."

Boies himself was never around, and had little regard for the "face time" that associates are usually so concerned about. "There's no office; there's no center of gravity," Marsh said of the firm. And there was almost no direct exposure to Boies, a fact for which Marsh was told he should consider himself grateful. Others at the firm told him, "You will find him impossible to deal with." Boies operated almost entirely via cell phone, in communication with his secretary, Linda Carlsen. No one got through to David Boies without first encountering Carlsen, and that experience was trying at best. A slight woman with an extremely clipped voice, Carlsen answered calls for Boies from her perch on Fifty-seventh Street in Manhattan, in office space owned by Boies's client Sheldon Solow. Officially, it was the Solow legal department, for Boies's firm did not officially have a Manhattan office and did not pay taxes there. The "office," such as it was, mostly served to house documents from Solow's many lawsuits. There was a room with a Colonial desk, where Boies made an occasional phone call when he stopped by. His son Christopher sometimes worked there. But most often, Carlsen toiled in solitude, acting as Boies's gatekeeper and making entries and changes to Boies's schedule. The schedule listed Boies's court dates, meetings, social events, and vacations, and it was likely to change at a moment's notice. The schedule was a prized document within the firm, sought after by partners—it was one way of physically locating an otherwise virtual boss. Eventually, the sharing of the schedule fell victim to office politics, when Boies's team of support staff deemed that they, and only they, should have access to it.

The firm advertised itself to young lawyers as a place that offered them entrepreneurial opportunities not available anywhere else. Salaries, the firm said, would be competitive with the big Manhattan firms, but associates could also earn a bonus based on their profitability to the firm. They were offered the chance to take home 30 percent of their billings, once they earned back their base salary. Marsh found that appealing but discovered there was a lot of uncertainty about it. "A document floated around, but we never really knew," Marsh told me.

The problem was more than just a lack of transparency; the policy was a moving target. One policy offered associates who generated new business a piece of the business as part of their bonus. When one enterprising associate did just that, the associate was told that the firm had changed its policy regarding this aspect of it.

Complaints and questions about the way that compensation worked kept cropping up, and Boies finally addressed the matter in a memo entitled "Staff Legal Bonuses" in December 1999, shortly after the firm's annual retreat at Disney World. The language of the memo contained several choice Boiesisms, among them, "The Firm recognizes that different lawyers may be more or less risk averse." This was a term Boies used a lot—some people were more "risk averse" than others, he liked to say. The way he put it, the phrase had the sting of an antiseptic, coming from a man known to eat risk for breakfast. At the time, one of the risks associates were worried about was the bonus they would receive for working on class actions, contingency fee cases in which the firm sometimes would not receive its legal fee for years. The memo tried to spell this out, but it failed, for instance, to mention that the firm's partners would take half of any contingency fee as their cut before any calculation of a bonus. There were some associates who didn't want to roll the dice with contingency work at all. Boies's memo did little to resolve the associates' questions, and Boies convened a meeting at his Armonk estate in March 2000, where he gave a speech about the firm's entrepreneurial spirit. The associates got a $20,000 raise to put their base pay in line with the New York firms, and the option to make a written request to opt out of the contingency fee work. The questions persisted. One associate told me that his bonus check was not as large as it should have been. "The math is not right," this associate said. Another told me that if you ask Boies about money, "You're not going to get a straight answer."

There was a fundamental difference between the law firm Boies founded and the Cravath establishment he had left behind. The compensation system set up by Boies made becoming a partner there much different from achieving that milestone at almost any other law firm. None of the lawyers at the firm, with the exception of those in its name, had any equity. Only three people shared the profits: Boies, Schiller, and Donald Flexner, who joined the firm in December 1999, when the name changed to Boies, Schiller & Flexner. Flexner was a former head of the Justice Department's antitrust division and a respected D.C. lawyer. Flexner brought substantial business with him from such clients as Northwest Airlines; he operated his own domain within the firm.

The firm had grown rapidly in 2000, mainly through its merger that July with Barrett, Gravante, Carpinello & Stern, a Manhattan law firm founded by ex-Cravath associates. The firm was originally called Duker & Barrett. One of its founders, William Duker, worked with Boies on the Westmoreland case and kept in close touch with him. In 1997, Duker pleaded guilty to federal felony charges for overbilling his client, the FDIC, by $1.4 million, by inflating bills in his work on lawsuits that the agency filed in the aftermath of the savings and loan crisis. Duker went to jail. The firm's remaining partners, David Barrett and Nicholas Gravante, also ex-Cravath associates, carried on and continued to litigate cases with Boies. The word, among some of the associates at Boies Schiller, was that Barrett Gravante had stayed in business mainly through "Boies leftovers." Barrett Gravante also worked on several cases with Mary Boies, including her class action against the U.S. pharmaceutical giants and another class action against the nation's casinos.

When the partners gathered for their annual meeting in a conference room at the Grand Floridian that December, it was clear that many of them didn't know each other. Each of them made a brief introduction, introducing themselves around the horseshoe-shaped table. Boies dominated the event with a few spare words that sent a chill through the room. "We want to be identifying early opportunities for contingency fee work," he told the assembled lawyers, with the disco hit "Staying Alive" blaring from the next room, where a wedding reception was in progress. He urged the assembled lawyers to think about how the firm could develop contingency work "more effectively." Boies pointed out that three of the top five clients at the firm would likely have substantially less work for the firm in 2001. His speech showed just how precarious this juggernaut venture was; in the end, it was a litigation boutique, and when the cases ended, so did the business. Boies made it clear that he wanted the firm to remain as conflict-free as possible, so that it could jump into class actions. He reminded the partners that it was "very important" that they not take on any work for a client until they first cleared the matter with him, Schiller, or Flexner. "We are one of the few major firms that is in a position to sue General Electric, Chase, Citibank, Goldman Sachs," he said. Boies wanted to keep that freedom for as long as possible.

The firm retreats were as much a chance to party as anything else. Boies held them at Disney World so the lawyers could bring their families. The Boies family loved to party. They were truly fun to be around. There was an easygoing casualness about them, a strange mix of Kennedy clannishness blended with the breeziness of Boies's California roots, which somehow coexisted with a desire to spend all hours at the craps table. This spirit infected the other lawyers at the firm, who seemed to know how to have fun while enduring the chaos. This was important to Boies.

At the firm's annual dinner dance, toward the end of the night, as he and Mary were about to go to bed, he looked around and told me, "They're a nice group of people." (The Boies children stayed up.) In the wee hours, a group of young associates gathered around one of the banquet tables at the Grand Floridian in a feeble attempt to play the college game of quarters. Everyone at the table, including myself, was having a hard time accomplishing the goal of the game—to bounce a quarter off the table and sink it into a short glass filled with beer. Landing a quarter in the glass allowed the player to choose who at the table should drink the beer. But we were all missing, and having to force down the beer at the end of our turns. It seemed so much easier back in college! Then Christopher Boies wandered over to the table. Plop! He slapped the quarter into the glass on his first shot, and again on his second, and chose his victims. Then his sister, Cary, arrived. She promptly smacked the quarter in the glass perfectly, and forced her brother to drink. In the Boies family, the taste for competition runs deep.

PART II

Microsoft

SEVEN

The Show

In 1990, lawyers at the Federal Trade Commission, the federal agency that shares antitrust enforcement with the more glamorous trustbusters at the Justice Department, began investigating Microsoft. The FTC's staff lawyers wanted to go after Microsoft, but the commission's political appointees deadlocked 2–2 over whether to bring suit. At the time, in 1992, Microsoft's Windows operating system ran on 80 to 90 percent of the world's personal computers.

Anne Bingaman, the first woman to head the Justice Department's antitrust division, wrestled the Microsoft case from the FTC, appealing to her friends on Capitol Hill, among them Senator Jeff Bingaman of New Mexico, her husband. Bingaman didn't sue Microsoft. In the summer of 1994, she settled potential claims against Microsoft with a consent decree. Microsoft admitted no wrongdoing, but the company vowed to end some of its most egregious practices. The company's enemies in the software industry complained bitterly—and anonymously—that the government's settlement with Microsoft was toothless. Stanley Sporkin, the maverick federal judge who reviewed the deal, refused to approve it. But the appeals court reversed, finding that Sporkin had overstepped his bounds by scotching the consent decree.

Microsoft's competitors continued to take their gripes to the government. Netscape Communications created something called a "browser," software that allowed computer users to surf Internet sites on the nascent World Wide Web. The new technology in browsers threatened the Windows monopoly, and Microsoft set out to destroy Netscape.

In October 1997, Anne Bingaman's successor, Joel Klein, sued Microsoft, alleging that the company violated a key provision in the consent decree, which prohibited Microsoft from tying other software—a tactic known as "bundling" in the computer industry—to its monopoly Windows operating system. Microsoft was insisting that PC makers take its Web browser, Internet Explorer, along with Windows. Microsoft claimed that IE was merely a Windows upgrade, an "integrated product" allowed by the consent decree.

In court before U.S. District Judge Thomas Penfield Jackson, Microsoft and its lawyers treated their government adversaries and even Judge Jackson with arrogance and disdain. When Judge Jackson sided with the government and ordered Microsoft to offer Windows without IE, the company complied, literally. It took all of the software code that invoked IE out of Windows, which crashed the operating system.

The Justice Department lawyers asked Judge Jackson to find Microsoft in contempt. At a hearing in January 1998, David Cole, a Microsoft engineer on the witness stand, shrugged when Judge Jackson asked Cole, point-blank, whether the company really believed that the judge's order was designed to crash Windows. Translation: It's not Microsoft's fault that judges are technological morons. Members of the press in the court gallery guffawed at the company's temerity.

Microsoft agreed to make Windows available without IE and without crashing, while it pressed forward with an appeal of Judge Jackson's preliminary injunction. Meanwhile, a team from the Justice Department's San Francisco office was putting together what they called "the Big Case." David Boies came on board as a consultant in December 1997.

The Justice prosecutors filed the Big Case on May 21, 1998, accusing Microsoft of violating sections one and two of the Sherman Act. The section two case, charging Microsoft with "illegal monopolization," would render the company subject to the worst of all possible sanctions—a breakup. The complaint essentially repeated the narrative of the government's consent decree case: in Netscape, Microsoft perceived a threat to its Windows monopoly, and set out to destroy the company, to preserve its lock on the PC market, and to extend that lock to the Internet. The complaint sought to block the rollout of Windows 98, which, the government contended, bolted IE into the operating system so that it could never be removed.

Less than a month later, the federal appeals court in Washington, D.C., issued a 2–1 ruling that seemed to pull the rug out from under the government's theory. That court overturned Judge Jackson's ruling, pointing out that he had not held a hearing before imposing his order on Microsoft, a flagrant violation of due process. The court could have stopped there. But in sweeping language it agreed with Microsoft's view of judges as technological idiots. Noting that courts are "ill-equipped" to second-guess the design decisions of software makers, the majority opinion said Microsoft's decision to bundle IE into Windows should pass muster under the antitrust laws if there was a "plausible benefit" from the integration. The decision suggested that Microsoft had carte blanche to put anything at all into the Windows operating system, and it took the guts out of the government's main case—that Windows 98 amounted to an illegal technological tie-in under the antitrust laws.

Klein had raised expectations by hauling Microsoft into court, only to be slapped down by judges who adhered to the "Chicago school"—shorthand for the revolution in antitrust thinking that began at the University of Chicago, which overwhelmingly favored antitrust defendants. The appeals court win for Microsoft suggested that antitrust enforcement in the technology industry might indeed be dead. The attorneys general from nineteen states and the District of Columbia had joined the case—mainly, they said, to make sure that the federal government didn't let Microsoft off the hook as easily as the last time around. And now the case seemed impossible to win.

The atmosphere in the hallway outside Judge Jackson's courtroom on October 19, 1998, the opening day of *U.S. v. Microsoft,* was electric. On the right wall, the fifty reporters lucky enough to obtain official press passes queued up. On the left wall stood yet more reporters and industry lobbyists, some of whom had lined up in the dark at five o'clock that morning to make sure they would get one of the remaining fifty seats allotted to the "public."

Most of the lawyers filed soberly by the press lines, taking notice of the throng, to assume their places in the courtroom. Some of Microsoft's lawyers, from the New York firm of Sullivan & Cromwell, were hauling what are known in the legal profession as trial bags. Shaped like large breadbaskets, the tops of which are embossed with the firm's name in gold, they are designed to hold heavy transcripts and thick motions. The trial bags are symbolic: the law is a weighty business, and lawyers bear the burden of lugging around their clients' problems.

David Boies did not carry a trial bag. His briefcase of choice—to use the term loosely—came from the Lands' End catalogue, in navy blue canvas embossed in green with the letters DB.

In fact, nothing, not the daunting task before him or the apparent death knell that the appeals court had sounded for the case, seemed to weigh Boies down. Bouncing up and down on the balls of his sneaker-clad feet, Boies stopped to chat with the reporters lined up on the right wall. Someone mentioned his beloved New York Yankees, who were on their way to winning their record twenty-fourth World Series. Boies had missed most of the games owing to the crush of work before the trial, he said, looking truly disappointed. (From the outset, Boies seemed to be having a tremendous amount of *fun*. Later that week, I caught a glimpse of him stealing a kiss from his wife in the courthouse hallway.)

Boies was also battling a cold. This was the hardest he had ever worked, he said. But another lawyer on the Justice team had worked "30 percent harder," Boies said. That was Philip Malone, the Justice Department lawyer who had headed the Microsoft investigation, and whom Boies was supplanting as lead trial lawyer.

This morning Boies was excited, pumped up. This, he promised, was going to be fun, his blue eyes laughing. It was the beginning of his Charm Offensive.

As the court came to order, Judge Jackson took up an emergency motion from the Justice Department. A team of prosecutors was holed up in Seattle, waiting to sift through Microsoft's sales data, Malone explained.

Microsoft was balking at the prosecutors' demands, which, Microsoft said, went well beyond what they had asked for in their written request. There it was again: Microsoft never gave an inch, no matter what the issue. Responding to the government's complaints, Steven Holley of Sullivan & Cromwell quickly proved just how tone-deaf Microsoft could be: "The entire history of this situation proves that I was right back in early August when I said to Mr. Malone, 'It's a very complicated database. Why don't you just ask me to get the information you need and we'll do it.' "

The judge ruled that Holley was entitled to a written statement of exactly what the government wanted. The judge touched on a few other bits of minutia, and then it was time for the show to begin. Stephen Houck of the New York State attorney general's office, the lead lawyer for the states who were co-plaintiffs with the Justice Department, went first for the government. It was Houck's job to explain why Microsoft had monopoly power.

Houck, a tall man with salt-and-pepper hair and a thick mustache who favored double-breasted suits, had a low-key manner. The speech he delivered to Judge Jackson was an exercise in caution. Houck quoted from cases and legal treatises. Invoking the government's chief theme of the harm caused by Microsoft—that innovation had been stifled—Houck quoted at length from a thirty-five-year-old landmark case involving a shoe factory. It went on for some time. The best bit was neatly eloquent: "Some truth lurks in the cynical remark that not high profits but a quiet life is the chief reward of monopoly power."

Admitting that it was "premature" to talk about what sanctions should apply if Microsoft were found liable for illegal monopolization, Houck cited the standard legal treatise. The court's duty, it said, would be to assure the monopolist's "complete extirpation." In plain English, that sounded like "breakup."

Houck's greatest moment of bravado came when he turned to the videotaped deposition of Microsoft chairman Bill Gates. That deposition, as the trial moved forward, would come to personify Microsoft's intransigence, its arrogance, its belief that it was a law unto itself. But for now, Houck noted Gates's repeated refusal to answer questions, and the defense's decision not to call him as one of their twelve witnesses at the trial. "His failure to appear here can only be explained, we believe, by a lack of intestinal fortitude and a fear of subjecting his story to the crucible of cross-examination," Houck declared. He then suggested that Judge Jackson "should feel entitled" to hear Gates's explanations for himself.

The tenor of Houck's speech was standard fare for what this case was: a fight over business practices presided over by a judge rather than a jury. It was as staid as the paneled windowless box we found ourselves in. It felt like work.

Now it was Boies's turn. Early indications of Microsoft's trepidation about their adversary came from the Sullivan & Cromwell senior litigation partner, John Warden, the defense's lead trial lawyer. When Judge Jackson prompted Boies to begin his opening, Warden rose to complain that the defense had received "a huge binder of exhibits" that morning, apparently intended for the government's opening, and that the defense hadn't had the chance to sift through them.

Boies dispatched this complaint quickly, managing to make Microsoft seem slippery in the process. "Just to make the record clear," Boies said, the documents were all part of the exhibit list. His colleague Phil Malone had tried to exchange the exhibits with Microsoft earlier, and he had left voice-mail messages in Boies's presence. And the government hadn't gotten any copies of exhibits that Microsoft intended to use in its opening. Still, the government gave them their documents. "But I don't think there's any doubt about where these documents have come from largely," he said, meaning Microsoft's own files.

Boies began methodically, taking the judge through each of the claims in the government's complaint. There was nothing dazzling in this, but it was a breath of fresh air. Boies was *talking* to the judge, *talking* to the gallery, and, despite his hoarse throat, he compelled us to listen to him. Lawyers on their feet in the courtroom can preach; some pour on the schmaltz; some are flamboyant; some are sophisticated. But by and large, they all possess a single unifying characteristic: their words sound canned. They are reading from a script. Not Boies. He is a performer—with a story.

And his story, this day, began with the government's most explosive charge: that Microsoft, at a meeting on June 21, 1995, tried to cut a deal with Netscape that would have divided the market for Internet browsers. Such a deal would have amounted to a flat-out violation of the antitrust laws. It also offered a lens through which to view the company's subsequent campaign against Netscape.

Moments into the opening, Boies announced that he had a video clip from Gates's deposition, a three-day marathon during which Boies himself grilled Gates for more than twenty hours. The tape rolled, and from that moment on, the credibility of Microsoft's founder and chairman—a key player in the events, but one who chose not to testify—was placed in doubt. Only Gates, sullen and slouching in a green suit, was filmed. The questioner remained off camera.

On the tape, Boies asked Gates if he was aware of the assertion that Microsoft attempted to divide markets with Netscape. Gates responded that his "only knowledge" of that was a recent *Wall Street Journal* article "that said something along those lines." Then Boies asked Gates if he had read the government's complaint in the case. Gates responded, "No." This, in itself, was incredible. Gates was said to be obsessed with the government's pursuit of Microsoft, and yet he had not read the document that could, at least theoretically, lead to the breakup of his company? No, Gates hadn't read a summary of the complaint. He had talked to his lawyers about the case.

Boies moved from there to an even more preposterous statement from Gates's deposition. The tape rolled again: in the short clip, Gates was asked about an internal Microsoft email that said Netscape appeared to be "moving fast" into businesses that would compete with Microsoft's. "Do you recall whether you agreed that that's what Netscape was doing back in June '95?" came the question. Gates answered, "At this time I had no sense of what Netscape was doing."

There were groans in the gallery. Looking back on it, Gates could simply have been parsing his words literally. But on that overheated morning, in a walnut box that was beginning to feel like a movie theater, the words had the ring of an outrageous lie.

With the stage set, Boies began to choreograph what would be his relentlessly consistent theme for the course of the trial: What should you believe? What Gates says now that he's on trial? Or what Gates and his henchmen said in their damning email exchanges and documents as they waged their campaign against Netscape?

Another clip from the videotape rolled. On it, Gates was asked for his recollection of the "principal purpose" of Microsoft's meeting with Netscape back in June 1995. Gates responded with a nonanswer. He said he "wasn't involved" in setting up the meeting, and then muttered something about the emails before him. Boies warned Judge Jackson that the

defense would argue that this meeting was the work of Microsoft underlings. Mere employees.

A moment later, Boies was referring to an email from Gates to his top
executives, written a month before the Netscape meeting and dated May
31, 1995. Boies had it blown up and flashed on the ten-foot screen in Jackson's courtroom. Gates began by saying, "I think there is a very powerful
deal of some kind we can do with Netscape." Gates described a potential
two-year deal, written in computerese. It envisioned Netscape doing "certain things" for Microsoft in the "client" [computer-speak for the browser
software], while Microsoft helped Netscape build its business in servers for
large companies. The Gates email concluded, "I would really like to see
something like this happen!!" And Boies pointed out the two exclamation
points that flashed on the screen.

By now, Boies had the gallery on the edge of their seats. He had one
more clip from the Gates videotape. On it, Stephen Houck asked if Gates
recalled any reports about the June 21, 1995, meeting with Netscape "as
you sit here today." Gates remembered that "somewhere about this time"
someone asked if it made sense for Microsoft to invest in Netscape. Gates
didn't think that made sense, he said. Asked if this was before or after the
meeting, Gates said, "Oh, it would have been after the meeting."

Once again, Gates was caught on tape trying to distance himself from
another of the proposals that Microsoft made to Netscape, which was that
Microsoft would take an equity position in Netscape as part of the deal.
"And he says, It didn't come from me; when I heard about it, I thought it
was a bad idea. And, in any event, nobody brought it up until after the
meeting," Boies said. In the next moment, Gates's May 31, 1995, email was
back up on the screen, showing Gates suggesting that Microsoft could offer
to buy a piece of Netscape. Boies had framed the drama: this trial boiled
down to the credibility of Bill Gates, the world's richest man. The one character destined not to enter the courtroom in person would haunt it.

Boies poured on the emails and other documents in the government's
case. There were the notes of Netscape's Mark Andreessen from the June
21 meeting, which describe Microsoft offering a "special relationship" to
Netscape. Once Netscape rejected the offer, Boies explained, Microsoft
made good on its threat to crush the company, by embarking on a preda-
tory pricing campaign. Microsoft offered its browser with the Windows
operating system. The price was zero on a product that the company admit-

ted, during pretrial discovery, it had spent a $100 million a year developing. Microsoft was even willing to pay companies to switch. There were the notes from America Online, which reported on a January 1996 meeting with Gates at which he offered to pay AOL to carry its Internet Explorer browser over Netscape's Navigator. Boies read from the AOL notes, "Gates delivered a characteristically blunt query. How much do we need to pay you to screw Netscape? This is your lucky day." Boies uttered these words with an equal amount of understatement and relish. They were thugs, software thugs. He didn't have to say it.

Boies laid bare the underworld of Microsoft's dealings with its customers and even its closest partner, Intel, the maker of computer microchips. He flashed on the screen a raft of Microsoft emails pondering how the company could make it more difficult for the Netscape Navigator icon to appear on the desktop screen of personal computers. Computer makers wanted to offer their customers choices, but they had nowhere else to go. They had to have the Windows operating system. Up went a letter from Hewlett-Packard to Microsoft: "If we had a choice of another supplier, based on your actions in this area, I assure you, you would not be our supplier of choice."

Another raft of internal Microsoft emails went up on the screen. This chain of emails, from late 1996 to early 1997, would become the most damning evidence against Microsoft as the trial proceeded. For now, Boies, in his conversational style, easily created the impression that what Microsoft said now about its objectives was "inconsistent" with the candid communications between its executives during the browser wars. "On the one hand, they say 'All we wanted to do was improve the operating system,' " Boies told Judge Jackson and the now rapt audience in the gallery. But Microsoft's real goal was "crystal clear as you look at these documents," Boies said. Top executives, among them Paul Maritz and James Allchin, two witnesses the defense planned to call at trial, are seen in the emails talking about the need to "leverage" Windows in order for IE to win in its browser war with Netscape. Boies read from several emails by Allchin, ending with one in which he concluded, "I am convinced we have to use Windows. This is the one thing they don't have. We have to be competitive with features, but we need something more—Windows integration." And then Boies built the drama toward Maritz's response. "Does Mr. Maritz say 'That is a really great idea, because if we integrate Windows in

IE, we're going to have a really great product'?" No, Boies told the crowd. Boies read from another Maritz email, in which Maritz had said, "The pain of this strategy" was that it required Microsoft to "subordinate" other Windows objectives to it, but Maritz said he saw "little option" but to do it. "So in order to tie IE and Windows, they are prepared to inflict pain on their core monopoly asset," Boies continued. "And they can afford to do that, your honor," he said, because Microsoft's customers, the computer makers, had nowhere else to go—as, Boies promised, we would hear at length in testimony introduced at the trial. Out came another of Maritz's emails: "To combat Netscape, we have to position the browser as quote, going away, close quote and do deeper integration on Windows." That Maritz chose to put the words *going away* into quotes put the words in an ominous light, and Boies repeated them. And then he wrapped up this portion of the narrative: "They have got two separate products, an operating system and a browser. They have got a major competitor in the browser market that does not have an operating system, because nobody else has a competitive operating system. And if they know they can tie these two products together—if they can tell people that the browser is simply *going away* and it's becoming part of the operating system, that is the way they can combat Netscape." Boies brought out ever more emails from the underlings of Allchin and Maritz, confirming that they did not believe IE could win "on the merits of IE 4.0 alone." Boies savored these documents, but the illegal-tying claim was just part of Microsoft's lengthy pattern of bad acts.

As the Microsoft executives plotted internally to bolt Internet Explorer to Windows in their upcoming Windows 98 rollout, it continued to cut deals that effectively exiled Netscape. AT&T, Prodigy, and Intuit all agreed to bundle the IE software—and not to promote Netscape—in order to get access to Windows. Up went the internal Microsoft email of company executives describing these terms as "nonnegotiable." Microsoft's enemies in the software industry often described the Windows monopoly as a plantation. And here were vivid illustrations of life on that plantation. Yet Boies never described the situation in those terms. He never coined a slogan for the case. He was a master of understatement. He let the documents speak for themselves.

Boies moved on to Bill Gates's relationship with Intel chairman Andy Grove, arguably the second most powerful man in the computer industry.

Intel made the microchips that powered Windows computers, and their partnership was often referred to as the "Wintel" monopoly. Boies talked about several Gates memos of conversations with Grove, while the documents were blown up on the huge screen. Boies read from one paragraph in which Gates wrote, "I thank Andy for pushing his Web people in our direction. I said it was very important for us that they NOT"—and Boies noted here the "capitalization by Mr. Gates"—"ever publicly say that they are standardizing on Netscape's browsers." More moves to exile Netscape, came the notion. Boies continued, suggesting that Gates was using his relationship with Grove to stop Intel from supporting Netscape or Java, the computer language created by Microsoft rival Sun Microsystems. The Java language was intended to run on any operating system—a promise that, if it came true, would threaten the Windows monopoly, and which, according to the government's complaint, Microsoft set out to sabotage. Up went another email from Gates to his top executives. At that time, Microsoft was being asked by ADM, a chief competitor of Intel's in the chip market, to support ADM's technology. "I would gladly stop supporting this if they would back off their work on Java," Gates wrote. So this was how the industry really operated, it seemed from the gallery. The puppet masters traded favors. Boies translated Gates's email for us: "In other words, Mr. Gates is proposing a deal with Intel. 'You stop supporting my competitor and I will stop supporting your competitor.' A clearer example of the kind of thing the antitrust laws are designed to prevent—indeed to criminalize—is difficult to imagine."

Now that was Intel, Boies told us. Microsoft did the same thing with Apple, he went on. Then Judge Jackson called for the noontime recess. The judge, we would find out, didn't like to keep too rigorous a schedule. The story of the bullying of Apple would have to wait until after lunch.

The reporters in the gallery were stunned and exhausted, yet clearly moved. We had been scribbling madly for more than two hours, hanging on Boies's every word. I had the sense that the lights had gone up in the courtroom, but it was just an illusion.

Dan Shaw, a reporter from the Los Angeles *Daily Journal*, a legal newspaper, put it best: "I could listen to him all day," he said. It was true. The man drew you in. He choreographed the facts in such a way that there was no need for overblown rhetoric or slogans, the common tools of the trial lawyer. He was a seductive conversationalist, and at that moment, he held

us all—the judge and the de facto jury, the press in the gallery—in the palm
of his hand.

When we returned to Jackson's courtroom at two o'clock, the judge
announced that he would be attending the robing of a new colleague at
four o'clock, and that his preference would be to finish Boies's argument
that afternoon and take up Microsoft's opening statement the next morning.

Boies picked up where he had left off: "This was not business as usual,
your honor," Boies said. Up on the screen went more damning emails. At
one point, Gates asked his henchmen whether Microsoft had a "clear path
on what we want Apple to do to undermine Sun?" At another point, an
email to Gates admitted it would be "tough" to get Apple to do anything to
disadvantage Netscape. "MacOffice is the perfect club to use on them."

It went on for another twenty-five minutes or so. At the end, Boies
promised there would be much more. And when inevitably Microsoft's
defense attacked the evidence, Boies asked the judge to remember this: "Is
what I'm being told something that can be squared with the written record
that people left behind at the time they were actually doing these things?"
In other words, Jackson should ask himself whether Microsoft's witnesses,
nine out of twelve of whom were company executives, would take the
stand to lie.

"All right," Jackson said, and then offered Microsoft the chance to
begin its opening that afternoon. "What's your pleasure, Mr. Warden?"
Warden said it would be fine to begin the next morning. He wasn't about to
try to follow the Boies act.

In a lifetime of creating brilliant opening statements, Boies has a couple
of advantages. One is his photographic memory. The other, strangely
enough, is his dyslexia. Overcoming dyslexia has given him an extraordinary ability to concentrate—to focus on what matters, and shut everything
else out. In the ten days preceding his opening statement, Boies read every
government exhibit—and there were eighteen hundred of them. He read
every deposition excerpt the government planned to introduce; in most
cases, he read the entire transcript. He pulled two all-nighters. "It was like
cramming for an exam," he told me later.

The cramming played to what Joel Klein calls one of Boies's extraordinary strengths. "He essentially assimilates in his mind the contemporane-
ous record," Klein told me. "It's almost like he downloads five hundred or
so documents onto the hard drive of his brain, and those are the documents

from which he can tell the story that wins the case. And he basically makes sure that those documents remain intact and the story being told from the defense witness that contradicts those documents has to be challenged."

The day before the opening, Boies had scrapped a twenty-minute segment from the Gates deposition and started over. "I put it together and marked it out and listened to it on Saturday. And I came in on Sunday morning, and it just didn't make the point." That's when he decided to juxtapose the Microsoft documents and emails against Gates's deposition testimony. It was the day before the opening!

The weekend before the opening, Boies spent hours with the Justice Department paralegals who would be responsible for making sure that the videotaped clips would run and that the emails and documents would be blown up on the screen, all by a computer mouse. Boies didn't like the idea at first. He told them he had always used an overhead projector, so he could maintain control, marking documents with his own pen. The paralegals showed him that they could accomplish the same thing, even better, highlighting portions of emails on the computer. But Boies kept an overhead projector under the government's counsel table for the first few days of the trial, just in case.

It turned out that Boies loved the drama that the new technology could create for him in the courtroom. "He took to it amazingly. He was a demon," Phil Malone told me later. The day before the opening, Boies spent more hours with the paralegals who would run the computer equipment. That gave the Justice team a clue about what he would say, but his opening was as much a surprise to them as it was to the rest of us. There was no dress rehearsal, no mooting of the argument that many lawyers engage in before the real event. At one point, someone casually asked whether Boies would want to set aside some time to moot the argument. "And David just got that look that he sometimes gets like, ha ha ha ha!" Malone recalls. "He didn't say, 'No, I don't do that.' But it was just clear. It was not going to happen! And, you know, people had enough confidence in him to say okay."

The morning after Boies's blockbuster, Warden delivered a speech from the podium, reading from his notes. A portly man with a long southern drawl and courtly manners who favored Hermès ties and tailored pinstripe suits and bowler hats, Warden was genuinely likable. Both he and Boies were fifty-seven years old when the trial began. The two men knew each other, but they had never faced off in the courtroom. That Warden was leading the defense of the trial at all was curious. Richard Urowsky, of all the lawyers on the Sullivan & Cromwell team, arguably had the most comprehensive understanding of the case. He had fended off federal antitrust regulators for almost a decade. And he was said to have Gates's trust. But it was generally conceded that Urowsky was also poison in the courtroom before Judge Jackson, since, during the consent decree case, he had succeeded in antagonizing him over the smallest of matters. Warden, the expansive southerner, at least stood a chance of avoiding Jackson's instant irritation.

In his speech from the podium, Warden called the government's case "long on rhetoric and short on substance," and ridiculed Boies's "efforts to demonize Bill Gates" as "emblematic of this approach." The personal attack on Gates would be no substitute for proof of anticompetitive conduct and its effects, he said. While Boies conjured up a mood rather than coin a slogan for the case, Warden delivered several memorable turns of phrase. "The antitrust laws are not a code of civility in business," he bellowed. He dismissed Netscape as "the government's ward."

"Microsoft hasn't denied consumer choice," Warden said. "Microsoft *is* consumer choice." This was a tough sell: Windows had run on close to 90 percent of the world's computers since the early 1990s, including the computers in Jackson's courtroom.

Back in 1978, Sullivan & Cromwell, Warden continued, had Videx machines for word processing. "People thought they were going to be around forever. They were so great," he boomed. But only a few people knew how to use them, and they were replaced by IBM display writers, and then all the secretaries had *them.* Now everyone at the firm had PCs on their desks with the Windows operating system—except for Warden and a few others, who continued to use fountain pens and legal pads. (Boies and Warden had this in common.) The implication was clear: the field was open to the next computer geek who built a better mousetrap than Windows and became the next Bill Gates. It was the American way.

In fact, Warden asserted the internal Microsoft emails relied on by the government merely showed Microsoft was responding to competition from all quarters. Netscape "gouged" consumers with its $39 charge for its browser until Microsoft came along and offered it for free. "The undisputed victor in the so-called Web browsing war has been the consuming public!" he bellowed again.

Warden ended with fire and brimstone, calling the case "a return of the Luddites, the nineteenth-century reactionaries who, fearful of competition, went around smashing machines with sledgehammers to arrest the march of progress driven by science and technology!" It was the quote of the day. In a spin session on the courthouse steps that afternoon, Boies said he didn't "even know how to spell Luddites," his voice dripping with sarcasm.

Microsoft's stance on Boies's conduct of the trial has never varied: the government presented the case as if it were a jury trial, while Microsoft was intent on establishing a record before Judge Jackson, and, ultimately, for an appeal.

The video clips that Boies played in his opening were written about by the press, but they were not made available because they had not yet been introduced formally into evidence. At the end of the opening day, Boies attempted a cute maneuver. Calling it a "housekeeping matter," Boies mentioned to Judge Jackson that he had been asked by the press for copies of the documents and materials used in the opening. Boies claimed to be looking for guidance on the judge's order for conduct of the trial. Warden instantly rose to object, and the judge instantly agreed.

Before the trial, Judge Jackson had asked both sides to offer up lists of the portions of depositions they intended to introduce at trial. The government designated Gates's twenty-one-hour deposition in its entirety. On the opening day, as part of the warring motions exchanged by both sides, Microsoft objected. Microsoft wanted the entire deposition stricken from the record. "The government's effort to grant itself a thirteenth witness . . . brings new meaning to the word audacity," the motion complained.

When Judge Jackson took up the motion on the afternoon of October 27, a week into the trial, the hopelessness of Microsoft's situation became clear. Jackson immediately tore into Microsoft. He pointed them to the federal rule of civil procedure making it "virtually dogmatic" that the deposition of an officer of a corporation in a lawsuit could be used "for any purpose, period." The rules gave the government the "absolute right" to use all of Gates's deposition if they chose. In other words, case closed.

Warden was already trying to play catch-up when he rose to speak. The defense never meant to suggest that the deposition was not admissible. Oh no! But this was excessive! It ought to at least count as one of the government's witnesses! It just wasn't fair. Jackson said the defense could also have a thirteenth witness if it chose. But, most ominously, the judge also observed: "A witness of equal significance for this case doesn't immediately come to mind."

In defeat, Warden felt the need to explain himself: "This was such a big deposition that it pushed the scale out of bounds. That's all our point is."

Warden's next humiliation over the Gates tapes came during a bench conference before Judge Jackson on the morning of November 2. The argument occurred out of earshot of the courtroom gallery, but the government team encouraged the press to get a copy of the transcript for some good reading. The government intended to play a portion of the Gates deposition prior to putting its third witness, an Apple executive, on the stand. The tape would then go into evidence, and "would, obviously, be available to the press," Boies told the judge at the bench. "And I think Mr. Warden is raising a question as to whether or not that is desirable," Boies said, ever the gentleman, even as he was turning the vise.

Jackson, whose reputation prior to the trial suggested he was no fan of the press, was weary. "If it were open to me, Mr. Warden, I would probably adopt your position in toto." But the rules were the rules, and that meant that anything available in open court was also available to the press.

Warden lost on every point he made: he objected to Boies's new tack, which was to introduce the eight hours of the Gates deposition they planned to play in segments, as a backdrop to each new witness as the trial went along (and feeding new bits slowly to the cameramen outside). Finally, Warden lost all composure. "And I must say that I do take personal exception to the comment apparently made to the press that I was somehow filibustering last week to prevent the playing of the Gates deposition."

Jackson interrupted Warden's fit. "Let's not get into a war with the press, gentlemen," he said. Warden piped up, "Oh no. I have no desire to do that." Jackson continued: "Because it's one we're all going to lose, all of us." Boies said nothing. He didn't have to. He knew who was winning the press war.

EIGHT

The First Lesson

When Boies agreed to become the Justice Department's consultant in December 1997, he cut his $550 hourly rate in half. At $275 an hour, he was indeed a bargain. Once the government filed its case and preparations for the trial began, Boies became a "special" government employee, at the highest civil service grade. As a GS-15, step 10 employee, Boies was paid an annual salary of $101,142 a year. At the trial, the Justice Department press team broke the figure down to equate to a fee of $50 an hour, an even bigger bargain.

And the trial very quickly became something much more valuable than money to Boies: it was the longest running advertisement for a fledgling law firm ever seen. When the trial began in October 1998, Boies & Schiller was less than a year old. Boies's reputation as a litigation star, his courtroom victories in the 1980s for IBM, CBS, and Texaco, were historical fact. But those victories were inextricably tied to his former law firm, Cravath, Swaine & Moore.

The dividends, if counted in press clippings, started pouring in before Boies said a word at trial. On Monday, October 19, the date of the opening statement, Boies appeared on the cover of *Washington Business*, which appears weekly in the *Washington Post*. Beside the picture was a Boies quote: "Do you want to win or sleep?" Inside, the headline read: "The Thorn in Microsoft's Side: Litigator David Boies Has Steak for Lunch. He Plans to Eat the Software Giant for Breakfast." That Monday morning, Schiller asked Sam Kaplan, an associate, to go out and buy a stack of *Washington Post*s. It was Kaplan's first day in the office. Schiller promised Kaplan, a Harvard Law School graduate, he'd never ask him to do anything like that again.

When Boies brought the house down with his opening statement, he delivered on the advance billing. The videotaped excerpts gave the proceedings a dramatic structure: The case of *U.S. v. Microsoft* boiled down to *Boies v. Gates*.

The process leading up to the deposition of Bill Gates was as dramatic as the deposition's content. Microsoft was insisting on a one-day, six-hour limit to the Gates deposition. Judge Jackson had made it clear that he did not want anyone wasting Gates's time, and the Justice Department lawyers considered offering a two-day limit as a compromise. Boies nixed that; the government would not agree to any limit on the length of the questioning of Gates. "That was a strategic decision David made," recalls Phil Malone. "David's view was very clear." He wasn't going to settle for anything less than the time he needed. Judge Jackson reluctantly agreed, but invited the Microsoft lawyers to call him if they believed the government was dragging the deposition out, asking unnecessary questions.

Boies was prepared for the deposition by Karma Giulianelli. She was a 1996 Stanford Law graduate who did Boies a big favor on the day she met him: she got him past the security guards at the Justice Department building in Washington for his first meeting with the legal team working on the case. It was a freezing Saturday morning in early December 1997, and Giulianelli, along with the rest of the legal team, was in town from San Francisco. Giulianelli had heard that Boies had been hired, but had no idea what he looked like. When she arrived at the security gate at the courtyard of the main Justice building, she saw a disheveled man standing in the freezing cold arguing with the guards. As she approached the gate with her Justice ID card, she heard the man repeating that he was there to meet Joel Klein. "And the guard obviously didn't believe him," Giulianelli told me. She stopped and introduced herself and asked if he was David. She turned to the guards and said he was with her.

Giulianelli spent many hours preparing groups of documents, categorizing them and highlighting the important bits, and created an eighty-page outline for the Gates deposition. Like others on the team from Justice, she had learned that one of the tricks of working with Boies was figuring out where he will be. What city? What hotel? Giulianelli had a box of documents and a detailed outline. The question was, where to send it? "I think that the box went all around the country," Giulianelli recalls. Finally, it ended up at Boies's home in Armonk, where he spent the weekend poring over it. Of course, Boies had no box when he showed up at the deposition at Microsoft's headquarters in Redmond, Washington. But Giulianelli had copies of everything.

The Gates deposition took place in Building Eight on the Microsoft campus in an interior room. While the videographers were getting the tapes ready to roll, Giulianelli quipped, "Gee, Mr. Gates, I'm surprised. I thought you had windows everywhere!" The Microsoft chairman just glared at her. Attending the deposition for Microsoft were David Heiner, a Microsoft in-house lawyer, Richard Urowsky of Sullivan & Cromwell, and William Neukom, the company's general counsel. Heiner sat next to Gates, officially defending the deposition, lodging objections to the questions. That someone so junior to Gates was acting as his main lawyer in itself was deeply strange, and troublesome for Gates, who, it would turn out, could have benefited from some objective criticism over the three-day ordeal.

On day one of the deposition, August 27, 1998, Boies allowed Stephen Houck, the lead lawyer for the state attorneys general, to question Gates first, so Boies could study him. Boies did not begin questioning Gates until about three o'clock that day, some five hours later.

Houck began the proceedings by deferring to Gates. "I understand from your lawyers that you don't want to be here any longer than necessary, and I will endeavor to do my best to accommodate that," Houck vowed. From the outset, Gates appeared prickly and argumentative, offering rambling answers, rocking in his chair and drinking Diet Coke. Houck scored some points. Even so, Gates seemed to be the one roughing up his opponent. At one point, Gates chided Houck for reading only part of a definition in a dictionary of computer terms that Microsoft Press had published in 1997. When Houck presented Gates with an email from a Microsoft employee calling Netscape a "threat" to the Windows operating system, Gates insisted that employee, "wasn't involved in the Windows operating system and none of this is about the Windows operating system, so to try and read that in here is certainly incorrect!" Gates steamed.

Houck seemed nervous, often clearing his throat, shuffling papers for long intervals between questions. Gates took several opportunities to rattle him. When Houck asked Gates whether figures that *Business Week* had published about Microsoft's 1996 revenues—$8.6 billion in revenue and $2 billion in after-tax profits—were correct, Gates took Houck to task for asking him to guess. "If you're at all interested in the facts, just give me a few minutes and I'll go get them." Gates ripped off his microphone and stormed out of the room to check the numbers himself in Microsoft's files. He returned ten minutes later. "It looks like the numbers in the *Business Week* article were accurate." It was apparent that Gates had decided that if he was going to give precise answers, he was going to demand precision from his questioners, and that they could not possibly give him the precision required to answer their questions. He always needed a "context."

When Houck turned the questioning over to Boies, it took only a moment for the dynamic in the room to change. Boies began by asking Gates to turn back to the *Business Week* article that Houck had questioned him about. Gates had previously testified that he could not remember making a statement attributed to him in the story. The statement was this: "One thing to remember about Microsoft, we do not need to make any revenues in Internet software." Around this time, Netscape's main source of revenue was the retail sale of Navigator, its browser, which Microsoft, according to the government's allegations, set to destroy by pricing its own browser at zero and broadcasting that Netscape was in trouble in interviews with the press.

"I don't remember saying that," Gates responded, sitting back in his chair.

"Did you *say it*, sir?" Boies asked.

"I don't remember saying that," Gates repeated. Boies moved in quickly, as Gates began to shake his head, looking up at Boies: "That wasn't my question, sir. Did you *say it?*"

Malone recalls this moment in the deposition vividly. "Right off the bat, boom!" he said of Boies's question, which, as Malone put it, telegraphed, "We're not in Kansas anymore."

Gates's lawyer jumped in, accusing Boies of "harassing" the witness. Boies gave nothing. "I'm not harassing the witness. I want to know whether he had a recollection of . . . He may not know whether he said it. He may think he didn't say it! I'm trying to clarify what the witness's testimony is!" he announced, a bit haltingly, but still relentless. Heiner had the question read back and told Boies, once again, that the witness did not remember saying it. But Boies pressed on. "Do you *doubt* that you said it, sir?" he asked. Gates paused, but said, "Same answer," all the while shaking his head no and staring down at the table. Boies began to turn the psychological vise. "Well, my question, *sir,* is whether you doubt it, and I'd like the best answer that you can give to me—on the question of whether you *doubt* saying it." Gates hazarded the response, "You're sort of asking me to make some kind of guess? I mean all I have—" and Boies quickly cut him off and moved to strike the answer as "nonresponsive."

Heiner interrupted once more. "You'll probably have to accept that as part of the examination," Heiner said. "Absolutely!" Boies agreed politely, adding that he would reserve his right to "preserve the record" by moving to strike unresponsive answers.

Gates took a long time, a solid sixty seconds according to the clock that ticks on the bottom left-hand corner of the videotape, to answer Boies's next question. "Do you have any reason to believe that *Business Week* would make this quote up?" he asked. Slumped in his chair, leaning to one side, staring off into space, Gates seemed to be pondering something larger than the question put to him. Boies was content to wait as long as it took for an answer. Finally, Gates said, "They have made mistakes in the past, but I'm not suggesting that I know they did in this case."

"He was very much in control of the situation," Malone recalls. "He knew his rights; he knew he was entitled to get an answer." Before Gates's deposition, the Microsoft lawyers had the chance to witness Boies's style. Earlier that month, Boies had deposed Paul Maritz, one of Gates's chief lieutenants. It was, indeed, the first chance that the Justice Department lawyers got to see Boies in action, other than in the meetings he had attended to discuss the case with them. Maritz was a more responsive witness, and, looking back on the transcript of the deposition, Boies hadn't extracted much from him that would be useful at the trial. But Boies's tenacity and his ability to call down the exact words of a witness's answer, as if a real-time transcript were running in his head, were very much in evidence.

For the better part of the afternoon, Boies tortured Gates over a single exhibit that had been introduced by Houck earlier in the day, a July 1996 article from the *Financial Times* of London. Boies read from the article, which quoted from an interview with Gates. " 'Our business model works even if all Internet software is free,' says Mr. Gates. 'We are still selling operating systems.' Netscape in contrast is dependent upon Internet software, he points out." Earlier, Gates had told Houck that he did not remember these words and told the lawyer, "You should get the transcript of it and get the context of what I said" from Louise Kehoe, the reporter who conducted the interview. When Boies took up this exhibit—an exhibit that would have little, if anything, to do with the truly explosive documents introduced at the trial—he asked Gates at least twenty questions about this one quote before he moved on (temporarily!) to another topic. Literally, it was a game of twenty questions. And in this game, Boies established that he would not give his subject any chances to look up the tape of the interview with Ms. Kehoe of the *Financial Times;* there would be no opportunity to put the situation in "context," as Gates preferred to call it.

Boies pressed Gates again and again about whether he had "any reason to doubt" that he had said the words. Boies simply wouldn't give up. "I don't remember not saying it; that's kind of an unusual memory to have, but I think that's what you're saying—is there a specific memory in my head where I go and look up in my memory where it says, I have never said those words—and I don't have a memory of that either." Apparently, Gates believed that he could control the situation with remarks like these, that he could outwit Boies at his own game. Boies calmly pressed on. Did he recall the "substance" of what was in the article? Was the substance of the article "inconsistent" with what Gates had said? "I think you're asking me to check for consistency with all of the statements I gave during that twelve-month period, and I'm not able to do that," Gates announced. Malone also recalls this line of questioning; he remembers that Neukom stood up at one point, fuming that if Boies asked *the Financial Times* question one more time, the Microsoft team would walk out of the room. Gates claimed that he could not tell what "Internet software" meant as it appeared in the article. (This moment does not appear on the videotape.) What Gates failed to understand—and would continue to fail to understand over three harrowing days—was that this deposition was not Gates's chance to offer his perspective on browsers. This was Boies's show; he was the one who was in control, and he was there to pin down Gates on only the questions he put.

"I have as much time as I need to finish this examination, sir, and I am prepared to spend as many days as I have to to do that," Boies warned Gates.

Boies called Klein at the first break of the Gates deposition to tell him that the Microsoft chief executive would never come to the courtroom to testify—Boies would have his videotaped deposition to cross him.

Boies would take three days to finish. And if you watched all of the videotapes, as I did in reporting this book, there were many moments when Boies's relentless questions seemed as ridiculous as Gates's quibbling answers. But Gates did not "present" well, as lawyers like to call it; he was a caviler, and each time he asked for a context he offered Boies yet another opportunity to use some of his favorite lines. If Gates could not recall saying something, Boies would shoot back his "Do you doubt saying it?" or "Did you say it in words or substance?" leading up to the dramatic and ominous "Is it your testimony, sitting here today under oath?" Arguably, day two of the deposition was the most productive. Boies said good morning to Gates, but Gates refused to return the greeting, a tidbit that inevitably made its way into Jackson's courtroom, and was duly noted by press accounts. Boies began the day's questioning by asking Gates whether he intended to appear as a witness at the trial. Objection! Heiner got into an immediate lather over this question. The witness list was not due with the court for another week! Gates's refusal to say whether or not he would come to the trial gave Boies the opportunity to torture him on the most irrelevant points—such as whether Gates recognized the stamps used to mark documents produced in discovery—on the ground that this was his only chance to test the "credibility" of the Microsoft chairman.

But Boies also grilled Gates on documents that would be central to the trial. Gates insisted, for instance, that Microsoft's primary goal in a 1997 deal in which Apple agreed to promote Microsoft's Internet Explorer as the default Web browser on its machines was to get Apple to drop its long-running patent lawsuit. But there was no internal Microsoft email that said the patent dispute was key in the deal. There were only emails describing the "threat to cancel MacOffice" as a bargaining point that would "do a great deal of harm to Apple immediately" and as the "perfect club" to use against them. Gates recalled none of this, and kept insisting that the patent issue was paramount in the negotiations. Boies didn't trap Gates, but none of the documents spelled out Microsoft's concerns over the patent dispute, and the contrast had the sting of a lie.

But Boies was equally content to string Gates up on matters of semantic lunacy. Chief among them was a rope-a-dope series of questions on day three of the deposition, Monday, September 2, 1998. Boies spent most of the morning questioning Gates about a single email from January 1996, in which he wrote, "Winning Internet browser share is a very very important goal for us." Boies employed one of his standard tacks, questioning Gates about ten times over whether he had communicated that browser share was a "very very important goal"—thus dragging out the suffering before he finally and mercifully produced an email for Gates to look at. Ever precise, Gates noted that Boies kept using the words "very very." Was Boies asking him about the times he had used those words? Boies said he would begin with that question. "I don't remember using those words," came Gates's response. Had Gates communicated the *substance* of that to people within Microsoft? "Help me understand. You communicate to people that something is important. Is the substance of that identical to communicating to people that it's very very important?" Boies put the burden on Gates to answer. "Would it be in *your view,* Mr. Gates?" Gates said it would not be identical. "What would be the difference?" Boies asked. "There are two verys," Gates responded. "What significance in terms of substance would those two verys have?" Boies asked. "It would speak to a tendency towards hyperbole," Gates offered. Boies shot back, "Other than your tendency, if you have one, to hyperbole, would there be anything different that you would be communicating to people if you were to say browser share is a very important goal or browser share is a very very important goal?" And Gates said, "You'd have to look at the context." Well, Boies had at least one context—out came the email that Gates had written!

The session became more absurd as it dragged on, and Boies would use selected bits of it on November 16, five weeks into the trial. It was the third installment of the Gates tape shown in the courtroom. The first, a two-hour excerpt that Boies played on November 2, two hours of Gates saying "I don't remember" or "I can't recall" when presented with documents about

Microsoft's alleged bullying of Apple, became front-page news the next morning. "Gates on Tape: Scant Memory of Key Details," read the headline in the *New York Times*. Installment three was meant to counter Microsoft's assertion that it bundled Internet Explorer into the Windows operating system mainly to benefit consumers. Boies played it on the morning that the government called an expert to the stand, one of its weakest witnesses. But it was the Gates tape that inevitably made the headlines the next day. On the tape, Gates quibbled when Boies asked if Microsoft tracked browser "market share." Gates said he had browser "usage share," which was not "market share," prompting Boies to ask the Microsoft chairman for his definition of the term "market share." Boies then asked Gates if he was "aware of documents within Microsoft" describing browser share as the company's number one goal. Gates said no. He was aware of "documents within Paul Maritz's group that may have stated that." This led to a series of questions establishing that, yes, Maritz did work for Microsoft and held a position of responsibility. Boies asked Gates how it was that Maritz "came to the view" that browser share was the number one goal, and Gates offered a long answer, suggesting that Maritz saw the value of innovating the Microsoft browser because of the increasing popularity of the Internet. At this Boies pounced. "Mr. Gates, isn't it the case that *you told* Mr. Maritz that browser share was a very very important goal and that's why he believed it?" Gates wasn't about to be bullied. "I guess now we're delving into the inner workings of Paul Maritz's mind and how he comes to conclusions?" He was huffy. Boies was not. "Well, let me try to ask you a question that won't require you to delve into anybody else's mind," he said calmly. "Did you tell Mr. Maritz that browser share was a very very important goal?"

The excerpts played in court did not include the bits of Boies and Gates fencing about what, indeed, the significance of "very very" was. The tape cut to the point when Boies whipped out the Gates email with this language. Though Boies did not appear on the videotape, which broadcast his disembodied voice, he seemed to be licking his chops, and everyone in the gallery knew what was coming. Out came the "Winning Internet browser share is a very very important goal for us" email from Gates.

Boies asked if Gates remembered writing it. Gates answered, "not specifically." If Microsoft was looking for browser share, there were other browsers in the total pie that comprised the market, he said. What were the other browsers? Gates responded, "I'm not getting your question. Are you trying to ask what I was thinking when I wrote this sentence?" Perfect. Gates was beginning to ask the questions for him. "Let me begin with that," Boies said.

Boies barely got the first part of his question out when Gates sputtered, "I don't remember specifically writing this sentence." That was fine by Boies. So that meant that Gates couldn't answer what he was *thinking* when he wrote the question? "That's correct," Gates responded. Boies continued, "You don't have an answer to that question, let me put a different question." But Gates interrupted, "I have an answer. The answer is I don't remember."

Boies took stock: "So you don't remember what you were thinking when you wrote it and you don't remember what you meant when you wrote it; is that fair?" Gates leaned forward on the table and added with a smirk: "As well as not remembering writing it."

Boies moved quickly on: he asked Gates what non-Microsoft browsers he was "concerned about." "I don't know what you mean 'concerned,'" Gates said. The situation had turned farcical, and Gates was the butt of the joke. "What is it about the word 'concerned' that you don't understand?" Boies asked. Then Gates offered, "Is there a document where I use that term?"

The whole courtroom—the gallery, the judge, even the Microsoft lawyers—had to laugh. Surely, if there were a document in which Gates used that term, he would have forgotten writing it. He would have forgotten what he was thinking when he wrote it.

Boies still wanted an answer to his question. He methodically soldiered on; he was relentless. He would make the witness answer. "Is the term 'concerned' a term that you're familiar with in the English language?" That drew a simple "yes" from Gates. Boies made sure. "Does it have a meaning that you're familiar with?" Another simple "yes" from Gates. That left Gates with no alternative but to answer the next question: "Using the word 'concerned' consistent with the normal meaning that it has in the English language, what Microsoft or non-Microsoft browsers were you concerned about in January 1996?" Gates finally answered. "Certainly Navigator was one of those." But the bloodletting continued. When Gates tried to offer that Microsoft was concerned with "competitive products," Netscape's Navigator among them, Boies drilled him about whether he understood the meaning of the word "competition." The whole point of the exercise was to get Gates to say that Netscape was *the* browser whose market share Microsoft was worried about when Gates wrote, "Winning Internet browser share is a very very important goal for us." But Gates just wouldn't do it. "You keep trying to read Netscape into that sentence, and I don't see how you can do that," Gates protested at one point, and Boies icily replied, "I'm just trying to get your testimony, *sir.*"

With Gates humiliated, the last bit on the tape cast an evil light on the hour's evasions. Boies presented Gates with a March 1997 email from Microsoft executive Brad Chase to Gates and others. In it, Chase wrote, "We have to continue our jihad next year." In other words, the browser war continued. Gates took a long time to answer. The seconds ticked by. Judge Jackson rolled his eyes and shook his head. Gates finally answered: "I think he is referring to our vigorous efforts to make a superior product and to market that product."

The tape sent the Microsoft team into overdrive at the spin session on the courthouse steps. At the noon recess, Microsoft dismissed the tape as a "sideshow." But there were signs of real trouble. Microsoft had on hand its latest hire, attorney Joseph diGenova, a former U.S. attorney and familiar talking head on the cable networks. DiGenova offered his observations about the Gates deposition. "A deposition is fundamentally a very ugly thing. These aren't works of art. They aren't designed to be," he told reporters. When Boies took his turn at the microphones that day, he said it would be "inappropriate" to comment on the Gates deposition. Asked if the three-day affair had been "typical," Boies simply said no. The next morning, the headline on the front page of the *New York Times*'s business section read, "On Tape, Gates Seems Puzzled by Words like 'Market Share.' "

After this incident, Warden, once again, sought a hearing before Judge Jackson on the subject of the videotapes. This conference was held in the judge's chambers before court began on November 19, where he pleaded with Jackson to end the Gates show. "It has become apparent, at least to me, and it is the strongly held view of my client, that there is no legitimate purpose vis-à-vis the trial, in playing this deposition in bits and pieces, and at least it appears that it is being done—and I say at least appears—for the purpose of an audience outside the courtroom and for the purpose of creating news stories day after day." Jackson overruled Warden's objections, and in doing so made no bones about what he thought of Gates on tape. "If anything I think your problem is with your witness, not the way in which his testimony is being presented," Jackson told Warden. "I think it is evident to every spectator that, for whatever reasons, Mr. Gates has not been particularly responsive to his deposition interrogation."

The government's case was going very well. James Barksdale, Netscape's CEO and the government's lead witness, had been unshakable under four days of cross-examination by Warden. Barksdale, with his silver hair and southern manners, had gravitas on the witness stand. And he was unshakable on cross. He admitted that Microsoft never used the words "divide the market" at the June 21, 1995, meeting. So there was no explicit proposal? "It was as explicit as you can get!" Barksdale boomed. When Warden barked that Netscape's Marc Andreessen had "invented or imagined" the proposal to divide the browser market in his notes of the June 21 meeting, Barksdale was appalled. "Is that a question?" he shot back. "It is," Warden drawled. "Well, I absolutely disagree with you. That's absurd!" Barksdale shouted. "I was in the meeting. I was a witness to it. You weren't!" When it came time for Boies to question Barksdale on redirect, there was little left to do.

Witnesses from AOL and Apple were also strong. The nadir, for Microsoft, came with Avidis Tevanian of Apple. Tall, dark, and handsome, Tevanian was cross-examined in staccato fashion by Theodore Edelman, a thirty-five-year-old Sullivan & Cromwell partner. The writer Michael Lewis, who filed a daily diary for *Slate* at the beginning of the trial, called the encounter "Interview with the Vampire." Edelman lost control of the questioning early on. He stumbled badly, and his questions annoyed Judge Jackson, who ordered Edelman to stop "mischaracterizing" the witness's statements. Tevanian engaged in lengthy conversations with the judge, gesturing with his hands and looking at him directly as he explained the technological issues to him, while Edelman stood by helplessly.

The very fact that Edelman was questioning a key witness suggested that Microsoft had come to the trial riding the wrong horse, employing the wrong law firm. Sullivan & Cromwell, whose most important client was the Wall Street investment banking firm of Goldman Sachs, prided itself on avoiding litigation rather than trying cases. Its litigation record was less than stellar. Warden had made a name for himself early in his career with a

1979 appellate victory, persuading the Second U.S. Circuit Court of Appeals to reverse an antitrust judgment against the camera giant Eastman Kodak. The decision overturned a jury trial, which had awarded $87 million in damages against Kodak's illegal tying together of its 110 Pocket Instamatic camera with new film. The Kodak decision remains a key antitrust precedent for the argument that technological tying claims—one of the central theories the government pursued against Microsoft—are difficult, if not impossible, to prove. Warden had won that fight, but his trial record, especially in the years leading up to the Microsoft trial, was checkered. "They are very good paper lawyers," one New York litigator told me. But, he added, "they have not been very good on their feet. . . . If they can't get up and read a presentation to the court, they are not that good."

At the Microsoft trial, Warden did, in fact, read his opening statement. He did a competent, if plodding, job of cross-examining Barksdale and the government's second witness, AOL's David Colburn. Warden questioned the witnesses paragraph by paragraph from a thick binder of prepared questions. But after crossing the first two witnesses, Warden sat there, and, some observers thought, worked on the daily crossword puzzle at the counsel table. He did not sit at the head of the defense table, the spot that Boies occupied for the government. Rather, it was the general counsel, Neukom, a former real estate lawyer, who was clearly calling the shots, passing notes around the table as a string of thirty-something lawyers—cutting their teeth on the antitrust trial of the century—bungled the defense's chance to shine in cross-examination. I found it hard to fault Warden himself, who joined the Microsoft defense team just before the trial, and Boies agreed with me that Warden was not entirely to blame for Microsoft's flameout. "He really was at the scene of the accident," Boies told me later. "But he was the driver," Boies quickly added. In Boies's mind, the problem with the defense was more fundamental than Warden's backseat role at the trial. "They were never prepared to stand up to Microsoft, their client," he told me.

David Boies had gotten under Bill Gates's skin. That was clear from the videotapes. But Gates revealed this to reporters himself when Microsoft went on a public relations counteroffensive, with a press conference at the National Press Club. Gates appeared via a satellite video link. He blamed his performance at the deposition on Boies. "I had expected Boies to ask about competition in the software industry," Gates said. "But no, he didn't do that."

Gates complained that Boies was "badgering" him "to give yes-or-no answers when he knew the questions were ambiguous." The richest man in the world was whining about a lawyer in a cheap blue suit. The only questions that reporters had for Gates involved the deposition, and the Microsoft team was desperate to wrap up Gates's satellite session. Joseph Nocera of *Fortune* put the last question to Gates: If he had to do the deposition over again, would he have done it a different way? "I answered truthfully every question," Gates protested. "You have to understand that Mr. Boies had made it clear in the negotiations leading up to the case that he is really out to destroy Microsoft. He is really out to take all the good work that we have done and make it look very bad." (In fact, at the last-ditch effort to settle the case at a meeting in D.C. before the government filed its complaint in May 1998, Gates "became quite agitated" when Boies began to talk, according to a senior Justice Department official. The talks ended abruptly after that. Boies recalls telling Gates that once a monopoly case was brought against him, everything would change.) Now, before the satellite cameras, Gates himself made Boies into a larger-than-life character. The moment crystallized the David and Goliath theme that the press had already established for the Microsoft story: Boies had single-handedly brought Microsoft down.

This simply wasn't true. The Microsoft case had been painstakingly put together by a group of extremely dedicated young prosecutors in the Justice Department's San Francisco office. They had spent hundreds of hours putting together modules of evidence, organizing the case, coming up with the material that Boies used in court, and making sure that he understood the significance of it. Boies often checked with the team to make sure what assertions he could make in court. Wayne Dunnim, a Justice economist, was forever warning Boies about what he could and could not say about the market data in the case.

Boies parachuted in before the trial, and benefited from this vast amount of teamwork. "David is the one standing up in court and doing the stuff that looks so great, but the only reason that works is the combination of his talent, his ability to master stuff and know when a witness had a vulnerability and to put questions together and all of that—with tremendous material," Phil Malone told me. Malone believed that Boies's parachuting approach spoke to one of his strengths. "He doesn't have to be the micromanager. He can take what he needs . . . transform it into the language he speaks, and get up and do brilliant things with it," Malone said.

The Justice team was, in fact, disappointed with Boies's handling of one of their witnesses, James Gosling, a vice president at Sun Microsystems who created the software language Java. In the government's case, Java represented the second threat that Microsoft set out to destroy. Java had the promise of allowing software developers to write applications that could work across platforms—that is, with all computer operating systems—or, in the lingo of the eventual Sun marketing campaign, "Write once, run anywhere."

In order for Java to work, Gosling's written testimony explained, Gosling also created the Java Virtual Machine, which ran on top of a computer's operating system. A Java program could "run anywhere" because it was connecting, through an Internet browser such as Navigator or IE, with the JVM rather than an operating system such as Windows. Java licensed its technology to Netscape in 1995, and in 1997, Microsoft also got a limited license for the Java technology for Internet Explorer 4.0, the version of its Web browser introduced in September 1997. Sun entered the deal with Microsoft to obtain the widest distribution for the JVM. But, according to Sun, Microsoft rigged the JVM so that it was dependent on Windows to run.

Gosling was eager to testify. The afternoon before he was to take the stand he came to court to familiarize himself with the scene. He had big hair that fell to his shoulders, a bushy long beard, and thick glasses. In his T-shirt, jeans, and Birkenstock sandals, he looked as if he belonged at a Grateful Dead concert or a Ben & Jerry's stockholder meeting. He returned the next morning in a dark suit, with his hair pulled back in a ponytail.

Tom Burt, the Microsoft lawyer in charge of defending Sun's pending private lawsuit against Microsoft in California, cross-examined Gosling for four days, pressing him with questions that suggested Microsoft had simply created a better version of the Java machine using the code available in Windows. It countered Gosling's story quite effectively.

Boies conducted a very brief redirect examination of Gosling, asking the computer scientist the most basic and general of questions, and mostly using the redirect to introduce Microsoft internal emails sprinkled with "kill Java" language. One read: "Strategic objective: Kill cross-platform Java by growing the polluted Java market." Gosling gave rambling answers, and Judge Jackson kept interrupting the redirect with his own questions. After Boies finished, Jackson made it clear that the super-lawyer had not done his job. He turned to Gosling and pointed out that a "goodly portion" of Microsoft's cross presented evidence that Microsoft simply built "a better version of what it was that you were working on, and they simply couldn't wait for you to catch up."

Gosling left the witness stand in dismay. Afterward, Steven Holtzman, one of the senior Justice Department lawyers from the San Francisco office working on the case, talked to Gosling and his lawyer. "They were kind of shocked," Holtzman told me later. Gosling was prepared to testify at a specific and highly technical level, and he had very good material. But Boies wanted to stick with broad themes. The reason? Holtzman says the episode shows Boies's "risk-averseness."

"This was a case of David's not understanding what this case was about," Holtzman says. "He fakes a lot of stuff."

The Justice Department team didn't think Gosling's testimony had gone well. But that didn't register with the press in the gallery. "It's like he's charmed," Holtzman says of Boies. "He screws up, and nobody notices."

In any case, Gosling's cross-examination had been upstaged by the half hour of Gates videotape that Boies played before the scientist took the stand. There were emails calling Sun a "major threat," and more emails assessing how Microsoft would "put obstacles" in Sun's path. Boies saved the most absurd bit for the last moments of the tape. He confronted Gates with an email that one of his top executives wrote in March 1997: "This summer we're going to totally divorce Sun." Gates claimed he didn't know what that meant.

The email went on to suggest ways of attacking Sun. It listed some Java technologies, "which we're going to be pissing on at every opportunity." Gates replied that he did not "specifically know" what the writer meant by "pissing on." Boies drilled on: "When you get these kind of emails, would it be fair for me to assume that 'pissing on' is not some kind of code word that means saying nice things about you, that it has the usual meaning in the vernacular?" Gates snapped back testily, "I don't know what you mean 'in this kind of email.' " On it went, until finally Gates agreed that while "pissing on" was a term of "multiple meanings, in this case I think it means what you've suggested it means." The gallery was in stitches. With that, Boies announced, "That concludes today's readings." Judge Jackson didn't miss a beat. "The first lesson," he chuckled from the bench.

NINE

The Doctrine of Retribution

David Boies enjoys the Japanese game of Go, which is played with stones, one player taking black, the other white, on a board with a grid of intersecting lines.

"The goal is to encircle and capture your opponent," Boies told me one day during the Microsoft trial. Boies was spending the noon recess alone in a dank, windowless room that Judge Jackson had designated the government's witness room.

Boies often skipped lunch during the trial. When he did eat, he'd buy a bag of bagels from the nearby Au Bon Pain and an orange juice, or gulp down Diet Cokes. (Boies ate the crusts of the bagels only, leaving behind piles of bagel innards, prompting one of his Justice colleagues to call him the Hannibal Lecter of bagels.)

The Microsoft legal team reserved a private room At The Mark, a swank restaurant blocks away from the courthouse, and at noon, the team often taxied there, or to the Sullivan & Cromwell offices near the White House.

But Boies didn't like to waste precious time. His standard procedure at the beginning of every trial was to pull out a map and make sure that everything—everything—from the legal team's war room to its living quarters, was located within seven blocks of the courthouse. The logic was geometric, much like the lines on a Go board.

When I talked with Boies in the witness room, it was late January and the government had rested its case, giving Microsoft the long-awaited opportunity to tell its side of the story.

To open its defense, Microsoft called as the first witness the economist Dr. Richard Schmalensee, dean of the Massachusetts Institute of Technology's Sloan School of Management. Schmalensee had been Microsoft's economic expert since the beginning of its antitrust troubles with the government. In antitrust trials, the economist is usually the last witness called to the stand, the "cleanup witness," who explains why all of the facts in the case impact competition and justify the intervention of the antitrust laws, or not.

When the time came to question Schmalensee on the afternoon of January 13, Boies said he'd like to dispense with "some housekeeping matters" first. He asked Schmalensee how many years he had been working with Microsoft, and on how many cases. Schmalensee said he had been giving Microsoft advice since 1992. He listed a handful of matters in addition to the company's big fight with the government. Schmalensee didn't think that rendered him "Microsoft's *house* economist," did he?

This question wasn't really directed at the witness, but at Sullivan & Cromwell's Michael Lacovara, who had tried to discredit the government's chief economist, Franklin Fisher of MIT, by attacking Fisher's previous relationship with Boies and Cravath. Lacovara had tried to make the most of this, but failed. It was true that Fisher, who was IBM's economist in its epic antitrust battle with the government, had been hired eighteen or nineteen times by Boies's former law firm. Had Fisher ever been referred to as "Cravath, Swaine & Moore's in-house economist?" Lacovara asked. The congenial professor—white haired, plainspoken, and comfortable on the stand—didn't miss a beat. "Nobody says that to my face," Fisher said with a smile, getting the last laugh. The gallery had joined in.

There were chuckles once again when Schmalensee agreed with Boies that he did not consider himself Microsoft's "house" economist. "I don't live in Redmond. I'm not on retainer. I'm not on salary," Schmalensee announced, but this time the joke seemed to be on him. Boies had had his sneer at Lacovara, so he did not ask the economist how much he made from his work for Microsoft. He would save that question for later, when the MIT dean was frazzled.

Boies moved quickly on to a discussion of monopoly power. Schmalensee maintained that, despite Microsoft's 90-percent-plus lock on the world market for PC operating systems, the company did not have monopoly power. In his 327 pages of direct testimony, Schmalensee had maintained that Microsoft faced "intense dynamic competition" to be the leading software "platform." Schmalensee asserted that it didn't make sense to analyze Microsoft market power by looking at its share of the PC operating systems market, and that one could not, in fact, define a market for PC operating systems. This assertion was so ludicrous it was ridiculed by the press even before Schmalensee took the stand. Schmalensee entered the witness box with his knees cut off. Boies finished him.

Boies zeroed in on the market share issue. Would the dean agree that looking at high market share was a "standard" way of assessing monopoly power? It was one way, Schmalensee allowed. Well, Boies pressed on, would you agree that it was "the traditional and most common approach?" Schmalensee huffed, "I haven't done a survey."

Boies showed the dean a copy of his own expert testimony for Microsoft in another antitrust case. The deposition testimony went up on the courtroom's big screen. Asked how an economist determines market power, Schmalensee had answered, "the traditional and most common approach" was to first look at whether the company had large shares of the market. Gotcha!

"Do you see that, *sir*?" Boies inquired, as the professor stared down at his own language.

Boies would use the dean's own language against him again before the day was out. Over and over, Boies posed the question of whether Schmalensee thought that Red Hat/Linux, a tiny company that offered an alternative operating system to Windows, was presently "a viable competitive alternative" to Windows. The dean tried to fence and dodge. Not now, he allowed, but it was a matter of months, not decades. "Let me be sure I understand what you're saying," Boies began. "But my first question is in the present time. You understand that I'm not now talking about the future." Well, if Boies had in mind a "more wholesale substitution" for Windows at the present time, Linux "would not be sensible," Schmalensee allowed, trying to parse the term Boies had thrown at him.

"Actually," Boies said, "I had in mind 'competitive alternative' in the way you and I used it during your deposition last October." Had the witness changed his view since his deposition? Schmalensee had unwittingly dug himself into another hole. He started to address his interrogator as "Mr. Boies," in an indignant voice.

Boies continued to hammer away at Schmalensee's main thesis—that products like Linux were big threats to Microsoft's dominance of PC desktops. Schmalensee admitted that Linux was not a big competitor to Microsoft "today," estimating that a large percentage of the seven million Linux copies that were in use ran on big business servers. Late in the day, after Judge Jackson had called a recess, Boies returned to the subject of Linux. Schmalensee took the opportunity to correct himself. Linux was mainly for desktops. He said there were only about ten million servers in existence, so he did not think that all Linux machines were servers. Schmalensee tried to offer that he had not really thought through his previous answer, but Boies immediately pounced. Had the witness discussed the issue with anyone? Yes, Schmalansee said. One of Microsoft's lawyers "reminded" him of the number of servers at the break; he had been coached. Boies was stern now. He looked up at Jackson and asked for an instruction that the witness not confer with defense lawyers during the cross, standard practice at any trial. "The instruction is administered," Jackson decreed.

The day soon came to an end, with the witness and the company lawyers equally flustered: Warden went to the bench, pleading with Judge Jackson for mercy, and Boies followed for a conference at the judge's side-bar. Wasn't the defense entitled to forty-eight hours' notice of what documents would be displayed on the courtroom's big screen during the cross? "Now if I'm wrong, I'm wrong," Warden pleaded. "I think you're wrong," Boies said. The parties had agreed to give each other forty-eight hours' notice for the use of videotaped excerpts, but not written documents. Hadn't the government witnesses talked with "everybody"—including the Justice Department team—during Microsoft's cross-examinations of them?

No, Boies said. Warden lost on each point. The ruling stood: for the remainder of the trial, Schmalensee and every Microsoft witness to follow would be without the benefit of counsel once they submitted themselves to the scaffold of Boies's cross.

Boies continued to string the dean up for three more tortured days. When Boies confronted him with a *Harvard Law Review* article that he had written in 1982—which flatly contradicted his assertion in court that Microsoft's enormous profits had no bearing on whether the company enjoyed monopoly power—the dean stammered, "My immediate reaction is 'What could I have been thinking?' " At one point, Schmalensee apologized for mumbling. "I'm sorry, I don't usually mumble," he said. Boies embarrassed the dean, making him seem like a shill for Microsoft who was willing to make silly assertions in return for his $800 hourly fee.

In the middle of questioning Schmalensee about Microsoft's profits from the sale of Windows as opposed to its other software products, Boies called the bloodletting to an abrupt halt. The company, the dean said, had told him that profits weren't broken down that way. Boies pressed on. Didn't the dean even try to find out? "Mr. Boies, they record operating system sales on sheets of paper." This, from the most powerful technology company on the planet.

Boies looked up at Judge Jackson. "Your honor, I have no further questions," he said.

Boies's high school friend Robert Gosney told me that Boies had put a name to this technique one day, on a drive through Fullerton. Gosney was nursing bruises on his face, black eyes from a fight he had at school. Looking at the horrible bruises, Boies asked Gosney why he kept getting into fights. Gosney said he wanted the school's bullies to know he meant business. Boies took a different tack: if someone offended him, he wouldn't do anything then. He would wait until the right moment, then find a way to devastate the transgressor. Boies got pleasure out of the fact that the victim wouldn't know who did it. "He called it his Doctrine of Retribution," Gosney told me. "If everybody operated that way, the world would be a very scary place, wouldn't it?"

Microsoft's Paul Maritz was about to find out. Third in command at Microsoft, Maritz was supposed to be the company's star defense witness. If Maritz, known as brilliant but much more disciplined than his petulant boss, could tell a compelling story, he could move the case beyond the shifty images of the Gates videotape. The Justice Department lawyers were nervous at the outset. "This is a very important week for us," one senior government official told me at the beginning of his testimony. "Maritz is a very smart guy; he's very well prepared." Maritz was the other Microsoft executive, aside from Gates, whom Boies had deposed in Redmond.

Burly and bearded, Maritz leaned forward in the witness chair with the determination of a boxer entering the ring, as if to challenge Boies to bring his questions on. Unlike the MIT dean, Maritz did not fence or parry. His answers were short and disciplined, with the lilt of an accent from his native Rhodesia. Maritz took the stand as a "summary witness," which meant that he could testify about all of the company's dealings, including those in which he wasn't present, based on what other Microsoft executives had told him. Boies did not proceed chronologically. He spent most of his first afternoon of cross-examination grilling Maritz about Microsoft's August 1997 deal with Apple—an event relatively late in the alleged campaign to destroy Netscape—in which Microsoft agreed to create a version of its Microsoft Office program for the Macintosh in exchange for Apple's agreement to promote Internet Explorer rather than Netscape Navigator. (Long before Maritz took the stand, Boies had made hay from that damning Microsoft email describing the threat of withholding the popular Microsoft Office program as the "perfect club" to threaten Apple with.)

Maritz had not negotiated the Apple contract. But in his written direct testimony, he asserted that Microsoft's main focus was to end Apple's threats of patent litigation. In fact, according to Maritz's written testimony, the subject of IE only came up while Steve Jobs, Apple's chief executive, was standing under a tree in Palo Alto, and only after the two companies had settled the patent dispute. Boies reveled in subtle sarcasm, but his first question to Maritz about the agreement backfired. What kind of tree was it? Maritz told Boies that the Microsoft executive had not gotten into that kind of detail, "but I'm sure if you would like to know, we could ask him." Boies moved on, and Maritz explained that Jobs had no shoes on while standing under the tree. Boies repeated that.

Then Boies employed a subtle trick, using language that would be featured prominently in the daily newspaper accounts the next day. Pulling out the company's own internal emails, he confronted Maritz with the fact that none of them referred to "patent terrorism." The fact was that Maritz, in his written testimony, had referred to Apple's "threats" of litigation, but had never called them "patent terrorism." This was Boies's term. Maritz repeated the term in an answer, and Boies used it twice more. It was inevitable that it landed in the newspapers the next day.

There were emails that cited Microsoft's goals for IE prominently and barely mentioned the patent problem. Maritz tried to suggest that the emails did not discuss the patent issue because that was something for the lawyers. "I'm pointing out that this merely represents how the parties chose to write things down," Maritz said of the eleven-paragraph email, which mentioned the patent issue at its very end. The answer offered Boies a straight line: "Now one of the parties choosing to write things down was Microsoft, correct, sir?" he asked. "Correct," Maritz responded, to laughter at his expense in the gallery.

As the proceedings drew to a close for the day, Boies said he would "briefly" address another topic. He probed Maritz about a quote that had appeared in the *New York Times,* and was, by then, infamous. According to the *Times,* Maritz had said that Microsoft would "cut off Netscape's air supply." One of the government's witnesses, Steven McGeady of Intel, had sworn on the stand that Maritz had said just that. In his written testimony, Maritz stated he "never" said that or words to that effect. "I believe that Mr. McGeady's accusation in this regard speaks volumes about his attitude toward Microsoft and the credibility of his testimony." Boies was making the credibility of Microsoft the central issue of the trial, and this written statement, in bold black and white, gave him ammunition.

The written statement should never have been approved by Microsoft's lawyers, because Maritz, at his deposition with Boies, had said it was "possible" that he said it but that he just couldn't recall. Boies reminded Maritz of his deposition. The day ended shortly after that, and the two sides headed to the spin cycle. At the end of his remarks on the courthouse steps, Boies put Microsoft's credibility directly, if subtly, on the line: answering a reporter's question about the discrepancy between McGeady's testimony about the "air supply" comment and Maritz's denials from the witness stand, Boies said that McGeady "doesn't have an incentive to lie." The credibility card, first put into play during Boies's opening remarks, would remain the centerpiece of the trial.

Boies respected Maritz, but he eviscerated him. By the end of Maritz's second day on the stand, John Warden rose to complain that Boies kept interrupting the witness before he could finish his answers. Judge Jackson didn't agree. "The witness is awfully difficult to get an answer to a question from," Jackson said, shaking his head in disbelief.

How does Boies do it? Boies gave me a quick course when I joined him in the dank witness room where he often spent the noon recess. "A lot of my cross depends on tying something down absolutely," he told me. "I try to tie something down and then move on. Tie something down and come back to it."

The first thirty minutes and last thirty minutes of any cross-examination are the most dangerous for any witness, Boies said. During Maritz's first half hour on the stand, when Boies was in the middle of sparring with him about whether Netscape in fact posed a threat to Microsoft, he tossed a question to Maritz about a Web browser called NCompass, which used Microsoft technologies. A browser like that would not be viewed as a threat to Microsoft, fair enough? "Correct," Maritz responded. The trap had been set. Then Boies told Maritz he was "just trying" to distinguish between browsers like NCompass and Netscape. "Go ahead," Maritz said.

The next afternoon, Boies made Maritz regret the exchange. It was inevitable that Maritz face the damning emails he had written in the days leading up to the June meeting when the company allegedly made its illegal offer to Netscape to divide the browser market. Confronted with his own emails, stating that it was "imperative" that Microsoft "keep control" of the computer code in Internet browsers, Maritz began to parry. Microsoft was only trying to make sure that Netscape was "using technologies in Windows."

"Let me try to use your language," Boies said. "You were trying to convince Netscape to use Windows technologies in these meetings?" Maritz responded with a simple "yes." In other words, Maritz was trying to render Netscape a nonthreat on the order of the Windows-dependent NCompass browser. His answer to Boies's early innocuous question in his first moments on the witness stand came back to haunt him. If Netscape had agreed to such a deal, Boies asked, would that have rendered the company "a less significant platform threat"? Maritz responded, "On one level, yes."

Maritz refused to concede the ultimate point. Faced with clear-cut emails on the goals for the meeting, like "move Netscape out" of the Windows space, Maritz insisted that Microsoft was merely "persuading" Netscape to build on Microsoft's technologies so as not to duplicate them.

Maritz was holding his own, but the emails produced by Boies proved his undoing. "Well, when you see this thing here, 'Avoid hot or cold war with Netscape. Keep them from sabotaging our platform revolution,' is it your testimony to the court that you don't know whether that has *anything to do* with reducing the platform threat that they posed?" Boies asked, incredulous.

Maritz had insisted all afternoon that the deal offered to Netscape at that fateful meeting back in June 1995 was merely part of Microsoft's crusade to get the world to use Windows. Boies pressed him again and again about the deal, until Maritz finally said, "If you're asking, is there another deal that has similar—all the similar elements to this deal, I can't recall one." The deal, by then, had been painted as so darkly illegal by the government that Maritz's reply seemed like an admission of guilt.

"I think that's as well as we're going to do," Judge Jackson observed. "I think that is, your honor," Boies agreed.

Joel Klein, who was attending the proceedings that day, had a huge smile on his face, his elbows resting cockily on the back of the courtroom bench, as he watched Boies in action, the lawyer whom he had described as Yo-Yo Ma to his Justice Department staff. Across the aisle, the Microsoft team was morose. Mich Matthews, the company's head of corporate communications, in town from Redmond to observe the proceedings, looked unhappy.

As Boies headed out of the courtroom and down the hallway toward the spin session, he pumped his fists into the air. Before the microphones and cameras, Boies put the nails in Maritz's coffin. "I think they are going to have a tough time walking away from what he has said," Boies told reporters. The beleaguered Microsoft team was flailing. Neukom, tall and debonair in his signature bow tie, tried to put the best face on Jackson's own frustration with Maritz's failure to answer questions. He blamed Boies. "What you heard a lot of today, frankly, is embellished, repetitive questions," he said. "The judge understands the give-and-take between trial counsel and witnesses. The judge was, I believe, acknowledging the fact that this was a give-and-take relationship."

On cross-examination, there are always three things Boies is trying to accomplish. "First, you want to identify the one, two, three, four, five critical points from that witness's testimony. And there are never more than four or five really critical points. If you've got twenty points you want to get from a witness, you're not prioritizing. You've got to confront the core of his testimony." The second goal is to seize on what Boies calls "targets of opportunity"—to get points from the witness for your own case, in effect, "almost making him your witness." It may come from a document, or from what the witness testified at his deposition. "You may think you can get it just from your read of what he's likely to say. But there will be a series of points that are affirmative points, that he may not have even mentioned in his testimony, or he may have mentioned it in passing." Boies's third objective on cross is to undercut the witness's credibility. "What you have is this core that you've got to confront; you've got these points that you're trying to make," he says. Boies never knows, and doesn't plan, the order in which these three goals will be accomplished.

At the Microsoft trial, Boies approached the podium each day with only a manila folder, with an outline in pen of the questioning he wanted to pursue. For each witness, there was a box of manila folders with the deposition excerpts and documents relating to that witness, arranged alphabetically, that Boies could delve into when the opportunity arose. "That allows me, when he says something, to jump on it. That's what damages a witness's credibility and a witness's confidence. I'm going to talk to him. Wherever he goes, I've got something to go with him."

And then there was the thrill of the chase. It was that thrill that led to the humiliation of James Allchin, Microsoft's third witness. Allchin, who was then forty-seven years old, was the Microsoft Windows man who oversaw the technical team for Windows 98. It was his job to refute the government's case by explaining that the company integrated Internet Explorer into Windows to offer technological benefits to consumers. Maritz had entered the witness box with the determination of a boxer; Allchin, frail and pale skinned, with a shock of thick white hair that made him look vaguely like Andy Warhol, came to court with a videotape. On the tape, a succession of young Microsofters in button-down shirts with open collars cheerfully explained the benefits of integrating IE into Windows. The tape ran for almost two hours and displayed a series of demonstrations. The final one attacked a government expert, Edward Felten, a Princeton University professor who created a software program showing that Internet Explorer could be removed from Windows, which helped to prove there were two separate products that Microsoft had tied together illegally.

Allchin's videotape showed that, even after Felten's program ran, IE was still in Windows. Moreover, Felten's program slowed Windows down.

The tape allowed the defense to tell Allchin's side of the story in the courtroom—and to the press—despite Judge Jackson's rule that direct testimony be filed in writing to move the trial along. Boies had masterfully grabbed the drama back for the government by playing the Gates tapes regularly before submitting government witnesses to cross-examination. The videotape demonstrations were Microsoft's attempt at the same sort of coup. Allchin's tape, in particular, gave the Justice Department lawyers a vast amount of material to work with to prepare the cross-examination. The weekend before Allchin took the stand, Boies remained in Washington rather than returning home to Armonk, immersing himself in the videotape with the Justice Department lawyers, Professor Felten, and his two former students.

Allchin's tape ran until the noontime recess on February 1, the day he took the stand. When Boies rose to cross Allchin after lunch, he asked whether Allchin was present when the tape was filmed. No, he wasn't. "I'm sorry, what?" Boies said, to echo the point. Allchin repeated his answer. Were the demonstrations filmed from a script? "I think the answer would be yes," Allchin replied. Had Allchin ever seen the script? No. Allchin expected that the presenters were reading from a teleprompter, but he didn't know for certain. There were probably different versions of the script, Allchin allowed. Boies asked if the witness would check on that overnight.

And, yes, there were lawyers involved in the making of the tape, Allchin admitted. "Now, did there come a time when you checked through this to satisfy yourself that the demonstration was, as near as you could tell, fair and accurate?" Boies asked. Allchin said he checked the tape himself several times. Boies had Allchin where he wanted him.

The questions were also meant to back Allchin into vouching for the videotape. They had less to do with Boies's interest in the facts than his desire to play with Allchin psychologically. Boies told me later that the questions were designed "to make him feel uncomfortable about it so that he's now going to embrace the video more than he might have otherwise." Boies now started to transform the videotape into a piece of evidence for the government. At the heart of the government's case was its allegation that Microsoft had illegally tied two separate products, IE and Windows, into Windows 98 to force computer makers and consumers to use IE, thus combating the threat it perceived in Netscape Navigator. Boies had a Justice Department paralegal roll the segment of the videotape that demonstrated the supposed benefits of the integration of IE in Windows 98. The tape stopped at the first benefit, and Boies asked Allchin whether a customer would get the same "rich experience" simply by loading the retail version of IE 4.0 into a Windows 95 machine. Allchin hemmed and hawed, but finally said wearily, "Yes, I believe that's correct." Boies ran the videotape eighteen more times, stopping at all of the purported benefits of deep integration in Windows 98, and eighteen more times, Allchin gave the same answer, admitting that it was "correct" that one could get the same benefits from combining IE 4.0 and Windows 95. Allchin grew more and more frustrated with each response. "Correct, but we are playing a word semantic game here, but the answer is yes," Allchin fumed at one point. The entire exchange took an hour's time, and ended just as Judge Jackson called his midafternoon recess. That was exactly how Boies had planned it. He did not want to give Allchin the opportunity to regroup. "He was panicked," Boies told me later.

When the opposing camps hit the spin cycle on the courthouse steps that evening, Boies was triumphant. He told the eagerly waiting throng of reporters that there was "no benefit that we did not debunk today." Boies joked with the reporters that the nineteen questions got a bit repetitive. But he was confident that Allchin's answers showed that "you don't have to weld" IE and Windows together to get the very same benefits that Microsoft attributed to its alleged "deep integration." Allchin had come to court with a simple but fundamental task—to demonstrate to Judge Jackson that Microsoft had merely created an "integrated product" with Windows 98. His testimony was meant to capitalize on the sweeping victory that the appeals court had handed to Microsoft in June 1998, when it held that courts should adopt a hands-off approach to software design as long as the purported "integration" offered a "plausible claim" of consumer benefit—a small hurdle if ever there was one—and the lengthy videotape was meant to clear it by a wide margin. At the media session, the Microsoft team desperately pointed the reporters to the appeals court decision. The reporters made note of it in their stories, but the headlines belonged to Boies. "U.S. Pushes to Get a Microsoft Defense to Boomerang," screamed the headline in the *New York Times*, over a story pronouncing that the

Microsoft video demonstration "appeared to have backfired." The report in the *Washington Post* was even more passionate, calling it a "searing destruction of the video presentation." The *Wall Street Journal* ran with a lead that began, "The government turned Microsoft Corp.'s own evidence against it."

The Microsoft team had a right to be flummoxed. Arguably, if you looked at the words of Allchin's answers, the witness tried his best to hew closely to what the appeals court had said would be good "integration." At one point, he referred to Internet Explorer as an "upgrade" of Windows, which is exactly how the appeals court had described it. At another point, he told Boies that IE was merely a "distribution vehicle" for code that existed in Windows. This, too, referred back to the appeals court decision, which had found fault in the government's assertion that IE was separate from Windows because it was distributed on a different CD-ROM. If all software were judged that way, the appeals court had said, no software product could ever be counted as "integrated." Flailing in the face of Boies's nineteen questions, Allchin told the lawyer that he was "correct" that the benefits of Windows 98 could be had by combining IE 4.0 with Windows 95. "We're taking two pieces of Windows and putting them together," he offered.

This was the theory that the Microsoft defense team believed would take them home. But the appeals court decision, in its lengthy discourse on the topic of "integration," had also pointed out that it was not enough for a manufacturer to "metaphorically 'bolt' " two products together. A genuine "integration" had to show something beneficial when it was compared to a purchaser's combination of the two products. Boies and the Justice Department, when they came up with their nineteen questions, were determined to show that there was illegal tying even under the appeals court decision, a decision they believed to be wrong.

At any rate, it did not matter. The drama of the trial had moved the case far beyond the dry pages of the appeals court decision, so devastating for the government's tying claims and so comforting to Microsoft. You could quibble about the details of the 2–1 ruling. Boies wisely chose to ignore it altogether, while the Microsoft team clung to the decision, even as they sunk into deep water. Boies had a much broader picture in his mind about the chess game that this trial amounted to: he knew that the appeals court decision was just one piece on the board, and he had effectively checked that piece with the nineteen questions. The Microsoft team would never trump his check. They kept waving the appeals court decision in the air, passing out copies of it to reporters, never quite grasping that the trial was not a static affair, and that Boies had successfully moved the game beyond the doctrinaire language set out by the appeals court.

The morning after the session of nineteen questions with Allchin, Boies moved on to that portion of the lengthy video that focused on the so-called Felten program—the program created by Princeton professor Edward Felten, which purported to show that Internet Explorer could be successfully removed from Windows 98. On the video, Yusef Mehdi, a young Microsoft programmer in a blue button-down shirt with an open collar, demonstrated that the Web-browsing functions were in fact still on the Windows machine. Boies played an excerpt from the video. "It's taking a very long time, however, unusually long, to access that Web site. That's a result of the performance degradation that has occurred because of running the Felten program." Boies got Allchin to admit that the navy blue title bar at the top of the desktop on the computer screen would read "Windows 98" instead of "Internet Explorer" if, in fact, the Felten program had run. Then Boies had the Justice Department paralegal run the videotape again, and freeze it. The title bar clearly showed "Microsoft Internet Explorer." It was still running! "They filmed the wrong system," Allchin had to admit wearily. "And when they were filming the wrong system and they were purporting to show the degradation and how long it took, they were showing how long it took on a Windows machine without the Felten program being run, correct?" Boies demanded. "I can't be sure. I am going to have to go back and look at it," Allchin stammered. "The performance problem exists."

"Well, sir, you say this problem exists, and I know that's what you *say*, okay. But this video that you brought in here and vouched for and told the court how much you'd checked it . . . *that's just wrong*, right?" Allchin said he would have to go through all the videos. Perhaps they filmed the demonstration several times and ended up "grabbing the wrong screen shot," he said. "To some degree, all this doesn't matter. The truth is, there are—those problems exist," Allchin offered shakily. "Mr. Allchin, you say it doesn't matter." Boies leaned in. "Do you understand that you came in here and swore that this was accurate?"

It was painful to watch.

Moments later, Microsoft's Tod Nielsen, who was monitoring the proceedings, bolted from the courtroom, cell phone in hand. It was time to call Redmond. The time was 10:51 a.m.

Moments later, Judge Jackson announced his midmorning recess. As the reporters in the gallery headed out of the courtroom, Gina Talamona, the Justice Department spokeswoman, took a deep breath and whispered, "You guys get ready, you're going to get pushed really hard." Neukom was in a fury, his tall, lean, elegantly dressed frame jutting down the hallway at a forty-five-degree angle as he took huge, pacing steps. "This is cross-examination by gotcha!" Neukom sputtered. "I don't think he's being inconsistent in any of this. He wasn't there on the ground at the time the tapes were made." By the noontime recess, the Microsoft team was more composed. Mark Murray, the Microsoft spokesman, dismissed Boies's Perry Mason moment as "nibbling around the edges and nitpicking." Neukom said that "inadvertent mistakes" did not impeach Allchin's 135 pages of written direct testimony. "What we're witnessing is not an effective cross, but a virtuoso performance by a great trial lawyer," he said.

Allchin was so shaken by the end of the day that he literally ran with his pretty young blond wife into a cab, stalked by a photographer from the Associated Press who caught the shot. Having drawn blood from Allchin on the witness stand, Boies was careful to be genial on the courthouse steps. He wasn't about to make too much of it. The press would do that for him anyway.

"The real point is not that Mr. Allchin is a bad guy," Boies told the throng of reporters. "He came into court with unreliable information, and for that, I think we gave him a justifiably hard time." It didn't really matter whether the video was deliberately false or not, he said. "Either way, it's unreliable evidence."

Members of Microsoft's legal team refused to discuss how the tape made it into the courtroom with these errors. This struck me, as a reporter who covered Wall Street law firms, as the cardinal sin of sloppiness, from the white-shoe Sullivan & Cromwell. The firm could be forgiven for having walked flatfooted through the trial, outfoxed by the wily Boies. But the sin of sloppiness was unforgivable at a firm like Sullivan, and corporate observers were aghast. No one, then or since, not even Boies, has ever suggested that it was anything other than a clumsy mistake, but Boies drilled at it nonetheless. Steve Brill told me later, "He is just the luckiest man alive, because he got to oppose the most incompetent lawyers God created." Brill said that if he had been at the *American Lawyer* during the Microsoft case, he would have written a piece attacking the press for deifying Boies. (This statement ignores the fact that Brill was editor of a magazine called *Brill's Content* at the time, and the subject of the press's coverage of the Microsoft trial might have made a fitting topic.) "No one is that good, and what really made him that good was the other side was hopeless," Brill told me.

The press was simply enthralled with the show. After Boies's sensational undoing of Allchin, Judge Jackson's courtroom was packed the next morning with reporters eagerly awaiting the next installment in the Case of the Phony Videotape. On redirect, Allchin, clearly exhausted, explained that he had spoken in person with the Microsoft employees who conducted the demonstration. They had been flown in from Redmond. He had a simple explanation for the snafu: there were many demonstrations under way, and during a rehearsal, the machine shown on the tape had Prodigy software installed on it. The installation of the Prodigy CD had the effect of changing the title bar to make it seem as if the Felten program had not run. But, in fact, the "actual machine" on the video was "Feltenized," Allchin said. "The video was correct."

Boies got up to recross Allchin after the luncheon recess. For two hours, Boies confronted Allchin with the many emails he had written, the most damning emails in the case. Boies returned once more to Allchin's fateful email from late 1996, Government Exhibit 47, in which Allchin had told his colleague Paul Maritz, "I don't understand how IE is going to win. . . . My conclusion is that we must leverage Windows more." In the heat of the trial, the notion that Microsoft wanted to "leverage" Windows sounded nefarious—it sounded like an illegal tie, it sounded like Microsoft wanted to preserve its monopoly. Out came another email written by Allchin several weeks later, in which he had observed, "We are not investing sufficiently in finding ways to tie IE and Windows together." When Boies pressed Allchin about whether he had given the "ordinary and reasonable" meaning to those words, the gentle-mannered Allchin offered this explanation: " 'Tie' is a term that we use, just like 'integrate' and 'leverage.' It certainly got us in a lot of trouble, but, you know, the 'tie' word here means integrate." At this Judge Jackson chuckled, "Because it's a word we use, too." It was a light moment, but its implications could not have been more serious.

Boies finally turned to the videotape and directed a Justice paralegal to play the four fateful minutes of the tape that purported to show how the

Felten program degrades Windows. Boies told Allchin that he would run the four minutes and asked the witness to tell him if the machines were switched in the middle of the sequence. "If I can see it," Allchin offered. "You mean, this wasn't run on the same machine," Jackson interjected, already alarmed. The judge wanted to know about the Feltenized machine, the machine that Allchin explained had Prodigy preinstalled on it to cause the wacky error. Allchin had testified to this only a few hours earlier. Now Allchin said Prodigy might have been preinstalled on multiple machines, always with the same problem with the title bar.

"Let's run the tape through. It's only four minutes," Boies said, and had the paralegal play the four minutes. The tape stopped, and Boies asked Allchin whether it, in fact, was a single machine or there had been multiple machines "slipped in and out." Allchin admitted that he couldn't tell. Were any other programs "added to or taken away" from this machine during the four minutes that the tape purported to show? Allchin said he didn't know that either—and Boies did not even bother to drill him on the fact that on those four minutes of video, Yusef Mehdi had stated unequivocally, "We have not made any other changes to this computer or Windows 98 except to run Dr. Felten's program." The screen shots would give him all the drama he needed.

Boies rolled the tape again and froze it on a shot of the green Microsoft desktop. In the second column of icons, two icons appeared, one of them being Microsoft Outlook, the email program that is part of Microsoft Office. Allchin stammered, "I think—I think I even mentioned that I thought [Microsoft] Office may be on this machine." Jackson interrupted again. Did all the machines have Office? Allchin said, "I believe that's the case, sir."

In these early moments, while the judge grew increasingly and obviously troubled by Allchin's answers, the counsel at the defense table sat mute. Now was the time to head off a true disaster. Now was the time to call a bench conference—to concede defeat and offer to do the tape over again—before the puppet master Boies used Allchin as a prop in his magic trick.

Boies rolled the tape again and froze it. On this shot, the demonstration blew up a Microsoft control panel, thus partially hiding the desktop. Was this the same machine? Allchin was already panicked. "We are just trying to show the demonstration," Allchin protested. "This wasn't in our lab being incredibly precise." Jackson cut him off before he could continue.

Incredulous, he asked, "How can I rely on it if you can't tell me it's the same machine or whether any changes have been made to it? It's very troubling, Mr. Allchin." Jackson was already troubled, and Boies had not yet pulled his coup de grâce.

Boies simply said, "Let's continue with the tape." The tape rolled again until Boies said, "Stop there, please." On the frozen screen shot, it was clear that the Microsoft Explorer icon had vanished. It was gone! "Now, that indicates that something has happened to this in the last two minutes, right?" Boies said. "Yes," Allchin replied.

Boies rolled the tape for the fifth time, and the sixth time. The Microsoft Explorer icon reappeared. Allchin now said that there were multiple machines involved. "Oh, now you're sure there are multiple machines involved," Boies sniped. Allchin tried to call a halt to the humiliation, offering to bring a machine in and show the judge himself. "Talk to your lawyers," Jackson said.

But Boies wouldn't let up. "Let me just continue briefly," he said. Three more times, he rolled the tape, to the bits of the tape where, in the morning, Allchin had testified that "Microsoft Internet Explorer" had popped up on the Feltenized machine because Prodigy had been run. Or could something else have happened? Allchin said he couldn't be sure; he wasn't there. Boies finally ended his questions. Allchin was finished.

"I just absolutely clobbered him!" Boies told me with glee that afternoon, clearly in an adrenaline rush. Over the lunch break, Professor Felten's two assistants had discovered the discrepancies and Boies went with it on the fly. All that he asked was this: "I said, 'Are you sure?' and they said, 'Yeah, we're sure.' "

Microsoft offered to redo the demonstration on the night of February 3. Their team purchased six IBM ThinkPad computers at a local shop, and Allchin himself conducted a new, live videotaped demonstration, watched by representatives from the Justice team. When it was played the next day, the tape showed that the Web-browsing functions existed in the "Feltenized" machine that was supposed to have removed Internet Explorer—which was Microsoft's point in the original video. The Case of the Phony Videotape, of course, had little to do with the real issues in the Microsoft case. But it didn't matter. Microsoft's credibility was in tatters.

Every Thursday night, from the outset of the trial, reporters headed to a local watering hole for drinks. Judge Jackson held no court on Fridays, so the reporters had the perfect excuse for a party. Boies was an early and regular participant in the ritual, and the younger members of the Sullivan & Cromwell defense team eventually joined in. Boies was usually accompanied by Gina Talamona, the Justice Department spokeswoman, who would watch nervously as Boies kept tabs on the number of cocktails he had had by collecting the straws from his drink of choice, the greyhound, in the breast pocket of his blue blazer. The reporters hung on Boies's every word, played rounds of pool with him, and hoped he would drop his guard and let them in on some Justice Department secrets. The drinks session after Allchin's evisceration was particularly raucous. Members of Microsoft's public relations team shared the absurdity of their predicament with the press corps: they regaled reporters with the details of their trip to the local computer store to purchase the machines so that Allchin could perform his demonstration live. The salesmen at the store had tried to steer them toward the fruit-colored iMacs, calling them a hot-selling item.

The press reports began to speak of Boies in superlatives. An article in the *New York Times* raved that Boies "has few equals" as a courtroom interrogator. "He cross-examines like a jazz musician, starting with a few themes but mostly improvising. He constantly probes for embarrassing weaknesses." A headline in the *Financial Times* read, "Lawyer Who Relishes the Taste of Blood," and began with the methodical way in which Boies tears into a steak. Joseph Nocera's biweekly *Fortune* diary of the trial surveyed the carnage. Boies had "opened Maritz's veins" and left Allchin "looking like the loneliest man on Earth," he wrote. Nocera declared that Boies "has completely taken control of this trial."

Paranoia seeped into the Microsoft public relations team, who became convinced that the reporters were all Boies's pawns. Late into the evening at one of the Thursday-night drink sessions, Microsoft's Vivek Varma asked Nocera when he was going to "come clean" and admit that he had been friendly with Boies for years, though this simply wasn't true.

As the trial progressed, there would be other victims of the Doctrine of Retribution. The Perry Mason moments kept coming. Boies toyed with Daniel Rosen, the Microsoft executive whose testimony was supposed to refute Jim Barksdale's account of Microsoft's "blatant" market division proposal at the June 21, 1995, meeting. Barksdale's testimony about the meeting had been compelling and unshakable. From the outset, Rosen seemed incapable of giving a straight answer. Rosen insisted that he did not view Netscape as a competitive threat to Microsoft—testimony that conflicted with that of Maritz, the most senior Microsoft executive to appear at the trial, testimony that Boies slowly and painfully confronted Rosen with. Rosen revealed his weakness as a witness early in the questioning. When Boies asked Rosen about whether Microsoft "was seeking to gain browser market share" from 1995 to 1997, Rosen responded with a nonanswer that ended with this line: "But I don't know that I understand what browser market share particularly means." Now this was positively Gatesian, and Boies knew by then that he had the canary halfway down his throat. Rosen was quibbling so much with Boies—disagreeing with what documents from other Microsoft executives said in the days before the meeting—that Boies was happy to drag it out, until Jackson signaled his annoyance. Jackson was worried that he was running out of time; the trial was set to recess by the end of February.

After the lunch break, Boies confronted Rosen with internal emails between Microsoft executives on their goals for the June 21 meeting. Rosen insisted that the language "Move Netscape out" of the Windows 95 platform and "Avoid battling them in the next year" referred to "interoperability problems." Incredulous, Boies repeated his question, and Rosen stuck by his answer, even adding that he had said "several times" that he did not think that "Netscape was competing in the platform space." At this, Jackson interrupted, asking about the email. "You mean that refers to interoperability problems?" he asked, and Rosen said yes, prompting the judge to gaze up at the ceiling and purse his lips.

It got worse. Boies confronted Rosen with one of his own emails on Microsoft goals in the days leading up to the June 21 meeting. His first goal read, "Establish ownership of the Internet client platform for Windows 95." Rosen offered to put the email in context—a page out of Gates's book!—and said, "I was fairly new to Microsoft, and the word 'ownership' in Microsoft terms means that you are going to deliver on something you say you will. It's akin to 'responsibility for.'" Jackson interrupted again, even more incredulous this time. "The word 'ownership' means delivering on something you promise, is that correct?" The witness promptly agreed. Throughout the day, Rosen quibbled with Boies over whether the "Internet client" in Microsoft's internal emails referred to Web browsing at all. Boies was in the middle of a question about one of these emails when he called his cross-examination to an abrupt halt. "To make this very clear—" Rosen began. Boies cut him off, and looked at the judge. "All right, your honor, I have no more questions." A hush fell over the courtroom. Boies hadn't even asked Rosen about the meeting itself.

The next morning, when Sullivan & Cromwell's youthful Lacovara rose to question Rosen, Judge Jackson remarked, "It is always inspiring to watch young people embark on heroic endeavors." Lacovara, a Harvard Law School graduate who was the one bright light on an otherwise lackluster defense team, made a valiant effort to rehabilitate the witness. The exchange suggested that Microsoft was merely attempting to "encourage Netscape to rely" on advantages already in Windows. "Outstanding job!" Neukom told Lacovara at the morning recess.

But Boies finished Rosen off on recross. Rosen testified that Microsoft did not become aware of the threat that Netscape posed until late in 1995, well after the June 21 meeting. Rosen said that he did not "personally" see Netscape's browser, which revealed the technological threat, until July. Then Boies showed Rosen a copy of an email from May 11, 1995, in which he asked to borrow a copy of Netscape's browser. "Do you see that?" Boies demanded. Rosen said it was just a "beta product" (industry lingo for early versions of software) that another Microsoft executive had gotten at a meeting with Netscape "to try out."

Boies pounced. "You don't remember that, do you, sir? You're just making that up *right now*, aren't you?" Rosen sputtered back, "No, I remember it!" Rosen protested that his colleague had gone to Netscape "in this time period" and had gotten the "beta code." What did "this time period" mean? Boies demanded. "Very early May," Rosen said. Boies pressed him, "And you're certain it was May and not before May?" Boies was accusing Rosen of perjury. He then asked the witness to look at Government Exhibit 1891. Boies did not bother to read from the exhibit, an email, or mention when Rosen had written it. He stood there as Rosen read the document to himself, turning ashen. "I stand corrected," he said finally. Rosen had, in fact, written the email on April 27—fully several days before May! And it read, "Do you remember who took the Netscape Win 95 browser that they gave us during our last meeting? I'd like to get a copy. Dan." This, in itself, was hardly relevant. But it painted Rosen as a liar, one among many.

On the courthouse steps that afternoon, Neukom was in a particular lather. He called Boies's courtroom stunt with Rosen an example of "one of our favorite themes—trial by snippet." This was "cross-examination by quarrel. Some little nit that you pick with the witness. Cross shouldn't work that way." That afternoon, Neukom suffered on the defensive; the previous afternoon, he had taken the offensive, telling reporters that Boies was "shortchanging his cross-examination," and leaving "the bulk of Mr. Rosen's testimony unchallenged." The change over a twenty-four-hour period was just one roller-coaster ride among many for the defense.

Veteran trial lawyers saw not just the brilliance of Boies's techniques, but fundamental shortcomings in the defense. "He was aided by a lot of Microsoft dumb moves," said Max Blecher, the Los Angeles antitrust lawyer whom Boies opposed in his first great victory, the CalComp case. "Microsoft made a lot of mistakes. They brought a lot of people to testify to things that were contradicted by their own writings, and if you're well prepared for trial, you don't do that." But there was an even more basic problem with the defense, in Blecher's mind: "On the whole Boies knew, as always, where he was heading, and they didn't seem to have thought through the case or understand where they were going." Boies had said the same thing to me, time and again, about the Sullivan & Cromwell defense: they worried always and only about the next news cycle, which left them to ricochet from crisis to crisis because the language of the documents defied their mantra that Microsoft's only goal was to innovate for its customers.

On it went. By the time Microsoft's eleventh witness, Joachim Kempin, took the stand, paranoia about the courtroom "tricks" that Boies played had gotten under the company's skin. Kempin oversaw Microsoft's licenses with PC makers. In Silicon Valley lore, Kempin was the guy who strong-armed the hardware guys with the threat of putting them out of business. The enforcer. Kempin, a tall, lumbering man with white hair and mustache, who spoke with a thick German accent, fit the part.

"I am not trying to avoid your qvestions! I have nothing to hide!" Kempin shouted at Boies early in the questioning. Boies was pressing him about what Bill Gates meant in a piqued email about PC makers featuring Netscape's browser "far more prominent" than Internet Explorer. It was just "semantic," Kempin kept repeating. Boies continued. Did Kempin know what Gates meant when he wrote the word "far," when he wrote the word "prominent"? Did he know? "I don't know vy ve are playing verd games here," Kempin sputtered, rising from his chair. "I am trying not to play verd games!"

No, this wasn't a game. Incredible though it was, it was really happening.

After Microsoft ended its case, there would be a recess until the "rebuttal" phase, in which both sides would replay the melodrama and try to recast the previous testimony. John Warden, Microsoft's titular lead counsel, granted me a sit-down interview just before the recess. "The plaintiffs have treated it as more of a jury trial–type case," Warden said. "Credibility is not much of an issue. The idea that there exists such a thing as corporate credibility is, I think, nuts. That, you know, Bill Gates's videotape somehow impugns Microsoft's corporate credibility." Warden said as much on the courthouse steps, for the benefit of the cameras and reporters present, calling the idea of corporate credibility "nonsense."

But Warden was wrong; he was wildly wrong. In November 1999, Judge Jackson issued his findings of fact in the case of *U.S. v. Microsoft.*

As the reporters gathered at the Justice Department briefing room for the announcement of the decision, the atmosphere among the Justice Department staffers was giddy. They filed into the room, beaming. It was clear, even as we attempted to leaf through the 207-page decision, that it was bad for Microsoft. Some referred to Jackson's decision, issued at 6:40 p.m. on Friday, November 5, as Microsoft's "Friday-night massacre."

At the press briefing that night, Janet Reno, the attorney general of the United States, and Joel Klein, her antitrust chief, made lengthy statements. But the reporters wanted to hear from the hero of the case, David Boies. Finally, Boies stepped forward to answer a question. In victory, Boies exhibited his characteristic grace. All he would say was, "I had my shot in the courtroom." The members of the prosecution team rallied around him. Richard Blumenthal, the attorney general from Connecticut, grabbed Boies in a bear hug, saying, "You're the man!"

Judge Jackson's findings surprised even the most stalwart followers of the case. "I am struck at how Jackson accepted Justice's narrative almost completely," said William Kovacic, a professor at the Georgetown University Law Center who had become a regular talking head for the trial. "He bought their story completely." This story included Boies's nefarious interpretation of the 1995 meeting where Microsoft allegedly made its blatant and illegal offer to divide the browser market. At oral argument in September 1999, Boies had told Judge Jackson that the meeting represented "an insight, if you will, into Microsoft's soul." In his findings, Jackson saw things Boies's way: Microsoft made its 1995 offer because it regarded Netscape as a "trespasser on its territory," he wrote. The soul of Microsoft, as revealed by Boies, was apparent to Judge Jackson, and it was evil.

Jackson's findings of fact held so fast to Boies's version of events that the judge failed to mention what was probably the worst moment for the government at the trial—when Franklin Fisher, the government's economic expert, testified, under gentle questioning from Boies on redirect on the morning of January 12. Boies asked, "At the present time have—in your analysis—consumers been hurt by Microsoft's conduct?" Fisher said, "On balance?" Boies said yes. And Fisher responded, "On balance, I would think the answer was no, up to this point." Boies took a deep breath and stepped away from the podium, rocking up on the heels of his black Reeboks. He looked as if he had had the wind sucked out of him. It was an admission gotten on his own friendly questioning—and it was an impossible gaffe! And yet, this moment got nary a trickle of press coverage. Neukom, for his part, had stormed the media at the spin session on the courthouse steps, crying out that the government's case was based on "raw speculation" of harm to consumers. But Neukom's comment dropped into a bucket. This admission—which, arguably, should have been front-page news, given that consumer harm is the ultimate matter of proof in any antitrust trial—landed on page C5 of the *New York Times,* and the *Wall Street Journal* did not even see fit to mention it for another day. No one pointed out that Fisher had made this admission on questioning by his *own* lawyer. And in fact, in the lore of the case, many would remember that Michael Lacovara had drawn this admission from the MIT professor. Holtzman was quite right; Boies indeed led a charmed life.

Judge Jackson made no reference to Fisher's gaffe in his findings of fact. At the very end of the 207-page finding, the judge inveighed against Microsoft's actions. The ultimate result of the company's illegal campaign to maintain its monopoly, he said, "is that some innovations that would truly benefit consumers never occur for the sole reason that they do not coincide with Microsoft's self-interest." That was the last line in Jackson's opinion.

For Boies, the accolades kept tumbling in from media outlets everywhere. At the end of 1999, the *National Law Journal* named Boies its Lawyer of the Year. By then, *Vanity Fair,* the standard-bearer of celebrity in our time, had inducted Boies into its annual hall of fame. His fellow inductees included the cast of *The Sopranos,* Bruce Springsteen, Hugh Hefner, and Jennifer Lopez. Boies's portrait showed him in jeans and a white flannel shirt, behind the wheel of the 1938 Chevrolet pickup truck that he bought at an auction to benefit his son's school.

The story I wrote for the *Law Journal*'s Lawyer of the Year issue told a tale that Boies had already told, and which had already been published by the *Boston Globe*: Boies, in the course of twenty-four hours, had won not only the Microsoft case, but two others. One of these victories was a verdict awarding $11 million in damages for asbestos damage on behalf of his client Sheldon Solow. The other was a victory for the state of Alaska, settling a dispute over antitrust concerns raised by the $28 billion takeover of Atlantic Richfield by BP Amoco.

There was another side to this "trifecta," as Boies called it. The $11.6 million jury verdict for Solow amounted to only a fraction of the $178 million in damages that Boies had been seeking. Moreover, the jury found Solow's own negligence accounted for 62 percent of his $30 million in costs for removing the asbestos. It didn't matter. The *Boston Globe*, the *National Law Journal*, and *Vanity Fair*, when it published a feature on Boies much later, in March 2000, all touted the three victories Boies had achieved.

By April 3, 2000, when Judge Jackson ruled that Microsoft was an illegal monopolist, the conclusion considered the kiss of death by most antitrust specialists, Boies was a media darling. Jackson had attempted to avoid this fateful day by appointing a mediator to broker a settlement. After the release of his findings of fact in November 1999, Jackson chose Judge Richard Posner, the chief of the Seventh Circuit Court of Appeals in Chicago. Posner and his colleagues on the Seventh Circuit, through their influential decisions, had reshaped antitrust law to adhere to the conservative principles of the Chicago school of economics. Posner was arguably sympathetic to Microsoft, and a polymath known for turning out several books a year. But after four months of negotiations, Posner informed Jackson that the talks had broken down, on Friday, March 31. After that, Jackson moved quickly: he issued his decision the next Monday, ruling that Microsoft violated sections one and two of the Sherman Act.

Jackson's ruling sent Microsoft's stock plummeting and roiled the entire stock market for the rest of the week. On the night of the decision, Boies was seated at a booth in the back of the Capital Grill in D.C., a power haunt that displays raw meat in its front window. By then, the wait staff of the Grill was well acquainted with Boies. The restaurant is several blocks from the courthouse where Judge Jackson sits, and from the war room that Boies set up for his trial team from the Justice Department.

His client, Joel Klein, wasn't there. In fact, the government had begun to chafe at all the attention Boies was getting. The producers of *Larry King*

Live wanted Boies as their guest that night, but the government asked that Boies decline the invitation, to avoid the prospect of Boies showing up Klein.

At the Grill, Boies's concern was about the selection of the wines: California cabernets. He started with a 1992 Cardinale from Napa Valley. His new law partner, Donald Flexner, arrived, and they moved on to a 1994 Caymus and finished with a 1994 Hess Collection. He had also convinced the Grill's kitchen to fix him an appetizer of potato skins, though they are not on the menu. They were fixed the way that Boies likes them—the greasier, the better. His son David III was with him.

As I joined them over dinner, the Microsoft trial barely came up. Father and son were arguing over the Elián González case; Boies thought the boy should remain in the United States. Why? "Because communist Cuba is a horrible place, a place that people escape on rafts, and a six-year-old boy shouldn't be sent back there." The conversation was wide-ranging—except that it did not touch on the Microsoft trial. As they ate, Boies and Flexner talked business. They pored over a business plan for the firm. In the midst of it, Flexner teased Boies about his liberal politics. Boies reminded him that he had been president of the Young Republicans Club as a student at the University of Redlands. The issue of civil rights made him break ranks with the party, he said. When pressed, Boies had to admit that the last time he voted for a Republican was some time ago: Nixon. "The first time," he added.

The waiter who came by to collect the check reminded everyone that the day was, in fact, historic. Boies dug into his Lands' End briefcase, but couldn't locate the credit card he had used hours earlier to pay for the shuttle from LaGuardia. His son, David III, offered his card. As the waiter took the credit card, he joked to Boies, "This is to make up for the drop in my stock." Everyone laughed.

Boies decided he wanted another dessert. He had already had his favorite, vanilla ice cream with chocolate sauce. Mary Boies once explained his love of ice cream to me. During law school, David was so poor he could not afford a new winter coat to brave the Chicago winter. He couldn't afford ice cream either. To this day, Boies doesn't pass up the chance for an ice cream.

That night, the Grill got it just right, serving the ice cream with hot fudge. (They left out the whipped cream.) "A second dessert?" I asked, facetiously. As we got up from the booth, he said, "You see, this is a big day for me."

Boies and I proceeded on to Olive's, one of the restaurants owned by celebrity chef Todd English, at that time the hottest new place in D.C. He never got around to his second dessert. Instead, we had a glass of champagne. Another journalist joined us, and Boies evinced the kind of detached attitude about the case that made him so popular with the press. "Microsoft and the United States government deserve each other," he said. "They're both bullies. They both have so much power that no one can litigate against them." Boies, like the journalists who covered the story, was *in* the case, but not *of* it. He could size up the battlefield along with us. Still, he was pressing his cause. With a Microsoft appeal of Judge Jackson's ruling inevitably on the horizon, he asked us to ask the question, "How many times has David Boies won a trial and had it reversed on appeal?" That number, he said, was zero.

The government had succeeded in the trial beyond its wildest imaginings, and sought the ultimate sanction against Microsoft. In late April, Joel Klein held a press conference in his private quarters at the Justice Department to announce the government's proposed remedy for the crime—the breakup of Microsoft into two companies, one for the monopoly operating system, and one for its software applications. Judge Jackson had put the case on a fast track toward a hearing on the proposed remedy. He scheduled a May 24 hearing, a date that both the parties and the press corps following the case believed would be the beginning of a lengthy evidentiary hearing weighing whether a breakup was in fact called for.

But Judge Jackson, it turned out, was much more eager to get the Microsoft case off his plate than anyone had understood. John Warden, Microsoft's lawyer, pleaded with Jackson to consider the defense's proposed schedule for a lengthy discovery period before the evidentiary phase of the remedies proceedings would begin. Moments into the proceedings, Jackson suddenly announced, "I intend to proceed to the merits of the remedy today." An instant later, the reporters from the three newswires were on their feet and bolting out of the courtroom to file the news flash with their editors.

Jackson broke for lunch. Michael Lacovara, the young Sullivan & Cromwell partner, stayed behind in Jackson's courtroom, as his colleagues made their usual trek to the private room at the Mark. Boies was also there.

Lacovara had heard that Boies was leaving the case—he did not intend to stick around for a lengthy remedies hearing. Over lunch, Lacovara asked Boies if he was happy to be leaving. Lacovara remembers this moment with relish: "And he looked at me with that David Boies grin and said, 'Michael, I'm getting out at the high-water mark.' " Lacovara described the moment as "quintessentially Boies—very funny and quite on the money."

Boies was right; the government, having vanquished Microsoft at the trial, would find itself foiled by the whims of Judge Jackson, who that afternoon called the remedies hearing to a halt, after less than a day of argument. Jackson stunned the packed courtroom when he announced, in response to a gingerly question from Warden about the schedule for the proceedings, "I am not contemplating any further process, Mr. Warden." An audible gasp filled the courtroom. Pens dropped. It was over! On June 7, Jackson issued a ruling giving the government its breakup order. The slim decision, just six pages long, quoted no legal precedents. In it, Jackson let his contempt for Microsoft rip. "Microsoft has proven untrustworthy in the past," Jackson wrote. To justify the breakup, Jackson lamely relied upon the notion that the victor deserved the spoils of this fight. "Plaintiffs won the case, and for that reason alone have some entitlement to a remedy of their choice." Boies was not even present among the government team for the grand announcement. On that day, he was in a federal courtroom in Miami, pleading with a federal judge that his group of lawyers should be the ones to lead a massive class action against the nation's HMOs.

Jackson's breakup order was doomed from the day it was released. The judge had not given Microsoft even close to a fair shot on the issue of remedies. But more ominous were the press reports published just days after the order. On June 8, just a day later, John Wilke of the *Wall Street Journal* published a front-page account of his wide-ranging interview with Judge Jackson, under the headline "For Antitrust Judge, Trust, or Lack of It, Really Was the Issue." Wilke drew some incredibly colorful remarks from Jackson. Among them was a statement about the breakup remedy: "Were the Japanese allowed to propose the terms of their surrender? The government won the case." Comparing Microsoft to one of the Axis powers at the close of World War II was one thing, but the *New York Times* upped the ante when it published a story on June 9, tracing what its headline called the "Missteps in the Microsoft Defense." The lengthy article, more than ten thousand words long, included many references to the *Times*'s interviews with Judge Jackson. Most scandalous was the fact that Jackson had talked to the *Times* reporters while the case was still pending. According to the story, Jackson had "agreed to be interviewed several times after the testimony at the trial had ended." The story mentioned that the interviews with Jackson had begun in September 1999, and that they were "friendly, informal and unstructured." Among Jackson's far-reaching comments to the *Times,* he said of Gates's deposition: "Here is a guy who is the head of the organization and his testimony is without credibility. At the start, it makes you wonder about the rest of the trial. You are saying, if you can't believe this guy, who can you believe, who else can you believe? It was a brilliant move by Boies." All of this redounded to Boies's greater glory. And all of this—Jackson's interviews with the *Times,* the *Journal,* the *Los Angeles Times, USA Today,* National Public Radio, *Newsweek*—was trouble for the government's case. (Jackson declined repeated requests to air his side of the story with the *National Law Journal.*)

Jackson's freewheeling interviews with the press arguably violated rules of ethical conduct for judges, but surely crossed into what most if not all judges consider forbidden territory. His transgressions, combined with the decision to break up Microsoft in the blink of an eye, would complicate the government's arguments as the case headed toward an appeal by Microsoft. But that was the government's problem, not Boies's. The giant killer had moved on.

PART III

The Annus Mirabilis, Act I

TEN

Kiss and Make Up

"Hi, sweetheart. Oh, you're such an important person, going to board meetings and all," David Boies cooed into the phone.

Boies was in his flirtatious mode, chatting up Linda Gosden Robinson, doyenne of the Manhattan public relations firm that bore her name, Robinson, Lerer & Montgomery. She and her husband, James D. Robinson III, the former American Express chairman, were the quintessential 1980s couple, on the A-list of society parties, along with the Kravises and the Milkens. Robinson was powerful in her own right; she had worked for Reagan's 1980 campaign and later served in his administration. When the government began its assault on Michael Milken, Milken hired Robinson to counter the attack with a media campaign. Blond and coiffed, Robinson was known as a diva among her staff, but she could be quite charming. She made Boies popcorn when he came to her Rockefeller Center office, and he became a darling there; through him, the firm landed several big clients.

The client that day was the fashion designer Calvin Klein, who was attempting to rid himself of his longtime licensee Linda Wachner, by suing her in federal court, accusing her of tarnishing the Calvin Klein brand name by producing shoddy jeans and dumping them in low-rent warehouse stores like Costco. The suit promised to dish the dirt on the rag trade as never before.

When Boies filed on behalf of Calvin Klein in May 2000, it became the Lawsuit of the Moment. The complaint, very much in Boies's style, told a detailed narrative rather than laying out the allegations on a skeletal frame, as most complaints do. Most of the legal claims concerned Warnaco, the company Wachner headed. But the sixty-three-page document also amounted to a personal attack on Wachner, a woman uniquely despised in the fashion world. It called her management style "vulgar and unprofessional," and accused her of "abusive treatment" of her employees. Page one contained the buzzwords that would later appear in the news stories about the case. The companies under Wachner's control, and Wachner herself, "have become a cancer on the value and integrity" of the Calvin Klein brand name, read the complaint.

In late July 2000, a reporter from *Fortune* magazine was at work on a long feature about the Klein/Wachner fight, and Robinson was pressing Boies to return the reporter's phone calls. Boies was in San Francisco, fresh from his drubbing by Judge Marilyn Hall Patel, who was overseeing the Napster case, Boies's *other* Lawsuit of the Moment. To prove to Robinson that he was indeed returning the *Fortune* reporter's call, he dialed the *Fortune* number on a landline while talking with Robinson on his cell phone. "I'm all psyched up!" he said playfully. "Kill! Kill! Kill!"

Calvin Klein did not hire Boies to kill Wachner, exactly. But he wanted to draw enough blood so she would hand back the license to manufacture and sell his jeanswear, which under their contract ran until 2044. This remedy was the most radical a designer could seek against a licensee, one that would carry an extraordinary burden of proof. In the fashion world, where clothing is produced on a frenzied schedule, licensees are accorded a fair amount of freedom in the day-to-day decisions they make in producing garments. If Klein prevailed, many in the industry worried that his victory would put all licensees on tenterhooks, called onto the carpet for every change they made.

When Klein's problems with Wachner came to a boil in late 1999, Boies was not his lawyer. Martin Lipton, a corporate lawyer known for broker-ing megadeals, was representing Klein in an effort to sell his company. Tommy Hilfiger, the all-American sportswear company, came close to buy-ing Klein's business in early 1999, but the deal collapsed. Warnaco was another potential buyer, but Klein shuddered at the prospect of selling to the woman who he felt had tarnished his brand name. When Klein decided to sue Wachner, he knew he needed a shark, and sought advice from his close friend David Geffen, the record industry tycoon. Geffen was quite familiar with Klein's business: in the early 1990s, Geffen lent Klein $60 mil-lion when the company did not have the cash flow to pay its debts. Geffen told Klein: call David Boies.

Klein's fight with Wachner was much more than just a dispute between business partners. It was clear he was emotionally upset by her mere pres-ence. He believed she had lied and lied, and lied again. When Klein and Boies reviewed the *Fortune* reporter's questions and the answers drafted by Linda Robinson and her public relations staff, Klein took it upon himself to write one of his own responses. He was especially peeved that Wachner was defending herself by claiming that he failed to provide her with designs that would sell. Klein read Boies his essay: he had provided the exact same designs to European licensees, and they were selling very well. Boies liked that point. It was crystal clear.

But Klein had just gotten going. In one absurd episode with Wachner, Klein had interviewed a candidate whom Wachner was considering hiring as a jeanswear merchandiser, and discovered that the woman was not a merchandiser, but a designer. Wachner, confronted by this discrepancy, asked Klein to explain to her exactly what it was that merchandisers do. Klein was shocked. The woman didn't understand the main function of her own company!

Boies had known Klein only a short time, but spoke of him with great affection. "He's such a sweetheart," Boies told me. "All he really wants to do is to make beautiful things, to make people happy, you know. And he hates this kind of conflict, but he also is a person of enormous integrity who is not prepared to see his life's work undercut." Boies talked fondly about Klein and Barry Schwartz, the company's chief executive and Klein's child-hood friend, who has been at Klein's side for thirty-two years. Both men were in their fifties but attacked each collection as if it were their first. Boies believed he had something more than a business relationship with them.

Boies told me he had been lucky in his clients because they were committed to working as hard as he did. That approach, he said, was partly generational. He grew up in the law in a more genteel era, before it became a bottom-line business like any other. "I think they understand that my commitment to them is not just as a commercial matter," Boies told me. "When I take on a representation I am committed to that representation, and I am committed to that representation if it works out well and I'm committed to that representation if it works out badly. And probably my highest and best use is in cases where something bad happens."

The Calvin Klein case would begin to head south shortly, and while Boies was always ready to talk strategy with Klein or Schwartz, he was, as usual, largely absent from the day-to-day litigation. That job was taken over by his partners Schiller and Hayes, and by a long list of assorted associates and members of the firm's Barrett Gravante division.

A crucial hearing occurred in early August 2000, before U.S. District Judge Jed Rakoff, on motions to dismiss various counts in Calvin Klein's lengthy complaint. I assumed that Boies would be arguing the case, but his assistant, Patrick Dennis, corrected me. "People have to understand that they are not always going to get David Boies," he said. Schiller and Hayes spoke for the firm.

Rakoff heard the motion late one August evening, as a storm kicked up around the federal courthouse in downtown Manhattan. Before his appointment to the bench in 1995, Rakoff had been among the super-lawyers and represented the titans of Wall Street in his white-collar-crime practice. He came from a family of overachievers; his brother Todd was a law professor at Harvard.

On the bench, Rakoff kept himself and the lawyers before him on a maniacal schedule. He sometimes held court until eleven o'clock at night, and pushed out legal opinions with ferocious speed. Before Boies Schiller appeared before him on behalf of Calvin Klein, Rakoff had already dealt the Boies firm a stinging defeat in another case, involving a rogue Internet company, Jurisline, that wanted to offer lawyers access to cases for free, in much the same way Napster gave free music to the people.

The Jurisline case came into Boies's office through Ted Normand, a rising associate, who had gone to law school with one of the company's young founders. Jurisline entered into licensing agreements with the owners of the online research service LexisNexis, a vast and costly directory of almost every legal decision a lawyer would want to cite as precedent, leaving the casebooks in most law libraries uncracked. Jurisline offered the Lexis library of cases free on their new Web site. They were promptly sued, and Boies Schiller came to their defense. Boies himself argued before Judge Rakoff to keep the case in federal court as a copyright dispute that invoked First Amendment issues, but Rakoff believed this was basically a case of fraud and breach of contract—namely, the blatant breach of the Lexis license committed by Jurisline's founders—and sent it back to state court, where Jurisline was sure to lose. Jurisline gave up its quixotic fight shortly after that.

Rakoff's fierce intellect and blunt manner were on display the afternoon he heard arguments on the defense's motion to dismiss many of Calvin Klein's claims. One claim drummed up by the Boies Schiller lawyers sought to hold Wachner personally liable for the damages Klein had suffered at the hands of her company, Warnaco. The complaint named Wachner personally as a defendant in addition to the company, meaning that Klein could go after her house and her personal bank account to collect on his judgment. Corporate executives are usually protected from personal liability when they are sued for their management actions, short of allegations that they used the corporation's coffers as a personal piggy bank. In legal jargon, that sort of conduct is known as "piercing the corporate veil," in which an executive in effect turns a company into his or her alter ego. Klein's lawsuit essentially accused Wachner of being a bad manager, but Boies Schiller also concocted an alter ego claim on the slimmest thread of a theory: they charged that she made shoddy products to pump up her bonus. It was an absurd application of the alter ego theory, a bit like random mudslinging in an ugly divorce, and Rakoff lit into it at the hearing.

The judge did not mince words. He ridiculed Klein's personal claims against Wachner, calling them nothing more than "disguised name-calling." He told Hayes that this allegation was "the functional equivalent of saying I'm a goody and you're a baddy, nyah, nyah, nyah." As Hayes stumbled through his case, the judge kept interrupting him. Rakoff suggested that his arguments "would make a mockery, it seems to me, of corporate law." Rakoff quickly threw out Klein's attack on Wachner's personal wealth—so she would not need to hock her jewels after all.

An overwrought Klein appeared on *Larry King Live* on Monday, June 5, 2000, just days after his lawsuit was filed. "He's shocked the socks off some folks with some of his ads. He's Calvin Klein, he's here for the hour," King said, introducing Klein. "You even made the news just for your appearance on the show, right?" The designer, known for minimalism in black on the runway, sang like a diva for King. "This is a very painful, difficult moment for us, Larry"—whereupon King cut him off, reading to him Warnaco's press statement reacting to the lawsuit, which described the litigation as a "desperate attempt by Calvin Klein to cover up and distract focus from the highly deteriorated business state of CKI. Throwing stones at Warnaco is not the answer to CKI's problems." On the program, Klein proceeded to throw those stones. He attacked the horrible mess Wachner had made of his designs—the designs that customers were then buying from stores—and whined about how he and his partner Schwartz had "been lied to," claiming that the product in stores was "not up to standard." Larry King asked the obvious question: "Are you saying to people, don't buy the Calvin Klein jeans tomorrow?" King's question pointed out that Klein seemed to be on a suicide mission, intent on announcing to the world that the jeans bearing his name on the racks of stores everywhere were of crappy quality. Klein's statements to King provided Wachner's lawyers at the Washington, D.C., firm of Williams & Connolly with some delicious ammunition.

At first, the lawyers at Boies Schiller were amused that Wachner had turned to Williams & Connolly. The team she hired included Brendan Sullivan Jr., who had served as Oliver North's counsel in the Iran-Contra investigation; Nicole Seligman, who had defended President Clinton in his impeachment hearings; and Gregory Craig, the lawyer who represented the family of Elián González in their quest to bring the Cuban boy back to his family. Boies Schiller viewed Wachner's choice as a sign that the lawsuit had put her in deep trouble.

In truth, Williams & Connolly was the most formidable firm that Boies Schiller could have faced in this case. Williams & Connolly were masters of libel law—on retainer, for example, by the *National Enquirer,* the supermarket tabloid routinely sued by wounded celebrities. And they creatively turned the screws on Klein after his emotional outburst on *Larry King:* they countersued for trade libel and defamation. By besmirching his own brand and Warnaco's name on the show, they claimed, Klein made false statements, intent on destroying his licensee's reputation, to advance his own interest to "get our license back," as he told King on the broadcast.

The trade libel claims put Calvin Klein's personal wealth potentially on the line. And Boies Schiller lost its bid to dismiss these charges. It failed to convince Rakoff that Warnaco had become a "public figure" under the libel laws by "injecting" itself into a public controversy, a ruling that would have put Calvin's diatribe on *Larry King* under the "actual malice" standard and that would have required Warnaco to prove that Klein had actual knowledge that his statements were false or that he made them with reckless disregard for the truth, a standard considered almost impossible to prove in court. But Rakoff wouldn't buy the theory: he found that Warnaco could not rise to "public figure" status merely by defending itself against Klein's attack.

The libel claims remained, but they were hardly the biggest worry for the Boies Schiller team as the case headed toward trial. The Williams & Connolly lawyers offered a compelling counter-story to Klein's claim that his brash licensee had cheapened the prestige of his name by dumping jeans at Costco. A raft of testimony and internal Calvin Klein documents suggested that Klein had been selling to discounters since the early 1990s, through the licensee Designer Holdings.

The trial promised to dredge up the substantial weaknesses in the designer's business. The pretrial discovery showed that, as Klein tried to manufacture his own products, with his sales plummeting, his friend David Geffen eventually urged him to find a licensee for his jeanswear business. In 1994, Klein found Designer Holdings, which turned the business around. Sales picked up dramatically: Klein had managed only $59 million in sales in 1994; Designer Holdings boosted sales to $367 million in 1995. Annual royalty payments to Klein under the license steadily increased, from $25.5 million in 1996 to $50.2 million in 1999. Much of the money was coming from sales to discounters; Calvin Klein complained about it, but he kept cashing the royalty checks.

In late 1997, Warnaco bought Designer Holdings, a move Calvin Klein hadn't seen coming. Warnaco already owned the trademark to Klein's underwear outright; in 1994, Warnaco had purchased the brand from him for $62 million when his finances were reeling. Warnaco now also had possession of the license to make his jeans, until 2044. He occasionally complained about the sales to Costco, and about designs that had not been approved by him, but he was still happily collecting the royalty checks.

At trial, the Williams & Connolly lawyers were preparing to attribute a cynical and calculating motive to Klein's sudden desire to rid himself of his most important licensee: he realized he could get much more for the sale of his business if it was not shackled by the license. Joel Horowitz, the CEO of Tommy Hilfiger, said in deposition testimony that his firm had come close to purchasing Klein's business in February 1999. During the negotiations, Hilfiger pressed Klein to clarify terms of the license. "The intent was for them to deliver us a clean license," Horowitz testified.

Other testimony suggested that Klein and Geffen were wringing their hands over the lack of clarity in the jeanswear license terms that had been negotiated by Klein's lawyer, Arthur Liman—the very terms that Boies's firm would have to prove were violated. At his deposition, Geffen testified that "Calvin had been upset because I believe Arthur was responsible for those negotiations and that they had not been as clear or as thorough as was intended."

The greed counterplot woven by Williams & Connolly climaxed when it was revealed that Hilfiger had offered Klein a "tantalizing prospect," raising its $888 million offer (by some enormous sum that remains sealed by the court) if Klein could recoup the rights he had bargained away to Wachner in 1994. At that time, Williams & Connolly alleged, Klein came up with the idea of a lawsuit against the most unpopular woman in the fashion industry.

It was not enough for Williams & Connolly to suggest that, hiding under that perfectly even tan, that impeccably styled hair, those elegantly monochromatic suits and shirts, Klein was just a greedy businessman—and nefarious as well. At Klein's deposition, Brendan Sullivan, the patrician head of the Williams & Connolly team, questioned the designer about the representations his company made about his ongoing disputes with Linda Wachner and Warnaco. These assertions were contained in the book that Klein's investment team had put together for potential buyers as they assessed Klein's business. The document contained no information about Klein's many troubles with Wachner. "I didn't think that the purpose of that book was to talk about every complaint that we have, you know, with any licensing partner," Klein testified. He was worried that the book would get into the wrong hands, he said. "I didn't feel that it made sense to put information in that book that would be detrimental to us," he said, adding that he thought the information was better conveyed verbally.

Sullivan's questions for Klein hinted that the designer might have defrauded potential purchasers. Companies are required to make full disclosures of their businesses in such documents, warts and all, but Klein told Sullivan that he thought the book was supposed to "point out the good things." Worse yet, a draft purchase agreement between Klein's company and Tommy Hilfiger described any disagreements with Warnaco as to design and distribution as "in the normal course" of business. Klein was not only greedy, he was shifty too! The Williams & Connolly team announced they would call Klein's lawyer for the Hilfiger deal and his investment bankers as witnesses at the trial. They were the henchmen for the man who wanted a billion dollars for his company and realized the only way to command that sum was to get his licenses back, according to the Williams & Connolly team.

How would this play to a jury? Whose story would hold up at trial? Williams & Connolly whipped up the greed theme, and the Boies Schiller team amassed evidence that Wachner's fabric supplier, an Arizona company called Azteca, shipped a lighter-weight fabric for the jeans that it produced for Costco and other warehouse clubs. Wachner insisted that the fabric was the same, but there was an email buried in the twenty-two boxes of documents that Warnaco produced that referred to "the special lighter weight fabric that we make for Sam's Club, Costco and BJ Wholesale Club." It was another Boies "Gotcha" moment in the making, and Wachner cooperated handily, when he took her videotaped deposition in late December 2000, and she denied that this fabric differed from the material used to make jeans sold to other retailers.

As the case headed toward trial, the differences in style between the two law firms became apparent. Brendan Sullivan essentially moved to New York from D.C. in the fall of 2000. Known for his relentless preparation, he led the Warnaco trial team as if it were a small special forces unit. He held meetings each morning during the entire time that the lawsuit was pending.

And as the trial approached, where was Boies? Indeed, where *was* Boies? He was in Florida, each day dazzling America's cable television audiences with his nuanced and loquacious explications of election law before the cable TV networks, whetting the ears of listeners. Meanwhile, the Boies Schiller team inquired gingerly of Judge Rakoff about a possible postponement, given that their star lawyer was otherwise engaged, representing the vice president in the Florida recount. They made the request informally, when the parties were at a conference in his chambers. It took some hubris to even venture the request: Klein was the plaintiff, after all. No dice, said Rakoff, who had warned them from the outset that a trial date in January 2001 was set in stone.

To prepare for the trial, the team from Boies Schiller had holed up at the Wall Street Regent Hotel, in keeping with Boies's policy of setting up a war room close to the courthouse. The Regent was an Old World hotel with a spooky feel. Space in the war room was so tight that the trial team had to keep many documents in the hotel's ballroom, where the temperature was freezing. The bellman and concierge were enlisted to do photocopying. Williams & Connolly set up its war room at Wachner's midtown offices. Paul Gaffney, a member of the Wachner team, traveled down to the Regent to meet with Boies Schiller associate Clayton Marsh. "He was kind of looking at me in amazement," Marsh recalls. The two teams had radically different approaches to the all-out war that was about to take place.

"It was really like the British and the colonists," Marsh said. "A large institutional army and a bunch of freewheeling guerrillas."

On the morning of January 22, 2001, the day on which Judge Rakoff was to pick a jury and proceed rapidly to opening arguments, Roseanne Baxter, a Boies Schiller associate, nervously paced the hallway outside the courtroom, watching as paralegals from the firm moved the last of the 150 boxes of documents to be used at trial into the adjacent storage and witness rooms. She was relieved when she saw David Barrett arrive. At least he was a partner!

What Baxter didn't know was that Boies and Schiller, the lead guerilla warriors, were in the midst of settling the case with Kevin Baine, the Williams & Connolly partner that the firm designated as its "peace department." Baine had spent all weekend brokering the settlement with Boies, while his partner Brendan Sullivan, head of the firm's "war department," honed his opening and continued to prepare the case. Boies Schiller had no separation between its war and peace departments. Both resided in one man: Boies. He was the primary negotiator of the settlement with Baine, and at the same time the lawyer who would deliver the opening statement to the jury if Klein and Wachner failed to reach a deal.

As nine-thirty approached, associate Clayton Marsh stood at the plaintiffs' counsel table alone. Behind him stood the Williams & Connolly war department, ready to fire. Marsh could feel them "drilling holes into the back of my head," he said later. As Rakoff took the bench, Marsh was still standing there, surreally, alone. Boies came bounding into the courtroom, a sky blue sweater tossed over the shoulders of his usual courtroom uniform, his thinning hair catching the wind of his step. Marsh felt his wave of panic subside. (When Marsh resigned from the firm a short time later, citing the "chaos level" at the firm, Boies told him that he compared his approach to litigation to jazz, whereas Thomas Barr's was more like Wagner. Marsh later quipped to me, "I'm no Wagner fan, but . . .")

A truce was about to be called in the war. "We are very close to a settlement of the lawsuit; we've been working all night," Schiller announced. "All right," Rakoff said, and adjourned the proceedings until 10:05 a.m. Boies sat at the counsel table, writing out some terms, while Schiller chatted with Klein. There was laughter. It was clear this case was over. Those of us who had come for the showdown between the designer and his brash garment licensee would be disappointed. (A close friend of Klein's, writer/comedian Fran Liebowitz, came to the trial to support him. Liebowitz, who would be Klein's date at Boies's sixtieth birthday party later that year, decided it was time to go outside for a cigarette.)

By 9:55, Klein was shaking Brendan Sullivan's hand, then offered an air kiss to Wachner, who that morning was clad in a black pantsuit and a leopard-print scarf, wearing oversize red-framed glasses that clashed unfortunately with her pink lipstick. Wachner also gave a kiss to Klein's partner, Barry Schwartz. Boies could be overheard saying graciously, "Thank you, thank you very much," to Baine.

When Rakoff came back onto the bench, he asked where things stood. Told that the case was settled, Rakoff wanted to make sure. He did not want to find any loopholes in this sudden reunion between two parties who days ago were clawing for a nasty divorce. Once he was assured that they were filing papers to dismiss the case "with prejudice," the legal term that made it final, he was happy. "My law clerks are devastated," Rakoff joked.

Wachner and Klein were going back to work together. They had kissed and made up, literally. The fact of the air kiss itself would be widely and prominently featured in the news reports about the settlement. "Now they can get back to making good products without this litigation mess," Boies announced to some of the reporters who had begun to crush around him with questions. "We go back to work!" Schwartz trumpeted. Klein greeted his supporters in the first row of the courtroom gallery. "I'll take you for some breakfast! Let's go to Odeon." (Klein and company landed instead at Balthazar, a French bistro in SoHo favored by fashionistas and the frequent choice of Ralph Lauren for his postshow celebrations with his design staff following the staging of his spring and fall collections.) As we headed down in the elevator, Fran Liebowitz announced, "It's a shame, we were all getting along so well."

Several cameramen from the cable channels were staked out near the courthouse steps, waiting to buttonhole Boies. At first, Schiller began to answer their questions, but the reporters urged Boies to go before the camera. They wanted a Boies fix; the image of his charismatic, daily presence before the cameras in the election wars was still fresh in their minds. He could have made a statement about the weather that day and they might have considered broadcasting it. Boies told the press that the details were "confidential," but that the settlement "would assure an increase of sales to stores that reflect the image and prestige" of the Calvin Klein brand.

What happened to all the rancor? How could the mudslinging have come to such an abrupt end? Boies looked into the camera and assured the world that "nobody is going to be taking potshots," employing his Abe Lincoln delivery to assert the unlikely notion that the parties had suddenly found peace and harmony. Half a block down the street, the Williams & Connolly team was heading toward their Lincoln Town Car. Sullivan, dressed in a black topcoat and a black fedora, got into the car, oblivious to the Boies spin session. But Nicole Seligman took a moment to assess the camera interview in progress, an ironic smile on her face. She knew that her team had had the Boies Schiller folks nailed, and that Boies had realized he needed to settle once he found the time to focus on it. Williams & Connolly had won, but it was Boies that the media wanted.

ELEVEN

Big Money

David Boies floated, rather than barged, into the murky world of the class action bar. The firms that made up that section of the law were not on the radar screen of the *American Lawyer*'s annual list of the top one hundred law firms in the country, the annual benchmark of prestige among the nation's corporate lawyers. They didn't hail from the Ivy League like many of their counterparts at the *Am Law* 100. Their résumés didn't boast a stint as editor of a law review or a prestigious clerkship with a federal judge. And often, they ran their businesses, not from major cities, but off the beaten path, in locales like Charleston, South Carolina, and Pascagoula, Mississippi. But the money that class action lawyers made often dwarfed the salaries of the lawyers who labored in the dark-paneled offices of firms like Cravath. And with that money, they purchased yachts, private planes, Bentleys. They also showered money on Congress, which has invariably blocked efforts to stop what big business sees as abusive tactics in "mass tort" litigation like the suits brought against asbestos companies and breast implant makers. At Cravath, class action lawyers were derided as "strike-suit" lawyers, for their ability to strike with record speed, churning out lawsuits sometimes the day after bad news about a company has appeared in the press.

Boies got into the class action game through his son David III, who had decided early in his legal career that he would not follow his father's path as a corporate lawyer. David III was a partner at the Birmingham, Alabama, law firm of Bainbridge & Strauss. In December 1997, the firm filed the first of many class actions alleging a price-fixing conspiracy among the world's largest makers of vitamins. The lawsuit by David III's firm followed a *Wall Street Journal* article, published in November of that year, breaking the news that there was a grand jury investigation of possible price-fixing in the vitamin industry. This class action began as many others before it had—a lawsuit following on the heels of bad news in the press.

The government's action against the vitamin makers ended in a spectacular victory when the companies pleaded guilty to criminal charges and agreed to pay fines totaling $725 million—a record in the prosecution of an antitrust case—for their participation in a global cartel to fix the prices of nutritional supplements. When they outlined their case to the press, federal prosecutors called the case the largest price-fixing conspiracy in U.S. history. The gist of the allegation was that over a period of ten years, executives of the companies met at European hotels or their homes to divide the market and set vitamin prices. The conspirators took to calling their enterprise "Vitamins Inc.," and it cut a wide swath through the American market, impacting products from breakfast cereals to horse and pig feed.

The multinational defendants included Swiss pharmaceutical giant Hoffman-LaRoche, BASF of Germany, and Rhone-Poulenc of France. There was no question that these companies would settle the class actions. The only question was, for how much?

The guilty pleas in the vitamin case occurred just as Boies was making headlines as Microsoft's slayer, when Boies made a regular habit of dining with the media. On one occasion he let slip that he had attended a summit of class action lawyers pursuing the vitamin makers held in a lobby ballroom of the Mayflower Hotel. Boies guffawed at the fact that the meeting at the Mayflower—a place frequented by most of the lobbyists and journalists in town—had not been discovered by any of the city's press corps. Days later, the *Washington Post* ran an item from its legal affairs correspondent, David Segal, touting the May 17 "summit meeting" that Boies had held. The Boies bug had bitten Segal, like the rest of us in the media. Of the vitamin class action, he wrote: "The case is the brainchild of David Boies, the multi-tasking partner of Boies & Schiller, and a litigator who apparently engineers the Justice Department's case against Microsoft in his spare time."

Boies offered me what sounded like a rare opportunity: he allowed me to read the briefing book for the Mayflower summit meeting—a chance, I thought, to look at the smoking-gun evidence that Boies and his team claimed to have amassed. "We mounted a massive investigative effort that in some senses preceded the government case," he told me. He would repeat this theme many times, not only with members of the press but, more brazenly, before the judge presiding over the case, to the ire of the team of prosecutors, both from the main Justice headquarters and the Dallas field office, where the grand jury investigation of the vitamin makers had originated. They fumed privately about Boies stealing the credit from their investigation, but they were in an awkward position, given Boies's heroics for the government in the Microsoft case.

I rode the train from the *National Law Journal*'s office in Manhattan to Boies's suburban office in Armonk with anticipation. Well into the night, I copied the words from the blue briefing book presented at the "summit" meeting at the Mayflower, expecting that the words would come together to suggest powerful evidence against the vitamin makers; but there was no smoking gun. Instead, there was page after page of the vaguest descriptions and conclusory statements. A typical entry read: "We have evidence (which we did not have a year ago) of direct explicit communications in which the defendants agreed on the prices they would charge for vitamin C." But where were these meetings? Who participated in them?

The blue briefing book contained no details, but perhaps the eighty or so class action lawyers who met at the Mayflower didn't need them. The meeting's purpose had nothing to do with the merits of the case. By hosting this summit, Boies hoped to avoid the usual slugfest that class action lawyers run through in big-money cases, in which many law firms file competing lawsuits in various locales, placing them like chips on a craps table, vying for their number on the board.

At the Mayflower, the class action lawyers came to terms. They agreed among themselves that the case should be tried in Washington, and came up with a leadership structure. The meeting was a Boies family affair. His wife, Mary, herself a plaintiffs' lawyer, his daughter, Caryl, and his son Jonathan all participated. "Each Boies took a vitamin," laughed one of the lawyers who attended. (David III, whose firm filed the first case, was curiously absent.)

Boies & Schiller and two other law firms took the lead in the case, and it settled rapidly. On November 3, 1999, Boies and his cocounsel presented a $1.17 billion settlement agreement to U.S. District Judge Thomas F. Hogan, who was overseeing the class actions consolidated after the Mayflower summit meeting. The sum was believed to be the largest settlement in the history of antitrust class actions. The press heralded the deal, and crowing by lawyers from Boies & Schiller suggested that the firm had beaten federal prosecutors to their investigation. "In this case the private enforcement contributed in critical ways to breaking the case and showed how effectively it could complement a Justice Department investigation," Boies's partner Robert Silver told the *New York Times*.

Boies himself was even more brazen later that month, when Judge Hogan held a hearing for preliminary approval of the settlement, the first step toward the court's signing off on the deal. "The investigation of this case by class counsel commenced substantially before the government investigation. Indeed, the results of what had been done by class counsel may well have contributed to the government investigation," Boies said. Beyond the members of the adoring press in the court's gallery, Boies had another audience: Many large companies, among them Tyson Foods, General Mills, and the Kellogg Company, were members of the class. These corporate giants, advised by their own skilled counsel, were coming to the conclusion that Boies had settled for too little in the trumpeted deal, which offered the companies between eighteen and twenty cents on the dollar for the overcharges. The companies believed the actual overcharges were twice that amount.

In this, Boies's first foray into the class action game, he negotiated two highly unusual provisions in his settlement with the vitamin makers. While Boies's name was never tarnished in the news coverage of the settlement, the deal would become known within legal circles as a failure, one that his colleagues at the bar believed was a hard lesson for Boies. Ultimately, more than 75 percent of the companies abandoned the deal—they "opted out" of the class, in the legal jargon—convinced they could do better by filing their own lawsuits. The record-breaking $1.17 billion shriveled to a much less spectacular $242 million by the time Hogan finally approved the settlement, in March 2000. In a series of separate settlements with additional defendants, Boies negotiated an additional $225 million for the class. In hindsight, other lawyers would speculate that Boies, largely off the scene in the vitamin case and relying on Jonathan Schiller and William Isaacson, had too readily accepted the defendants' lowball calculations of the overcharges from the price-fixing conspiracy. One lawyer involved in the case repeated a frequent observation: "David is the best unprepared lawyer I've ever met. He does things on the fly. He pulls it off most of the time; in the courtroom, you would never know how thin his knowledge is."

Ironically, the vitamin case would also lead to a $123.1 million fee—a staggering 50 percent of the final settlement—for Boies and his cocounsel. As I continued to travel with Boies and keep tabs on his activities, I became convinced that such a turn of events was part of his charmed life. In the vitamin case, Boies got extremely lucky in the judge who drew the case; Hogan was known as a pragmatist, a jurist who, unlike many of his counterparts on the federal bench, saw his role not so much as shaping the law, but as passively refereeing the disputes presented to him.

Judge Hogan vetted the two unusual provisions in the deal with an eye toward efficiency. The first of these provisions, known as a "most-favored nations" clause, said that if a member of the class opted out and got more money from the defendants, the defendants would be required to pay the difference to the class. The clause ran for two years, meaning that if the defendants entered into a more lucrative settlement with any of the opt-outs during that time, they would also have to kick in more money to the remaining members of the class.

The intended effect of this clause became the subject of a great controversy before Judge Hogan. One lawyer became Boies's nemesis in the case. Kenneth Adams had already signed up Tyson Foods, Quaker Oats, and a host of other companies, comprising 20 percent of the class, by the time of the hearing on preliminary approval in November 1999. Adams ultimately convinced about half of the companies in the class that he could do better for them if they opted out. Adams argued that the most-favored nations clause worked as a "tax" on opting out, and was really meant to coerce companies into remaining in Boies's class. Boies, on the other hand, insisted that the clause was meant to ensure that the class members got the benefits of other settlements that piggybacked on his tremendous and speedy deal with the defendants.

Adams's arguments were complicated by a legal technicality: once the member of a class opts out of a class action, that member has no grounds, under the law, to complain about the deal on the table, because he or she has elected to file a separate lawsuit and pursue a new claim. In the end, Judge Hogan took to heart the threat that Boies and his cocounsel raised in their papers: the deal would "be undone" if the most-favored nations clause were stricken from the settlement. Judge Hogan never called their bluff; faced with a rich settlement, he wanted the case off his plate.

When the case was called for a hearing on final approval of the settlement on March 28, 2000, Adams was still pressing Hogan to overturn the most-favored nations clause. It fell to Steven Susman to counter Adams's arguments.

Tall, tanned, and impeccably attired, Susman, in his Texas drawl, put on the hokum. He leaned his coat-hanger frame into the podium, his voice booming, and gave his own, personal reasons for negotiating the clause: "I am sure there are people that said we wanted a most-favored nations clause to discourage opt-outs. That didn't have a thing to do with my asking for the most-favored nations clause. I wanted it to prevent from being embarrassed by having some guy who is not a real trial lawyer to hustle some clients in the newspaper, or wherever the hell they hustle them, and come in and make a better settlement than I did, and then go around crowing that Susman gave up easily." This was a not so indirect dig at Adams, who by then had lured half the class away from the settlement. Seated at the plaintiffs' counsel table, Boies turned to the side, laughing and shaking his head in disbelief. Susman's brand of sound and fury, exactly in keeping with the class action bar, was exactly the opposite of Boies's casual intelligence and technical precision.

The entire gallery broke into laughter, and Susman turned around as if to say, damn straight! Susman, of course, was beyond embarrassment. Aside from a few members of the press, the courtroom was full of lawyers, and each of them knew it was just a show. The packed table of defense lawyers, all of whom hailed from top-tier law firms of Cravath's ilk, sat mute, billing $400 or $500 an hour to their price-fixing clients. They had not a word to say about the MFN clause, which had by then failed their hopes of keeping more companies in the class and tied to Boies's deal.

Judge Hogan gave his final approval to the settlement from the bench that afternoon. His written opinion, issued a few weeks later, exhibited his practical side: in part, he was able to justify the MFN clause based on the actual experience of those companies that had opted out of the settlement and taken deals equal to or slightly less than the 18 percent overcharge in Boies's deal. (Adams, meanwhile, was confident that he could prove overcharges of 36 percent.) But Hogan took much more time—while Boies and his cocounsel sweated it out and plied him with briefs to bolster their case—to approve the most eye-popping provision of the settlement: the defense lawyers had agreed that a fee of $122,438,032 was "reasonable" for the plaintiffs' lawyers.

The previous fall, when the settlement was purportedly worth $1.17 billion, this sum represented a demure 10 percent of the settlement. By the next spring, the situation had reversed itself. "Do you realize that your fee request will be reported in the papers as asking for 122 million, after getting 242 million for your clients?" Judge Hogan asked in March 2000. Michael Hausfeld, a Washington lawyer who rounded out the three-man team leading the class action, had the thankless job of defending the fees. "Well, again it depends upon what the papers report and how they report it," Hausfeld offered. He said that "in context," the fee was "nothing that we're ashamed of." At that point, Boies rose and piped up. "We hope at least, Your Honor, that all of the reporters who are present here will report it accurately." There were mild chuckles from the gallery.

The defendants, whose hopes were dashed when the MFN didn't meet their expectations, never dreamed that Hogan would approve Boies's $122 million fee once the settlement shriveled to about a quarter of its original sum. The fee clause in the deal specifically said that the defense could not object to it. The defense lawyers were banking on a sentence in the lengthy clause on attorneys' fees, which provided that they were "committed to the sole discretion" of Judge Hogan. But Hogan was caught in a bind by the fee provision: if he reduced Boies's fee, the money would not go back to the class, but to the price-fixers. On July 16, 2001, he finally issued an elaborate opinion justifying the $122 million fee, plus another $850 thousand from another settlement. "Importantly, the proposed fee does not diminish the Plaintiffs' recovery," he wrote. In this, he was correct. Boies had negotiated his fee separate and above the money allotted to the victims of Vitamins Inc.

That move, in itself, is a red flag to the public interest lawyers who keep tabs on the class action bar. For as long as the class action mechanism has been in place, there has been fear that class lawyers will place the size of their fees above the interests of their clients. For this reason, most class action lawyers avoid the kind of bottom-line floor for fees that Boies, according to one defense lawyer, "insisted upon" in negotiating his deal with the vitamin makers. In a multimillion-dollar settlement like the vitamin case, a fee of 10 percent is average, and 15 percent is considered high. Boies's $122 million amounted to an unheard-of 50 percent.

No one complained about the fees in the vitamin case; the defense lawyers just took their medicine quietly. And the small companies from hometown America—companies like David III's original client, the J & R Feed company—did not make a peep. The case also fell below the radar screen of public interest groups like Public Citizen, a Washington, D.C., watchdog affiliated with Ralph Nader that intervenes in class actions when it determines that the plaintiffs' lawyers have abused their roles. I phoned Brian Wolfman, one of Public Citizen's senior lawyers, and asked him to read Hogan's opinion. Wolfman said it was merely convenient to say that Boies's enormous fee didn't reduce the class's recovery. "The only reason to set it up this way is to create this fiction that the class is not being harmed," he said.

There was evidence, even among the ranks of Boies's firm, that the fee was not the kind of triumph that would garner the best publicity. Bill Isaacson, the young partner who did most of the legwork on the case in its early stages, traveling to remote farms in places like Texarkana, admitted as much. When I called him shortly after Judge Hogan's opinion was released, he was immediately concerned that I would draw the press's attention to the story of the fee approval. "I'm sure we're not going to publicly say anything because it would be in bad taste," he said. But there were no stories in the press about the fee.

The villains in Vitamins Inc. would never incur the sort of wrath that the tobacco industry engendered. The lawyers had already played out their lawsuit against the tobacco giants by the time Boies got into the class action game. But his timing was perfect, in the fall of 1999, for the next assault—against another vilified business, the nation's health maintenance organizations.

In the fall of 1999, the lawyers who pocketed multimillion-dollar fees in the settlement against the tobacco makers decided to invest some of that war chest in a new campaign against the HMOs. In late September, as the lawyers were preparing lawsuits that would be filed in jurisdictions around the country over the next few days, the *Wall Street Journal* ran a lengthy story about the massive new effort, picturing, in its classic drawings, three lawyers: one was Russ Herman of New Orleans, who had represented Louisiana in a tobacco case that brought the state a $4.6 billion settlement; the second was Richard "Dickie" Scruggs of the $246 billion nationwide settlement with Big Tobacco; the last was David Boies. Under Boies's drawing, the *Journal* cited his credentials from the Microsoft case.

Going after the nation's HMOs—alongside Dickie Scruggs, no less—put Boies in a far more public view than his relatively obscure lawsuit against the vitamin price-fixers. It landed him on the opinion pages of the *Wall Street Journal*, which on October 7 labeled him "a simple ambulance chaser." In short, Boies had become one of the "Lawyers from Hell" a term coined by *Fortune* in 1995. Those words had appeared in block letters across the magazine's cover over a picture of the lawyers who went after the makers of silicone breast implants. Inside was a scathing article by Joseph Nocera detailing the tactics of the lawyers who swooped down on Dow Corning and eventually drove the company into bankruptcy. The catchy phrase stuck; it may not have been as universally understood as "trophy wife," another epithet launched by *Fortune,* but corporate America painfully understood what it meant. And this time around, the Lawyers from Hell had an audacious plan—to reform the nation's health care system through the courts.

Boies himself had little to do with the HMO litigation. It was the passion of his partner Stephen Neuwirth, who came up with the idea while still at the Clinton White House. Shortly after he joined Boies's firm, Neuwirth hooked up with another Washington lawyer, Joseph Sellars, to investigate the case. Teaming up with Sellars made practical sense: Sellars was a lawyer with Michael Hausfeld's firm, Cohen, Milstein, Hausfeld & Toll, and Hausfeld made it his priority to wrangle his way into a leadership position in many of the major class actions pending at any given moment. The firm of Cohen Milstein was steeped in the class action game long before Boies arrived on the scene. Hausfeld was among the group of lawyers who sued Swiss banks on behalf of Holocaust survivors to collect fortunes stolen by the Nazis. In 1997, Hausfeld was part of the team of lawyers who negotiated a $176 million deal with Texaco to settle allegations of race discrimination, the largest such award in U.S. history. (His young associate Cyrus Mehri, a former member of Ralph Nader's Raiders, uncovered the tape recordings of Texaco executives plotting to destroy evidence and making racist comments, which triggered the spectacular settlement.)

Because the stakes were so high, the struggle among the lawyers vying to lead the assault against the HMOs was far more rancorous than it had been in the vitamin litigation. Scruggs assembled the largest team, and called it the REPAIR group, an acronym that stood for RICO and ERISA Prosecutors Advocating for Insurance Company Reform. The group filed a pile of lawsuits in Mississippi against various HMOs. Scruggs was striving to bring a super–class action against all the nation's HMOs to Mississippi, and become the top dog in the mega-suit. The first of these was against Aetna.

Meanwhile, Neuwirth sought out Linda Peeno, a former claims reviewer for Humana turned whistle-blower, who had become a star expert witness in suits against the managed care industry. Peeno put Neuwirth in touch with Theodore Leopold, a lawyer from West Palm Beach, Florida, who was suing Humana on behalf of a local police officer, claiming that Humana denied treatment to his daughter, who suffered from cerebral palsy. Leopold won a $79.5 million verdict against Humana in January 1999, and most of that—$78 million—was imposed as punitive damages by the judge who oversaw the case, because he found that Humana had not turned over crucial documents in a timely fashion.

Leopold had strong ties to the local police community, and two members of the local police force became plaintiffs in the class action the Boies team filed in Miami on October 4, 1999. Another of the plaintiffs was Ramón Ortiz Rosario, who received his Humana health coverage from his employer, Nical of Palm Beach. Nical was a lawn care company owned by Amy Habie, a close friend of David Boies who had received pro bono legal help from him for a decade. The named plaintiff in a class action is put forth as a representative of all the others injured. Critics claimed that the people named in these complaints were not "clients" in the sense that the rest of the legal profession understood the term, people who hired a lawyer and sought legal advice. They were merely individuals known to the class lawyers who could serve as plaintiff on the document that would start the ball rolling. Rosario's appearance as a plaintiff suggested that Boies's firm was doing exactly that.

The complaint filed in Miami by Boies was the first against Humana. Several other Humana lawsuits also piled up in Miami, all by law firms with a close connection to Boies. The most curious of these—if anyone had stopped to question it, which no one did—was filed by James Fox Miller, the Hollywood, Florida, divorce lawyer who considered David Boies his best friend. The number of lawsuits in Miami gave that forum the appearance of critical mass. One defense lawyer called it a "total cheap-shit thing to do. They were all shilling for Boies."

The jockeying for position between Scruggs and Boies landed before the Judicial Panel on Multi-District Litigation (MDL), a bench of seven federal judges from various parts of the country who meet every few months to sift through stacks of class actions, and face the unenviable task of sorting out the arguments of lawyers competing for the lead position against their corporate prey. Understandably, the panel allows each advocate about five minutes to make his case. The proceedings are reminiscent of a long day in line at the passport office. Mary Boies quipped at one of these hearings that her husband said they reminded him of plaintiffs' bar conventions. At the Boies-Scruggs hearing, in Palm Springs on March 30, 2000, Scruggs pushed for a mega-case against all of the HMOs in his Mississippi backyard. The panel chose a narrower path, transferring only the cases against Humana to Miami, where they were assigned to U.S. District Judge Federico Moreno. That decision gave Boies leverage against Scruggs's much larger and more powerful REPAIR group.

When the panel gave the nod to Miami, the jockeying for position in the mega-case began in earnest. The plaintiffs' lawyers still had not agreed to a management structure when they convened for a hearing on the subject before Judge Moreno on May 22. Several in Boies's circle came forward to sing his praises and say that they, too, had filed cases in Miami against Humana and believed he should be part of the leadership team. Stephen Zack, the head of a Miami plaintiffs' firm that bore his name, introduced Boies. Zack was fast becoming one of Boies's most eager acolytes. "All you need is a television set or a newspaper to know who David Boies is. Anybody who follows the legal landscape knows that one of its brightest stars is David Boies," Zack fawned before Moreno.

Humana's lawyer, John Beisner, pleaded with Moreno to appoint a single lead counsel. As with many hearings involving class actions, all was not what it appeared: there was already a move afoot to lump together all of the actions against the HMOs—actions involving giants like Aetna and Cigna—to Miami. Scruggs and company had determined, in the wake of the MDL panel's decision, that the die was cast for Miami, and that they would have to negotiate with Boies. They just hadn't hashed the management structure out by May 22. Beisner, on the other hand, was trying to hang on to the simple notion that the MDL had transferred only the case against Humana. The stakes in this subtle undercurrent at the hearing were enormous: it meant the difference between a class action against one company and a mega-class—possibly including eighty million HMO customers from as many as seven different corporate giants—before one judge.

Judge Moreno gave the plaintiffs' lawyers another couple of weeks to work out their management differences.

Dickie Scruggs and David Boies made for an unlikely team. Scruggs had taken home a billion dollars in fees from the tobacco settlement, but he still presented himself as a hick from Mississippi. He had taken his assault against the HMOs to Capitol Hill, and made conference calls to analysts on Wall Street who covered HMOs, intent on scaring them about the effect a mega-suit would have on stock prices. At one early hearing before Moreno, he declared: "The patient's bill of rights is not going anywhere this year or next year, so Congress is not going to fix it. They are counting on this court to fix it." Scruggs made no bones about wanting to use the court system to regulate the HMOs without the benefit of congressional legislation. Boies was just the opposite. "Boies is more of a law and record guy," Beisner said. The law and record guys usually represented corporate defendants, intent on establishing a record on appeal.

But Boies and Scruggs shared one defining characteristic: they were both super-lawyers; and in the end, they came to a logical and Darwinian compromise. On the eve of the June 8, 2000, hearing before Moreno, the plaintiffs' lawyers finally agreed to a management structure. Boies and Scruggs would colead the case. The plaintiffs' lawyers hand-delivered a hastily written letter to Judge Moreno on the morning of the hearing. Just as the lawyers were hashing out the terms, the Justice Department was holding a press conference in Washington to announce that Judge Thomas Penfield Jackson had agreed to their historic request to break up Microsoft. The press was eager to hear from Boies, but the team from Justice, bracing for a disappointed reaction, quietly informed the crowd that Boies was otherwise engaged in a case in Miami. Superman had moved on—and he was breaking bread with the Lawyers from Hell.

The management structure included various committees, all of whom would share in the legal fees. These committees featured the friends and family of David Boies. Among them were James Fox Miller, Boies's best friend and gambling buddy, who all but admitted to me, before one hearing, that he had no qualifications for the job: "I am a divorce lawyer; they are going to program me." Also on the list were Ted Leopold, the lawyer who fed Boies the Humana documents and clients; Steve Zack, the emerging Boies acolyte; and Bainbridge & Strauss, the law firm where Boies's son David III was a partner.

For at least a decade, the HMO industry, with its contemptible cost cutting and potentially deep pockets, remained insulated from an assault by the class action bar for a simple reason: the decisions made by a doctor constrained by those cost-cutting measures, and the resulting injuries, were in every case unique. These highly individual circumstances could not be lumped into a class action, which by necessity asserted damages suffered anonymously and commonly by thousands of people.

Boies and Scruggs found a way around this sticky problem by seeking damages on behalf of people who had *no* medical problems. The idea was that the HMOs, by failing to disclose their cost-cutting methods and their financial incentives to doctors for withholding treatment, had deceived subscribers about the true worth of their health insurance policies. That deception, Boies and Scruggs claimed, fell under the provisions of the Racketeer Influence and Corruption Organizations (RICO) Act, a federal law enacted in 1970 to assist the FBI in going after the mob. For decades, plaintiffs' lawyers had employed RICO with wily determination to charge many corporations with a "pattern of racketeering activity." All that it required was proof of the use of mail or wires as part of the fraud. Boies and Scruggs could easily establish that. Presto, there were hundreds of millions of HMO "victims"—victims of the failure to disclose the cost cutting, victims with none of the complicating physical injuries at the hands of managed care that would render them impossible to be lumped together in a class action. And civil RICO claims carried the threat of triple damages. Brilliant!

This ingenious theory had occurred, a bit earlier, to the class action kings at Milberg Weiss, which had filed a class action against Aetna before the tobacco lawyers turned their sights on the HMOs. As a result, Milberg was not part of the mega-suit developing before Judge Moreno. With remarkable timing, the Third Circuit Court of Appeals in Philadelphia upheld the dismissal of the RICO claims against Aetna on August 11, just six days before Judge Moreno was to hear arguments on Humana's motion to dismiss the claims brought by Boies and Scruggs. The Philadelphia case, *Maio v. Aetna*, was not necessarily binding upon Moreno, who sat in the Eleventh Circuit. But the case was directly on point. Boies's team scrambled to write a brief explaining how the Miami case was different from *Maio*, an effort that stretched the contortionist capabilities of even a Harvard-trained lawyer like Neuwirth.

As Boies touched down in Miami on the evening of August 16, the night before the Moreno hearing, he had other pressing deadlines on his mind. A brief for Napster, the online music service he was charged with rescuing from copyright infringement claims, was due at the federal appeals court in San Francisco, and Boies was not happy with the product delivered by Napster's California counsel. At the hearing, Humana's lawyer, John Beisner, ridiculed the plaintiffs' attempts to explain away the *Maio* ruling, saying the papers reminded him of the speech his high school debate coach gave, warning students not to fall into the trap of the "delusional debater" who could pick up a mirror and assert that the person he was seeing in it was someone else. When Beisner finished laying out the many reasons why the case should be dismissed, Judge Moreno looked out onto the courtroom packed with plaintiffs' lawyers—so large in number that they overflowed into the jury box—and asked, "Who is going to be the delusional debater?" Boies demonstrated his ability to defuse the most damning parts of a case with a casual witty remark: "I would be delusional, your honor, if I thought the *Maio* case was a helpful case for us. I don't think it's a helpful case."

It was a bold admission, so simple as to be obvious, and one that most other lawyers would not have dared to make. Boies was possessed of such an unlimited reserve of confidence that he could trust his instincts and give up the points that he knew he would lose for the larger picture. And it turned out to have saved the plaintiffs; Judge Moreno rejected the motion to dismiss and allowed the claims against the HMOs to proceed. In his decision, Moreno credited the breath of fresh air in Boies's argument: "The Plaintiffs in their pleadings attempted without success to distinguish *Maio* on its facts. However, this acknowledges the merit of the argument by

Plaintiffs' counsel during oral argument that the reasoning in *Maio*, rather than be distinguished, should simply not be adopted."

Moreno lingered over the motion to dismiss longer than anyone anticipated. He did not issue his ruling until June 2001, and by that time, the case against Humana had metastasized into the mega-litigation against the entire managed care industry that Boies and Scruggs were aiming for. Boies and Scruggs accomplished this, according to one defense lawyer, "through the most amazing chain of procedural chicanery." Once Moreno approved the duo's management structure, they filed a complaint purporting to amend the class action against Humana, including claims against six other HMOs. The other HMOs had nothing to do with Humana's complaint, but Judge Moreno did nothing to stop this. "He played along because he wanted to be the managed care czar," one defense lawyer told me. When the MDL panel took up the competing claims as to where cases against such giants as Aetna and Cigna should be "transferred," these cases were already up and running before Moreno. And he seemed eager to hold on to them. The opponents of Boies and Scruggs still hoped to turn back the clock and transfer at least some of the cases now before Moreno to another courtroom.

The MDL panel met on September 22, 2000, atop the federal courthouse in lower Manhattan, in the ceremonial courtroom reserved for the swearing-in of new citizens and other grand occasions, which could accommodate the sea of plaintiffs' lawyers and their opponents from the Wall Street firms. The arguments proceeded at a staccato pace until the end of the day, when the panel dispensed with their stopwatch mentality to consider the HMO litigation. The session ended when the chief judge announced, "We understand, most seriously, how awesome these cases are." Arthur Miller, the legendary civil procedure professor from Harvard Law School, who argued at the hearing for Milberg Weiss against the movement of the cases to Miami, stopped on the way out to greet Boies. "Take care of yourself," he said. "You're a one-man universe!"

A month later, the panel left the cases before Moreno in order to avoid, as they always sought to do, duplication of the arduous discovery process and to save resources. Boies and Scruggs now had the entire industry before one court. The case meandered along until late July 2001, when Boies touched down by private jet for another crucial hearing in the case, the hearing that would prove fatal to the pursuit of a mega-case against the HMOs.

In every class action, there comes a time for a motion for class certification, when the plaintiffs' lawyers are required to establish that the alleged injuries ought to be lumped together. The requirements of proof, under rule 23 of the Federal Rules of Civil Procedure—the rule that created class actions—are extraordinarily complicated. A vast body of case law exists on what rule 23 requires. In the easiest cases, such as a class action on behalf of investors based on false information that a corporation sent into the stock market, class certification can be a simple matter. A class action against a single HMO would have been hard enough; the HMO's disclosures to subscribers changed from year to year, and were often modified by their subsidiaries. Boies and Scruggs compounded the difficulties when they decided to pursue a case against *all* of the nation's major managed care companies at once. The contracts that each of the HMOs issued were vastly different. And the number of people in the potential class—a number that ranged anywhere from 40 million to 140 million—was unprecedented, indeed uncountable.

The class action lawyers, once again, packed themselves into Judge Moreno's courtroom, filling up the gallery seats and piling into the jury box on the morning of July 24, 2001. Early on in the daylong hearing, Moreno showed he could be an aggressive and skeptical jurist. Scruggs, who went before Boies in the arguments, displayed his Elmer Gantry approach to oral argument. Moreno asked, "Where is the link between one defendant and another?" and Scruggs boomed back that the HMOs were engaged in "an unholy alliance; a race to the bottom." Scruggs employed the language of an evangelist or a politician, reminding Moreno that he had been "impolitic enough" at a previous hearing to refer to the cash bonuses that HMOs granted for the denial of claims as "bribes." Scruggs described the HMO system as "a one-size-fits-all, that takes no account of the medical necessity in an individual case," voicing the ire of subscribers. But the judge shot back, "I thought that was what HMOs were supposed to do."

It fell to Boies to make the argument at the heart of the lawsuit—that the HMOs' alleged failure to disclose their true cost-cutting measures could be lumped together in a class action. If Scruggs was the preacher, Boies was the cautious tactician. The hearing took an ominous turn late in the day, when the defense lawyers bombarded Moreno with the vast differences in knowledge even among the few people put forth by the plaintiffs' lawyers as representatives for the mega-class. Some of the class representatives handpicked by the plaintiffs knew that the HMOs used cost-cutting guidelines; others knew nothing at all of their coverage, and simply took what their employers offered, or learned about their coverage from their employer rather than the HMO. "There are forty-six million stories in the naked city, and they are all going to have to be litigated," said John Quinn, a lawyer for United Healthcare. Quinn suggested that there would need to be trials on each individual's reliance on the HMO disclosures—disclosures that Boies and Scruggs insisted were "uniform"—and that process could "take years and years" to litigate," long enough, Quinn said, that his "grandchildren would be involved."

Moreno took this in, and announced: "The case really revolves, then, on whether or not I will find reliance." Boies recognized that Quinn's arguments had resonance with the judge. In his argument, Quinn had used a copy of the United Healthcare contract. The document, blown up on a ten-by-twelve-foot screen, showed that United Healthcare spelled out to subscribers that its definition of coverage "differs from the way in which a physician engaged in the practice of medicine may define medically necessary." The document was just one of a series that Quinn used to show that the disclosures were so varied and many that lumping together a class of millions based on them was ludicrous.

As Quinn wrapped up his argument, Boies turned to his litigation team, his face taut, his body rigid, his eyes piercing. He ordered Kent Ankar, a young associate, to find a copy of the United Healthcare contract. At moments like these, Boies's intensity could frighten even seasoned lawyers. Ankar was panic-stricken. As Boies looked around for Neuwirth, the partner with daily responsibility in the case, Boies became more agitated, and the tension thickened when Boies demanded to know whether the same version of the United Healthcare contract was in the judge's book of exhibits for the hearing. Nobody on the team knew why Boies was so intent on finding the contract. Mary Boies, who was seated next to me in the gallery, turned to me and whispered, "It's a funny business—you work for weeks, and find one document."

Like the rest of us, Mary was wondering what Boies would do next. When Boies rose to the podium for rebuttal arguments, he meant to land a "Gotcha" punch at Quinn's successful arguments. Boies guided Moreno down to the date at the end of the page of the United Healthcare document used by Quinn, showing Moreno that the document was created *after* the plaintiffs sought their motion for class certification, and suggesting that the document was rigged to serve as a defense. "They cannot escape class certification by later-created documents," Boies said, implying that the defense had manufactured evidence in its favor. "Check and see whether those documents predated the litigation." Moreno was unmoved. Whatever the documents said, the defense arguments stuck in his craw. Disclosures to subscribers could be impacted by so many things. At one point, Moreno suggested to Boies that the plaintiffs might need to bring employers in as defendants, if, indeed, the disclosure documents to corporate employers purchasing the health benefits offered by the HMOs revealed their cost-cutting measures. Left unsaid between Moreno and Boies was that bringing in the nation's employers would have destroyed the simple strategy of Boies and Scruggs, who wanted to gather the HMOs together as defendants so they could strong-arm them.

Boies seemed to recognize that he was making little headway with Moreno. He asked the judge to consider his own legendary ability to extract admissions from witnesses. Boies suggested that Moreno allow the case to proceed to the discovery phase—a move that would allow the plaintiffs to issue massive requests for the files of each of the HMOs—while reserving his decision on whether the case deserved to proceed as a class action. In class actions, discovery is usually curtailed until the class is certified, a practice intended to curb plaintiffs' lawyers from filing the flimsiest lawsuits just to go on a fishing expedition against a defendant. Boies was now asking Moreno to take this extraordinary step. "They have made all sorts of assertions that have been untested by cross-examination or discovery," Boies said. Boies was playing his favorite card with this move—the credibility card. But Moreno wasn't likely to bite at this suggestion; it would have amounted to the most colossal fishing expedition in the history of class actions.

Scruggs got up once more, fuming over the defendants' picking apart the knowledge of benefits—or lack thereof—held by the class representatives. The defendants, as was their right, had deposed the named plaintiffs and had made the most of what they learned in those depositions. Scruggs took it as an insult. "They sort of assume that we should get our class members from central casting!" Scruggs harrumphed.

The hearing came to a close. Judge Moreno then sat on the motion for class certification for many months, and in the interim, the team of Boies and Scruggs suffered one last bit of bad luck. The HMO pursuers had escaped the Maio decision, but there was no escaping the impact of the ruling from the court of appeals for the Eleventh Circuit, in *Sikes v. Teleline Inc.*

Until *Sikes* came down, Boies and Scruggs could rely on the idea that there should be a presumption of reliance on what they described as the allegedly "uniform" disclosures about coverage made by the HMOs. But the Sikes decision ruled that there could be no class action status for the ten thousand victims of AT&T's "Let's Make a Deal" campaign, who got their information from 119 different television commercials, print advertisements, and direct advertising mailings, making it impossible to establish a mass scheme to defraud. The claims by the HMO plaintiffs—based on widely different disclosure documents, often filtered through many different employers and their benefits consultants—could not possibly pass the test set by *Sikes*. In the end, when Moreno issued his ruling denying class certification, in late September 2002, the judge could not get past a simple but practical fact: each of the HMOs, and their subsidiaries, had "vast differences" in their plan documents, a situation creating highly individual instances of fraud on the HMO consumers, impossible to aggregate on a class basis. It was over. The plaintiffs' lawyers filed a motion to appeal Judge Moreno's denial of class certification with the Eleventh Circuit, but that was a Hail Mary pass.

The super-regulation that Boies and Scruggs sought to impose on the HMO industry, and their visions of hundreds of millions of dollars in fees, went up in smoke. All that Neuwirth could muster, in an interview with the *Wall Street Journal,* was the faint hope that the plaintiffs' lawyers would look into their options. Putting the best spin on the situation, he said, "We certainly feel that our suit exposed practices and that exposure forced the companies to change some of what they were doing." There was no public reaction from Boies himself.

TWELVE

Getting to $512 Million

BIDDING UP THE CASE AGAINST CHRISTIE'S AND SOTHEBY'S

The auction house case was like many other chapters in Boies's career: Boies arrived on the scene after the case had been pending, took control away from the lawyers who had been litigating it, and achieved spectacular results. Usually, the decision to switch to Boies was made by a corporate executive—from IBM or Texaco or Westinghouse—leaving Boies to work alongside (though in isolation from) the lawyers he had supplanted. The result was often wounded egos and strained work relationships. Here, the selection of Boies would be made by a judge and veterans of the class action bar were left out of the money.

There was never any doubt about the liability of London-based Christie's and Sotheby's of New York for price-fixing. In mid-January 2000, Christie's and its former chief executive Christopher Davidge turned over a pile of documents, including handwritten notes, detailing a conspiracy between the two art houses to fix commissions which had been going on since the early 1990s. Christie's got leniency from the federal prosecutors in return for its cooperation, which transformed a moribund investigation into a rapid-fire prosecution.

The case against the auction houses promised to lay bare the seedy underbelly of the clubby art world. The nearly five hundred pages of documents detailed years of collusion between Davidge and his counterpart at Sotheby's, Diana Brooks, known as "Dede." Davidge documented his secret meetings with Brooks, a starchy blond ice princess of relentless ambition, known best for presiding over the auction of the estate of Jacqueline Kennedy Onassis. Davidge and Brooks often met in the backs of limousines, at her apartment, or at restaurants, where they discussed fixing prices and dividing up their super-wealthy client lists.

Christie's made a terse public statement acknowledging that it had delivered the documents to the government on January 28, 2000. Two days later, Christopher Lovell, a Manhattan lawyer who had figured in several mega-cases, filed the first class action against Christie's and Sotheby's. Together, the two auction houses controlled 90 percent of the $4-billion-a-year auction business. In the following weeks, scores of other suits were also filed. Among them was one filed by Boies and Steve Susman. Susman's firm had a client who was an avid art purchaser.

The auction house case landed before U.S. District Judge Lewis Kaplan of Manhattan, who had been appointed by Clinton in 1994. Kaplan relished his work, and his hands-on approach to the auction house case had the plaintiffs' lawyers running in circles. They often joked that they wished the judge would get a hobby.

From the outset, Kaplan seemed to look on the auction house case as a laboratory. He sized up the lawsuits seeking class action status that flooded into his courtroom for what they were—plaintiffs' lawyers out to make big, easy money. The predicament of the auction houses had all the makings of a quick settlement—one that would earn the lawyers millions but possibly shortchange the class.

Dozens of plaintiffs' firms attended the first status conference, held in February 2000, and five of them proposed themselves as the leaders of the consolidated cases. Kaplan appointed six lawyers, including Christopher Lovell, who had filed first, to serve as the "interim executive committee." But it was clear that Kaplan was toying with something different.

The judge mulled the situation for some months, announcing that he would hold an auction to determine who would win the coveted role of lead counsel. This procedure disrupted the unwritten rules that class action lawyers established, wherein the lawyers with the most clout set up a leadership structure, and at the end of the case divvied up the pie, often fighting over the booty. The foot soldier law firms got their fees from the leading law firm that they had aligned themselves with. There were more than fifty firms, all told, sharing the $123.1 million bonanza in the vitamin case. In the auction house case, the firm that won the bid to represent the class would take home the inevitable multimillion-dollar fee, every last cent, without having to share it with other law firms. It was a tantalizing prospect.

Auctions had been employed before in class actions, but the procedure was still controversial. The lawyers on the interim committee balked, pleading with the judge to leave things as they stood. "We do have *real* trial lawyers here, your honor, that will take this case to the maximum result," declared Frederick Furth, a San Francisco lawyer who had a Texas accent and Texas attire, right down to his calfskin boots, and whose class action riches had allowed him to start the Chalk Hill Estate Vineyards in Sonoma County. *Real trial lawyers.* Members of the class action bar were forever reminding people that they fell into this category, as if, on some level, they realized that everyone else suspected they did not.

When he released his decision explaining why he chose an auction to select lead counsel, Kaplan said the "class action mechanism on occasion has proved to be Janus-faced," and the case presented him with "an occasion to ease this tension and improve the class action as an instrument of justice." As the case continued, Kaplan turned his blunt wit and sharp pen on the class lawyers, calling them on the games they played. Eventually, even Boies found himself skewered by Kaplan.

Boies won the auction, which required firms to submit bids with an "X" figure, representing the recovery that would go to class members before the lawyers received a dime. Kaplan appointed Boies's firm in mid-April 2000. Under the bidding procedure, the lawyers would be paid 25 percent of any recovery above the X figure. Boies's X figure was $405 million, a number that remained secret throughout the case and Boies's settlement discussions with the defense lawyers. It became known only when Judge Kaplan revealed it at a final hearing.

The lawyers on the interim executive committee were livid about

Boies's appointment. "Kaplan wrote Boies a big, fat check," sniped one anonymous lawyer in an article in the *New York Observer*, the salmon-colored weekly broadsheet that chronicles Manhattan's media elite and high society with bitchy delight. Boies, it turned out, offered two other law firms, including Susman's, the chance to work with him to achieve the X figure. They alone knew the amount. Both firms declined. "I turned him down," one lawyer told me at the time. "I hope they reach their X, but it's a huge, huge risk," he said.

Boies reveled in this story, which reflected a spin he very much wanted to foster—that his firm was unlike others in the class action bar. "When we take on a class action, we approach it in the same way as an individual client," Boies told me in August, just as he was beginning settlement discussions with the art houses. Had the case proceeded to a trial verdict, he said, the jury's dollar award for the art customers would have been tripled automatically, as the antitrust laws require. "The individual client is not going to say, 'We want single damages,'" Boies said. He suggested he would not settle for less than triple damages on behalf of the 130,000 customers in the class.

A year later, I would look back with amusement on this conversation with Boies, when I filed a motion before Judge Kaplan to unseal the competing secret bids. Boies urged me on in this endeavor; he knew the files would show his bid was much larger than those from the other firms. But when Kaplan granted my motion and I finally got a look at the bids, it struck me that Boies's firm had won, not by taking an audacious risk, but because his expert had made a miscalculation in his preliminary estimate of damages.

Boies's expert, the economist Jeffrey Leitzinger, relied mainly on the financial disclosures that Sotheby's, a publicly traded company, reported to the Securities and Exchange Commission. He used two methods: First, he calculated the revenue effects of the auction house overcharges during the conspiracy. That method yielded damages of $533 million. Then Leitzinger prepared an alternative method, in which he compared the gross margins earned by the defendants during the conspiracy with their gross margins from before the conspiracy began, and came up with damages of $550 million. He concluded that this alternative method "serves to confirm the reasonableness of the overcharge method."

The interim lead counsel, who had already begun settlement discussions with the defendants before Kaplan made the lawyers compete for the right to handle the case, had gotten some data on actual auction transactions from the defendants. The data suggested that the total damages—sellers' and buyers' sides—amounted to about $270 million. All of the law firms competing for the case were given access to this data, but Boies's firm chose to ignore it. Leitzinger's report states that his estimates were "based solely on publicly available data," and that "a more accurate calculation can be done when discovery commences."

Boies's firm, as well as the twenty or so others that bid to become lead counsel, knew this much for certain: the documents Christie's had turned over to the government established, without a doubt, that the two auction houses had conspired to fix the commission rates charged to sellers. The prosecutors had solid evidence of meetings between Brooks and Davidge, beginning in April 1993, at which they conspired to publish new, nonnegotiable sellers' commissions in the spring of 1995. Christie's announced its new schedule that March; Sotheby's followed a month later. The higher commission rates remained in effect at both companies at least until December 1999. The houses exchanged customer information to monitor and enforce the nonnegotiable fees. They also agreed to limit or eliminate other perks formerly offered to sellers on their consignments, such as interest-free loans.

But the case had a tricky variable: in 1992, Christie's and Sotheby's had set identical buyers' fees, increasing the commissions from 10 to 15 percent on the first $50,000 of the hammer price, and 10 percent above that figure. Sotheby's announced this change in November 1992, and Christie's made the same change that December. But prosecutors were struggling to establish proof of collusion on these fees. (In fact, when Sotheby's and Brooks finally pleaded guilty to price-fixing in October 2000, the charges did not include the buyers' commissions.)

The lack of evidence establishing a buyers'-side conspiracy should have been problematic for the class action because most of the damages were on the buyers' side. Preliminary estimates by the interim class counsel suggested a figure of about $200 million from the 5 percent overcharge on buyers' commissions. The estimates from the fixing of sellers' commissions were much lower, between $30 million and $80 million.

The law firms that lost the case to Boies discovered that a little knowledge could be a dangerous thing. Boies's bid made it clear that his firm had done little investigation. The few facts that the firm claimed to "understand"—such as documents evidencing meetings on the sellers' as well as the buyers' conspiracy—were never established during the litigation. Of the bids that were unsealed, the most cautious and sober assessments of the case came from the two interim lead counsel who had spent the most time on the case, Christopher Lovell and Robert Kaplan, who had interviewed a number of former Sotheby's employees. Lovell's bid was the more aggressive; he put his X figure at $180 million, although he had grave reservations about the ability to prove a buyers' conspiracy. Among the bids, one X figure was the same as the $405 million Boies offered, from the law firm of Shapiro, Haber & Urmy of Boston. Their damages estimate came to $346.2 million, but they were willing to bet on $405 million—in other words, they were willing to press for more than actual damages, something the Boies firm considered unreasonable, at least according to the papers it filed with Kaplan. Boies's submission to Judge Kaplan stressed that the firm was "not aware of any defendant ever settling a case, including an antitrust case, for more than actual damages, no matter how strong the facts might be." To preserve the prospect of a settlement, the Boies firm explained that it was setting its bid in relation to actual damages, rather than the treble damages the plaintiffs could collect at a trial. Boies's bid had not been the most audacious; it just turned out to be the most fortunate. The night before the final bid was due, Richard Drubel, the partner handling the case, wanted to bid $400 million; but Boies suspected that other firms would round their bids out to even numbers, and decided that an odd number would give his firm an edge.

As the case proceeded, and Boies discovered that his expert was wrong, he had to press for triple damages on the sellers' commissions if he had any hope of reaching his X figure. And it turned out that treble damages was exactly what Judge Kaplan was looking for: in one of his decisions, he disagreed with the prevailing case law that applied to review of settlements in antitrust class actions. "The received wisdom is that the adequacy of antitrust class action settlements is to be tested against an estimate of single rather than treble damages," Kaplan wrote, citing a leading case from the 1970s. But, in his view, the justifications set forth in the precedents were "not persuasive." To merely accept single damages, he observed, would place the court approving a settlement—whose role was to look out for all of the absent class members—"in a position in which it may be forced to approve a settlement that no non-representative plaintiff would accept in similar circumstances." The defense lawyers came to believe that Judge Kaplan was, in effect, playing God in the case; Boies was his messenger, and the auction houses were the objects of his lesson.

During the bidding, Boies's firm set $26 million as its fee in the case. Originally, Kaplan had the competing firms submit an "X" figure, representing the amount that would go to the class members, and a "Y" figure that would go to class counsel. Boies had set "X" at $410 million and "Y" at $26 million. Kaplan changed the rules and had firms submit just an "X" figure, providing that the winning firm would get a fourth of any recovery beyond "X" as its fee. This, in effect, upped the ante. To make $26 million, as I discovered when Kaplan granted my motion to unseal the bids, meant Boies would now have to extract a settlement of about $500 million from the auction house defendants. The number had alarmed Susman when Boies asked him to become his cocounsel. Susman's art collector client worried that Sotheby's, a public company already in financial turmoil over the scandal, could not survive such a settlement. In fact, this prospect was very real. The number of the final settlement was $512 million—which happened to give Boies a little more than the $26 million he had named as his "Y" figure!

Boies got the defendants to this outlandish figure in negotiations that took place over a frenzied month beginning on the Friday of Labor Day weekend 2000. After the experience, one of his opponents vowed never to do business with Boies again. To get to the $512 million figure, the defendants pledged $100 million in coupons that could be used at the auction houses to offset the price of sellers' commissions. The auction houses, which had been negotiating with Boies separately, finally decided to meet with him jointly because, in the end, both wanted to hear the same story. A combination of factors—that Boies was playing Sotheby's, a public company on the brink of bankruptcy, against Christie's, a private company with unlimited access to cash—created a unique opportunity for Boies. One plaintiffs' lawyer from the interim lead counsel described the deal as "a once-in-a-lifetime thing, where all the planets and the moons were aligned, and it will never happen again."

The entire course of the settlement talks was shaped by a single factor: Christie's, which had beaten Sotheby's to the door of the Justice Department and gained leniency by turning over the treasure trove of documents, had decided it would not play ball with Sotheby's. Defendants in antitrust cases commonly enter into a "sharing agreement" soon after the case is filed. These agreements typically provide that the defendants will split the cost of damages among them equally. These agreements protect defendants from the draconian effects of the antitrust laws, which can force one party to an alleged price-fixing conspiracy to foot the bill for the entire cost of liability, including the treble damages that apply to antitrust verdicts, without any right to force their codefendants to share the burden under what is known in the legal jargon as "joint and several liability." Once a sharing agreement is signed, the defendants are yoked together against the demands of the class lawyers, and the class lawyers lose the ability to play one defendant off another by using the threat that the last man standing will carry the whole burden, including treble damages. The Sotheby's lawyers sent a draft of the sharing agreement to Christie's counsel in June 2000, but never heard back from them. "All Boies had to do was play one against the other," said one lawyer involved in the case. "Boies got them into an auction. Boies played them like a fiddle, basically."

Boies approached Christie's first. Boies and Leitzinger made a trip to the office of Christie's lawyers at Skadden, Arps, Slate, Meagher & Flom. The Christie's lawyers rejected Leitzinger's calculations, and Boies soon agreed with them. His main purpose was to convince Christie's that he preferred to settle with them first because, among other things, they were based in Europe, where treble damages could not be enforced in any rate. By mid-August, less than three months after Kaplan had appointed him as lead counsel, Boies was engaged in serious settlement discussions with Christie's. They culminated in a meeting on the Friday afternoon before Labor Day, held on the veranda of Boies's home, overlooking the back acres of his estate. Boies preferred to do business this way. It lent to his ostensibly informal style, and it also meant that those who came to do business with him were his guests.

The Skadden lawyers left Boies's house with many variables still up in the air. From their perspective, it was a beginning, but there was no deal. The Skadden lawyers also asked, point-blank, whether Boies and his firm were talking to Sotheby's, and were told no. Boies reiterated: he preferred to settle with Christie's first. In fact, that very morning two lawyers from Boies's firm, Drubel and Philip Korologos, who were also seated on the veranda that afternoon, had paid a visit to hear a presentation from Weil, Gotshal & Manges, the law firm representing Sotheby's.

Sotheby's lawyers had emphasized that there were real limits on the company's ability to pay. Sotheby's net revenues in its best years hovered between $40 million and $50 million, and they told Drubel and Korologos Sotheby's could not possibly pay more than $50 million in cash. The Weil Gotshal lawyers believed Boies's firm was talking with Christie's, but Drubel and Korologos did not say they had a deal at the meeting. The next morning, Drubel called one of the Weil Gotshal lawyers and told him they were about to sign a deal with Christie's. Then, Drubel made a stunning demand: Sotheby's and its chairman, A. Alfred Taubman, could settle the case, together paying $400 million. "$400 million or your life," one of the Sotheby's lawyers recalled. Taubman, a shopping mall developer and self-made man, had bought Sotheby's in 1983 for $125 million, and took the company public in 1989, remaining its controlling shareholder. Taubman's personal wealth was said to be more than $700 million. There were reports that he would be indicted, along with Dede Brooks, on price-fixing charges.

Drubel's demand shocked the Sotheby's lawyers. The auction house still had not settled the criminal case, while Christie's had gotten amnesty from the prosecutors. And the two auction houses were in vastly different financial situations; Christie's, privately owned by the French billionaire François Pinault, who also had stakes in Gucci and Yves Saint Laurent, had unlimited access to cash, while Sotheby's had to answer to its shareholders. If Christie's settled the class action, while the suit against Sotheby's remained open, Christie's was sure to take advantage of that uncertainty with art customers. "The auction business runs on confidence," one Sotheby's lawyer told me. "And if we were left there with unresolved liability, Christie's would be able to say to potential customers, 'Who knows if Sotheby's is going to be around?' That would have been enormously precarious."

After Drubel's alarming phone call, the Weil Gotshal lawyers realized that it was imperative to reach David Boies. The firm turned to its own star, Ira Millstein, who had dealt with Boies on other matters, to place the call. Boies agreed to meet at Weil Gotshal's Fifth Avenue office in the Trump Tower on Wednesday, September 6. He came alone.

Boies outlined the terms of his deal with Christie's. They had agreed to pay $230 million to settle the case, but there was an important caveat: they had to pay $140 million in cash. For the balance, Boies gave Christie's the opportunity to "earn back" some or all of the rest by helping him obtain greater damages against Sotheby's. This kind of deal is known as a "Mary Carter" agreement, named for a 1967 case in which one of the defendants secretly agreed to settle a case and help the plaintiff pursue a case against another defendant. Highly controversial, Mary Carter agreements were a favorite tool of plaintiffs' lawyers, and it was Drubel, the veteran class action lawyer, who came up with the idea.

Millstein and Richard Davis, one of Sotheby's lead lawyers in the courtroom, listened as Boies outlined the deal. Boies told them that the deal with Christie's was essentially done, but that he could control when it was actually signed. It was subject to a "proffer"—a show of evidence by Christie's as a first proof of its intent to cooperate. Boies had to review the proffer, and he could always claim he was traveling. That much, at least, was true—on Friday Boies was headed to San Francisco to prepare the final brief in the Napster case.

When Boies left the Weil Gotshal offices, he and the Sotheby's lawyers had arrived at the rough outline of a potential settlement: the number was $230 million, and Sotheby's planned to pay that astronomical sum by raising $100 million in cash. Sotheby's also had a potential claim against its own chairman, Taubman, for his violation of fiduciary duties as chairman of the company. Sotheby's would turn over its potential claims against Taubman to Boies in order to get to the $230 million. "We want to make it perfectly clear that we are taking at face value that you need the 230," Millstein told Boies in a telephone call upon Boies's arrival in San Francisco. "We don't want to wake up some morning and read that they settled for two dollars and eighty cents," he quipped. Millstein was still clearly nervous that Boies would leave Sotheby's out in the cold by settling with Christie's first, leaving his client potentially on the hook for the entire cost of treble damages. He told Boies that he thought he could get a "firm commitment" on the deal by the following Tuesday, and that the Sotheby's board of directors would meet to discuss it on Wednesday.

Boies reassured Millstein. Boies would not return from California until the next Tuesday, and would be unable to review the proffer by Christie's until Wednesday, or talk to the Christie's lawyers until Thursday or Friday. Millstein sounded relieved, and the two lawyers ended their conversation with banter about another case. Boies had a new client, Echostar, the number two satellite television company in the country, which was suing DirecTV, the number one satellite company, and a subsidiary of General

Motors, one of Weil Gotshal's most important clients. Millstein would be working on the case. "I will take it as a compliment that they want to bring you in!" Boies remarked. Their conversation could not have been friendlier—they communicated as one super-lawyer to another. There wasn't a hint, at least on the surface, that Boies, in class action mode, had requested the fantastic sum of $230 million from Sotheby's, $100 million of which it would need to raise in hard cash, a demand that put the auction house on the brink of financial disaster.

By now, Boies was confident that he would be able to settle this case. "Oh, we're going to settle it," he told me while we were traveling together in San Francisco. "The real question is how much we're going to get from Taubman."

Getting funding from Taubman was in the end the key to the deal. On one hand, Taubman and Sotheby's interests were aligned; both the chairman and the company had been left out in the cold when Christie's dumped documents with the Justice Department. On the other hand, none of those documents directly implicated Taubman, and he had decided to hang tough with the government prosecutors. He never pleaded guilty, and ultimately went to trial on price-fixing charges.

The week of September 10 proved fateful to the case. Monday, September 11, Boies chatted with Taubman's lawyer, Scott Muller of Davis, Polk & Wardwell. From an office in San Francisco that he borrowed from cocounsel in the Napster case, Boies told Muller that he wanted to get to $500 million in the settlement, and to do that, he would need $125 million from Taubman. This was in addition to the $130 million that Sotheby's had already promised they would get from Taubman for its claims of breach of fiduciary duty against the former Sotheby's chairman. Boies was asking Taubman to personally fund $255 million of the settlement!

Muller had dealt with Boies before in the vitamins class action, and now he wasn't giving an inch. He talked about a potential trial of the civil case, and how difficult it would be for Boies to prove damages. Boies conceded the point, as he always did with a losing argument. But the case would still go to a jury. "Frankly, your client is going to get on the stand and he's going to say, 'I don't remember.' He's going to say 'I don't remember' to enough questions so that . . ." Boies's voice trailed off. "There's so many things, with DeDe and stuff . . ." The ruthless cross-examiner was remarkably nonconfrontational in his out-of-court dealings with other lawyers.

Meanwhile, the Sotheby's lawyers were intent on selling Boies a deal before he signed with Christie's, and came up with another approach that required Taubman's participation. Sotheby's and Taubman would guarantee that Boies would get X amount for the entire settlement. The Sotheby's lawyers proposed an amount of $460 million, but Boies countered with $512 million. "The 512 was Boies's figure," one of the Sotheby's lawyers told me. "He pressed for the 512."

In the course of their sales pitch to Boies, the Sotheby's lawyers also brought up documents that were buried among the boxes of materials produced by Christie's in response to discovery requests. These documents came from the files of Stephen Lash, the chairman of Christie's in North and South America. Lash was prone to taking copious notes, which recorded his mounting suspicions that his colleagues were conspiring to divvy up clients and fix the terms of commissions. Boies's partners had also discovered the Lash papers. Sotheby's lawyers argued that these documents proved Christie's to be less than credible in its vow to help Boies amass the proof in the case with a proffer of evidence. If the Skadden Arps lawyers left Boies to discover the Lash documents for himself buried in the stacks of files produced in discovery, it did not bode well for their cooperation under the Mary Carter agreement as the case went forward. "Boies was pissed off," one Sotheby's lawyer recalled. "He didn't feel that they had been candid with him."

By the week of September 11, Shepard Goldfein of Skadden Arps believed he had a done deal with Boies for Christie's. On Thursday, September 14, he sent a settlement contract for Boies's signature. Friday, Goldfein got a call from Korologos, who explained that circumstances had changed. An angry Goldfein asked whether they still had a deal, and Korologos said, "Don't worry, don't worry!" By Sunday, Goldfein still had no signed papers, and he phoned Korologos again. Korologos told him that Boies himself would call that evening. When Boies called from his Armonk home, Goldfein told him that they had a deal. But Boies was blunt—there was no deal. A screaming match ensued.

The next morning, Monday, September 18, Boies quietly put the screws to Goldfein, who by that point was on the defensive about the Lash documents and facing the prospect that Christie's would be left out in the cold. "I don't want to make a big point of this now, but I, certainly, did not have a sense that these kinds of documents existed, and maybe you didn't either when we were talking," Boies told Goldfein. Goldfein tried to explain, tried to play down the Lash documents. He was getting nowhere with Boies. Finally, he said, "I still maintain that the proffer, if our deal were to stick, the proffer would be quite valuable to you." But Boies had moved on. He reviewed for Goldfein the terms of his $512 million guarantee agreement with Sotheby's, which required the firm to pay $200 million in a deal, with Taubman's participation. The deal stuck Christie's with $312 million, or risk facing a trial. If Christie's ended up paying less than $312 million at the trial, Boies would go back to Sotheby's for the difference under their guarantee. (The guarantee agreement never came to pass, and the Sotheby's lawyers said that drawing up such a document would have been impossibly complicated.) But on the phone to Goldfein, Boies announced that he would settle with the defendant that offered the highest guarantees.

Goldfein finally suggested that Christie's and Sotheby's could get together in a room to "whack it up." That would end the bidding war between the defendants, which was now spiraling out of control. In lawyerese, whacking it up translated into a bargaining session in which the defendants hashed out how much each was willing to pay toward the $512 million. "There's obviously a pretty strong incentive to whack it up," Boies said, signing off with Goldfein.

That afternoon, Boies was scheduled to attend a status conference in an Atlanta case involving Philip Morris. The hearing was canceled, and Boies immediately instructed his assistant, Patrick, to book him a flight to Florida, where the firm had a potential new litigation client. On the way to the airport, Boies phoned Drubel, informing him of his latest triumph with Goldfein. "Right now, we're in the happy position of having people throw money at us," Boies told him. Ideally, the two auction houses would agree to split the 512 figure. Boies was still not sure whether he could get Sotheby's to pay $256 million—half of the $512 million—in a whack-it-up session. At the least, he had convinced Goldfein to consider matching the $512 million guarantee that Sotheby's had offered. I found the process dizzying, and on the ride to the airport tried to take it in. Why would Goldfein accept such a reversal of fortune? I asked. "He is willing to do that now, as opposed to being the person who is on the outside," Boies told me.

That week, both firms decided that they could not trust Boies to not leave either of them out in the cold in the negotiations. On Tuesday, Millstein called Goldfein, and they agreed the two firms should meet to discuss the situation. The Weil Gotshal lawyers went across town to Skadden's posh offices at 4 Times Square, where the law firm was the other major tenant in a gleaming new tower known as the Conde Nast Building. There, the lawyers for the art houses agreed that the only way to deal with Boies was in a joint negotiation.

One irate defense lawyer told me: "He played two ends against the middle and he made misrepresentations to both sides to get a result. One could call that good lawyering or one could call that dirty pool. It depends on your perspective. You can do that once, but you can't do that twice."

On the night of Thursday, September 21, Boies and the defense lawyers convened at Weil Gotshal, where the art houses tried to offer Boies $465 million. Boies was adamant about the $512 million figure. The auction houses, now together in the negotiation, could have chosen to hang tough; they could have told Boies no. But they didn't. In the end, they relented, agreeing to split the figure down the middle: each agreed to fund the settlement with $206 million in cash, with Taubman agreeing to pay $156 million of the Sotheby's payment. To get the remaining $100 million, the houses each agreed to issue $50 million in discount coupons that art sellers could use to offset their commissions. That was the only way to get to the $512 million that Boies insisted on, the figure that translated into a $26.75 million fee for his firm. Boies did not even stick around to sign the settlement papers that night. He left that task to his partner Bob Silver.

There was, of course, a catch.

The next morning, Boies presented the terms of the agreement, a four-page document, to Judge Kaplan in his chambers. The spectacular settlement appeared on the front page of the *New York Times* the next day. But Kaplan waited and waited for the final document confirming Boies's deal with the auction houses. The few sheets of paper presented in his chambers were just a bare-bones outline, and Boies told Kaplan that the parties would deliver a final deal to his chambers by October 4. That date came and went. By October 17, Kaplan was sufficiently annoyed that he ordered the parties to come back into court.

Behind the delay was what became known within Boies's firm as the Super Spuds crisis, a crisis born of a central provision in the deal. The auction houses demanded "global peace" from Boies in exchange for the $512 million. In any settlement, defendants are seeking one legal document in return for their payment of damages, the document releasing them from further liability for their alleged wrongs. It makes the present lawyers go away, and insulates the defendants from an onslaught of more lawsuits based on the same claims. Boies, in his complaint and investigation, had focused on the domestic activities of the auction houses, not their vast businesses abroad. Still, Boies signed off on a deal that released claims against the auction houses, "wherever occurring or located" in exchange for the $512 million. In plain English, this release would present the globetrotters who had the misfortune of buying or selling at the auction houses both in the United States and overseas with a Hobson's choice: any auction house customer who chose to participate in Boies's rich settlement for his or her domestic purchasers had to release whatever claims they had against the auction houses for their purchases abroad. They would never get any damages for their overseas transactions.

The broad release was never in contention during the otherwise heated negotiations. There was no question that the auction houses would be sued for their foreign activities, but the houses wanted to limit where. After handing over what they thought was a ridiculous sum to Boies, they wanted to be done with their liability in the U.S. courts. But the veteran class action lawyers who lost when Boies won the auction to handle the case had other ideas. Milberg Weiss, which had bid just $75 million, wanted a piece of the action. Milberg led several law firms in filing new cases before Judge Kaplan alleging damages based on the overseas business.

Within a week of the settlement announcement, a lawyer from Milberg Weiss was on the phone to Drubel, citing him the case of *National Super Spuds Inc. v. New York Merchantile Exchange*, a decision in the Second U.S. Circuit Court of Appeals, which governed Judge Kaplan's actions. The 1981 case, a landmark opinion by the distinguished jurist Henry Friendly, threw out a class action settlement involving Maine potato futures contracts. Friendly nixed the deal because it required class members to give up their claims to damages based on unliquidated contracts, even though the class lawyers had filed complaints based only on executed contracts. Judge Friendly decided that the class lawyers had no power to do that, and Boies seemed to be doing precisely the same thing by releasing the foreign claims.

Drubel, the class action veteran, took one look at the Super Spuds opinion and realized the seriousness of the situation. He envisioned an army of the class action lawyers who lost out when Boies became lead counsel marching into court to derail the settlement based on the overly broad release, unraveling the deal and the firm's $26.7 million fee with it.

But Boies wasn't worried. "If Kaplan disagrees with us, then we've got no settlement," Boies declared. Boies believed that the class notice, which would spell out to auction house customers that they would lose their foreign claims should they take part in the $512 million settlement, was enough to get around *Super Spuds*, where the plaintiffs' lawyers had given no such notice to the class members. None of his partners agreed. But Boies was adamant about one thing: the firm would not agree to pay a cent of the settlement toward the foreign claims. "We don't want to be in that role," he told Drubel, "because there's a real good argument that anything we pay these people gets reduced from the amount we get a fee in." It was that simple. Drubel, along with Silver and Korologos, yammered on about the problems, and finally, Boies could stand it no more. "Let's just do it!" he said. "Let's get the defendants, because we've got to talk to them about it."

Boies held a conference call with the defense lawyers, in which they, in fact, did suggest that the easy way out of the Super Spuds problem was to pay something for the foreign claims from the settlement fund. Drubel announced nervously, "I think we're very, very clear that we cannot pay these claims." Rich Davis, the Sotheby's lawyer on the call, was disgusted. "You can't allocate, even in a settlement of 512 million bucks, you can't allocate any percent, any money?" Davis asked, incredulous. Boies suggested that the other plaintiffs' lawyers were looking for leverage, hoping to get some piece of the pie in return for going away. Davis said, laughing, "The reality is that you took all our money so we're all in trouble."

Boies signed off on the conversation, and, by the next afternoon, clad in his bicycling gear, was ready to fly to France for a week of cycling, and then on to Monaco and St. Tropez. Meanwhile, the remaining members of his team, still anxious about the Super Spuds problem, filed a "motion for clarification" with Judge Kaplan. The motion asked Kaplan to recognize that Boies had the authority, in his role as lead counsel, to resolve *all* claims—domestic and foreign—of the class of U.S. auction house customers that he was selected to represent. The motion hung its request for clarification on two little words in the complaint which started the lawsuit, that the conspiracy between the auction houses resulted in higher prices in the United States "and elsewhere." It was a cheap legal move that the Boies firm hoped would cut off the debate on the release before a storm of complaints arrived in Kaplan's courtroom during the public hearings reviewing the fairness of the deal. Kaplan saw right through it and ruled that Boies represented the domestic purchasers—but pointed out that he could not pass judgment on any proposed settlement, because no settlement papers were before him.

Kaplan's ruling, issued on October 10, 2000, was arguably crystal clear about the scope of Boies's charge. The judge wrote, "There is no doubt whatever that the Court intended Lead Counsel to act on behalf of the Class that was certified—persons who purchased or sold through Christie's or Sotheby's at non-Internet auctions held in the United States during the relevant period." The judge then pointedly added that, just because he had consolidated the Milberg Weiss case on foreign claims for practicality's sake, he did not intend to expand Boies's role. Arguably, that should have put an end to the matter. Boies could easily have read Kaplan's ruling and concluded that he didn't have the authority to release the foreign claims. Since the defendants were adamant about getting that release, the deal might well have imploded.

Boies went ahead and gave the defendants the broad release they were asking for. Over the fall and winter, the Super Spuds issue percolated unattended, while Judge Kaplan raised his eyebrows about the coupons, which would allow those victimized by the auction houses to obtain discounts on sellers' commissions in their future dealings with the price-fixers. Long before the time of the auction house case, coupons had become a dirty word in class actions, roundly criticized by courts and legal scholars because they forced victims of the defendants to do business with them yet again, while the lawyers walked away with millions of dollars in fees. In Boies's case, the settlement had a rich cash component of $412 million. But Boies was able to get to $512 million—and the prospect of that $26.75 million fee—only with the coupons. Kaplan was well aware of this, and taunted Boies with the prospect that he would be taking most of his fee in coupons. At a December hearing, Kaplan suggested that the cash portion of Boies's fee might amount to just $1.7 million—or 25 percent of the $7 million in cash in the settlement above his $405 million bid to take the case. Boies would get the rest of his fees in coupons, Kaplan chided, "if they are so wonderfully valuable, or *even if* they are not."

Boies argued that his coupons were different from those offered in other class actions. (Of course they were different; they had been negotiated by him!) The coupons could be redeemed to offset consignment and commission costs by sellers at either of the houses for a five-year period. But during the five years, the coupons could also be traded on the open market, exchanged for cash by anyone who wished to do business with the auction houses. Boies hired the renowned economist William Landes, who issued an expert report concluding that the $100 million in coupons "are likely to equal their face value," dollar for dollar, in the secondary market. Kaplan didn't buy that. In fact, he was so skeptical that at the defendants' expense he hired his own economists, who were not nearly as confident about the liquidity of the coupons. They concluded that 60 percent of the coupons would land in the hands of either buyers or onetime sellers, who would be forced to trade them on the open market. The report concluded that the coupons were worth about 80 percent of their face value.

Christie's and Sotheby's agreed to issue $125 million in coupons to assuage the judge. As Boies headed toward a hearing on final approval of the settlement, Judge Kaplan issued a ruling that seemed to make the Super Spuds problem all but go away: in late January, he ruled that there was no jurisdiction in the U.S. courts for litigating the foreign claims of the auction house customers. The judge dismissed the claims that Milberg Weiss, which was out of the money and desperately seeking to get into the money, had filed on behalf of the foreign purchasers. On the morning of the final hearing, a chilly gray day in early February 2001, Boies seemed jubilant. As a crowd of some fifty lawyers hovered at the door of Kaplan's courtroom, Boies wandered the hallway alone, his sky blue sweater tossed over his cheap blue suit, toying with his bifocals and holding one of the exhibits he intended to offer at the hearing.

"This is my favorite chart!" he told me with glee. It showed that, if the plaintiffs proved liability at trial on both the sellers' and the buyers' case, the $512 million settlement would represent 179 percent of total damages. When plaintiffs' lawyers settled a case rather than risking a trial, they usually compromised on damages. Boies had done just the opposite! And most of those damages came from overcharges on buyers' commissions, a case that federal prosecutors conceded they could not bring because they didn't have enough proof—claims that Boies would surely have had difficulty establishing if the auction house claims had gone before a jury at trial. The settlement defied all the odds. Nobody made that kind of settlement! Nobody but David Boies.

The hearing started, and Kaplan reviewed the complaints of a parade of objectors to the deal, a common occurrence in many large class actions. Most of the complaints came from lawyers left out of the action. But two of the objectors were individual customers of the auction houses—real citizens who mainly came to complain about Boies's fee and the discount coupons. Thomas Broussard, a distinguished and elegantly dressed elderly man, traveled from his home in Los Angeles to appear in Kaplan's courtroom. Broussard's objection suggested that Boies take only $1.7 million of his fee in cash—representing 25 percent of the settlement above his $405 million bid. Broussard was appalled by the notion of the coupons that required customers to continue to do business with the price-fixers. "They are compelling the plaintiffs, their victims, to continue to trade with the enemy in order to obtain any benefit from these coupons," he told Kaplan. Broussard said he would rather take his business to the Phillips auction house, a third player in the market that struggled to compete against the Christie's/Sotheby's duopoly. When Broussard mentioned that the coupons he got in the airline cases were worthless, the judge wholeheartedly agreed. "Mine were, too," Kaplan sighed. Broussard's sense of injustice was palpable, genuine, and articulate. At one point, Boies turned to look at him. This was what it meant to be a class action lawyer. Inevitably, one of your erstwhile "clients" would show up in court to rail against the deal you cut with the devil.

But Boies's real problem remained the global release. When the Super Spuds issue came up, Kaplan's observations seemed to give Boies more reason than ever to stop worrying about it. Kaplan was blunt about why Milberg Weiss and its contingent of plaintiffs' firms had suddenly filed their lawsuits on behalf of the foreign customers. "Anyone who devotes three seconds of attention to the chronology in this case knows exactly why," Kaplan said. "The usual folks decided who was going to be lead counsel, and everybody was happy," and that changed once Kaplan held his auction and appointed Boies lead counsel. "A lot of very entrepreneurial people went looking for a way to get into the game. . . . And the way they were going to try to get into the game was the foreign claims." As a reporter who had covered many class actions, I found Kaplan's blunt honesty about the antics of the class action bar highly refreshing. But it also lulled Boies into believing that the Super Spuds crisis had passed, which, in fact, it had not.

Judge Kaplan spent the latter part of the day extolling the spectacular result that his bidding process and the efforts of Boies's firm had produced for the class. The judge made no mention that Boies had based his bid on Leitzinger's incorrect preliminary damage estimate. (In fact, as Judge

Kaplan noted in a later opinion, Leitzinger revised his assessment, finding that actual damages were $85 million on the sellers' side and $201 million on the buyers' side, for a total of $286 million.)

Last up were the interim lead counsel, the plaintiffs' lawyers who worked on the case initially. They were there, mainly, to convince Kaplan that they deserved hourly fees for the amount of time they had worked on the case until it was taken away from them. They were obsequious, one and all, in their praise of the talents of David Boies. "Your honor, we feel like we teed up the ball for the new Tiger Woods of the plaintiffs' antitrust bar," boomed Frederick Furth, the outsize Texan lawyer. The judge delighted in interrupting Furth: "Give credit where credit is due," he said, alluding to the fact that Christie's lawyers from Skadden Arps had told their client to turn over their documents to the Justice Department. Kaplan was still aware that this central fact made going after the auction houses something like shooting fish in a barrel.

Furth was undaunted. "I've been in the plaintiffs' business for forty years," he continued, and "this is the most ooout-standing result I have ever heard of in the history of the antitrust laws!" Furth then demurely asked the judge for "a fair and reasonable fee" for the interim lead counsel.

Boies left the hearing believing that the settlement was substantially out of the woods. In late February, Kaplan issued an opinion "conditionally" approving the settlement. But, the judge said, the global release had problems under the Super Spuds case. By then, the judge had dismissed a separate case based on the foreign claims. Even so, he ruled, the global release asked the foreign art house customers to give up something of value because it expressly forbade them from pursuing their claims in the U.S. courts. Kaplan's opinion noted that approval of the settlement, "as long as it contains this objectionable feature," would be "inappropriate."

Boies incurred Kaplan's ire when he offered a solution: the defendants would allocate $7 million of the questionable coupons to the foreign claims. Boies still did not admit the obvious: he had no authority to release foreign claims; they were not part of the class he represented. In a decision that chastised Boies for failing to strike the global release from the deal, Kaplan attacked as cynical the firm's move to try to preserve its fee by offering up a few lousy coupons. Once Boies and his firm arrived at their 512 figure, Kaplan wrote, they gained "a powerful incentive to protect the settlement and thus their large fee." In other words, Boies turned into the

"Janus-faced" class action lawyer that Kaplan had warned of at the beginning of the case, once Boies sensed that his $26.75 million fee was near.

The auction houses did not give up their desire to get the broad release,
a desire so fervent that it suggested the foreign claims must be worth *something* after all. The houses could have walked away from the deal at that
point, but they didn't. They were desperate to get price-fixing behind them
and restore confidence in the market, a factor that Boies had preyed upon
during the negotiations. And it was their desperation that allowed Boies to
ease himself out of the Super Spuds crisis. The auction houses agreed to
take out the offending global release. Kaplan then approved the settlement,
but gave the defendants the right to appeal the issue of the release to the
Second Circuit. He approved the $26.75 million fee—in the same ratio of
cash and coupons as the class members, 80 percent in cash and 20 percent
in the coupons. The appeal put the fee on hold, but Kaplan approved
Boies's request to receive half of it while the case went to the Second Circuit.

When the case arrived before the appeals court judges, Boies turned the
screws on the auction houses one last time. Throughout the case, Boies had
argued that the global release was valid under *Super Spuds*. But once
Kaplan approved the deal without the global release, Boies completely
changed his tune. The firm's brief to the appeals court declared: "Lead
Counsel's prior arguments against the application of Super Spuds were
based on Lead Counsel's mistaken belief that foreign auction claims were
among the Class' claims in this litigation, which the District Court has now
decided definitively to the contrary." How convenient! Having gotten his
settlement approved, Boies turned his back on the defendants on the Super
Spuds issue on appeal. The argument was about as transparently self-
serving a reversal of position as one could find in a court case, and it did not
escape the attention of the appeals court judges who heard the case on July
17, 2002. One of the members of the three-judge panel pressed Boies on
how there could be any confusion about the claims he represented. "Well,
the complaint didn't have an ambiguity. The complaint is domestic?" asked
U.S. Circuit Judge Chester Straub. Boies had to admit that the complaint
was "basically domestic" but that it "made some references to the foreign
claims." On that basis, Boies said, there was "sufficient ambiguity" to seek
a motion for clarification. Once Kaplan made it "very clear" that Boies had
no right to represent "mixed" claims of auction house customers who had

transactions both in the United States and abroad, "at that point" Boies and his firm realized that it "was not possible for us to release any claims with respect to foreign auctions." The argument put Boies in the bizarre position of siding with the Milberg Weiss arguments that he had so adamantly opposed before Judge Kaplan.

Less than two weeks later, the appeals court issued a ruling approving the settlement. The judges issued what was called a "summary order," which would not be published in books of case law or quoted as precedent. In other words, it was unimportant, except to the litigants before them. The judges found that the global release that Boies cut with the auction houses fell exactly within what was forbidden by *Super Spuds*. And the issue was much more than a philosophical debate over the kind of release Boies had the power to give: by then, the second circuit had reversed Kaplan's ruling dismissing the foreign actions. In a March 2002 decision, they had decided Kaplan was wrong in concluding that the U.S. courts had no jurisdiction over the foreign claims. But by then, the case for damages based on foreign transactions was revived, though the auction houses' ability to pay the Milberg Weiss contingent was vastly impaired by the huge sums of money they had already turned over to Boies.

Did Boies know, before anyone else, that the Super Spuds issue, which should have nuked his settlement, would wind up mooted by this bizarre turn of events? While his colleagues whined about the problems, did Boies's preternatural confidence in his course of action save the day? Or did he simply lead a charmed life?

THIRTEEN

Glamour

David Boies was seated across from Charlie Rose, the talk show host, at the circular table in midtown Manhattan at which Rose interviews the personalities of the moment for his nightly program, broadcast on public television. Boies was, on Monday afternoon, July 31, 2000, doing what he does best: spinning the media. He was fresh from a trip to San Francisco on behalf of Napster, the online music service that had, at that time, attracted more than twenty million users to its Internet site. The technology created by Napster allowed users to "swap" songs for free, by downloading files available on the site to one's own computer. To the record industry, which had promptly sued Napster, the site was simply a vehicle for wholesale copyright infringement. To its large music-loving following and its many supporters in the press, Napster represented a social revolution: it was free music for the people.

On the previous Friday, Napster was facing an order from Judge Marilyn Hall Patel, San Francisco's chief federal trial court judge, to shut down its service. But that afternoon, the federal appeals court granted a motion filed by Boies and issued a temporary stay of the trial court ruling, while it mulled over the appeal.

Boies regaled Rose with some of his favorite statistics about the uses of Napster's Web site. According to Boies, about 70 percent of Napster's users downloaded songs for the purpose of what he called "space-shifting." Once they listened to the songs, these users went out and bought the music, Boies said. "In fact, every independent study that's been done has demonstrated that Napster increases music sales," Boies averred.

"For some reason, those numbers are suspect to me," Rose said, looking like a Cheshire cat. Boies, true to form, quickly responded: "Right. I know they are!" Rose bantered with Boies for a few more moments, finally tossing him a softball, observing that the record industry believed it had "driven a stake" through Napster's heart with Judge Patel's order to shut Napster down. "Fortunately, they were a little premature in that," Boies responded, with characteristic understatement. Rose returned the favor. "Yeah. Boies had not gone into action!" Rose said with a laugh.

Boies wrapped up his interview and sprinted several blocks to his makeshift office at Fifty-seventh and Park Avenue, the war room space lent to him by his client Sheldon Solow. There, his longtime secretary Linda Carlsen greeted him. "I saw you on CNN," Carlsen said, referring to his interview with Lou Dobbs the previous Friday, just after the appeals court issued its Napster reprieve. Carlsen continued to ooze compliments, speaking about Boies in the third person: "That's why he's the king. He can make you think what is totally wrong is right!"

Boies was on his cell phone to Mary. He called to tell her that the deal to share an apartment with Charlie Rose in Paris was done. Boies had not known Rose long. The two met when Rose devoted a whole show to an interview with Boies in November 1999, after Judge Jackson issued his devastating findings of fact against Microsoft. The two became fast friends. Now at the war room, Boies settled into his chair, seeming quite self-satisfied. The apartment, on the Left Bank, would be shared by Boies, Rose, and Mort Zuckerman, the real estate magnate and publishing tycoon who owned the *New York Daily News* and *U.S. News & World Report*. Life was good—a fairly painless interview with a winking Charlie Rose, and a pied-à-terre in Paris. Apparently, neither Rose nor Boies paused a moment to consider whether this kind of mixing of business and pleasure between journalist and subject was appropriate.

When Boies agreed to represent Napster, the company was soaring. A May cover piece in the *Industry Standard,* the Internet news magazine at that time thick with advertising pages and media hype, pictured Godzilla in flames, carrying a guitar. The headline was a mock movie advertisement for the monster thriller *Killer App: Unstoppable Internet Titan of Terror.* The next month, Napster's nineteen-year-old creator, Shawn Fanning, hovered on the cover of *Fortune* magazine in an issue dedicated to "Hot Companies, Cool Ideas." *Fortune* said Fanning could "fly high—or crash and burn." Either way, the magazine declared, "the technology he's unleashed is the Next Big Thing." Fanning's heady press was made more dramatic by foreboding doom: Napster had a big problem—it existed so millions of people could steal copyrighted music. A lot of clever observers ginned up various rationalizations for Napster's apparent illegality. In an essay in the *New York Times* on June 11, 2000, British bad-boy writer Andrew Sullivan admitted that "a sharp, unexpected twang of conscience" had hit him as he was downloading the "umpteenth" Pet Shop Boys tune from Napster. "Was this theft?" Sullivan pondered. No, Sullivan declared, this was "dot communism." It was what Marx dreamt of. "So what if there's no money in it? That's the point!"

Around the time that Sullivan was writing his dot-communist manifesto, Hummer Winblad, a San Francisco venture capital firm that had invested $15 million in Napster in late May 2000—intent on turning Napster into a profit-making engine of capitalism—was trying to pin down David Boies and his firm as their new lawyers. "They were very much on our mind even before we made the investment," Hank Barry, a Hummer Winblad partner and lawyer by training, told me.

Barry's partner, John Hummer, called Boies's office on May 23, and encountered the first challenge that anyone who has ever dealt with David Boies knows all too well—simply tracking him down. Hummer finally called Jonathan Schiller at home on a Sunday afternoon. Hummer and Schiller knew each other, having played college basketball in the Ivy League, Schiller for Columbia and Hummer for Princeton. When Schiller asked Hummer, "What's Napster?" his son Joshua, who had just come home from his freshman year at Yale, jumped out of his seat.

Hummer told Schiller to listen to his son for ten minutes and call him back. Joshua had downloaded two thousand songs from Napster before arriving at Yale, which was one of four universities sued by the rock band Metallica, and which became the first to cut off Internet access to Napster. Joshua told his father that there was one record store in New Haven and that it charged "ridiculous" prices. Surfing on Napster introduced him to music he would never otherwise have bought, CDs by artists like Bob Dylan and Tracy Chapman. "I think he saw the way I felt about it. That excited him," Joshua told me.

Meanwhile, Boies's twin sons, Christopher and Jonathan, the latter of whom was already an avid Napster fan, researched the Napster case for their father. After two weeks, the twins reported back: the press had gotten it wrong on Napster. Napster didn't copy anything; its users were simply sharing music with each other. Napster had a potential defense under what is known as the fair use doctrine. A law called the American Home Recording Act, passed by Congress in 1992, allowed noncommercial copying of music. And there was very helpful language from an important appeals court decision in the Ninth Circuit, where the Napster case was pending. "At the end of all that, I was convinced they really had the better part of the argument," Boies told me.

Their kids made them take the case. And as members of the press lined up for the inevitable round of interviews with Boies, this notion had a nice ring to it. "Probably very few other cases matter as much," Boies told the *New York Times Magazine* in August 2000. "And it didn't hurt us in making the decision that every one of our children insisted on it."

Boies's second wife, Judith, laughed when she heard that her former husband had agreed to represent Napster. "It's hard for me to believe that another intelligent adult thinks there's an argument to be made for Napster," Judith told me. "It certainly wasn't principle; I think it was amusing to him."

On July 16, 2000, Napster announced that it had hired Boies. His appearance on the scene transformed the way reporters treated the story. In the days before the announcement, the recording industry had sought a motion before Judge Patel to shut Napster down, and it looked like the end was near. But Napster's prospects brightened, according to the news reports, before Boies even uttered a word in court.

"Can Microsoft's Nemesis Save Napster?" a *BusinessWeek* headline asked. The story gushed that the government's case against Microsoft had seemed far from certain until Boies arrived on the scene, and that Napster was hoping "the courtroom Houdini can work some magic" in its case.

The legal writer Roger Parloff snagged the first "extended" interview with the "superlitigator" for the Web site Inside.com. Boies held forth like the Voice of Reason, admitting that Napster raised important policy questions that Congress should address. Boies embraced the notion that Napster users were engaged in unauthorized sharing of copyrighted music. But the law as it stood—particularly *Sony v. Universal City Studios Inc.*, the U.S. Supreme Court's 1984 decision rejecting the movie industry's claims that Sony's Betamax VCR was a copyright infringement device—would uphold his new client's right to continue their service.

Interviews like the one with Parloff were not a sidelight to Boies's work; they were a central part of it. Parloff was not overly convinced by Boies's arguments, and his articles reflected that. But the details didn't matter. The man who slew Microsoft was about to take on the Big, Bad Record Companies. The coolest company in America had the country's coolest lawyer on its side.

The hiring of Boies left Fenwick & West, the San Francisco law firm that had represented Napster from the outset of its troubles, in a demoralized state. Napster had put them under a gag order. No one but Boies could speak to the press for Napster. Laurence Pulgram, the head of the Fenwick & West team, accepted the turn of events with calm resignation. Tall, affable, and quintessentially Californian, Pulgram's easy manner belied his impressive résumé. He graduated summa cum laude and Phi Beta Kappa from Duke University, went to Harvard Law School, graduating magna cum laude in 1983, and had experience with difficult copyright cases. Pulgram understood why Napster had hired Boies. The company intended to plead its case beyond the Ninth Circuit, to Congress, and Boies's miracle-worker image fit perfectly into that plan. "It's in the client's interest to put David Boies forth as the champion," Pulgram told me. "That has really given Napster a great podium."

A mob of reporters began queuing up in the hallway outside Judge Patel's courtroom early on the morning of July 26, 2000. The hearing on the record industry's bid for an injunction to shut Napster down pending a trial was set for two o'clock. It wasn't exactly like a rock concert, but it was close. Most of the seats in Patel's tiny, windowless courtroom went to the two sides and their armies of lawyers and public relations people. Only a handful of reporters got in; the rest watched the proceedings on videotape from the courtroom next door.

The teams of lawyers made their way through the mob. Peeking out from the courtroom, a stern woman in uniform called for the defense attorneys. Boies raised his fist and cheered, "Yeah! Defense attorneys!" as the Napster team filed in. Boies looked like he was ready to have some fun.

Russell Frackman, the Los Angeles lawyer for the record labels, spoke first. Frackman often said he had been representing the industry since the days when the record companies were seizing eight-track tapes from people's garages. Tall, bearded, and bespectacled, Frackman was decidedly unhip. Making the case for an immediate shutdown of Napster, he noted that in the few moments since the hearing began, "maybe fifty thousand recordings had been downloaded from the system."

Judge Patel listened passively, asking just one question, about evidence that Napster users sampled music and then bought it, suggesting that Napster actually enhanced sales for the recording industry. Frackman took the opportunity to read from one of Napster's own incriminating documents: "What are Napster's goals?" an internal email read. "Napster brings about the death of the CD." This gem was one of several Napster emails that rivaled Microsoft's, and this time Boies was on the wrong side.

"Your honor, my name is David Boies. I'm one of the counsel for Napster." Boies began, as he always did, by introducing himself with the genial formality that suggests a respect for the process and often unnerves the witness he is about to cross-examine, who by then is well aware of his name and reputation. Boies's manner at oral argument is often tutorial, an effort to alert the court to some obvious point that the other side has stupidly missed or intentionally overlooked. And today was no exception. "Your honor, I want to begin with a subject that was conspicuously absent from the plaintiffs' presentation, and that is whether or not they have any reasonable likelihood of success on the merits." This language is the legal standard that Patel was required to meet in order to issue an injunction against Napster before a trial. It was true that Frackman had devoted most of his twenty minutes to the vast harm that would occur in the absence of an injunction. He seemed to have made a judgment: Napster's exchange of "pirated music" was obviously illegal.

If this was a gaffe on Frackman's part, Judge Patel certainly didn't seem to agree. Boies handed up a binder of excerpts from court cases that he would mention in his argument. (Boies, as usual, had no notes and cited from the binder from memory.) Patel was unimpressed. She snarled that she had complete cases before her at the bench, and she'd rather look at them than selected excerpts. She didn't even trust Napster with the excerpts!

Boies started with tab 2 of the binder, a list of the many uses Napster "is capable of" that did not infringe copyrights. "And as the court is aware—" Boies began, but found himself cut off immediately by Patel. "What does that mean 'is capable'?" she asked. Boies was attempting to flesh out Napster's argument under the U.S. Supreme Court's decision in the Sony case, which held that the VCR was "capable of substantial noninfringing uses," such as allowing viewers to time-shift the watching of television programming.

Patel was clearly more interested in the apparent hypocrisy of Napster's arguments. If the service had all these legal uses, she demanded, then why did the defense complain that an injunction forcing Napster to block copyrighted works would put it out of business? "Isn't that inconsistent with the fact that it's capable of doing all these other things?" Patel demanded of Boies.

Boies tried to cite a decision from another federal trial judge in Los Angeles, who found no practical way of separating out the infringing and noninfringing uses of an online bulletin board. But that was dicta, Patel pointed out. Dicta, the parsley of legal decisions, could dress up a ruling but was never necessary, and was therefore irrelevant. Boies admitted that the language, was, in fact, dicta. Concessions like this from Boies usually found admirers among judges and the media alike. The appearance of frankness from the mouth of a lawyer was like a breath of fresh air.

But Patel wasn't seduced. "I like my dicta, but I don't necessarily have to follow someone else's," she said, to laughter in the courtroom gallery. "Right," Boies said, moving quickly to another topic. He pressed on with the Sony case, the case that Napster believed would take it home. Napster had a variety of uses, and therefore couldn't be guilty of contributing to copyright infringement, "even if certain people" used it to infringe copyrights, Boies said.

Certain people? How about *twenty million* people?

Patel didn't let that go. "Well, isn't that the guts of what Napster was all about?" she asked. It was in the company's documents. "I mean, piracy was uppermost in their mind; right? Free music for the people; right?" she stared down at Boies, her velvety voice dripping with sarcasm.

"Free music for the people," Boies repeated. "And I would say, though, that what is piracy or is not piracy, what is legal or what is illegal is obviously something for the court to decide not based upon what some nineteen-year-old, however talented, wrote." This was a tough row for Boies. It was simply too soon after the Microsoft trial, where Boies strung up Microsoft on its own emails and preached to the judge and the press that we should believe the written record rather than the dissembling witnesses on the stand.

Boies had more dicta for Judge Patel to consider—this time, at least, from a higher authority, the Ninth Circuit federal appeals court, where Judge Patel's decisions were reviewed. The case Boies cited concerned a product called the Diamond Rio, a gadget roughly the size of an audiocassette with headphones. You could transfer music files from your computer hard drive to the Rio and listen to them elsewhere.

The record industry had tried to block the manufacture and sale of the Rio, claiming the device did not meet the requirements of the Audio Home Recording Act of 1992, and lost. In June 1999, the Ninth Circuit ruled that the record industry had no AHRA claims against Diamond Multimedia, the maker of the Rio, because it was not a recording device under the law as it was written. The AHRA specifically exempted computer hard drives from its definition of a recording device, and so the recording industry was doomed to fail in its claims to enjoin the Rio and collect royalties. This ruling helped Boies not a whit. But he loved one passage in the decision interpreting the AHRA. "In fact, the Rio's operation is entirely consistent with the Act's main purpose—the facilitation of personal use." The judges then referred to the legislative history, a Senate report on the law, which said that the purpose of the AHRA was to "ensure the right of consumers to make . . . recordings of copyright music for their private, noncommercial use." In the language of copyright law, this was known as the fair use exception to copyright violations. Boies was intent on using this one sentence to hone the point that Napster's millions of users were simply engaged in making recordings for their personal use, and he had one sentence on his side.

Patel became irritable from the moment Boies mentioned the act, which, throughout the argument, he incorrectly referred to as the American

Home Recording Act. Patel did not allow Boies to finish his first sentence about the act before interrupting him. "Where is the digital recording device in this case?" she snapped. There was no direct answer to the question, for Napster, just as the Rio before it, involved computer hard drives and therefore could not be considered a device under the AHRA. Boies tried to steer Judge Patel to the dicta of the Diamond Rio case, which suggested that all noncommercial copying ought to get a pass under the copyright laws. He employed his standard tactic—that of conceding the obvious. "The plaintiffs say that's dicta. It is probably dicta. . . . But it is certainly recent dicta," Boies said.

Boies had a legitimate point, and Patel didn't throw "dicta" one-liners at him this time around. Instead, the wily judge engaged him. The Diamond Rio case noted that the Rio device merely allowed consumers to "space-shift" musical files already residing on their computers, just as the owners of VCRs had engaged in "time-shifting" by taping copyrighted television programs, an activity that the U.S. Supreme Court sanctioned in the Sony decision.

Napster, unfortunately, was an entirely different animal—it allowed the wholesale copying of licensed songs by millions of people each day, and Patel let Boies know it. As the hearing spiraled downward, Boies tried vainly to pluck nuggets from the Supreme Court's decision in the Sony case. When he noted that 80 to 90 percent of what was being copied by Betamax users was copyrighted material, Patel shot back, "They weren't sharing it with the world."

Patel's last question seemed to catch Boies completely off guard. When she asked him how his arguments under the Sony case squared with a 1994 Supreme Court decision interpreting it, Boies stumbled, then asked her to repeat the name of the case. He sat down shortly after that, yielding the floor to Daniel Johnson Jr., one of the lawyers from Fenwick & West.

Johnson had not rolled over quietly when Napster hired Boies and gave him the lead role. "Virtually all of the work to date has been done by us!" he huffed to me over the phone when I called to ask how the two law firms would be handling the case. Napster was losing badly before Patel. But Johnson, a tall black man with a booming voice, made matters worse by behaving belligerently. When he told Judge Patel that Sony touted its VCR as giving consumers the ability to record films and "watch them at home" with their friends, she sneered, "All seventy-nine million of them, right?"

At that, Johnson snapped back, "Hey, seventy-nine million or seven." In the end, he told her, "You're not listening." She told him, "You're finished. You may have a seat."

Patel took a ten-minute recess, and the spinning began. When reporters approached Hank Barry, Napster's interim CEO, he said, "Talk to David; David speaks for us." Jonathan Schiller didn't know how to put on a poker face. "We just came into this three weeks ago," he told me nervously. "It's hard to turn things around in three weeks."

When Patel came back to the bench, she read from the decision she had clearly prepared before the hearing had even begun. She accepted none of Napster's defenses, and ordered the company to block the infringement of copyrighted music. Period. End of story.

Boies rose to suggest "with respect" that he did not see how the injunction could be "fairly implemented." Napster didn't even have a list, he said, of what the record labels claimed was copyrighted. "That's the system that has been created," Patel shot back. "And I think you're stuck with the consequences of that." Boies opened his mouth, and Patel cut him off again: "I mean, they can have their chat rooms and they can solicit all those new artists," she said, leaning over the bench to address Boies with a maniacal smile. Those were, after all, the "substantial noninfringing uses" that Boies had offered to show Napster was capable of something other than massive copyright infringement.

Patel ordered Napster to comply with her order by midnight that Friday, July 28, 2001. And no, she said, before Boies got the chance to speak, she would not stay her order pending Napster's appeal to the Ninth Circuit; Napster could ask the appeals panel for that. As the masses of people departed the hearing, Hank Barry asked, "Where's David?", searching in the crowd for Boies. "I just want to go home."

There were eleven cameramen from cable and television stations waiting for Boies in the courthouse lobby. He faced them, as always, with an air of preternatural calm and forthrightness. No, Boies had no advice for Napster's users. Had he been keeping track of the hits on Napster's site? And did he expect increased activity between now and the midnight deadline? "I have not been keeping track of it. And I'm not sure anybody is. Although everybody seems to track hits at every service," Boies said, pausing a half second, and adding: "I took a few hits today myself."

It was a bloodbath. As Boies explained that it would be "essentially impossible" for Napster to comply with Judge Patel's order, John McChesney, technology correspondent for National Public Radio, asked Boies whether he found "any analogy" between Microsoft and Napster: the two companies created software code and then claimed they could not fix it. Boies said it was up to the record companies to tell Napster which songs to block, and the companies would not even do that. This was a thin answer, and the Abe Lincoln of the Microsoft trial now sounded like a hired gun.

Boies remained patient as he answered questions about every last inane detail from the huddle of reporters. In fact, Boies was anything but calm. Fanning, Barry, and the rest of the Napster team had sped from the courthouse in a Lincoln Town Car. Boies, along with Schiller and Schiller's son, Joshua, the college freshman who had prodded his father into taking the Napster case, started the long walk back to the Fenwick & West offices on Battery Street in downtown San Francisco, near the city's waterfront. Boies raced ahead in his sneakers. Schiller suggested they hail a cab, but Boies just ignored him, creating the unlikely sight of a group of white men in suits blazing their way through the city's seedy Tenderloin District. Irritated, Boies said to Schiller, "Now they're going to see why they hired us."

When he arrived at Fenwick & West, Boies started immediately on the introduction to Napster's motion for a stay of Patel's order. "He operates extremely well at that level," Pulgram told me later. "He's too stretched to know the details. What was remarkable was that we had just been slammed."

Just after Napster had filed its emergency motion for a stay before the Ninth Circuit, I met with Boies, on the afternoon of July 27, in the windowless conference room at Fenwick & West that served as his war room for the Napster case. The clock was ticking toward the Friday midnight deadline when Napster would be shut down. Boies placed a call to John Hummer. Napster was in free flight, and Boies began with a joke about the predicament. "Well, as they said by the eighty-fifth floor, jumping off the Empire State Building, so far so good!" Boies started off lightly. Hummer had some information for Boies relevant to a possible Napster counterattack. Boies was encouraging. But he also wanted to brace Hummer for the worst and let him know the plan going forward if the worst happened: "If we don't get the stay then what we really have to do is we have to go into court and tell the court we want a trial as fast as we can, we want a trial date and we want accelerated discovery. We have to send a message to the court and to the other side that this is not the end of it," Boies told him.

Boies was already looking beyond a probable defeat, but Hummer was still exercised about Judge Patel's swift decision to pull the plug on Napster from the bench. Boies empathized, struggling to figure out where he had gone wrong; but ultimately he put the blame on Patel for coming to the hearing with her decision already written. "It was intemperate on her part; it reflected both a mind that had been made up and a sort of an unwillingness or at least a reluctance to open up. We brought her right up to the point where I thought we might open her mind. And I mean one of the things that you always do is you try to figure out what could you have done differently, you know. She walked on the bench, she walked on the bench with her opinion written. She won't give us an evidentiary hearing and she hasn't read all the papers. I mean it's disconcerting, you know, for everybody. You know this is not a bad judge. I've been in front of bad judges, I've been in front of corrupt judges. But she had her mind made up and in a very unfair and really irresponsible way." With that Boies signed off from Hummer.

There were indications that—as Boies's ex-wife Judith believed—he looked upon Napster's quixotic battle with some amusement. On the phone with Linda Robinson, the public relations executive working with him on the Calvin Klein lawsuit, Boies said, explaining why he had taken so long getting back to her, "I am trying to preserve the freedom of the American people to listen to music," his voice dripping with sarcasm.

Boies reveled in working with executives like Hummer and Calvin Klein. In fact, he believed he had reached the point where he could choose his clients rather than have his clients choose him. That day he told me, "It's a blurring of sort of business and personal relationships. And I think one of the things that they understand is that I am committed to them. When we lost yesterday, they were surprised that I came back to the office to work. We were supposed to go to John Hummer's house for dinner." And Boies believes that his highest and best value is in cases where something bad happens. "Mary says that I enjoy it, and that's not so. Like everyone else, I'd rather win easily, but what she is reacting to is that when things happen like yesterday I am better, faster at responding than most people are, and I enjoy it more."

Boies loves the action, always expecting the thrill of victory, ever willing to turn his back on the agony of defeat. On Friday afternoon, July 28, as the midnight deadline approached, the lawyers and executives convened a conference call to assess the alternatives for complying with Patel's injunction. The miracle happened. Word came from the clerk's office that the Ninth Circuit had granted a stay.

After Boies boarded an American Airlines flight home to New York on Saturday, the plane was delayed for hours on the tarmac. A passenger asked Boies if he was, indeed, the Napster lawyer. When he said yes, there was a round of applause in the cabin.

FOURTEEN

In the Bunker

When the Ninth Circuit issued the emergency stay of Judge Patel's order, it put the Napster case on a fast track, requiring the company to file its appeals brief by August 18, ordering the record companies to file an answering brief by September 8, and giving Napster a mere four days to file its final brief on September 12. Boies flew to San Francisco the weekend before the final deadline to oversee the marathon brief-writing session for Napster's plea.

Boies had a packed schedule for the week that ended August 18. He had sent the brief off to San Francisco, expecting the Fenwick & West lawyers to "fill in the cites" and nothing more. But the Fenwick lawyers made many additions, a fact that Boies discovered as he was en route to Miami for a crucial motion to dismiss in the mammoth class action against the nation's HMOs. Boies stayed up until about two a.m. the night before the hearing to undo Fenwick's changes. On a steamy Miami morning, Boies piled into an elevator in the federal courthouse with his fellow class action lawyers, on his way to the hearing. "At about 1:45 a.m., we were at about nineteen thousand words, which is about two thousand words too many," Boies declared to the crowd in the elevator. Boies was referring to the word limit that the Ninth Circuit imposed on the lawyers who argued before it. A deep southern voice boomed from behind. "How ARE ya' doing?" It was Dickie Scruggs, Boies's Mississippi cocounsel for the HMOs, who did not inquire further about the word count of the Napster brief.

Boies delivered an impressive performance at the HMO hearing on the motion to dismiss, one that convinced Judge Moreno to rule in his favor. But throughout the day, he was preoccupied with the Napster brief. He ordered his assistant, Patrick, to have the folder of Napster materials ready so that he could work on the brief while arguments from other lawyers in the HMO case went forward. When the class action lawyers decamped for a powwow at the office of Steve Zack, Boies discovered another problem with the brief. The count of nineteen thousand words was incorrect. It was really twenty-four thousand! Apparently, someone at Fenwick & West had forgotten to check the box on the Microsoft Word software program so it would count the footnotes.

By cell phone to his partner Bob Silver, who was slaving away on the brief at the firm's Armonk office, Boies bellowed, "Don't call me back, find it!" about one case cited in the brief. Boies was agitated; the brief was far too long, and there were still some basic citations missing. "The thing is, do the simple things first. As a forward-looking thing, do the simple things first, so if worst comes to worst, we've got a product." The crisis over the brief sprang from Boies's arrogance about the firm's own work. Boies chose to ignore the fact that his new firm was a lean operation. It had none of the extravagant resources that Boies had grown accustomed to, in a crisis, at Cravath. I imagined the team in Armonk experiencing a meltdown. A little criticism from Boies had a powerful impact.

The struggle over the number of words continued: the Ninth Circuit's rules allowed a brief of only fourteen thousand words, but permitted a 20 percent increase for cases of "expedition or first impression." Napster was both. Still, twenty thousand words put the brief considerably over the limit, so Fenwick called the clerk's office for the appeals court, where the person who answered the call told the firm that she "would be stunned" if the

Ninth Circuit would not accept such a brief in the Napster case. That news relieved Boies. "That's good to know, because I was about ready to either shoot myself or do graphic surgery," he said.

The day dragged on, and Boies kept working on the brief, waiting for lengthy faxes that, once again, got confused and complicated by the lawyers' love of footnotes. Jimmy Miller hung around, watching. "I have to tell you," Miller said to Boies, "it was more fun when you were at Cravath." Miller turned to me and bragged that he could have dinner with his best friend as many as a hundred nights a year in the Cravath days. Boies was barely listening. "Well, I certainly had more time," Boies muttered, going over the brief. The two made plans for dinner, and Miller headed home.

By seven o'clock, with the cleaning people's vacuum humming in Steve Zack's office, Boies had a draft he was happy with. He asked Patrick to fax it to Armonk, and got testy when Patrick explained that one of Zack's assistants was doing the faxing. "I don't want you to hand it to him; I want you to go with him, get it on the machine. If he gets distracted, it's twenty minutes. Minutes make a difference!" Boies snapped, as Patrick shrank away to find the fax machine. Boies took a moment to phone Mary to tell her how the Fenwick team had added to the brief, then miscounted the words. "I mean, the client wanted to fire them, you know, both before and after the district court hearing," he told her. "Schiller thought they were terrible. I liked their work. I thought their work was good." It was clear that his wife thought Boies was being too soft on the Fenwick team. "They don't know how lucky they are not to have to deal with you!" he said, laughing.

Miller called to check in on the dinner plans. "So the brief is good now, right?" Miller asked from the speakerphone, attentive as always to Boies. "This has been a pretty productive day," Boies announced. "My God, David, there's no reason for you to do that by yourself. That would never have happened at Cravath!" Miller sighed. Boies heatedly disagreed. "This exactly would have happened. It's exactly what would have happened!" he said. "Nobody else could have turned this around at this stage."

The real crunch for Napster came on the weekend of Friday, Sept. 8, when the company had just four days to produce its final brief. When I arrived at Fenwick's offices that Saturday morning, I found Boies camped out in one of the firm's empty offices, at a desk strewn with a selection of pretzels and four cans of Diet Coke. Boies grabbed the arguments under the Audio Home Recording Act for himself and spent a lot of time honing his arguments under the AHRA, time that would prove to be wasted. The judges at the Ninth Circuit would not ask a single question about the AHRA, which was not so surprising, given that the law, by its explicit terms, did not apply to Napster's situation. But Boies felt the need to attack the arguments of the Justice Department's amicus brief agreeing with the record industry's position that the AHRA had no application to the Napster case.

By Sunday morning, Boies had been through his AHRA argument two or three times, while the young associates were still hemming and hawing over their research. Boies simply plunged in. "People spend so much time researching and analyzing," he told me. "Just write it down." That was his motto. "And if I had to file that first draft, I could, and sometimes I do. On the other hand, the more time I have, the more elegant the argument, but it's basically the same thing."

From my fly-on-the-wall position, I discovered that writing a brief over four days was a messy process. The main action took place in a cramped corner room at Fenwick's office, where Bob Silver presided over the Boies Schiller troops: young Ivy Leaguers, all of them men, making lists and assigning topics to research. If one of them wanted to add to Boies's work or make a suggestion for the brief, they drafted a "rider" for him to review. The rider authors were like supplicants.

By Sunday noon, the tension was building. Boies asked Silver for the latest typed additions to his AHRA section, which was sacrosanct given that Boies had taken it on. Silver discovered that the Fenwick & West staffer on duty this Sunday did not know how to log on to the computer system, and the friction between the Boies Schiller team and Fenwick began. Silver told Pulgram that the firm would need four or five people on call to man the computers and process the revisions to the brief as they came.

By Sunday at four o'clock, the tension hit a new high. Boies was reading drafts of the Sony section of the brief—the guts of Napster's arguments—and not liking them. Silver pleaded that there had been no time at all to edit, and suggested to Boies that they work on it overnight and present a new draft to him in the morning. No, that would be too late. How about another draft in two hours? Boies nixed that idea too. He asked Silver to send in the troops from their cramped quarters on the other side of the floor.

The lawyers filed into Boies's temporary office, and he explained the record industry's position as he saw it: the industry was arguing that Napster had no "fair" uses for the unauthorized copying of songs. Under the copyright laws, a "fair" use was an unauthorized use that was deemed acceptable because it had some redeeming value. In the Sony case, the U.S. Supreme Court found that the Betamax's ability to allow viewers to "time-shift" by taping television shows that were broadcast for free was a fair use. Napster had argued that its users, likewise, were merely "space-shifting" by downloading computer musical files (known as MP3s) of CDs that they already owned legally onto their computer hard drives, and then sharing them with others. Boies looked around the room and asked if he had missed anything.

There were few volunteers. Steve Holtzman spoke up. He had worked with Boies on the Microsoft case, had recently joined Boies's firm, and was an independent-minded guy. He pointed out that the record industry's brief talked a lot about Napster's "ongoing relationship" with its users, a potential problem if Napster intended to rely on the Sony case. Sony sold its Betamax VCR to the public, and the relationship ended there. Sony had no ability to control the consumers who purchased it.

Boies acknowledged Holtzman's point, but said that the Ninth Circuit would not decide the Napster case solely on that ground. I had to admire Holtzman for trying. Boies claimed that he wanted feedback on his own work—he wanted, in his words, to see if there was "anything wrong" with what he wrote or suggested—but few people ventured to challenge him. "We ought to be attacking what they say, we ought to be figuring out what they say, what's wrong with it, and how do we attack it," Boies told the troops. Whether that advice gave them any real help on the brief was dubious at best.

Boies was flipping through the pages of the opposition's brief and read the following passage aloud: "Any Napster user who downloads a song to 'space-shift' obtains it, in the first instance, from another Napster user who lacks authority to distribute it," he said. "That's true," said Sam Kaplan, one of the young Ivy Leaguers. Kaplan got his head handed to him. "No! It's not necessarily true!" Boies shouted. For Boies's space-shifting argument to work, he needed to assert that at least some portion of the Napster crowd downloaded music files they already owned, and therefore were engaged in a fair use. Boies wanted the brief to explain just how badly the other side had gotten it wrong. He also wanted to ridicule Judge Patel, who had commented in the written opinion she issued on August 10 that "there may be a lot of space-shifting going on" at the July 26 hearing, but concluded that space-shifting was "de minimus." "Every time we cite that, we then want to cite her oral statement in which she said there's lot of space-shifting going on. That makes it clear how stupid she is, okay? She can't have it both ways," he said.

The meeting came to an abrupt end. Silver reminded Boies that they had a 4:45 p.m. conference call with Echostar, a new client. Boies apologized, and the team filed out. The Echostar call—a meet and greet, really, between Boies and Dan Moskowitz, Echostar's general counsel—was only one of many interruptions over these several days. In addition, Boies was in the throes of negotiations with the auction houses over the class action settlement.

Monday came, and the pace became more hectic. Boies had to catch a three-thirty flight from San Francisco back to New York: he would not be onsite for the final preparation of the brief and spent little time on it in the hours before his flight. The course of the day proved how thinly stretched Boies was; as the head of his own law firm, he was the rainmaker at an exploding enterprise—quite an ironic turn of events, given his reputation for disinterest in generating new business at Cravath. Moreover, Boies insisted that new clients be vetted by him, and he kept watch on the secretive billing process, all of which took up precious time. Boies seemed oblivious to these practical problems as he plunged into the most important and difficult cases on the legal landscape. Today, there were more negotiations on the auction house settlement, and a phone call to Jodie Egelhoff, the Boies Schiller assistant who handled the firm's billing, who apologized for not being at the office over the weekend because she had a wedding to attend that she had completely forgotten about. "That's okay. We've really got to get this done now, though," he said.

Egelhoff told Boies she had faxed the bills to his San Francisco hotel, along with a *Wired* magazine story about him. "It was a great article!" she cooed. Boies had not received it. She faxed it again to Fenwick. Boies signed off, asking her to include the final bills in a package the firm was set to deliver to his house in Armonk that night when he landed from San Francisco.

The *Wired* "article" was not really an article at all. Billed on the magazine's October 2000 cover as an "exclusive"—with a graphic that featured

Napster's computer data shaped like the American flag—the piece, in fact, was an edited transcript of a question-and-answer session over several hours that tech writer John Heilemann had conducted with Boies in Napa Valley as they sat in the sun and "drank near-fatal quantities of Diet Pepsi." In the interview, Boies explained at considerable length that the record industry had to win on four issues to prevail. If they lost on any issue, Napster would win. For five pages, Boies held forth with no challenge from Heilemann. The piece left Ricki Seidman, Napster's publicist, ecstatic. Boies later told me that, of all the stories that had appeared about him, people mentioned the *Wired* piece the most.

Boies's partner Schiller called, and Boies explained why he had been trying to reach him over the weekend. Boies had been talking with John Hummer, partner in the investment firm that had sunk $15 million into Napster, over the weekend. They thought it would be a good idea to get Ricki Seidman to plant an editorial, perhaps in the *Wall Street Journal,* complaining about the increasing politicization of the Justice Department. The piece would chide Justice for signing the amicus brief attacking Napster's position under the AHRA. Boies had subtly (or not so subtly) done that in his brief, with this footnote: "Whatever the limits of appropriate advocacy by a private litigant, this court has a right to expect more from the Department of Justice when it appears as an asserted amicus."

Next up was a call from his law partner Paul Verkuil, with a potential piece of new business—representing Park Place Entertainment, a casino operator, in a case against the Mohawk Indians for a botched real estate deal in upstate New York. Boies was interested. Verkuil told Boies that the other side had retained Joe Jamail, the Houston trial lawyer with whom Boies had hooked up in the failed antitrust case against American Airlines, to the chagrin of his Cravath partners. The mention of Jamail sealed it for Boies. "You ought to get into it right away," he told Verkuil. "If Joe is in this case, we're going to have to really get into it." Boies hung up and placed a call to another of his partners, David Barrett. Boies asked Barrett if he still represented the Mohawk Indians. Barrett hedged. There were two cases, extremely dormant. "Good!" Boies pronounced. "Let's not restart them," he said, laughing.

Boies spoke at length with a reporter from *Fortune* magazine about the Napster appeal. After that, there was precious little time to talk with Pulgram about the hearing that was about to take place, in Los Angeles, in a related Napster case. The Los Angeles judge had agreed to patch in Pulgram and Boies by conference call. Boies was gathering his things as the call wrapped up, ready to head to the San Francisco airport. Silver followed him into the elevator that would take them to the Lincoln Town Car awaiting Boies, as Boies barked out the orders. "Move! Move!" he kept saying.

Boies was off and running. He was always running. The next afternoon, Tuesday, there was an Arthur Andersen board of partners meeting that Boies had to attend. His secretary tried to set up an appointment to squeeze in drinks with another client. Tuesday night, he would fly to Washington, D.C., for meetings and a hearing the next day.

The fact that Boies had boarded an airplane gave his underlings about four hours, give or take, to finish a draft of the Napster brief that could be faxed to Boies's home upon his arrival in New York, around midnight. Silver blew up at about eight-fifteen. A Fenwick partner assured him that five word processors would be on call to help with the brief preparation. "Well, that's good!" Silver shouted. "It would have been good if they were here on Saturday or this morning, but good!" Silver stormed back into the office formerly occupied by Boies. "I hate these people!" he said. "It's a resentment thing; they're trying to fuck us, they're trying to fuck us!"

Later, when Silver took over the case and dealt with the consequences of Napster's loss at the Ninth Circuit, he grew to like Pulgram. But now, Silver had the arrogance of a favored child, an outgrowth of his boss's natural superiority. Silver rejected even the most minor changes that Pulgram suggested to Boies's AHRA section, and insisted that Boies's language on the Sony case be put back into the brief. "No, no, no, no!" Silver said, aping his boss's habit of repeating the word several times to put a point on his displeasure. "Why would you hire David Boies to write something and then take out what he wrote?" Silver asked, mystified. To Silver, Boies's precise, handwritten briefs were the work of genius. "It's like Mozart," he told me.

D day came on Tuesday, September 12. That morning, the entire team began working off a brief that was 9,500 words—or one thousand words longer than the limit of what they could file as a reply brief. At about ten-thirty p.m., Napster's Hank Barry called in. A lawyer by training, Barry had read the brief and thought the team ought to do what he called an "adjective dilution." Silver agreed heartily. "Adjectives suck! They're so anti–David Boies." Silver also relayed another change, per instructions from Napster executive Milt Olin, who, like Barry, was a lawyer. Olin wanted to change the verb "copy" to "transfer," and the noun "copies" to Napster "uses" whenever possible in the brief's Sony arguments.

Silver was exhausted and getting ready to leave. He took one last phone call from Schiller, who was checking in on the brief and updating Silver on Napster's negotiations of a possible settlement with the record label BMG and its German parent company, Bertelsmann. Silver told Schiller that Hank Barry had called to say that he liked the brief. "And he told me to watch out for Fenwick people taking out the good stuff," he added, laughing. The rest of the troops, and Pulgram, would finish the painstaking work of checking cites and putting the brief together, crossing their fingers and praying as the word processor counted. They filed it in the nick of time, just before midnight. Pulgram offered the Boies Schiller troops a round of Anchor Steam beer, and the young Ivy Leaguers gathered around a computer and logged onto a Web site of cartoons that ridiculed the record industry and Metallica's anti-Napster assault.

Boies traveled to Capitol Hill on September 20 to make Napster's case in an informal gathering of congressional staffers. He traveled with Silver, who was on a new diet and seemed quite a bit thinner under his dressy shirt and lavish suit. Napster, even then, was already expecting, and preparing, for the worst—a loss in the courts and an appeal to Congress. As Boies was headed into the Dirksen Building, he ran into an old political hand, a Teamsters representative with whom he had worked while on Senator Kennedy's staff in the late 1970s. "Keep sluggin'!" the rep cried out, as Boies and the Napster entourage made their way through the door.

Boies's presentation before the Hill staffers went smoothly enough. There were laughable technical difficulties when Shawn Fanning, Napster's creator, tried a demonstration of Napster with the song "Sundown" from a Radiohead concert. One questioner asked Boies about the "standing ovation" he had received on an American Airlines flight. But another attempted to nail Boies with "glossing over the specifics" in his arguments under the AHRA. A pert young woman with long blond hair pointed out that the section of the AHRA immunizing home recording did not immunize the *distribution* that Napster users were clearly engaging in. "You're just glossing over that!" she declared, with all the sureness of someone in her twenties. The woman cited the portions of the record industry's appeals briefs making the point. Boies smiled and deflected the answer casually. "I thought the more honest argument they made was that Congress never envisioned the scale of the Internet," he said. The session ended, and Fanning autographed Napster T-shirts offered for the congressional staffers. Silver told Boies that people said he had been "brilliant." Boies caught the shuttle back to New York, with Silver in tow, and Silver took the opportunity to complain to Boies about his ridiculous workload, and about the management of the Armonk office. Silver got hot under the collar, and Boies kindly admonished him. "Don't raise your voice, Bob; nobody ever listens to you when you raise your voice." It was wise advice from the master.

In no time at all, the Boies Schiller troops were back in San Francisco, preparing for the October 2 arguments before the Ninth Circuit. Coincidentally, Boies had another argument scheduled before the Ninth Circuit that day, in a case called *Pincay v. Andrews.* When Boies realized he had two arguments in one day—one scheduled for a federal appeals court panel in San Francisco and the other before the Ninth Circuit panel in Pasadena—he was thrilled.

"I have another argument that day!" he told me with glee in late August, when the Napster date was announced. The prospect of jetting from one case to another excited him. In the end, the Pasadena panel agreed to listen to Boies's argument by video, from a room at the San Francisco courthouse where the Napster case was being heard.

The Pasedena case concerned Laffit Pincay Jr. and Christopher McCarron, two renowned jockeys who had sued their former business manager, Vincent Andrews, for fraud. Andrews, and before him his father, had been the jockeys' advisor from 1967 to 1988, when the jockeys terminated the relationship. A jury found Andrews guilty of fraud and various violations under the federal RICO statute, and they awarded the plaintiffs more than $4 million in compensatory and punitive damages and almost a million dollars more in attorneys' fees. Boies was representing Andrews on the appeal. He told me he felt that Andrews "had been screwed" at the trial.

Boies had been traveling for a solid week by the time he arrived in San Francisco late on Friday, September 29. Midweek, he made an emergency flight from Dallas to Palm Beach, Florida, to deal with the arrest of José Habie, the former husband of his longtime client Amy Habie. Almost a decade earlier, José Habie had absconded from the United States to his home in Guatemala with the couple's twin children. Now he had returned to the States as a show of good faith regarding a settlement of their myriad legal battles, and had been arrested at the border on sealed federal kidnapping charges.

At the Fenwick offices, the troops gathered intelligence on the three appeals court judges assigned to the Napster case, while Boies, ensconced again in Fenwick's windowless conference room, juggled the arguments for the two cases. The truth was, Boies thought the Napster argument was a loser, and he said as much on the phone with his client Sheldon Solow. "I am going to get my head handed to me!" Boies said to him, laughing.

One of the problems, as Boies saw it, had to do with the judges on the panel. When Napster got its emergency stay from the Ninth Circuit, U.S. Circuit Judge Alex Kozinski was one of the two judges who signed the order. Kozinski was a maverick, libertarian in his politics, sometimes eccentric, always fiercely independent. But he was not one of the three judges who would be hearing Napster's appeal: instead, the case drew, among others, Chief Judge Mary Schroeder. In 1996, Schroeder wrote a decision called *Fonovisa Inc. v. Cherry Auction Inc.*, finding the operators of a "swap meet" where vendors sold bootleg musical recordings liable for contributory copyright infringement. Russell Frackman, Boies's opponent, had argued and won the Fonovisa case for the recording industry. And Judge Patel agreed with him that Napster was essentially an "Internet swap meet." The Fonovisa case, if applied verbatim to Napster, would render the online service nothing more than a worldwide parking lot filled with bootleggers, albeit in cyberspace.

On Saturday afternoon, Ricki Seidman, Napster's publicist, popped in for a word with Boies. "The bottom line," she said, "is that most of the stories are going to say that we don't have a prayer." At least fifty reporters were credentialed to cover the argument, and Seidman was hoping to put the best face on the situation in backgrounders with these reporters and in the session with the television cameras that would follow the hearing. "What do you want to accomplish?" Boies asked, barely looking up from his papers. Seidman said she would like a replay of the "brilliant" *Wired* interview. Of course, she was praying that the judges would come out "loaded for bear" against the record labels, but wasn't expecting that.

"Not with Schroeder on the panel," Boies said bluntly. Seidman, ever optimistic, told Boies that his associate Sam Kaplan had convinced her that the Fonovisa case could be explained away "in a poof." That was not the problem, according to Boies. "Yeah, I can distinguish it away," he said. "It's not the case that's hard to distinguish. It is that the judge who decides the case that way has a certain view of the relative importance of copyright protection and other things. So it's not the analytical stuff that's hard. It's where the judge is coming from." Was there anything that she could pass along to reporters on background heading toward the hearing? Boies laughed. "I don't think there's anything that we can say that's helpful. Without Kozinski on the panel, we're going to get our heads handed to us," he said once again. As they continued to discuss the judges, Seidman mentioned one of the other members of the panel, Robert Beezer, a jurist Seidman described as in the same realm but more passive than Kozinski. Seidman, savvy, affable, and every bit as casual as Boies in her dealings with the press, pointed out that the team should not speculate about any judge. Boies looked up from his papers and let his arrogance rip. With dripping condemnation, in a clipped tone, he bluntly told Seidman: "*Nobody* is going to say *anything* about any judge. *Nobody* is going to say *anything* about how the court is going to rule. *Nobody* is going to say *anything* about what arguments they like." This dressing-down was gratuitous; Seidman's opening remark agreed with all of this. Still, Boies's chilly stare could have frozen water.

Seidman gamely forged on, snacking on a banana. She proposed her strategy. She would try to convince Hank Barry to focus the press on the view that this case should not be decided by the courts, but by the parties in settlement discussions, where Napster had made detailed and real proposals to both compensate the recording artists and benefit consumers. "Good, I think he should do that," Boies said, and then Seidman left Boies alone.

Boies worked by himself. He didn't want to talk. He didn't want to consult. "What I want is a piece of paper with everybody's hardest question and the answer to it," he told Silver. "I don't want to listen at this point; I want to read. Give me the points and what you want me to say." On Saturday night, the troops worked until three a.m., drumming up menacing questions and answers for Boies's review. He was much more concerned with his own list of eight questions, to which he sought answers from his colleagues. Though nobody realized it at the time, Boies wanted to make sure that the answers to all of his questions were in the negative—because the answers to these questions would form the beginning of his argument.

Boies was crafting the first point of his argument to appeal to Judge Schroeder. The commercial flea market operator in that case entered contracts with the vendors who sold thousands of bootlegged cassette tapes. In other words, the operator had a commercial relationship with the direct copyright infringers. Napster didn't charge anything to its users; it didn't even ask them to post their own music in exchange for the privilege of downloading music. Napster had no "commercial" relationship with its users, and therefore could not be held liable for contributory copyright infringement for the millions of songs they copied.

Unfortunately, the young Ivy Leaguers turned up several cases that seemed to suggest that there need not be a commercial relationship to impose contributory liability. On Sunday afternoon, Boies came out of isolation for a rare discussion with Bob Silver, who tried to point out to him that, under the case dug up by the associates, the idea that Napster users were not engaged in "commercial activity" would be invalid at the moment that Napster (and its investment banking backers) decided to charge subscription fees to Napster's users. In his wonky fashion, Silver said, "The question is when it gets monetized, what's the IPO, what's the business plan?" When Silver tried to suggest that a commercial relationship need not necessarily be present for a defendant to be held liable for the acts of another, Boies just got testier. He demanded that Silver cite him a case where a court imposed such vicarious liability. When Silver mumbled that parents could be held vicariously liable for the acts of their kids, Boies exploded. "You know that's a red herring! Now, just listen to the question." Silver admitted that he could not, off the top of his head, come up with a case. "This debate is over, all right? It's a silly point, you know," Boies snapped at Silver at the end of several painful minutes. Silver rose to the occasion. "It's not!" he said, slamming his hand on the table. "I'm worried that you could be walking into something." Boies dismissed him quickly. "I'm not walking into anything, all right?" he snapped back. "Leave this alone, all right?"

Kaplan, who was on hand for the outburst, dared to venture that one of the cases, an opinion from a California district court, plainly went against Boies's argument. Boies waved Kaplan off, saying he was much more concerned about appellate court rulings than rulings from district courts. As Boies wrote out in longhand—and without ever crossing out a word—the points he would make at the beginning of his argument, it became clear why. Boies had eight bullet points. He intended to begin each with the phrase "No appellate court has ever . . ." For the court, he was asserting the same position that he held in the *Wired* interview, making it appear that the record industry, rather than Napster, had the uphill battle.

By Sunday afternoon, the strain of preparing two arguments at the same time was beginning to show. Boies kept passing his questions for answers to the troops, but they were not providing him with the precision he wanted. "Who did these?" Boies asked at one point, looking up, his blue eyes narrowing. The cases cited in the answers did not include the "jump cites," legal jargon for the relevant page of the decision. "Somebody take it back and read it through. Nobody takes any responsibility for the damned thing!" At one point, Kaplan came into the conference room, trying to explain one of the decisions referenced in the answers. Boies blew up. "I don't want to talk about it! We're running out of time," he told Kaplan. "Just find me the reference."

Kaplan, a 1998 Harvard Law School graduate, and the rest of the team were hardworking and intelligent. But the lean staff lacked the military efficiency that Boies had grown accustomed to at Cravath.

The fact that Boies was preparing two federal appeals court arguments in one weekend did not stop him from dealing with another pressing matter. The $512 million that Boies had negotiated in his class action against the art auction houses was under attack. The plaintiffs' lawyers left out of the action were planning on upending the settlement, based on principles espoused in the Super Spuds case.

On Sunday, Boies's partner Richard Drubel was frantic about the Super Spuds problem. Over the course of the day, Boies had a conference call with Drubel and his other partners, and another call that evening, as the clock was ticking toward the next morning's California arguments. Boies was sanguine, if sarcastic. "Yeah, well, you know, I'd sort of like to spend some time preparing these arguments," he mentioned to Drubel. But for Boies the auction house case, with its $26.75 million in fees on the line, merited the distraction.

When the Super Spuds crisis popped up, I realized Boies believed he could do anything, and everything at once, and he had proof that he was often right about that. Pulgram checked in with Boies at about seven o'clock on Sunday night and ventured to ask the master what his opening line would be the next morning. Boies offered a coy "Oh, I don't know; but there's still time." Boies left Fenwick's offices at 9:10 that evening. "Tomorrow should be a good day," he said lightly, and I believed that he meant it.

It *was* a good day; in fact, it was a *great* day. The Ninth Circuit relaxed rules against cameras in the courtroom in the federal courts and allowed the filming of the Napster arguments, which were broadcast live on cable and over the Internet. As Boies entered the grand neoclassical federal courthouse, he stopped to take in an exhibit on the civil rights movement called "Marching Toward Justice." His argument in the Andrews case came first. It seemed to go well for him, and I told him that I thought so. "Yeah, but that was the easy one!" Boies grinned to me as we moved through the crowd for the Napster hearing. It was a ticketed event, and courthouse officials had issued badges of various colors, to be worn as necklaces by the attendees.

"It's show time, it's show time!" Fenwick's Don Johnson kept repeating as the lawyers took their seats at the Napster table. Johnson irked the Boies Schiller troops by his mere presence at the counsel table, a position he had insisted upon. And he violated a rule that Boies had decreed for the rest of the Napster team. There was to be no conversation during the argument; people were to pass their questions and comments with written notes.

Boies worked his usual magic. He had no notes that anyone could see, although he was carrying two flashcards in the breast pocket of his jacket. On one of the cards, there was a quote from the Sony case. On the other were the dictionary definitions of the word "such" as an adjective, pronoun, and adverb, definitions that Boies hoped would help him in his argument over the applicability of the AHRA. The word "such" was crucial because in the section of the AHRA on which Boies wanted to rely, the provision of the law referred to "such a device or medium" when it granted immunity to home copying activities under the 1992 law. Boies intended to show that with "such" a device, Congress had meant any "such" device, including Napster's online service. But the subject never came up. None of the judges on the three-member panel asked a single question about the AHRA, the topic that the writer Roger Parloff referred to as Boies's "Hail Mary" argument in his Inside.com column following the hearing. Parloff suggested that the lack of questions about the AHRA from the panel was a "bad sign" for Napster.

But few people at the arguments picked up on such subtleties. It was Boies's lightness on his feet and his simple language, more than anything, that held the judges' attention. When Judge Schroeder pressed him on how Napster could claim it had "substantial" noninfringing uses, Boies said, "Remember in *Sony* . . ." and reminded her that the U.S. Supreme Court had given Sony a pass on the Betamax based, in part, on one uncopyrighted movie, *My Man Godfrey,* and on one public television show, *Mr. Rogers' Neighborhood,* that had no objection to the copying. That, according to the Supreme Court, was significant. "The Supreme Court said, no, it doesn't matter what the predominant use is," Boies told her. "And that's particularly important in a changing technology. . . . And what the Supreme Court was saying is you can't take a snapshot and say how it is being used today. What you've got to ask is what is it capable of being used." Boies began to refer to the Sony case at length, and when Judge Schroeder looked suspicious, Boies said, "I'll get the quote, because I can see the court raising its eyebrows," quickly referencing page 441 of the Sony decision. The judges continued questioning Boies, and he responded as if in rapt conversation. It was part of his gift.

Boies's opponent, Frackman, came to the podium with a black binder of notes. Throughout his argument, he kept shuffling through his papers. Frackman began with something that Boies would never have done: he fawned over the last observation made by one of the judges. "You had it absolutely right!" Frackman told Judge Beezer. Beezer had pressed Boies, but he pressed Frackman harder: How was Napster supposed to have knowledge of what was coming off of some kid's computer in Hackensack, New Jersey, for transmission to Guam? "They designed it to be a pirate system," Frackman insisted. "No. They designed it for fair use!" Beezer shot back, playing the devil's advocate. Frackman fumbled once again, when he raised the Fonovisa case, obsequiously calling it a case that he knew Judge Schroeder was familiar with. Napster was no different from the swap meet, where the owner of the meet didn't have his fingerprints on the cassettes, he said. Schroeder was not flattered.

Schroeder interrupted Frackman in midsentence. "Well, but you know this is *really* different from that," she said, adding that the defendants in that case could go into the parking lot where the swap meet occurred, physically, at any time and see what was going on. Frackman lost his footing momentarily, but kept returning to Napster's bad documents, the documents that said the basic purpose of the Napster system was to infringe copyrights. If Boies was cool, Frackman was the antithesis of cool. He recited his thirty years of experience chasing copyright infringers, years back when people were making eight-track tapes in garages.

His argument ended, Frackman gathered his clumsy binder and turned the podium over to a New York lawyer named Carey Ramos, who represented the recording artists. This was a colossal mistake. Ramos began by taking the judges down the memory lane of his clients, who included Mike Stoller and Jerry Lieber, authors of such Elvis Presley greats as "Hound Dog" and "Jailhouse Rock." "Yeah, we are—we are familiar with that. If you could get to the legal parts, we would appreciate it," Judge Schroeder said.

The hearing ended shortly after that, and the Napster team was flying. Andrew Bridges, a Palo Alto lawyer who represented Napster in other matters, stood up and declared "3–0," predicting that the panel would rule unanimously in Napster's favor. "It went really well, it went really well," Fenwick's David Hayes told Boies. Of all the Fenwick lawyers, Boies respected the gangly and cerebral Hayes the most. Boies gave Shawn Fanning a hug. As for the hearing's prospects, Boies was circumspect. "These are very hard questions," Boies told Fanning, as the team headed down in the elevator to face the media throng.

Afterward, on this crystalline day in San Francisco, Boies still had a gaggle of reporters around him as he waited for the car that would take him away. He was holding forth, taking in the scene, remarking that music touches people deeply in their lives. Just then, *Wired*'s John Heilemann sped past in his Saab convertible. "Now that's California!" Boies shouted after him. Boies was not at all weighed down by the burden this auspicious day presented. The outcome would determine the fate of his client, but Boies was enjoying himself. He looked like a kid who had just been to the circus, and for Boies, facing two arguments in one day was that much fun.

The Napster team repaired to the company's anonymous warehouse offices in nearby Redwood City, Boies taunting his assistant, Patrick, about the accuracy of his driving directions along the way. Napster's headquarters were in a squat building with no indication that it housed the most popular revolution in the music world in decades. Napster's logo, its sly cat, was nowhere to be found. A Napster executive explained that the anonymity was good—Napster still got bomb threats.

Boies was greeted by euphoric staffers who had watched the arguments over the Internet. One young programmer approached Boies sheepishly. "I

have to shake the hand of the Microsoft-slaying lawyer!" he said. The
staffer told Boies that morale at Napster was running really high. Boies
kept repeating, "This was the right case to take! We're on the right side of
the issue, we're on the right side of history!" Several staffers asked him to
sign copies of Heilemann's *Wired* piece, which were stacked in Napster's
reception area. Boies cheerfully autographed the copies.

At that moment, Boies was glowing, truly glowing. "I thought we had
a good day," Hank Barry offered. He grabbed Boies by the arm and told
him what his colleagues had said was the Napster CEO's main problem:
Barry was not the head of a company, he was the leader of a revolution.
Barry was about to introduce Boies, to answer a few questions for the
wildly curious crowd. Just then, Boies, who was already wearing a Napster
hat, began to rip open a box containing Napster T-shirts. A frantic Napster
assistant assured him that there would be plenty of T-shirts available later.
Boies pulled on the T-shirt as Barry introduced him, and stood on the stair-
case of Napster's warehouse. He gave no speech. "Any questions about
where we go from here?" Boies asked simply. In his Napster T-shirt and
Napster hat Boies, at that moment, seemed about the age of the Generation
Y staffers in the audience. Boies continued, "I second what Hank said. We
had a good panel. They thought about it, they listened, they asked tough
questions of both sides. They recognize that this is an unsettled area of the
law. There's never been a case like this." In such moments, David Boies was
the essence of grace.

At the airport, Boies discarded his blue Lands' End suit, throwing it in
the trunk of a rented Lincoln Town Car, and donned bicycle gear for his
trip to the south of France. John Wilke from the *Wall Street Journal* had
come along. Boies chatted with him about a new class action the Boies
Schiller firm had just filed in the Ford/Firestone case. As he waited for his
plane, Boies tried to persuade Wilke that the Boies Schiller class action was
different from all the rest of the many cases filed in the wake of the enormous scandal involving tires on Ford's SUVs. And then Boies was off to
France. Wilke wasn't convinced; the *Journal* ran a short item on its Washington Wire column that botched Boies's first name, referring to him as
"Donald."

Boies won at the appeals court in the Andrews case, reversing the jury's
verdict on behalf of the jockey Laffit Pincay. The Boies Schiller Ivy Leaguers, watching the months tick by, hoped that the Napster panel's lengthy

deliberation would bode well for their case. They were disappointed. The three-judge panel delivered its opinion against Napster on February 12, 2001. Boies was conveniently in New York, prepping a Philip Morris executive for his upcoming deposition. Meanwhile, his partner Jonathan Schiller stood frozen at the press conference on Napster's defeat, his eyes glazed behind his designer eyeglasses. Boies's former partners from Cravath snickered: they knew that David was never present for the photo ops of a defeat.

The appeals court decision shredded each of Napster's arguments. Its conclusions under the Sony case were devastating to Napster. Boies had failed to divert the judges from the obvious—that, whatever legal "space-shifting" of their own CDs Napster's users were engaged in, by download-ing music files online they were also sharing those files with the world—a fundamentally different activity from the time-shifting Betamax users who amassed videotape libraries of their favorite television shows. The decision, written by Judge Beezer, called the Sony case "inapposite" because it "did not also simultaneously involve the distribution of copyrighted material to the general public."

Boies's most technical argument—the one he seemed most attached to—was also shot down by the panel. Boies was so intent on focusing Judge Schroeder on it that he asked her for an extra minute at the end of his pre-sentation, as his time was running out. He reminded the court that under the Fonovisa case, there must be a "commercial relationship" between the direct infringer, in this case, the downloader, and the contributor infringer, in this case Napster, in order to impose vicarious or contributory liability on Napster. *Fonovisa* did not articulate this conclusion in so many words, but that was the way Boies interpreted it. However, the panel concluded that the evidence supported Judge Patel's finding that Napster's future rev-enue was "entirely dependent" on increases in its user database, and that alone was enough to prove that Napster was financially benefiting from the availability of free songs on its system. Bob Silver's worries came to pass; the panel focused on Napster's business plan, not on the fact that it cur-rently had no commercial relationship with its users.

The end came quietly for Napster, at a closed-door meeting on Wednes-day afternoon, July 11, 2001, in the chambers of Judge Patel. Ten days ear-lier, on a Sunday night, Napster had voluntarily suspended its online song-swapping service, citing technical glitches with new software designed to comply with Judge Patel's order requiring Napster to block all sharing of copyrighted music. Chat on the Web about Napster, already grim, turned funereal. One wistful Napster poster wrote, "Bye, bye Napster pie; used to get files in piles but the fountain is dry."

The final meeting in Judge Patel's chambers made it official. At this hearing, only the remnants of Boies's participation in the case were left. Steve Holtzman sat in the room, mute, as Napster's new lawyer, Steven Cohen, made the case for why Napster should continue to exist. Cohen had effectively taken over as lead counsel. Shortly after the appeals court entered its devastating ruling, Napster hired a new general counsel, Jonathan Schwartz, who convinced the brass at Napster that they had been overpaying for advice offered by Boies Schiller.

Vainly, Cohen asserted that Napster had blocked 99.4 percent of the copyrighted music on Napster. If that was good enough for Ivory Soap, he said, it should be good enough for Napster. Patel threw up her hands. "I am finished, counsel," she said, "I am finished. I think I've made one thing clear. One of the things that counsel has to learn is when it's time to stop. Go back and get what needs to be done done." Patel demanded total compliance. Until she got that, Napster would not operate. Hank Barry delivered the official news to the Napster community. The national media responded with a yawn. The *Wall Street Journal* did not publish a story the next day, and the *New York Times* ran a six-graph item buried on page six of its business section.

Boies was busy attending the official swearing-in of Theodore Olson, his adversary in the Bush-Gore battle. Olson had invited Boies to the occasion. Later that evening, there was a cocktail party given by Olson's wife, Barbara, an archconservative pundit and Clinton hater. The next day, July 12, as Napster prepared its final arguments, challenging Judge Patel's rulings once again before the federal appeals court, Boies was engaged in a deposition for his biggest client, Philip Morris. That evening, Boies attended a party hosted by Tina Brown, the editor of *Talk* magazine, honoring New York governor George Pataki. (*Talk* was published by Talk/Miramax, the publisher that had signed Boies to a seven-figure book deal.)

In June 2002, Napster filed for bankruptcy protection. The company listed the law firm of Boies, Schiller & Flexner as its second-largest unsecured creditor, with a bill of $2.1 million owed to it.

PART IV

The Annus Mirabilis, Act II

FIFTEEN

The Haymaker

On Monday, November 13, 2000, David Boies was in the middle of a meeting on the Napster case when one of his assistants gave him a message that Walter Dellinger was trying to reach him—about the presidential election.

Dellinger and Boies had been classmates at Yale Law School. Boies had not been close to anyone at Yale, even to Dellinger, who remembered Boies for his air of mystery. Dellinger went on from Yale to specialize in arguing cases before the U.S. Supreme Court. He served as acting solicitor general in the Clinton administration and, after that, landed at the law firm of O'Melveny & Myers, where he was a law partner with Warren Christopher, Clinton's secretary of state. Christopher had been summoned to Gore's Nashville home in the middle of the night after Gore refused to concede the election. More important, Dellinger was also a law partner of Ron Klain, who, at the age of thirty-nine, had been Vice President Gore's chief of staff, and for a time ran his presidential campaign. It was Klain who took on the impossible job of orchestrating Gore's postelection strategies from the bunkers of Tallahassee, Florida.

By the time Boies got the call, the Democratic and Republican Parties had deployed armies of lawyers in the hours after Al Gore, in the wee hours of election night, called Bush to take back his concession. Florida, Gore said, was too close to call. The nation awoke the next morning to discover that Bush led Gore in Florida by just 1,784 votes out of six million ballots cast, a margin that under state law triggered an automatic machine recount of the votes. Under Florida law, Gore also had seventy-two hours after the polls closed to ask for hand recounts. That Friday, November 11, was a holiday, Veterans Day; on Thursday, November 10, the Gore camp made the decision that would prove fateful to its cause—to seek manual recounts in four Florida counties: Broward, Miami-Dade, Volusia, and Palm Beach. The Gore campaign had learned that twenty-nine thousand ballots had been thrown out as "undervotes"—meaning that the voting machine failed to read the mark that the voter punched into his card, often because the voter failed to punch holes all the way through the ballot. This mark, over thirty-six days, would become famous as the "chad."

On Friday, the news broke that after the automatic recounts Bush's lead had dwindled to just 327 votes. On Saturday, the Republican Party made it into court first, filing a lawsuit in the federal court in Miami, claiming that Gore's selective recounts violated the equal protection clause of the Fourteenth Amendment. Meanwhile, the Gore campaign mulled over a lawsuit concerning the notorious "butterfly ballot" in Palm Beach County, where a confusing ballot design caused many liberal Jewish voters there to mistakenly vote for Patrick Buchanan.

For the Gore campaign, the shenanigans already in full swing at the local county canvassing boards, which were responsible for carrying out the hand recounts, were fast becoming disastrous. In the four counties where Gore had requested a manual recount, only one had begun counting, and the rest were embroiled in questions of whether they could or could not recount. On November 13, the office of Katherine Harris, Florida's secretary of state—who was one of the cochairs of Bush's presidential campaign in Florida—issued an advisory opinion that no manual recounts should take place unless the counties could show that the machines themselves or the "reporting software of the voting system" caused a counting error. This was the first assault against the chad, against the notion that a voter's intent should count, even if the voter made a mistake when attempting to punch through his or her ballot. In the Gore camp, Harris was quickly emerging as the villain of the election. The same day, her office issued another opinion, stating that the local boards had to submit their vote totals by five p.m. on November 14 or they would not be included in her statewide certification of the vote results. The state law was contradictory on this point; one section said that returns submitted after five p.m. on the seventh day after an election "shall be ignored," but another section said, "such returns may be ignored."

Desperate for more time for the recounts to continue, two counties raced into court on the afternoon of November 13 to argue that the "may" trumped the "shall" under the state's law, and the Gore and Bush teams intervened and took over the court proceedings. W. Dexter Douglass, a folksy, white-haired elder statesman of the Tallahassee bar and veteran political hand, argued the case for Gore, while Harris's lawyers insisted that absent an act of God, like a hurricane, nothing could delay the certification. The proceedings, before Judge Terry Lewis of Tallahassee, were broadcast to the world on cable television. Florida had the most liberal "sunshine" laws in the country, allowing cameras into all of its courts, making every skirmish in the election wars available to the world on cable. Ron Klain had already tapped his former professor from Harvard Law School Laurence Tribe for the fight with the Republicans over equal protection in the federal courts. Klain knew he needed another super-litigator for what he believed was an inevitable fight before the Florida Supreme Court. Klain called Dellinger at O'Melveny's offices in Washington for some advice. Klain told me, "I said, 'Who's the best appellate lawyer in America who isn't yet working on this matter?' " (Dellinger himself couldn't be in court for Gore in Tallahassee because he was preparing two imminent U.S. Supreme Court arguments.)

The two hashed over the choices. Klain immediately proposed Joel Klein, with whom Klain had worked at the White House counsel's office early in the Clinton administration. "And my mention of Joel made Walter think of David," Klain told me. Klein, after all, chose Boies for the Microsoft trial. "It's hard to think of one without thinking of the other," Klain said. Klain, at any rate, knew of Boies's reputation from another context: in one of his many political stints, Klain had served as chief counsel to the Senate Judiciary Committee, and said that Boies had "always been an icon." Klain said he would try to track down Klein, and Dellinger would call Boies. The campaign would hire whomever it reached first. As it turned out, Klein was on an airplane, en route to his delayed honeymoon with his new wife, Nicole Seligman, one of Clinton's lawyers in the impeachment hearings. Dellinger reached Boies's secretary, Linda, and Boies got back to him quickly. Dellinger put Klain on the phone, and Klain explained that the Gore campaign expected to be before the Florida Supreme Court the next morning. Could Boies come to Florida? Boies said sure. He didn't pause, didn't ask a single question, didn't consult his calendar or his partners. Boies had just one question for Klain: "I asked where he was. And he said he was in Tallahassee," Boies told me.

Boies hung up from Klain at about six o'clock, and had Linda book a private plane from the Teterboro Airport for nine that night. Boies wrapped up his Napster meeting, went on to a Calvin Klein meeting, and landed at Sheldon Solow's Fifty-seventh Street office, where Boies and Solow shared a bottle of white wine as Boies prepared Solow for his testimony in an ongoing trial. And then Boies was off to the airport. There was no time to go home to Armonk to pack a bag. In Tallahassee he met with Klain shortly before midnight in the lobby of the Governors Inn, an intimate, elegant place where the forty rooms were appointed with antiques. It was the only spot in Tallahassee that could legitimately claim luxury accommodations, and the Democratic Party had booked most of the rooms.

Klain expected that Boies would be arriving with the kind of entourage a partner of his stature at O'Melveny would have in tow—a junior partner, perhaps a couple of associates. Klain was expecting "David Boies Inc." But Boies was alone. (His assistant, Patrick Dennis, was on his way to Tallahassee, but no other lawyer from Boies's firm ever joined him in Florida.) Klain liked Boies instantly. "He just could not have been nicer, more down-to-earth, charming, engaging, all of those things that he obviously is. It was just a fantastic first meeting," Klain said. Boies had read some cases on the plane, and Klain had copies of the legal papers that the Gore campaign had filed in court. But that night, Boies mostly listened.

The Gore campaign expected to either lose or win before Judge Lewis the next morning and land before the Florida Supreme Court in short order. But that didn't happen. When Judge Lewis issued his ruling, just before one o'clock the next afternoon, it was a split decision: Lewis upheld the five p.m. deadline. He ruled that all sixty-seven Florida counties were required to file their vote totals by that time. He said it was within Secretary of State Harris's discretion to ignore late-filed election returns, but he also said she couldn't ignore late-filed counts arbitrarily. She had to consider all of the facts and circumstances. Boies and Gore exchanged brief pleasantries when Gore's lawyers placed a conference call to the vice president to discuss how to spin Lewis's ruling.

The Gore team decided to declare victory. The Bush team did the same. At the Gore press conference, Warren Christopher spoke for a few moments. Over the past week, he had been the Gore team's public spokesman, facing off against James Baker III, the consummate Washington strategist the Bush campaign had tapped as its top advisor on the recounts. Christopher called on the counties to keep counting. And then he introduced Boies.

Boies stood at the microphone, relaxed and engaged. "I don't have anything to add to what Mr. Christopher has already said, but I'd be happy to respond to any questions that anyone has." And so it began. Within about twenty minutes, Boies had effortlessly become the Gore team's public face and voice. From the start, Christopher, looking all of his seventy-five years, did not seem to have the heart or the stomach for what Gore had gotten himself into. Boies, on the other hand, ate it up. The reporters quickly learned that there was no question Boies would refuse to answer. Just as he had done so deftly at the Microsoft trial, Boies would hold forth as the upfront, plainspoken man of reason, making the other side look bad by default.

Boies pointed the reporters to page six of Judge Lewis's decision, the page that contained the most powerful quote in the Gore camp's favor. There, Judge Lewis chided the no-delay-absent-a-hurricane arguments made by Secretary Harris's lawyers. He pointed out: "To determine ahead of time that such returns *will* be ignored, however, unless caused by some Act of God, is not the exercise of discretion. It is the abdication of that discretion. An Act of God has long been considered to excuse even the most mandatory of requirements. Rather, the exercise of discretion contemplates a decision based upon a weighing and consideration of all attendant facts and circumstances." Rather than read the passage itself, Boies simply guided the press gallery to the page, and pointed out that the language there weighed "heavily in favor of considering the votes."

By November 14, the press was in a frenzy—it was Day Six without a president—and the questions came from all directions. Would the Gore team go to court again, given Lewis's split ruling, to force Secretary Harris to accept the manual recounts? Boies had only been on the ground in Tallahassee for about twelve hours, but he had already established his main principle: that for the will of the people to be heard, the state of Florida should count all the votes. Boies said, "We would hope that the secretary of state, having received the guidance from the court, would do the right thing," adding that if Harris arbitrarily refused to accept the recounts, Gore would be back in court. "But we all hope—we all hope—that what is going to happen here is that the will of the people is going to be heard." His tone was measured and thoughtful, his language was clear. As always the man had perfect pitch.

Toward the end of the press conference, one overheated reporter shot a staccato round of questions at Boies. "Are you suing Broward County? Are you suing Broward County? And are you trying to change the standards on which these recounts will be judged? And how do you justify that with previous statements that you want locals to handle it?" There were, in this blizzard of words, a few solid points: Republicans were alleging that the Democrats were pressuring the canvassing boards to loosen the standards, to count every dimple—any indentation on or near the place on Gore's spot on the ballot—as a vote for Gore. But Boies was ever light on his feet. "Yes, yes, no," he quipped, and the room broke out into laughter. Klain later described this as a "classical Boies moment." No one could remember the questions, but Boies delivered three monosyllabic answers no one would forget.

"That's where David Boies, in our world, went from being our lawyer to our rock star," Klain told me. After the press conference, Klain returned to the office and rang the vice president. Gore was "incredibly impressed," Klain said. He thought it was "great, fantastic, you know, he was just really, really happy about it." The campaign was in love.

After that first press conference, Todd Webster, the Democratic National Committee staffer in D.C. who was booking television appearances for the Gore campaign, could not keep up with the requests for Boies. Everybody wanted him. Klain talked to Boies about how much press he would be willing to do. Klain told him, "Look, that was fantastic. Our phone's ringing off the hook. You need to tell me what you're comfortable with. We could book you twenty-four hours a day, seven days a week." Boies had some rules about appearing on camera. For instance, he did not want to go on while a judge was contemplating a decision. But he was happy to do television. He told Klain that he considered it another way of helping him get ready to make his arguments.

I watched the Boies press conference from my apartment in Brooklyn, while making arrangements for a hasty flight to Tallahassee. When I arrived at LaGuardia for my flight, Boies was on the big TV screen in the terminal with CNN's Bernard Shaw. There was a small crowd gathered around the TV. By then, a couple of counties had begun the manual count of the ballots. "So we're very hopeful that things are now back on track and the lawyers can go home," he told Shaw, who blew right past that line, pointing out that Judge Lewis had, in fact, refused to extend the deadline of five p.m. Shaw was looking for an admission. But Boies demurred. "Well, that's not quite accurate," he offered, his midwestern accent flattening out the *r*s and making him seem all the more plainspoken. Shaw fired a last question at Boies about Lewis's ruling. "Do you regard the ruling as a psychological cudgel over the head of [Florida's] secretary of state?"

Psychological cudgel. Now there was the making of a nice sound bite, the kind that most lawyers cling to and Boies never engages in. Boies responded in the way he does best, which was to appear to be frank, while giving up nothing at all. "Well, you could say that," Boies allowed. "I don't think that's the right way to look at it." Shaw wasn't done yet. "Do you, in effect, *regard* it that way?" he pressed. "No, I don't," Boies responded. "I regard it as telling the secretary of state what the right thing to do is, and we assume she is going to do the right thing. . . . This is too late in the game for lawyers, it's too late in the game for partisan politics. The voters have spoken and the votes ought to be counted." Shaw cut to Ben Ginsberg, a top lawyer for the Bush campaign, who seemed to wear a perennial snarl behind his red beard. "I enjoyed the spin very much," Ginsberg sneered. It seemed the Republicans didn't care how they looked.

America was about to discover the blue suits. Over the next thirty days, as Boies became a ubiquitous presence on the cable channels, on the morning talk shows, on ABC's *Nightline,* much would be made of his uniform. Readers of the business pages were already acquainted with Boies's dress code when he arrived in Tallahassee. The corps of business reporters who covered the Microsoft trial, myself included, had catalogued and dissected Boies's idiosyncratic tastes in clothes (and food) repeatedly, endlessly, and almost dutifully. In Tallahassee, the process began again. One NBC *Nightly News* segment filmed only Boies's black sneakers as he was walking. The promo for the show called Boies "a high-priced lawyer in a cut-rate suit."

Mark Fabiani, Gore's deputy campaign manager for communications, dubbed Boies "The Haymaker." As the adulation in the press built, the Bush team began to deride Boies's popularity, referring to it as C.O.B.—Cult of Boies. Jim Baker had Bush's army of Republican loyalists deployed in a military fashion, while the Gore team came to rely on Boies to front their efforts both in the courtroom and before the cameras. "They thought they got both [PR man and advocate] with Boies, and they were quite infatuated with themselves," says Dorrance Smith, a former ABC news executive and advisor to the Bush team in Tallahassee.

Katherine Harris, meanwhile, made the most of her half of Judge Lewis's split decision, and took Lewis at his word about her power to enforce the five p.m. deadline on November 14. She held a press conference at about seven-thirty that night. Clad in a maroon suit and matching lipstick, Harris announced the vote totals. Volusia County had been able to finish its recounts by the five p.m. deadline, and the totals reduced Bush's lead to just three hundred votes. There were still three other counties tallying votes, and Harris announced that she would require a written statement from each of those canvassing boards, due at two p.m. the next day, explaining why they required a delay. This announcement was intended to fulfill the other half of Lewis's ruling—which warned that she could not ignore late-filed totals arbitrarily in the exercise of her "discretion."

Later the next day, to no one's surprise, Harris found each of the counties' reasons wanting. She held another press conference at around eight p.m. on November 15, saying that her staff and lawyers had "developed criteria appropriate to the exercise" of her discretion, and that she had applied the criteria "for the past six hours," a process that led to the denial of the requests for more time to recount the votes. A whole six hours! This, to the Democrats, was not the exercise of discretion. It was a sham. The Democrats took to calling Harris Cruella de Vil, the villain from Disney's *101 Dalmations*. Harris took no questions at the press conference, citing the ongoing litigation. As Harris made her harsh pronouncement and refused to answer questions, Boies was a stone's throw away from her, just outside the "Spin Room," in the lobby of one of Tallahassee's capitol buildings. The cable networks had pitched white tents and staked out small squares of the building's terrace. At the moment, Boies was before the CNN tent. "Let the people's voices be heard," Boies was saying, as Harris made a hasty exit from the Spin Room and the clamoring press.

Boies hung around the media tents after his CNN appearance, answering questions from Eric Avram, a producer from ABC News. Avram was looking ahead, to the inevitable next legal venue, the Florida Supreme Court. "Historically, they're pretty protective of the voting franchise," Boies told Avram. Boies was in no hurry. He could have stood there in the cold all night, going over the issues. As Boies and I made our way from the capitol complex to the law offices where the Gore team was holed up, Boies was a bundle of enthusiasm. "The thing I can't figure out is what they know that we don't know," he said. "They must know something that we don't know. . . . They are trying every single maneuver, including maneuvers that are now, I think, backfiring on them." Boies believed that the Republicans had the public's approval in the days after the election. "And they've squandered it; they've just flat out squandered it!" Boies said, talking as fast as we were walking. I listened and tried to take it all in, but by then I had realized that it was difficult to tell whether Boies was really caught up in the moment or spinning.

We moved on to Andrew's Capital Bar and Grill, the restaurant and bar that was the only game in that part of town. There were two items on the menu that Boies continually ordered: the fried chicken fingers appetizer, and a plain hamburger. His beverage of choice, on this trip, was a screwdriver, but well-wishers at the bar routinely sent him other drinks. Tonight, the waitress brought us a couple of Jägermeisters, as the crowd watched the dozen or so television sets suspended from the Grill's ceiling. On the screens, Gore delivered a speech from the vice presidential mansion, proposing that Bush agree to a statewide recount. Boies then began spinning me about legal maneuvers that were long in place before he touched ground in Tallahassee. "There was a lot of concern about whether in light of the ballot, the butterfly ballot, and blacks being turned away in several counties, but it was hopeless," Boies told me. These were the reasons that the Gore campaign turned its back on blatant problems with the election process and focused on the dimpled chads, believing that the chads would take them home. Boies had had no role in choosing to emphasize the chads over the butterfly ballot or violation of voting rights, but he quickly adopted the campaign's mantra, evincing empathy for those lost causes along the way. Just then, Boies's cell phone rang. Yes, he said, he had seen the speech given by Gore campaign manager William Daley, who had served as Clinton's secretary of commerce.

I squeezed in a question, asking Boies what he thought of the first volley of the legal fight, the Bush campaign's equal protection claims in federal court. The federal judge overseeing the case had rejected the claims out of hand. "I mean you'd have to have somebody who wanted Bush to put them on the Supreme Court!" Boies laughed. The matter of the federal claims—which at that moment Boies deemed so inconsequential—would ultimately decide the fight over the 2000 election. No one, least of all Boies, saw it coming.

At about noon the next day, November 16, the Gore team was back in court before Judge Lewis with an emergency motion attacking Harris once again. The Gore camp was seeking a clearer directive from Judge Lewis forcing Harris to allow the recounts to continue. Klain, Christopher, and Daley were watching on television from the local law office that Mitchell Berger, a Florida lawyer for the campaign, had donated. They were all waiting for David Boies to speak.

They had a long wait.

With the presidency in the balance, Judge Terry Lewis of Tallahassee had a very precise problem: Gore's motion called the exchange of letters between Harris's office and the county canvassing boards—the double whammy of letters that both forbade the manual counting on November 13 and enforced the deadline of five p.m. on November 14 after a whole six hours of consideration by her office—a "charade." But the Gore team offered little else to persuade Judge Lewis. The team had decided to come to court with rhetoric about Harris's tactics. The motion flatly pronounced, "it is clear that the Secretary continued to employ her arbitrary and unwavering view that under no circumstances will a Canvassing Board's decision to manually recount ballots permit the Board to amend its election results. The rejection was arbitrary on its face." In fact, the Gore papers made little or no effort to refute the case that Harris had cited in her letters to the counties supporting her denial of the manual recounts. In short, the Gore team presented no real evidence to prove up the standard articulated in Judge Lewis's split decision earlier that week—that Harris could ignore late-filed returns but "not arbitrarily."

At the hearing, Douglass spoke first for Gore. In his folksy manner, the seventy-one-year-old lawyer compared the contradictory opinions that came out of Harris's office to a traffic incident. "It's like the policeman says, 'Stop,' and you're driving along and you stop. And he stands there and you stop. A whole bunch of cars come up behind you. And then he comes over and he says, 'I'm writing you a ticket for blocking traffic.' And you say, 'But you told me to stop.' And he says, 'But the law is you're to go. You're not to hold up traffic. Here's your ticket. Take off.' That's what they've done here, basically," Douglass said. It was a nice little speech, but it clearly did not help Judge Lewis sort out the situation.

The hearing was taken over by the ramblings of the Republicans. Michael Carvin, a beefy redhead with the look of a Teamsters organizer, was one of the lawyers sent by the Bush team. In fact, he came from a Washington, D.C., law firm that was filled with members of the archconservative Federalist Society. Carvin had a simple point: The counties had missed the deadline. Palm Beach County had slacked off for days, he said. At the rate they were going, it would take seventy-five days for them to finish counting the ballots. The deadline was more important than the count. In one especially tone-deaf moment, Carvin compared the counting of ballots to the pro bono work that lawyers at large law firms donate. "Everyone knows that you can only do your pro bono work if it doesn't interfere with your billable work, and if you have time to do it, because the billable work takes precedence," he said. That analysis must have played well with the folks watching at home.

Back at the law office, Christopher and Daley were shouting at the TV. "Get David up there! Stand up, David!" they were shouting at the tube. Boies finally rose at the end of the hearing. "Your honor, my name is David Boies," he said, then he noted that within the hour the Florida Supreme Court would be taking up the issue of the conflicting legal opinions between Harris and Bob Butterworth, the state's attorney general, an ardent Democrat who had issued a letter to the county canvassing boards insisting that they could go forward with their manual recounts.

A moment after Boies spoke at the hearing, it became clear that Judge Lewis wasn't convinced the Gore team had made a case. "I don't know that it's necessarily relevant or essential," Lewis observed mildly, "but I haven't received any evidence of any *facts*." This, Boies knew, was a death knell. As the hearing was wrapping up, he rose, vainly, once again, to salvage the situation. Lewis had offered both sides the opportunity to submit additional materials. Boies said that Gore would gladly do that, but suggested that it wasn't necessary. "From our standpoint, this is not a question de novo of what standard the secretary should apply," Boies said. "The court made a ruling and set the rules." The other side, he pointed out, "didn't appeal" that ruling. "That's the law of the case," he announced, employing one of his standard tactics, which was to declare outright victory when the circumstances were in fact a lot more muddy than that. "The question is: Based on the undisputed record that's in those exhibits, did the secretary's conduct comply with what this court has said or not?" This was not an answer to Judge Lewis's stated problem of just a moment earlier, that the Gore team had brought *no evidence* to buttress its emergency motion. But Boies implied that all the evidence Lewis needed was already in the record. In other words, because Harris had so clearly failed in her duties, there was no need for more evidence—especially since the Gore team had brought none to the hearing! (Later that afternoon, Berger made a hasty motion to "supplement the record" before Judge Lewis.)

Klain told me later that he was surprised at how little Boies had spoken at that first hearing before Judge Lewis. Klain had asked Boies about it afterward. "And he gave me the classic Boies smile/giggle, shrug-of-the-shoulders thing," Klain recalled. Boies was, as ever, nonconfrontational to the core when outside the courtroom. It didn't bother Klain. He told me later, "It was David's decision, how much or how little he would do, and you know, I don't know."

When Boies returned to the Governors Inn that night, at about eleven p.m., he bumped into Doug Hattaway, the Gore campaign's spokesman, in the lobby. Hattaway had bad news. The Democrats in Palm Beach County were reporting that only twelve out of the thirty tables counting ballots were moving ahead with the job, because the Republican observers weren't showing up. "Remember, they have the *right* to be there, but they don't *have* to be there," Boies offered, trying to reassure Hattaway that this Republican maneuver would fail. Hattaway got back on his cell phone. "I just talked to a well-informed source," he began. As Hattaway was climbing the stairs to his room, Boies shouted up to him: "Remember," he said, "the Russians walked out of the Security Council and that's when we sent troops into North Korea. And then they tried to get back in, but it was too late!" That Boies conjured this memory and applied it to the ongoing Florida circus was extraordinary on its face. But that Boies didn't read much—a fact attributed to his dyslexia by his close friends—and was not only conversant in history but able to conjure scenes from it at will when the situation called for it made the reference spooky. Boies was in his glory. This was history, and Boies, son of a high school history teacher, was in the thick of it.

The Gore lawyers expected to lose the hearing before Judge Lewis, and on Friday morning, November 17, Lewis delivered. "On the limited evidence presented," he ruled, Harris appeared to have come up with criteria and had made a reasoned judgment that there should be no delay in the counting. The Democrats' failure to present factual evidence was lethal to them, Boies or no Boies. Worse still, the Gore legal team did not think there was any good basis to appeal Lewis's decision. This was no small matter. The final curtain was about to come down on Saturday, November 18, the date when Harris would certify the official results of the election after counting the absentee military ballots. The Gore people back in Washington regarded certification as the blow that the Gore campaign could not withstand. It would mean the erosion of political support, regardless of what legal fights Boies and company might pursue.

What could they do about the loss that Judge Lewis had handed them? On the phone from D.C. to Tallahassee, Daley, Gore, Gore's running mate, Joe Lieberman, and Lieberman's chief of staff, Tom Nides, were pressing the lawyers to get an injunction to stop the certification of the election that Saturday. Boies and Klain had to tell them no, no, no. There was no legal basis for an injunction. To get an injunction, one had to prove something called "irreparable harm," and Gore could not prove that because he still had a legal avenue available to him: he could "contest" the results of the election. This option, which meant challenging the results of the election after Secretary of State Harris had finalized them seemed, at least as of November 17, politically unfathomable to the Gore team.

Gore's lawyer filed a two-page notice that they were appealing Judge Lewis's ruling. At one o'clock that afternoon, Boies and Christopher hit the Spin Room and tried to put the best face on the situation. Boies was his typically unflappable self. He explained to the reporters that an injunction to block certification of the election results wasn't possible because there was no irreparable harm. Boies announced calmly that the Gore team would go to court to contest the election results—the very course that the team had viewed as political suicide just twenty-four hours earlier.

Eric Avram of ABC News gave Boies what he later called the best question, the question that he said gave him "an opening." Avram, trained as a lawyer, pointed out that Lewis's ruling established that Secretary Harris had, in fact, been right about the deadline of five p.m. on November 14. She was, in fact, right about not taking the manual recounts from the counties. "Is there anything out there, from a legal matter, anything at all that stops her from certifying tomorrow?" Avram asked.

Boies stood there, staring down more than a dozen cameras, in the small space of the Spin Room. The short answer to Avram's question was clear: no. But Boies gave the eight-paragraph answer. He began by pointing out that "everybody has said from the beginning" that the election dispute would be "decided by the Florida Supreme Court." Though Boies said this repeatedly, it wasn't true. Bush had filed the first motion and had lodged its equal protection case—ironically, given the Republicans' stance on the relationship between the federal Constitution and states' rights. But the Gore team knew that their best chance of victory was with the Florida Supreme Court, and Boies did his best to make it appear as if the justices from that court would decide the outcome of the legal fight over the election.

Boies, who liked to mark his life by numbers and time—such as the number of haircuts that a certain litigation would require—would later recall November 17 as one of the three dates when he was about to leave Tallahassee for Armonk but was called back into service. The state was in the throes of counting the last of the overseas military ballots, which would increase Bush's lead substantially, to 930 votes. But lightning struck late that afternoon, when the Florida Supreme Court agreed to hear Gore's appeal of the Lewis ruling on the deadline for vote counting and scheduled oral arguments for the next Monday. On its own motion, the court also issued an injunction blocking Harris from certifying the election on schedule. The court said its order was "NOT" intended to stop the counting of ballots. Gore could not have gotten more, even if his lawyers had asked for it. The miracle of the moment could not be overstated: the counting of the overseas military ballots had put Bush ahead of Gore, but the Florida Supreme Court's decision to accept the appeal mooted Bush's victory.

When Boies and Klain finally got the chance to brief Gore on the day's outcome, Gore took the opportunity to tease them about the situation. "I have the best legal team," Klain recalled Gore saying. "They're so good that the mere *possibility* that they might raise an argument in the court is enough to persuade a court to go along with us!"

If appearances counted—and the Gore team surely had decided that they did—the Democrats came out ahead that day: in the Spin Room, Baker hissed a brief statement for Bush saying that the Florida Supreme Court's order said nothing about the merits of the case. Given that the court had taken Gore's appeal, this was about as much as Baker could say. He took no questions and made a hasty exit, as the Republican handlers moved the eight American flags that they insisted on having on the stage of the Spin Room at their press conferences—the eight flags representing an official sign that the new president (official or not) was appearing in the room.

Baker refused to engage the media, but Boies was back on the cable circuit that night. In between TV appearances, Boies told me that he thought Baker and the Republicans were making a mistake by ducking questions. "There isn't anyone on the other side who is prepared to come out, as I did today, and last Tuesday, and deal with the difficult questions and let people talk about it. I think it damages their credibility." This was a very familiar note: Boies had often suggested to the reporters covering the Microsoft trial that the defense had the same problem.

By eleven o'clock, Boies had wrapped up his TV appearances. A crew from *60 Minutes,* which was working on a Boies segment, was still following him as he made his way toward the Governors Inn. A block party was in progress, the kickoff for the main event in Tallahassee that weekend— the annual Florida University–Florida State football game. The camera crew followed as Boies meandered through the crowd searching for something to eat. A woman holding a beagle and wearing a sign that read "Dogs for Gore" stopped to thank Boies. The shot of Boies petting the dog made it into the *60 Minutes* segment that aired months later.

On Monday, November 20, the nation tuned its collective television sets to arguments before Florida's seven justices in their pristinely white and elegant courtroom, adorned by historical portraits of their predecessors. The line to attend the proceedings, which were set to begin at two p.m., began forming in the early morning, and by midday the crowd extended down the block, under a crystal-clear sky. It reminded me of the day that Boies had argued the Napster case; the weather seemed part of his charmed life. As the day progressed, the protesters showed up in full force. Most of them were anti-Gore. One sign read "Lawless Recount" on one side, and "Corrupt Judges" on another. "Al Gore, Commander in Thief," read another. Another was a clever wink at the Oz-like nature of the times. It read: "Gore, Daley, Boies; Liars, Cheaters, Thieves, Oh My!"

The first question from the bench made it clear that Bush was going to lose. His lawyers came to the arguments seeking to enforce the strict Harris deadline. Under that deadline, the final curtain on the election should have come down on November 17, when the overseas military ballots were counted. But it was clear from the moment the hearing began that the seven justices were more interested in the ultimate deadline. They were ranging about for a framework for counting votes without jeopardizing Florida's twenty-five electoral votes when the electoral college met on December 18. They needed a timeline from Boies.

Paul Hancock, a lawyer for Bob Butterworth, the Florida Democratic attorney general, spoke before Boies. When Chief Justice Charles Wells pressed Hancock for "the outside date" for certifying the election so that Florida's electoral votes would not be put "in jeopardy," Hancock said that date was December 12, six days before the electoral college would vote, a date known as the "safe harbor" deadline for states to choose their electors. When Boies rose, the first question from Chief Justice Charles Wells was about the December 12 deadline. "What that date means is that all of the controversies and contests in the state have to be finally determined by that date. Okay. Do you agree with that?" Wells asked. "I do, your honor," Boies responded. He didn't pause over this issue.

Over the course of his argument, Boies embraced the December 12 deadline at least five times. Long afterward, in the aftermath of Gore's loss to Bush before the U.S. Supreme Court, when handwringing began over who was to blame for the outcome, the *New York Times* cited Boies's agreement about the December 12 deadline as a decisive moment that led inexorably to Gore's defeat. In a post-defeat analysis the *Times* published on December 14, William Glaberson looked back on Boies's November 20 argument before the Florida justices. "Back on Nov. 20, during what would be the first of a series of historic oral arguments, the chief justice of the Florida Supreme Court turned to David Boies and asked a question. In that exchange, Boies made a pivotal concession that, in retrospect, helped bring the vice president's defeat in the legal war for the White House," Glaberson wrote. The justices of the U.S. Supreme Court in *Bush v. Gore* used the December 12 deadline to show that time had simply run out on the recount. The majority opinion—issued at ten p.m. on the night of December 12—heavily relied on the Florida Supreme Court's choice of December 12 as the final date for all contests of the elections.

But at the hearing on November 20, Boies was just trying to get past Harris—he was just trying to buy some time for the canvassing boards to start counting ballots and examining chads. Boies empathized with the judges; he said he felt their pain. "Do we know how long it's going to take to do these things?" asked the crotchety justice Major Harding. "Are we going to reach up from some inspiration and put it down on paper?" Well, Boies said, "to be completely candid," there was "some information on the record," but "I believe there is going to be a lot of judgment applied by the court as well." Justice Harding pressed on. If Harris's deadline was wrong under the Florida statutes, then what was the time limit for counting the votes? "Your honor," Boies responded, "if I were sitting in your chair, that would be a difficult question for me. It is an even more difficult question standing where I am." Boies finally offered a firm timeline—seven days for the counting of the ballots—when he went back to the podium for several moments of rebuttal argument.

The next morning, November 21, I spotted Boies, almost running, as usual, toward Mitchell Berger's law office. I asked him about the chances for victory. "It is a difficult and complicated issue," he told me, "because what we're essentially asking them to do is to rewrite the statute" in order to extend the deadline for counting votes. That was precisely what the Bush team was arguing! Bush's legal brief to the Florida justices actually used these words, accusing the Gore legal team of framing an appeal that challenged Harris's exercise of her discretion as a disguise for the real objective, which was to ask the Florida justices "to rewrite the law."

That night, in the freezing cold, a pack of reporters held a vigil outside the grand courthouse building, waiting for the Florida Supreme Court's decision. The anti-Gore protesters became more colorful as the hours ticked by. "No more Gore! No more Gore!" they chanted. Several broke out into song. "All I want for Christmas is a president!" one reveler chanted. Another made his own lyrics to the Dylan tune "Blowin' in the Wind," singing, "How many times must we recount the vote? How many chads must fall to the ground before you don't count them again? The answer my friends may be on CNN, the answer may be on CNN!" The court released its decision shortly after ten p.m.

The per curiam opinion—legal jargon for a decision that no justice will put his or her name to—pushed the deadline for certifying the election forward to Sunday, November 26, at five p.m., just shy of the seven days that

Boies had asked for. The court noted that it was setting this deadline in order to allow the maximum time for legal contests after certification. The court also accepted Boies's argument on the dicey topic of what standard should be applied to determine whether the dimples, pimples, and partially pulled away chads on ballots should count as votes. In the days leading up to the appeal, the Gore team promised they would articulate a standard on which chads—ones with one corner, two corners, or no corners detached—should count as a vote. In the Spin Room, Warren Christopher promised that the Gore team would do just that. But reporters would search in vain for an articulation of an objective standard in the Gore team's legal briefs, which argued the most general of standards—that the intent of the voter should apply. There were no Florida cases on point, and the Gore lawyers cited cases from Massachusetts and Illinois as guidance. The justices quoted at length from the Illinois case in their decision.

The Gore and Bush camps played a game of chicken to see which side would hold its press conference first. Boies was lying down on a sofa in one of the senate offices borrowed as its Green Room. Boies watched as the vice president made a televised address at about eleven p.m., applauding the Florida Supreme Court ruling as a victory for democracy. As the time passed, in the idle chatter, Boies mentioned his severe dyslexia, and that he had not learned to read until he was in the third grade. At that, Douglass twanged, "Well, you sure CAN talk!" The room burst out into laughter.

In the Spin Room, Boies faced the cameras. He never gloated in victory. "We're very pleased with the opinion. It's what we asked the court for, we think it's the right opinion," he told the crowd of reporters. The battle was far from over, and Boies took the opportunity to put public pressure on the Palm Beach County Canvassing Board. Palm Beach was where Gore intended to pick up the most votes in the manual recount, but the chair of the board, Charles Burton, by refusing to count every dimple, was stymieing Gore's efforts. Boies mentioned a story in the *Chicago Tribune* that morning about *Pullen v. Milligan*, the Illinois case cited by the Florida Supreme Court. The *Tribune* story said that dimpled chads were counted in *Pullen*. "Many of you may have seen the *Chicago Tribune* article earlier today in which it referred to the fact that under Illinois law the indented chad or the so-called dimpled chad are counted under Illinois law, and the *Chicago Tribune* article referred to the exact Illinois Supreme Court case the Supreme Court of Florida referred to and relied on in its decision. Now we would hope that the Palm Beach County Canvassing Board would like-wise adopt that standard. They've been told that that was the right standard before and now the Supreme Court has indicated that as well." Boies's reference was something like a threat to the Palm Beach board. The court, in actuality, had not mentioned dimples specifically. They had ducked the issue by including a long quote from the Pullen opinion and leaving the issue at that. The Gore team's enthusiasm about the *Tribune* story—they took the story's reference about dimple counting at face value—was largely misplaced, and it would come back to haunt them over the next twenty-four hours. But for the moment, Boies was making the most of the coincidence of the *Tribune* story and the Florida Supreme Court's cite to the Illinois case.

Another question came from the scrum of reporters in the Spin Room. What about a Bush appeal to the U.S. Supreme Court? Boies dismissed that prospect out of hand, understandably—all the precedents said that state electoral procedure was a matter of state law. Boies was so confident of this that he made a bald statement: "There's no basis for an appeal, and any appeal to the U.S. Supreme Court is going to get denied." Boies, who was fast becoming the nation's wise professor in an ongoing civics lesson, took the high road as the questions turned ugly on the subject of the court's slamming of Secretary Harris. "Both sides have respect for the rule of law," he said, ending with a lie—"and when we had it, we would listen. Both sides. And now we have it"—that both sides wanted "a final rule from the Florida Supreme Court."

"It is terribly important that those votes be counted," he said. "It's obviously important to the candidates. But even more so to the voters themselves. And I think each of the canvassing boards will recognize that they have a duty to their citizens to make sure that they act in such a way that those votes do get counted by the deadline." Let the will of the people be heard—it was a bedrock principle of our democracy, and Boies basked in the halo of the history lesson.

Moments later, James Baker stormed into the Spin Room and issued a statement about the Florida Supreme Court that was so nasty in its tone, so full of disrespect for a judicial body, that it was hard to believe it was being said at a televised press conference, and from the Bush team's leading spokesman, no less. "Today the Florida Supreme Court rewrote the legislature's statutory system, interfered with the responsibilities of the executive branch, and sidestepped the opinion of the trial court as the finder of fact. Two weeks after the election, the court has changed the rules and has invented a new system for counting the election results," Baker huffed. "It is simply not fair, ladies and gentlemen, to change the rules, either in the middle of the game, or after it has been played, and therefore we intend to examine and consider whatever remedies we may have to correct this unjust result." Baker then made a not-so-veiled threat, observing that he would not be surprised if the (Republican-controlled) Florida legislature took some action. Under Article II of the U.S. Constitution, state legislatures could determine how their electors would vote in the electoral college, and there were members of the Florida State Senate milling about the Spin Room that night who appeared to be ready for that prospect.

It wasn't over yet. But Boies believed his work was done; he had delivered a victory before the Florida Supreme Court. The Haymaker was about to pack his bags, check out of his room at the Governors Inn, and fly home to Armonk on the Lear. But then the Democrats asked him to work his magic again.

SIXTEEN

3,300 Ballots

Gore's victory before the Florida Supreme Court would mean nothing if the canvassing boards failed to count the ballots according to the standards that Gore was hoping for. The Democrats in the south Florida locales where the votes were being counted were locked in a down-and-dirty battle each time a member of the board lifted a ballot into the air to examine its chads, pregnant, dimpled, or hanging. At around one a.m. on November 22, just hours after the Florida justices delivered the victory to Gore, Ron Klain got a call from Peter Deutsch, a Democratic congressman from Hollywood, Florida. Deutsch didn't like the way the count was proceeding at the Broward County Canvassing Board. The candidates' teams were scheduled to make final presentations on standards for the counting of ballots the following morning in Plantation, Florida. The county had been going back and forth on the standard. Could Klain send Boies to Broward

County? It could mean the difference between getting three hundred and one thousand votes in Broward, Deutsch said.

Klain told Deutsch he would sleep on it. "I was a little worried," Klain told me later. Klain believed that part of the campaign's success with Boies lay in "having a certain mystique" around him, which would be undercut by trotting him around to the local canvassing boards. But there was so much at stake. Klain didn't want to regret losing the election because Boies didn't go to Broward to argue before the board. So the next morning, Klain knocked on Boies's door at the Governors Inn. Boies was disinclined to appear before the local political bodies in Florida, but he had some connections to Broward County. His best friend, Jimmy Miller, was based in Hollywood. And his daughter, Caryl, lived in the area and worked for her father, out of an office that Boies, Schiller & Flexner shared with Miller's law firm. Boies told Klain he would go.

The trip would mean a stop in Fort Lauderdale en route to Armonk on the Lear. On the way to the airport, Boies made a call on his cell phone to his stockbroker. "What is CGMI doing today?" he asked. "Would you buy me ten thousand shares?" Boies was a true American. His fight for one of the men trying to get into the White House didn't stop him from tending to his investment portfolio. Apparently, Al Cardenas, chairman of the Florida Republican Party, was also headed somewhere in a private plane that day, and he was sitting in the lobby of the Tallahassee airport when Boies passed by. Cardenas looked up at Boies in disgust. The Wonder Boy was getting under the Republicans' skin. When I mentioned Cardenas's sneer to Boies, he said he hadn't noticed. He didn't even know who Cardenas was.

When we arrived in Fort Lauderdale, one of Mitchell Berger's law partners, Lenny Samuels, was waiting to pick us up. Wiry and hyperbolic, Samuels piled us into his car—Boies, Patrick Dennis, myself, and Jessica Biddle, a Democratic National Committee worker whom Boies had agreed to shuttle home for Thanksgiving in the Lear. Samuels started imparting the crucial information Boies would need for his appearance. We were headed toward the Broward County Emergency Operations Center in the nearby town of Plantation, a site normally used to monitor the area for hurricanes, where the canvassing board was counting ballots, and, according to some reports, eating chads. Samuels had been living with the infighting between Republicans and Democrats at the Broward board since November 7. His breakneck monologue brought home what the fight for Florida was really about: Gore needed to get votes from these boards. He needed three locally appointed officials to count chads his way in order to have a shot at the presidency.

Samuels ran down profiles of the three members of the Broward board. "Suzanne Gunzburger. Partisan Democrat. Golden. Okay?" Samuels told Boies. "Um-hum," Boies grunted back. There was a Republican judge on the board, Robert Rosenberg, who had been appointed that Monday, when Jane Carroll, the seventy-year-old Republican elections supervisor, quit for health reasons. The image of Judge Rosenberg, who would take off his eyeglasses and lift a magnifying lens, narrowing and bulging his eyes as he held the ballots up in the air, appeared often in newspapers and on the cable channels to demonstrate just how surreal the situation had become. That left the chair of the board, Robert Lee. "Judge Lee is the swing vote. He's the only person that matters," Samuels told Boies.

Samuels gave Boies the rundown on Judge Lee: "Openly gay. Trying to do the right thing. Democrat by registration—conservative, though, as I understand it from people who have worked with him in the past. He is not an ideologue. He would probably be just as easily a Republican or a Democrat. He just wants to know what the law is." When it came to the standards applied to the ballots, of course, the answer to that question was as murky as the Florida swamps. When Broward County started examining ballots, the board was told that two corners of a chad must be detached from the ballot in order for it to count as a vote. On Sunday, November 19, a county attorney informed the board that the two-corner rule was impermissibly narrow. They should count a vote whenever the voter's intent could be determined. Since then, the board had been doing just that. And on Tuesday night, the Florida Supremes reinforced their decision. Samuels handed Boies a transcript from the board's Sunday session and told him to read it carefully.

The Democrats had essentially already won in Broward. Boies's star presence and silver tongue were just added insurance. When we arrived at the Hurricane Center, it became clear why the Democrats felt they needed Boies. Bob Dole, the former Republican senator, onetime presidential candidate, and Viagra pitchman, was there, splitting his time between staring down the canvassing board as they scrutinized the ballots and granting interviews to the press. With Boies's arrival, the Democrats had their own celebrity. "Everybody there sort of treated him like a rock star at that point," says a lawyer for the Democrats who was on the scene. At that point, the Democrats were weighing an extreme option—whether to make a motion to disqualify Judge Rosenberg from the canvassing board. With so much at stake, every option was being considered at every moment, and the Democrats had some ammunition against Rosenberg: he was running for reelection as a circuit judge, and the treasurer of his campaign was a named plaintiff in one of the federal lawsuits filed by the Bush campaign to block the hand recounts. Rosenberg had also made statements about hand recounts that could have been used against him.

Boies made the call not to try to remove him. Judge Lee and Rosenberg sat on the same circuit; to remove one of them could be seen as a smear on the entire bench. And, had the Democrats moved against Rosenberg, the Republicans would have moved against Gunzburger, the staunch Democrat. They would be back in court and never finish the manual counting by the new deadline. When Boies made the call, his word was treated as if he were the oracle from Delphi. "The decision was made. Move on. That was it," recalls one Democratic lawyer. "His reputation preceded him at that time." The Broward board was set to hear from Boies and the Republicans after lunch. What would happen if the canvassing boards refused to count dimples? "Then we're fucked," Eileen Kotecki, the Gore campaign's national finance director, told me.

During lunch, another Gore crisis erupted. The Miami-Dade County Canvassing Board, facing a stampede by protesters from the Bush camp, voted to stop its hand recount, a huge blow. Earlier, the Miami-Dade board had at first decided to count only some 10,000 "undervotes," but then decided it would not be fair to count anything less than all of the county's 700,000 ballots. Since that could not be achieved by the Sunday deadline set by the Florida Supreme Court, it simply stopped counting. Boies got a panicked phone call from Mitchell Berger and Ron Klain. The campaign would be going to court in Miami to get the Dade board to begin counting again. John Sasso, the Gore campaign operative on the ground in Broward, began to worry that the lawyers in Tallahassee would redirect Boies to head to Miami on the Lear before he had the chance to speak before the Broward board. "I just want to make sure that Ron lets him stay here long enough so we can get to the issue!" Sasso spat into his cell phone.

Boies stayed, and delivered a dazzling performance. The Republicans' lawyer, William Scherer, spoke first, asking the board to consider the plight of voter William Rohloff, a person described by Scherer as "an interested individual who came up to us and volunteered" his story. Scherer held up a huge poster of Rohloff's affidavit, in which he attested to how he came to dimple his ballot. Rohloff, Scherer explained, was neither a Republican nor a Democrat, and entered the voting booth on election day thinking he would vote for Gore. But he was still uncertain. Rohloff put the stylet, the pointy instrument given to voters to dislodge the chads, over the Gore entry on the ballot, but he just couldn't go through with it. As a protest, Rohloff chose not to vote for either Gore or Bush, and he resented the notion that his ballot would be used as a Gore vote because he had probably indented a chad.

"Remember William Rohloff, because there are a lot like him," Scherer intoned. Then it was Boies's turn.

"Let me see if I can locate that form affidavit they had," Boies began, looking around for the monster poster—a "Gotcha" moment was in the making. There was nothing that delighted Boies more than turning the other side's evidence against it. At times like these, Boies was like a kid in a candy store, savoring his favorite M&Ms. The large exhibit on the poster board looked like a preprinted form. But just then, Boies showed that even Rohloff, now cast as a pawn in a Republican campaign to gather as many signatures against the recount as possible, would not go along with the verbiage that the Republicans had asked him to sign onto. Rohloff had crossed out the word "would" in the preprinted sentence about how he "would" have voted, and wrote in the word "could"—a tiny change, but Boies found it and presented it to the board. The Republicans, Boies pointed out, couldn't even find a single voter—a person who, by the way, was absent today, and therefore unavailable for cross-examination—to sign their preprinted form without making some changes! This couldn't have much evidentiary significance! Boies had his "Gotcha!"

Judge Rosenberg tried to string up the great trial lawyer by citing the rules of evidence. Suppose a voter had clearly punched through all of the chads on his or her ballot, but had barely indented the entry for president? Wasn't there a rule, maybe number 406, on inferences about a person's habit or routine, that would counsel against counting that indent as a vote? Boies said he didn't think that was true as a matter of law or logic. "It's 406," Rosenberg said again, intent on pinning Boies down. Unfortunately for Rosenberg, he added, "I don't have the rule here."

Boies turned it into a straight line for his punch. Well, Boies said, he wasn't sure whether it was rule 406 either. You could speculate about what someone was thinking when they indented a chad, he said. But why not use simple logic? "Jimmy Miller, who's a friend of mine, and lives around here, and many of you know him, says that if you hear hooves in the background, your first impression is not that you're being pursued by zebras. What the logical explanation is, is usually the right explanation," Boies said.

Boies was on a roll now. "I understand why Governor Bush's advocates want to distract from the natural and logical and obvious implication of that indentation," he continued. There were cases from Illinois and Massachusetts. Boies had an affidavit that indicated exactly what the Illinois court did on the indentations. "Wherever you go, people understand that when a voter makes that indentation, they are intending to vote." With that, Boies's presentation ended.

When the board finished their manual recount that Saturday, Gore gained 567 votes in Broward County, making Boies's visit well worth the trip. Now it was time to go. Boies made an appearance on CNN's *Inside Politics* from the lawn outside the Hurricane Center, and then we were off to the airport. Caryl, who had come to the hearing, was joining us for the trip to Armonk. Boies's assistant, Patrick, felt badly for her. He suspected that Boies was bringing his daughter home for the holiday so he would have one of his four grown lawyer/children in the picture on Sunday, when the *60 Minutes* crew was planning to shoot Boies en famille at his Armonk estate, though it certainly seemed as if Caryl was happy to go home for the holiday.

There ensued an ugly postscript to Boies's Broward County appearance, a sideshow that indicated how far the Bush side was willing to go to disrupt the recount. During the course of his argument, Boies presented the board with an affidavit from Michael Lavalle, the Chicago lawyer who had represented the election challenger in the Pullen case. Mitchell Berger had awoken Lavalle at around midnight on the night of November 21 to ask whether what he said in the *Tribune* story was true—that the trial court in *Pullen* had counted dented ballots. Lavalle said yes, and Berger told him that would be very helpful because the Florida Supreme Court had been unclear on the topic in its opinion extending the deadline for counting votes. Moments later, Boies got on the line and told Lavalle that an affidavit to the effect that dented ballots were counted in *Pullen* would be very helpful to them. Lavalle said he would have no problem with that, because that was what happened.

Lavalle signed an affidavit that had been drafted by the Gore campaign for him early on the morning of November 22. Lavalle corrected a few minor errors about his background and had his secretary fax it to Florida. It was this affidavit that Boies presented to the Broward board. In it, Lavalle swore that the trial court counted seven indented ballots for Penny Pullen, his client, and one indented ballot for her opponent, and that Pullen won the nomination for her race by six votes. Boies handed the Lavalle affidavit to the Broward board, citing it for the proposition that if you have a "discernible indentation," it should count as a vote. But the Broward board barely paid attention to it. Judge Rosenberg was much more intent on quizzing Boies about rule 406 of the rules of evidence. Still, there was trouble with the Lavalle affidavit.

Lavalle called the Gore legal team in a panic late on the evening of November 23, believing that his original conclusions about the counting of the dimples were mistaken. The *Tribune* reporter who wrote the original dimple story was getting feedback from the Republicans that the Pullen judge counted only ballots with light showing through. The reporter eventually dug out the trial transcript and read Lavalle portions suggesting that this was, in fact, true. Berger reacted to Lavalle's news with equal panic. "We're fucked," he said, insisting on getting a corrected affidavit drafted. That did not deter the Republicans from storming before the Broward County board at nine a.m. the next morning, Thanksgiving, accusing the Democrats of filing a "false affidavit" on the subject of the dimpled ballots. The Republican lawyers were in such a rage about the affidavit that Judge Lee, the board's chairman, asked for a deputy to stand by to remove anyone who was out of order. "I'm not basing my decision here on anything that anyone says in an affidavit," said the implacable Judge Lee.

But Gore's political enemies believed they had found a way to wound the Great One: the National Legal and Policy Center, a conservative think tank in McLean, Virginia, filed an ethics complaint against Boies before the Florida bar. The Florida bar rapidly dismissed the complaint, finding that there was no evidence to support the allegation that Boies had knowingly presented the false affidavit from Lavalle. Boies realized the ethics complaint was not something he needed to take seriously, and he paid it no mind, a fact that further maddened the Republicans.

Boies had been on the ground in Westchester for about a half an hour on the night of November 22 when Ron Klain called, asking him to return to Tallahassee. Klain thought the campaign might be back before the Florida Supreme Court, appealing Miami-Dade's decision to stop counting, by the next morning. In addition, Gore was looking past the Sunday deadline, when Harris was set to certify the election, toward a trial contesting the election results.

Boies reveled in these moments. We were back on the Learjet about twenty hours later, on Thanksgiving afternoon. Once seated on the plane, Boies got on the phone to Gore. The Palm Beach County Canvassing Board was continuing to count ballots in a manner much more restrictive than the Democrats had hoped. The campaign was now convinced that Judge Burton, who had been appointed to the bench by Bush's brother, Governor Jeb Bush of Florida, was in the tank with the Republicans and determined to count ballots in Bush's favor. With the deadline of Sunday, November 26, looming to finish the vote count, Judge Burton had his board take the Thanksgiving holiday off. The Palm Beach County board, as Broward had done, was set to hear arguments on the dimple question on Friday morning. On the phone to Gore, Boies was convincing the vice president that it didn't make sense for him to make a presentation in Palm Beach, as he had done in Broward County. On the basis of the numbers alone—and the recount amounted to numbers and only numbers—this advice didn't make much sense. Palm Beach, after all, was the county where Gore expected to gain the most, by turning its ten thousand "undervotes" into chads that registered votes for Gore. "I think there is a danger," Boies told the vice president. The Gore campaign was anticipating filing a lawsuit the next Monday contesting the election. The campaign would be arguing that whatever the Palm Beach board did should be overturned by a court. "It's facially inconsistent for me to go down there," he said, signing off.

After Boies got off the phone, he got whimsical about what his client was expecting of him. "So I go down and sprinkle a little fairy dust," Boies said, his hands shaking the imaginary powder for effect. The Broward County board had been open to persuasion, Boies said, "so it was worth the risk." This logic made no sense to me: from the outset, the Gore team had known that the treasure trove of uncounted votes was in Palm Beach. Why would Gore send Boies to Broward and not to Palm Beach? But there was no point in arguing with Boies. On the plane ride, I also learned that the Republicans were seeking an appeal of the loss of their federal equal protection case—the first lawsuit filed in the fracas, a case that the Republicans had lost and no one had paid much attention to—to the U.S. Supreme Court. When I ventured to mention this development, Boies snapped, "The U.S. Supreme Court is irrelevant. Nobody is worried about that. They're worried about Palm Beach." Then why didn't it make sense for Boies to go there?, I wondered.

The next morning, Boies trundled around the media tents in the dark, beginning before dawn, appearing on the morning talk shows on CBS, NBC, and ABC. The appearances that morning were crucial: the campaign had to find a way to brace the nation for the hard fact that the postelection nightmare would not end on Sunday with Harris's certification of the vote. Gore intended to drag it through the courts once more. After certification of the vote, the Florida law allowed a "contest" of the vote tally, and that is what Gore intended to pursue in the Florida courts. Boies hit the media tents to use all of his nonchalant powers of persuasion to make the case that this course of action was entirely reasonable, that anything less, in fact, would be premature because all of the votes had not been counted. Under Florida's law on election contests, Gore was entitled to challenge the results of any county in the state. But with the reporters, Boies was coy about which counties Gore intended to challenge in his lawsuit. He kept citing the clearest case, that of Miami-Dade, which stopped counting midway through. "The right way to fix that is a contest," Boies told Matt Lauer of NBC's *Today* program. "However it comes out, it comes out."

Boies made the rounds later in the day, after the Supreme Court—contrary to Boies's predictions that their say was "irrelevant"—agreed to hear Bush's appeal of the federal lawsuit. Margaret Carlson, a writer from *Time* magazine, a regular pundit on Beltway talk shows like CNN's *Capital Gang,* and a personality considered to be one of the most powerful in the media, came to Tallahassee to spend the day with Boies and record her observations for what turned out to be a glowing profile.

At this point, admiration for Boies among press and public reached a crescendo. The press could not get enough of Boies's boundless enthusiasm, and they soaked up his aura once again, often over drinks at the Grill. The *Washington Post* fawned over him, describing Boies as "the sort of man who could eat dinner with reporters and settle a multi-million dollar negotiation by cell phone at the same time." And what did Boies tell his fellow diners when he got off the phone? The *Post* wrote about that too. " 'It wasn't a very difficult negotiation,' he said suavely when he clicked off and turned to his companions,' " the *Post* reported.

Katherine Harris certified Bush the winner by 537 votes on Sunday night, November 26. In keeping with her diva image, Harris issued tickets for the event, which was held in a large forum beneath the capitol. Her tally did not include 168 net votes that Gore had picked up in Miami-Dade before the board there halted its recount the previous Wednesday. And Harris included no results from the Palm Beach board, which failed to make the five p.m. deadline imposed by the Florida Supreme Court, and sent a fax of jumbled numbers. When Palm Beach finally finished counting, at seven o'clock on the night of November 26, Gore had picked up as many as 215 votes, but far fewer than the Democrats thought he deserved. Democratic observers set aside 3,300 ballots they believed should have counted as votes for Gore. Gore's legal team planned, even expected, that it would regain these votes when the campaign pursued its legal contest and established that every dimple should count.

After Gore decided to contest the election, Boies and the legal team had held several press conferences, focusing on mechanical problems with punch-card ballot machines that failed to dislodge chads. The Democrats trotted out officials from Massachusetts, where these very problems had occurred and a court had ordered a recount. Boies was clearly headed toward asking for a recount of the 10,000 Miami-Dade undervotes, and a new recount of the 3,300 Palm Beach ballots under a more liberal standard. The team decided that nothing could be done about the butterfly-ballot disaster, and had long since ceased to consider the alleged problems that black voters had encountered at the Florida polls on election day.

But there were other problems the Gore campaign could have seized upon: in Seminole and Martin Counties, the Republican Party officials had almost surely violated election procedures. In both counties, the party had sent absentee ballot applications that omitted identification numbers, and Republican election officials in both parties had allowed party officials to correct this mistake. In absentee voting alone, Bush won more than six thousand votes in Seminole and Martin. Boies urged Gore to consider using the Seminole and Martin claims as leverage—Bush could not have it both ways, on one hand insisting that strict compliance with election procedures penalized voters who failed to punch through their chads, while on the other hand asserting that election technicalities didn't matter in Seminole and Martin. Boies saw the potential for a lawyers' trade, if Gore put the Seminole and Martin claims into the lawsuit: if the Bush team wanted to keep those thousands of absentee votes, it should allow the Gore team to count the ballots in Miami-Dade and Palm Beach. That was Boies's view. But Gore, the candidate who preached counting all the votes, believed this strategy was far too subtle to be understood by the American people. It was not an easy call. The Gore team did not make its final decisions on what to contest until a conference call on the morning of Monday, November 27, when Gore filed his contest lawsuit.

Gore's complaint relied mainly on a single, seemingly simple provision in Florida election law, which listed five possible grounds for contesting an election. One of them was the "rejection" of legal votes that could "change or place in doubt" the election results, the ground that the Gore team believed would take their candidate home: they would show that punch-card ballot machines cast the vote in "doubt" because they invariably failed to record votes. Boies, America's quintessential trial lawyer, now had a trial on his hands. But he had just the opposite plan in mind.

Boies wanted the trial to be over before it began. "David's theory was always crystal clear and exquisite," Klain says. "The trial was just an obstacle between us and the end zone, and the end zone was the Florida Supreme Court." Boies made the final call when the campaign drew Judge N. Sanders Sauls to hear the contest case. Everyone agreed that Sauls was the worst of the five Leon County judges for Gore's cause.

It would have been easy to knock Judge Sauls off the case. Under Florida law, litigants get one free pass to disqualify a judge. But Boies figured that the Florida Supreme Court would be much less inclined to help Gore if the campaign sought to replace Sauls with another judge. In addition to this, a bad ruling from a bad judge would give the Florida justices all the more reason to help Gore. "It was a brilliant strategic decision," Klain says.

At the Microsoft trial, Boies had drilled down on a single theme with relentless consistency—Microsoft's credibility. In Tallahassee, Boies's drumbeat focused on the ballots. Boies made the ballots witnesses; they were essential evidence. In his first move before Judge Sauls, Boies requested that Sauls bring the 10,000 undervote ballots never counted by

Miami-Dade and the 3,300 contested ballots from Palm Beach to Tallahas-see. Boies demanded that the counting of those ballots by an agent of the court begin immediately.

Boies came to court with the theory that once Gore filed his contest proceeding, the slate had been wiped clean. Whatever counting had been done by the canvassing boards was irrelevant, and the court should now count the ballots anew—or de novo—as a judicial question. This proposi-tion infuriated the silver-haired Tallahassee lawyer who became Bush's main lawyer in Florida, Barry Richard. "Counsel is trying to put the cart before the horse," Richard intoned. "It's asking your honor to begin to institute a very costly remedy before you decided anybody violated any-thing." Richard suggested that the first order of business was to hold a hearing to determine if the Miami-Dade, Palm Beach, or Nassau County boards did anything to abuse their discretion. "My client is entitled to a hearing before Mr. Boies's client gets relief!" he huffed.

Judge Sauls presided over the proceedings as if he were sheriff of May-berry R.F.D. "It's a little bit like getting nibbled to death by a duck!" Sauls told Boies, just as Boies apologized for "pestering" the court with so many papers, so many motions. On this first day in court before Sauls, the judge seemed to be denying Boies's motion to count ballots immediately, and all Boies wanted was a written order to that effect, a document he needed under the local rules to appeal to the Florida Supreme Court. Sauls wouldn't even give him that much. "If you want some ballots up here, we'll bring them!" the judge bellowed. "I'm not saying ANY-body is going to count ballots. We have to take some evi-DENCE." As I watched from my seat in what was normally the jury box, I saw something quite extraordi-nary in Boies, something I had never seen in all my time with him. His jaw was locked, his eyes narrowing. The expression on his face screamed what Boies really thought of Sauls. It said, "You idiot!" After Boies exited Sauls's courtroom, he appeared before the cameras in the lobby of the Leon County Courthouse. "Delay is on their side," he said of the Republicans. "Justice delayed here is really justice denied. Three days of counting could be critical." Then Boies made a dig at the Republicans. "You'll all remem-ber, Palm Beach County lost the right to have their votes counted because they were 127 minutes late. So this is something that we have to count every hour of every day." Even without Sauls's order, the Gore team appealed his denial of an immediate count to the Florida Supreme Court, which denied the appeal later in the week.

Sauls agreed to ship some fourteen thousand ballots requested by Boies to Tallahassee, and the next afternoon, the judge also agreed to the Republicans' request that all 1.16 million votes from Miami-Dade and Palm Beach be sent with them. Boies didn't object to this absurd request, and merely asked that the disputed ballots be separated. "I know when it's futile," Boies told Judge Sauls at the hearing. "All I'm asking is that they send our ballots up as soon as they can." But the Republicans, intent on wreaking as much havoc as possible, insisted that all the ballots should come up together. And Sauls chimed in that he didn't want to place "an undue burden" on the counties. Boies, exasperated, pointed out that the Democrats were paying for the expense of the trip. Once again, Boies found himself peering through his bifocals icily at the judge, grinding his teeth.

Phil Beck, a Chicago trial lawyer brought in by Baker for the contest, did a fine job of suggesting that the Democrats were somehow threatening Sauls with their appeal of his order denying an immediate count. "We're not threatening anything!" Boies insisted. "Even if you did, it wouldn't bother me!" Sauls shot back.

Boies wanted to lose the case in Sauls's courtroom as quickly as possible. The legal team had a witness list of about ten people. Boies slashed all but two names from it. Klain left it to Boies to orchestrate the trial, since Klain was busy preparing Gore's briefs for the U.S. Supreme Court arguments that were scheduled for Friday, December 1.

When the trial got under way in Sauls's courtroom on Saturday morning, Boies made an opening statement, and after that spent curiously little time on his feet. At one point earlier in the week, Boies told me that he planned on not being around on Saturday at all. His teenage son Alexander was scheduled to visit the prep school he was going to attend, and Boies was flying home to Armonk for it. He called the trial a "set piece" that the other lawyers could handle.

Boies brought in Steve Zack, a Miami trial lawyer who favored olive double-breasted suits, and who was working with Boies on the pending class action against the HMO industry and fast becoming a Boies acolyte. He canceled his Thanksgiving plans to join Boies in Tallahassee and was thrilled to be in his company, enjoying his fifteen minutes of fame. Zack called the first witness in Gore's case, Kimball Brace, a bearded man who testified about how punch-card ballots could malfunction to create dimpled chads. Zack had found Brace and prepared him as a witness. He was terrible on the stand, rambling and repetitive. When Zack and Brace returned to the Gore headquarters that evening, the other members of the trial team averted their eyes.

Sauls anticipated a one-day trial, but Brace was on the witness stand until one-thirty p.m. on Saturday. It was clear the case would drag into another day. Gore had one other witness, a professor from Yale who testified that the rate of undervotes was much higher in counties that used punch-card ballot machines rather than optical-scan ballots. The Bush lawyer, Phil Beck, proved to be the star cross-examiner of the proceedings. He humiliated Gore's Yale professor, who had signed a sworn statement that referred to a 1998 ballot. The rate of undervotes on the ballot showed that it was more difficult to punch through a chad in the first column of a ballot, which was where the Bush-Gore race was located. But the professor had never actually seen the ballot, and Beck got him to admit that on the stand while Beck had his sworn statement up on the overhead projector. This was a "Gotcha" moment for the other side.

As the Gore team was getting ready to rest its case, Boies was still worrying about the ballots; he didn't think they had been appropriately moved into evidence. This, in fact, was his only real concern. Boies wanted to make sure that the ballots were in evidence, so when Sauls refused to look at them, Boies would have his legal error to take up to the Florida Supreme Court. Jeremy Bash, a bright young lawyer, had the task of making sure that the ballots were part of the record. "I kept saying, 'I promise you they are in,' " Bash recalled telling Boies. Bash had double-checked with the office of the court clerk (who, by funny coincidence, had a son named Chad).

Boies cross-examined two of the nine Republican witnesses. His legendary cross-examination skills were not on display. He spent little time with Judge Burton, the chair of the Palm Beach board, and even less with the Republicans' statistician, getting his wrist slapped for pulling a cheap lawyers' stunt, when he questioned the defense expert about his work on behalf of lead paint defendants. The case dragged on into a marathon Sunday session, wrapping up at eleven-thirty p.m. Boies piled into a car with Zack. Ever clueless, Zack commented on the prospects for a victory before Judge Sauls—a victory Boies had no notion of obtaining. "The question is, will he have the guts?" Zack said. "I don't care! Just as long as he decides!" Boies blurted. Zack still didn't get it: Boies didn't care if he lost before Judge Sauls; he just needed a ruling, any ruling, to get back before the Florida Supreme Court.

The trial before Sauls, if you could call it that, obscured one crucial fact: Florida had no law "clearly" telling him to review the ballots de novo, as Boies insisted he should do. When Boies made his final arguments, he cited a 1932 case called *State v. Smith,* in which, Boies told the judge, the Florida Supreme Court "expressly stated that the ballots were the best evidence" to resolve an election contest. Boies, with no notes, as usual, had the cite for Sauls. Sauls peered down from the bench at Boies, looking out over his eyeglasses. "That is *State versus Smith,* you say?" Yes, Boies confirmed. The relevant portion was on page 336. The trouble was that the case, on that very same page, also said that the court "must find as a fact that a legal basis for ordering any recount exists, before ordering such recount." And Sauls quoted from that portion of the Smith case when he issued his ruling against Gore.

Boies's argument that the ballots were the "best evidence" would have worked beautifully if he had been appearing in Massachusetts, which has clear law on recounts, just as it had clear law on how to read the chads. In a 1996 case called *Delahunt v. Johnston,* cited many times by Boies, every dimple counted. In Massachusetts, there were cases dating back to 1961 that said, point-blank, that once a party contested an election in court, the court itself began counting ballots anew, de novo. If the trial judge's ruling was appealed, the appeals court started over again, reviewing the ballots for itself. But Boies was in Florida, and there was no clear Florida law on the subject. "The fact that they don't have de novo review hurt us," Dennis Newman, a Boston lawyer who was one of the army who trooped to Florida to help the Gore camp, told me later. Newman knew his chads; he had worked on the Delahunt case.

On Monday, the morning after the trial, the U.S. Supreme Court delivered its opinion in a case that became known as *Bush I.* The Bush legal team had appealed the Florida Supreme Court's November 21 ruling that extended the deadline for the certification of the election and allowed more time for the counting of ballots. The Bush lawyers had argued that the change violated two provisions of federal law, one of them being Article II of the U.S. Constitution, which gives states the power to appoint electors "in such a manner as the legislature thereof may direct." According to Bush, that meant that the Florida Supreme Court had no power to change the deadline for certifying the election—the Constitution left that power to the Florida legislature alone. Laurence Tribe, the Harvard Law School professor and renowned Supreme Court advocate, had argued against the Bush appeal on Friday, December 1, as Gore's Florida lawyers prepared for the contest trial before Judge Sauls. The justices of the U.S. Supreme Court punted on the Bush I appeal in the per curiam opinion they released on midmorning Monday. The Florida recount fight was giving a new context and meaning to the obscure tradition of per curiam opinions, a designation often used to signify irrelevant legal decisions but sometimes ducked under in controversial settings. In the fight for Florida, most of the decisions that mattered had no judge's name on them.

The anonymous ruling from the Court that Monday ran just three pages, and most of it was given over to a factual history of the case and the conflicting interpretations that the Bush and Gore teams had urged regarding the Florida election code. This much, they were forced to admit. The high court in the Rehnquist era—at least those within the five-justice majority—put a premium on the rights of the fifty states, a factor that almost always worked in favor of conservative causes in the important cases. Now Bush was asking the Court to ignore states' rights, citing what were arguably solid reasons under federal law. And while the justices waffled, failing to give Bush an outright victory by reversing the Florida Supremes, their noises boded well for him.

The decision quoted at length from one of its own precedents, dusting off the Court's 1892 decision in *McPherson v. Blacker*. The McPherson case interpreted what the Founding Fathers meant in Article II of the Constitution regarding the authority of the states to appoint presidential electors. Article II, according to *McPherson*, did not confer the power to appoint electors on the "people" or the "citizens" but on the legislatures of the states—unless there was a provision in a given state's constitution that circumscribed the legislature's power. And now, in the year 2000, the anonymous Court decreed that the Florida Supremes had perhaps failed to consider the impact of *McPherson*, had failed to clarify how the Florida Constitution allowed them to rewrite the election code to extend the certification deadline. The justices vacated the Florida Supreme Court ruling and remanded it for "further proceedings not inconsistent with it." Oblique as it was, the decision demanded that the Florida Supremes explain themselves, justify themselves, to the highest court in the land. The decision was a rebuke, a scolding, a word of caution that fell just short of accusing the Florida Supreme Court of handing a partisan victory to the Democrats in the presidential election.

That Monday, as the High Court was delivering its ruling in *Bush I,* Boies was spending the morning in leisurely fashion. He had a formal photo shoot for *Time* magazine at the Florida Supreme Court. The magazine was clearly considering Boies as its Man of the Year, if he managed to deliver the presidency for his client. Boies also stopped by a local videographer to make a mock television appearance for a video that his friend Steve Susman was planning to show at his law firm's Christmas party. Boies borrowed his assistant Patrick Dennis's sunglasses, à la Jack Nicholson, for the video, in which he appeared to be accepting a litigator of the year award, holding a trophy that looked like it had come from a high school gym. "I find I am now recognized almost everywhere I go and I'm sure that this will make it even more so. There are times, however, when I long for those days when I was just an obscure multimillionaire like my friend Steve Susman, toiling away for that occasional 25-million-dollar contingency fee, unknown and unappreciated." Boies then embellished on the script, making it much wittier. "However, fame does have its benefits and I'm sure that you'll all see me on the *Jerry Springer Show* and *Oprah* and other places." (Susman had cited the much more staid venues of *Time* and *Vanity Fair,* where Boies appeared in real life.) Boies then signed off, in accordance with the script, because Gore was on the line for him. Shortly after noon, Boies was in the lobby of the Leon County Courthouse in Tallahassee, appearing before the cameras once again, explaining what little there was to explain in the decision from Washington. "This would be a terrible mistake to take this away from the people," Boies intoned. The votes must be counted. That was his relentless message. The Supreme Court ruling, really, had nothing whatever to do with that, but he pounded the theme, and we all listened. At any rate, the ruling became a footnote for the high drama of that day.

Judge Sauls delivered his own ruling later that afternoon, calling the parties into his courtroom at four-thirty for a televised reading. Bash, the young Ivy Leaguer on the Gore team, had with him a notice of appeal to the District Court of Appeal, the first piece of paper that Gore would need to move the case to the Florida Supreme Court. As Sauls began reading his ruling from the bench, Boies passed a note to Bash. It read: "File the DCA papers." Bash bolted to the DCA, banged on the glass doors, and had the document filed before Boies left Sauls's courtroom.

Boies was masterful in defeat. "They won, we lost, we're appealing," he said simply, motioning with his arms. The press was in a frenzy. When would this all end? Were Florida's twenty-five electoral votes in jeopardy? Should the vice president concede? Boies returned the reporters to his relentless theme. "Remember, our position from the beginning has been that, consistent with Florida law, the ballots were the best evidence. And unfortunately, this ruling comes without the judge having looked at a single ballot." ABC News's Chris Vlasto blasted a question: "But Mr. Boies, the judge also said that you didn't make the case. I mean, you didn't present evidence that the ballots should be counted. Do you regret not presenting more witnesses?" At this, Boies went into teacher mode: "The point of the evidence is that, when you introduce evidence, that is part of the record to be reviewed and taken into account by the court. Now, what the court did was to decide that it was not going to even look at those ballots." Boies's performance at the press conference was so spectacular that the *New York Times* devoted an entire article to it the next day. "Gore's Lawyer, Steam-rollered, Looks at Bright Side," the headline read.

Later that night, Phil Beck and his partner, Fred Bartlit, were being toasted by Republican lobbyists at Andrew's Capital Bar and Grill, where Boies was also having dinner. "Congratulations!" Boies said to Beck and Bartlit. Boies was as gracious in defeat as he was in victory. To him, it was part of the game.

The next morning, the Florida Supreme Court agreed to hear Gore's appeal. No one on the legal team was surprised; Sauls's ruling was riddled with legal errors. The justices set oral argument for ten a.m. on Thursday, December 7. Briefs from both sides were due that Wednesday at noon. Meanwhile, Boies had a hearing in the Napster case on Tuesday afternoon, December 5. The San Francisco judge presiding over the Napster suit agreed that Boies could participate by teleconference from the Gore head-quarters. For the hearing, I slipped past the security guard. There, I discovered the true cult status Boies had achieved with the Gore legal team.

Gore called, as he often did, looking for Boies. It was clear that the two were close, though they had met only once before, in 1988 at a New York fund-raiser held by Victor Kovner, the West Side Democratic honcho. On the phone, Gore asked about Boies's son Alexander. And Gore had a tip for Boies: Gore's friend Randall "Sunny" Rawls, an investigative reporter, had some information on the maintenance of punch-card machines in Florida. Gore wanted Boies to talk to Rawls. Reports of Gore's micromanagement of his case were not overblown, I thought to myself. "Sure, absolutely," Boies told the vice president. "And the thing is, even though the evidence is closed, if something gets out in the press, the Supreme Court is going to see it." Boies brought Gore up-to-date on the team's work on the briefs due at the Florida Supreme Court the next day. "The court gave us the schedule that we wanted," Boies told Gore. "The time is not going to run out on us."

Several lawyers came into the room that Boies and Patrick had taken over as a makeshift office, where there were telltale signs of Boies's snack obsessions. Large plastic vats of pretzels were on hand, as were bottles of Stewart's Diet Root Beer, a current favorite. The room was equipped with a television set, and pictures of Boies yawning in court that Patrick had downloaded from Yahoo! were taped to the wall. Throughout the headquarters, there were several signs warning, "Nothing leaves here without Permission from a Paralegal!" This was the Democrats' attempt to run a tight ship.

Several lawyers came into the room, like supplicants, offering Boies cases and checking with him on parts of the brief to the Florida Supreme Court. Boies had done little work on the briefs during his time in Florida. But he made it a point, as was his practice, of working on the introductions. Boies was also participating by phone in the Napster hearing. Sam Kaplan had come to Tallahassee to brief Boies on Napster. Judge Marilyn Hall Patel, no shrinking violet, introduced Boies as the "other gentleman, who, I understand, is somewhere in the land we're in the process of ceding back to Spain." "Right! yes," Boies laughed. Boies, by then, had lost before Judge Patel, and his appeal on Napster's behalf had also failed. Patel seemed to be enjoying the current Florida predicament. "It sounds like you're underwater there," Patel noted, her tone suggesting that she did not mean the quality of the phone connection. "Well, I am a little more underwater today than yesterday," Boies admitted.

Little did Patel know that, as Boies was listening in on the conference call, with the speakerphone on mute, he was also attending to other matters, among them writing the introduction to Gore's brief to the Florida Supreme Court. The words, if you looked at them in print, did not jump off the page. "This is an election context pursuant to Sec. 102.168. This is the election contest that this court held in Palm Beach County Canvassing Board v. Harris that the Plaintiffs had a right to bring; this is the election contest that caused the court in Harris to set its certification deadline in order to permit this action to be completed by December 12." On it went. The document reflected the low-key and mathematical workings of Boies's mind.

Kendall Coffey, the Miami lawyer who was the team's local recount expert, entered Boies's inner sanctum. Boies was reading documents at his desk and never looked up from them as Coffey haltingly raised the subject of the Palm Beach count and the 3,300 ballots that the Gore camp wanted recounted. "Now I just want to make one quick point on this whole subject of discretion as far as Palm Beach is concerned," Coffey began. The fact of the matter was that there were no Florida cases demanding a de novo recount of ballots that had already been counted. As Coffey was trying to suggest that, even under an "abuse of discretion" standard, the ballots would have to be looked at again, Boies cut him off. Coffey was saying it was far from clear that Florida law mandated a de novo standard, and he tried to suggest that—even under an abuse of discretion standard—the Florida Supreme Court should revisit "a goodly number" of the 3,300 ballots that Palm Beach chose not to count. Agitated, Boies interrupted Coffey. "You've got to look at the evidence! You've got to look at the evidence!" he repeated. Back to Boies's theme: the ballots were the witnesses and all of them should be recounted. Coffey soldiered on: even under a much tougher standard of review demanding a finding that the Palm Beach board had acted in a "clearly erroneous" fashion, a "goodly number" of the 3,300 ballots that Palm Beach chose not to count would still be counted. "I'm not saying that's the standard, I'm not saying we give up the argument . . ." Coffey trailed off. He finished shortly after, telling Boies that he just wanted to make him aware of the cases. Boies seemed distracted. He thanked Coffey and sent him away.

Boies left at about eight-thirty that night, as the legal team pulled an all-nighter to finish the brief that was due at ten the next morning. Under the Florida rules, each side had fifty pages to make its case, but the Gore team had convinced themselves that the Florida Supreme Court would allow them seventy pages, given that there was no time for a reply brief, which could be twenty pages. But early on the morning of December 6, just hours before the brief was due, the Florida Supreme Court's clerk called to tell the Gore team to stick to fifty pages. At that point, the brief was seventy-five. Boies breezed into Gore headquarters at eight-fifteen a.m., and the panicked staff told him of the problem. Boies, who had never written more than three or four pages of any of Gore's legal briefs, amazed his colleagues by taking the brief in hand and whacking it decisively. Klain was bowled over: "He took out paragraphs, he'd replace an entire paragraph with a sentence that was even more persuasive than the entire paragraph. He would do some kind of lawyer cheating tricks where you take out parenthetical after cases. Some of it was cheap cheesy stuff, but that made it all the more impressive. It was the whole range of ways in which lawyers cheat on brief lengths. It was everything." Boies always seized the moment when it mattered most. He grabbed it, ate it up, his supreme confidence and uncanny instincts allowing him to take control while everyone else was in a sweat.

That night, Boies was seated in the lobby of the Governors Inn, reading over, once again, the cases at issue. Clad in a white turtleneck under his standard blue suit, Boies perused the cases while a photographer from *Time* magazine took pictures. Later, he joined the Gore team at the Governors Club for a final dinner, inspiring the team with a final speech about the rightness of their cause. Everyone was expecting to lose.

The Gore brief asked the Florida Supreme Court to begin an immediate count of the 9,000 uncounted Miami-Dade ballots, and the 3,300 ballots that the Democrats had set aside as challenged in Palm Beach. The hearing began ominously for Boies. It was clear that Chief Justice Charles Wells, a conservative Republican, had hardened his views against Gore since the last hearing. Boies had barely spoken his standard introduction—"May it please the court, my name is David Boies and . . ."—when Wells interrupted him. Wells was clearly furious about the rebuke his court had received from the U.S. Supreme Court earlier that week. He demanded to know, not just from Boies but from all the lawyers before him, how important *McPherson* really was. Luckily for Boies, Wells rambled on, asking a number of questions before Boies could finally respond, and Boies chose not to address the McPherson issue.

Justice Wells also tried to trip Boies up on his "ballots as witnesses" argument. That argument, Wells suggested, would, for instance, allow someone to "say that they lost by 130,000 votes in Dade County, and we would have to have the court count those votes." That was, in fact, what the Gore legal team wanted. They wanted the court to count the votes de novo, just as the Massachusetts court had done in *Delahunt*; but Boies didn't admit as much to Justice Wells. No, no, Boies replied to his question.

"This is a situation in which the evidence is clear and undisputed that there were voter errors and machine errors that create this undervote in punch-card equipment." To hone the point, Boies relied on one of his fail-safe maneuvers, guiding the justices to a page from Judge Sauls's opinion—page ten—where Judge Sauls had observed that the counties using punch cards "have been aware for many years" of counting problems with these machines. Sauls had gone on to say that the Gore team had failed to establish "a reasonable probability that the statewide election result would be different." Boies didn't mention that part of Sauls's ruling, but pinned him to the few words that worked for Gore.

As the argument continued, Boies found himself in trouble even among the Democrats on the seven-judge panel, who demanded to know why—if the punch-card machines were so unreliable—there should not be a broader recount. With the clock ticking toward December 12—and the panic over it increasing—Boies tried to focus the justices on the narrow confines of what Gore had sought at the trial before Judge Sauls, which was to count the 9,000 uncounted ballots in Miami-Dade and to recount the 3,300 challenged ballots in Palm Beach. Justice Barbara Pariente, a Democrat and the member of the court believed to be the primary mover behind the previous anonymous ruling for Gore, asked: "But why wouldn't that apply to all the other counties, at least the punch-card counties, where there are undervotes and those votes haven't been counted? If we're looking for accuracy, which has been the statement from day one." Well, Boies had a simple if insincere answer to that question: "I think the first difference is that that's where the ballots have been contested," he said. "This and other courts have looked not at the entire type of ballot that may have been involved but only those ballots that were actually contested by a party."

The Gore team had no real interest in a statewide recount, especially now, on December 7, with only five days left on the clock. Whether Gore had ever meant what he said on November 15, where he had made a televised offer of a statewide recount, was highly doubtful. In fact, back on November 20—a lifetime ago in this legal fight—Boies had punted on the prospect of a statewide recount in his first argument before the Florida Supreme Court. Mentioning Gore's televised speech in passing, Boies had told the justices, "We are not urging that upon the court."

As Boies's allotted time for argument was drawing to a close, the crotchety Justice Leander Shaw Jr., at seventy the oldest member of the panel, returned Boies to the stark realities of Judge Sauls's ruling, reminding him that Sauls had found no "competent substantial evidence" in Gore's contest. In other words, Boies had failed to prove his case. Once again, Boies relied on a favorite ploy, citing the testimony of John Ahmman, a witness for Bush and the punch-card inventor, who admitted that a manual recount was needed in a close election. That could be found at page 442 of the trial transcript, Boies said. He told the panel that Sauls was plain wrong. Gore had moved the contested ballots into evidence, and Sauls, by ruling before looking at a single one of them, had behaved in a manner "inconsistent with the way a trial goes, which is that you look at the evidence before you reach a conclusion."

Justice Wells reminded Boies that he was out of time; he had already used some of the precious minutes that appellants reserve for their "rebuttal" arguments. None of the justices posed a specific question about Palm Beach, nor did the court address the Gore team's insistence that the 3,300 ballots set aside there should be counted again because the ballots themselves were "proof." When Barry Richard, Bush's lawyer, got up to make his argument, he referred back to the principle, which he described as the standard "for time immemorial," that the decisions of the canvassing boards could be reviewed only on finding that they had abused their discretion. And in this case, Gore had simply failed to prove an abuse of discretion. When Boies rose for his rebuttal, he emphasized once again that the justices could limit the recount to what Gore had requested. "There's never been a rule that says you have to recount all the ballots in an election contest," he said.

Boies had dinner that night at Andrew's Capital Bar and Grill with Steve Zack, who was by then trailing after him like an eager puppy. Phil Beck and Irv Terrell, a Texas lawyer who was defending Bush in the ongoing lawsuits based on the problems in Seminole and Martin Counties, joined them. The lawyers were gaming how the justices would rule, and Boies raised his glass of wine, proclaiming a four-to-three split on the panel. The next day, Friday, December 8, dragged on, as everyone awaited a decision. The day had an air of finality to it; the legal circus was drawing to a close, and we could all go home. By midafternoon, the judges overseeing the Seminole and Martin cases had dismissed those lawsuits. Terrell bragged to a producer from one of the television networks that Governor Jeb Bush had called him on his cell phone after the victories, telling him,

"You're my Boies killer." Terrell reveled in this, though Boies had had no involvement whatsoever in those cases. Boies had lunch at the Grill, surrounded by a gaggle of reporters. Michael Isikoff of *Newsweek*, famous for breaking the Monica Lewinsky scandal, dominated the questioning, one alpha male to another. "Did you insist on being in charge?" Isikoff asked. Boies didn't quite answer that. "You're a supremely self-confident guy," Isikoff remarked.

Lightning struck shortly before four o'clock on Friday afternoon. In yet another per curiam ruling, the Florida Supreme Court had found for Gore. It seemed miraculous when Craig Waters, the court spokesman, read the statement. "By a vote of four to three, the majority of the court has reversed the decision of the trial court," he said. "The circuit court shall order a manual recount of all undervotes in any Florida county where such a recount has not occurred. Because time is of the essence, the recounts shall commence immediately," Waters announced. Outside the Gore headquarters on South Monroe Street, in the borrowed law offices of Dexter Douglass, streams of anti-Gore cars sped by, the occupants shouting epithets. One local restaurant owner, David Green, had become a Boies fan. "Heisman trophy! Heisman trophy!" he shouted in my direction as he drove past in his car.

At Gore headquarters, the legal team had been waiting around all day. They had spent the time signing each other's commemorative T-shirts, getting autographs, and saying their good-byes. Suddenly, Ron Klain's fists were in the air. The entire team started cheering. Ron handed Boies the phone. Gore got on the line. "Congratulations!" he said to Boies. "Congratulations to you!" Boies answered. Then he put the situation in his own, betting man's terms. "I told you the odds were fifty-fifty, and I think four to three is better than fifty-fifty." There were thanks all around, and the moment was over.

By eight o'clock that night, the parties were back before the trial court to iron out how the massive recount would go forward. Judge Terry Lewis was back on the scene; Judge Sauls, whose record and character had been excoriated on the front page of the *New York Times*, bowed out of the proceedings on remand from the Florida Supreme Court. The Republicans, true to form, did not hide their disdain for the court process. Ben Ginsberg, their red-haired talking head, glared in Boies's direction. Meanwhile, Boies was laughing with Phil Beck, who had clearly trounced Boies at the trial, fair and square, and Boies respected that. The two lawyers joked that, if they found a county in the recount they didn't like, they would send them either Kimball Brace, the Gore expert who bombed on the witness stand, or John Ahmann, the Bush witness who got nailed by his own patent application, in which he admitted that the punch-card machines resulted in potentially unreadable votes. Boies and Beck were trial lawyers, bonded in their cowboy roles, and they engaged in gallows humor when their witnesses died on the stand. Meanwhile, Ginsberg, the politico, pouted fiercely, sneering at one break in the proceedings, "Mr. Toad's wild ride in Tallahassee continues." Could he have been referring to Toad of Toad Hall, the boastful hero of the children's classic *The Wind in the Willows*?

Ginsberg was obviously fed up with Gore's fantasia before the Tallahassee courts. That afternoon's ruling directed the lower court to immediately add 168 votes found for Gore in the aborted Miami-Dade recount, and to add the votes found for Gore in Palm Beach, which were ignored by Secretary Harris because she said they were filed late. The number of these Gore votes was either 215 or 176—the Bush and Gore teams disputed the figure—and the supreme court left it up to the lower court to sort that out. At any rate, as Ginsberg sat pouting at the hearing, the ruling had dwindled Bush's lead to less than two hundred votes before the statewide recount of undervotes even began.

At Judge Lewis's hearing, Beck did his job for his client—which was to begin running the clock, raising any and every practical and due process concern related to the counting of some 45,000 undervotes that remained. The hearing went on interminably, the Republican lawyers spouting off as if they were speaking in tongues. Boies yawned frequently. He pointed out, accurately, that "hours make a difference." In all the sheer craziness, no one, it seemed, not even the Republicans—for whom it was a boon in an otherwise dismal decision—noticed the *defeat* that the Florida Supreme Court had handed Gore. The slim majority had refused to recount the 3,300 ballots from Palm Beach, the very ballots that the Democrats believed would put Gore over the top and would bring him the presidency. The court said Sauls "did not have an obligation de novo to simply repeat an otherwise-proper manual recount" that had occurred in Palm Beach.

The Florida Supreme Court had, for the most part, accepted Boies's "ballots as witnesses" argument. The majority opinion faulted Sauls for presenting the plaintiffs with "the ultimate Catch-22," by accepting "the only evidence that will resolve the issue"—in other words, by ordering the ballots onto the Ryder truck—and then refusing to examine them. The majority would not go the extra step and say that, in Florida, Sauls had the obligation to count those ballots de novo merely because the Gore legal team had asked him to. In other words, Boies had in fact failed to prove his case where his client thought it mattered most.

It's difficult to know whether the 3,300 ballots would have made a difference. The U.S. Supreme Court stayed the recount the next day. At the time, Boies was having lunch with Steve Zack and Michael Isikoff. Isikoff had a reputation as one of the most feared investigative journalists in the business, but Boies barely registered his existence. Later, when I asked Boies about the moment when he found out about the stay, he said he had been having a burger with "that Mike guy from *Newsweek*."

When Boies heard the announcement, broadcast on the fourteen televisions in Andrew's Capital Bar and Grill, he couldn't fathom it. "There's no irreparable harm!" Boies exclaimed in disbelief. Boies didn't think it was possible for the Republicans to prove that the mere counting of votes could establish the irreparable harm needed for a stay. This was a lawyer's response, and one that was quite apt—it was exactly what U.S. Supreme Court Justice John Paul Stevens would soon write in an unusual dissent to the 5–4 vote to stay the recount. "Counting every vote cannot constitute irreparable harm," Justice Stevens wrote. "On the other hand, there is a danger that a stay may cause irreparable harm to the respondents—and, more importantly, to the public at large."

Boies appeared for one last round at the media tents at the Tallahassee capitol building. He was headed back to Armonk, he told the gathered reporters. Boies was getting hooked up at the Fox News channel when Bill Hemmer, the CNN morning anchor and the network's man in Tallahassee, passed by. Boies had spent many a chilly morning with Hemmer, who had been nicknamed "Chad Lad" by *People* magazine.

"You're leaving town?" Hemmer shouted after Boies. "That ain't right!"

SEVENTEEN

"Well, I think that's a very hard question."

And so Boies was headed home to Armonk, this time, perhaps, for good. He wasted no time—he rushed back to the Governors Inn just after his spin pronouncements at the media tents about the stay decision. In fact, Boies had intended to leave the Florida capital early that morning. With the Florida Supreme Court decision in hand, and the counting of the nine thousand Miami-Dade ballots already under way, Boies figured his work was done. As the morning dragged on, the cable networks carried images from the local counties, where many of the canvassing boards in Republican strongholds were dragging their feet on the recount. Klain and company were particularly leery about Duval County, one of the areas where the largest number of undervotes existed, and where the canvassing board, composed only of Republicans, was wasting precious time by running test ballots through the counting machines. Democrats already harbored feelings of guilt about Duval, which had a ballot-design fiasco that rivaled the butterfly trauma in Palm Beach. The ballot, two pages long, had triggered as many as nine thousand undervotes in largely African-American precincts. Now the Gore team expected to be in court over Duval County, and they asked Boies to stick around for the prospect of a hearing.

The stay from the U.S. Supreme Court trumped that possibility. The Court had set arguments in the case for December 11, a precarious one day away from the deadline that Boies had argued and assured everyone was the final curtain for the 2000 election. Now, in the Spin Room, Boies maneuvered his way toward a new deadline, a bit of hypocrisy that Jake Tapper, the Washington correspondent for Salon.com, later flagged in *Down and Dirty: The Plot to Steal the Presidency,* one of the first books to appear after the recount fight ended. Boies said the timing was the "single most disappointing thing" about what the U.S. Supreme Court had done. "I think there's no doubt that December 18 is the final deadline," Boies said, referring to the date when the electoral college would actually meet to vote. "We've all been trying to get it done by December 12," Boies said, now sounding as if that date was merely the most optimistic time. "I think that in the last week, everyone has recognized that it would not be done by December 12," he said, ending with the note that "the December 12 deadline was not any magical end date."

Boies held a last interview with CNN's Mike Betcher, one of the best television correspondents in Tallahassee. "Is the Monday hearing the last one?" Betcher asked Boies. "Well, obviously that depends on what the United States Supreme Court says," Boies replied. If the Court ordered that the counts be completed—a completely unrealistic scenario, given the stay—Boies said he would be back in Tallahassee. But if it did not, the Democrats would have to respect that, he said. "The United States Supreme Court is the highest court in the land. Under the rule of law, we must accept that decision, whether we agree with it or disagree with it." Boies said he hoped to be back in Tallahassee soon, and Betcher wished him a good trip. All of us who had chattered in the cold waiting for court decisions, piled into the Spin Room, lined up before the Florida Supreme Court, and spent countless hours of dead time eating and drinking at the Andrews Capital Grill, waiting and wondering and contemplating every twist and turn that would resolve the presidency of the United States, had become one. There was giddiness about this moment in the Spin Room, part exhaustion, part letdown, part disbelief, and Boies was at the center of it. He had pushed so far, it seemed, to get the votes counted for Gore, only to have victory slip away with a wild ruling from the U.S. Supreme Court. That decision served to heighten his stature in the Spin Room. And then he was off.

Boies got on his cell phone almost immediately after we piled into a car for the airport. He dictated some of his ideas about what should be included in the Gore brief to the U.S. Supreme Court. Boies focused on the words of Justice Antonin Scalia in the stay opinion. It is highly unusual for the Court to issue any opinion at all prior to a final decision on the merits, but Scalia and Stevens took each other on in the stay order. Scalia believed that counting votes of "questionable legality" was enough to prove irreparable harm. But he also harped on the variances in counting standards from county to county. To Boies's mind, the Florida Supreme Court, by ordering a statewide recount of the undervotes, exacerbated this standards problem. Why not focus on the remedy that Gore had asked for—the counting of the nine thousand ballots from Miami-Dade—which was proceeding in relative calm at the Leon County library? "If it's wrong as a remedy, just leave it out," Boies suggested over the cell phone to the brief writers. Boies thought the best way to counter Scalia's concerns about inconsistencies in counting dimpled and hanging chads was to scale back from the Florida Supreme Court's statewide count. The Florida Supremes had found, contrary to Boies's pleas at the oral argument, that a statewide count was "absolutely essential" to determining the "will of the voters" in Florida—all the voters, not just the ones that Gore had selected. The Republicans insisted this process was fraught with constitutional peril, chaos, and confusion (a situation the Republicans themselves had a large part in stoking). Boies was ready to argue that the Florida Supreme Court had gone too far. "You don't throw out what we've done right."

Even then, as Boies was presumably heading home for good, he mentioned the possibility of going to Washington. "If I don't go down to Washington, I'll give you a call, okay?" Boies told one of the people he called from his cell phone en route to the airport. There was only one reason to go to D.C., and that would be to argue Gore's case before the U.S. Supreme Court, a task for which Laurence Tribe was already on board. But the dynamic between Gore and Boies altered the equation. Gore was believed to have been less than pleased with Tribe's performance at the first Court argument on December 1. Meanwhile, Gore had bonded with Boies in a way that few of Gore's intimates had seen before. "He took to David more completely and more quickly than I've seen him almost take to anyone," Klain told me. "I think that he was smart obviously made a big difference. David had a certain calm and confidence about this process that is always reassuring to a client. And I think Gore was incredibly grateful for David's sacrifice, in totally blowing up his life to come down there for a month."

Once we were on the plane to Armonk, Boies told me what he really thought of the stay decision. "This is partisan politics," he said. "The Supreme Court's made a lot of decisions over the years that have had political implications. But they've rarely, if ever, in modern times intervened in particular election contests to try to influence the election of a candidate they prefer." Why would they do it here? "Because you have at least three people on the Court—Rehnquist, Scalia, and Thomas—who have dedicated their lives to a particular judicial philosophy. That judicial philosophy is now dominant by, at most, a 5–4 majority. If you look at the ages of the members of the Court, the next president is going to select multiple people. You run a risk—what happens if Gore is elected and everything that Rehnquist and Scalia and Thomas have struggled for comes to naught? So it is almost irresistible, at one level, to use the power of the Court to influence the election of somebody other than Gore if they can do that."

The members of the Gore camp were holed up at the Watergate Hotel, where Laurence Tribe had a suite. They knew something was up on Saturday afternoon, as they were frantically preparing the brief that was due at the Supreme Court at four o'clock on Sunday afternoon, when Warren Christopher called. Christopher wanted to come over; he requested to speak with Tribe immediately. At first, Tribe believed Christopher was coming over to give him a pep talk. But that thought vanished after Christopher appeared at the Watergate, and announced to Tribe that he believed it was always better to give bad news in person. Gore had settled on Boies as the person to argue his final cause before the U.S. Supreme Court.

Gore made the call that Boies should do it. Klain had argued adamantly for Tribe, and had reminded everyone of Boies's last and only other outing at the U.S. Supreme Court. In that case, argued in 1987, Boies lost badly to none other than Laurence Tribe. The justices had rendered a 9–0 decision against Boies's client, Texaco. (Tribe had represented Texaco's competitor, Pennzoil.) Strangely enough, the broad issues in the *Pennzoil v. Texaco* case were similar to the case at hand: whether the federal courts could interfere with state proceedings.

In 1987, Boies was not known as the staunch protector of democratic principles who emerged from the Florida trenches. He was, in the words of the headline that appeared under his portrait on the cover of the *New York Times Magazine*, "The Wall Street Lawyer Everyone Wants." By the time Boies reached the Supreme Court, he had convinced a federal trial court judge in White Plains, New York, that the $12 billion bond that Texaco was required to post under Texas law to seek an appeal, an amount equal to the jury's staggering verdict, violated Texaco's due process rights under the Fourteenth Amendment. The federal appeals court in New York upheld the victory for Texaco.

There is evidence to suggest that Boies was poised to win once again for Texaco at the Supreme Court, up until the time of his argument. The papers of Justice Thurgood Marshall, which became public after his death, show that four justices, including Marshall, were inclined to affirm for Texaco when they agreed to take the case in June 1986. Marshall's bench memo, written days before the argument, said he was ready to rule for Texaco, albeit while holding his nose. He wrote, "This is the fallout of a fight between the new kind of robber barons: the faceless corporate management who gobble up one another's enterprises and when hurt go crying to Mommy, or the nearest high-priced litigator." That would be Boies and Tribe.

Marshall had little pity for Texaco. He called the company's flight to the federal court in White Plains, near the company's corporate headquarters, "the crassest kind of forum shopping." Marshall ridiculed Texaco's argument and the lower court rulings as saying, "How can you let a big, rich, important American corporation be wiped out by one little so-and-so of a Texas state trial court judge?" But Marshall was concerned about the impact a reversal would have on more deserving litigants. The most recent case on the issue involved the NAACP, which got relief from a $1 million bond requirement, but only after it had exhausted its appeals in Mississippi. Legally, Texaco's arguments were very close to the NAACP case, though factually they were very different, and Marshall decided to swallow hard and affirm—but changed his mind after the arguments.

Marshall penned his own opinion, and joined in another opinion written by Justice Stevens. Stevens's concurrence appears last in the decision, and he therefore has the last line, which reads, "our duty to deal with the rich and poor does not admit of a special exemption for multibillion-dollar corporations or transactions." It was not just that Tribe won, but the manner in which he won, that showed how intricate arguments before the U.S. Supreme Court had become by the 1980s. Tribe won 9–0, but the justices wrote six separate opinions.

If Boies gave a moment's thought to his defeat in the Pennzoil case as he boarded a plane in Westchester midmorning on December 10, he did not show it. He had spent the morning doing the rounds of the morning talk shows in appearances telecast from the library of his Armonk home. Even now, at the eleventh hour, Boies shouldered every role for Gore, facing off against Baker on the TV shows as the clock ticked toward the arguments before the justices. The Republicans would later say they were thrilled at the sight of Boies parrying with Tim Russert on NBC's *Meet the Press*—it meant he had that much less time to prepare for his appearance at the Supreme Court. Russert played a videotape from the Gore press conference following the Court's stay of the recount, in which Klain and Boies reported that Gore had picked up fifty-eight votes so far, indicating that Gore was headed toward winning Florida. Did that violate an order from Judge Lewis against reporting on the recounts while they were still in progress? Russert ended the session by asking about the disciplinary complaints pending against Boies in Florida, based on the so-called false affidavit of Michael Lavalle. "So you're confident that the Florida bar will take no action?" Russert asked. "I'm very confident of that," Boies smiled, signing off.

Boies boarded the plane with the fax of the latest draft of the Gore team's Supreme Court brief in hand. The briefs were due at four p.m. Boies placed a quick call to Tommy Goldstein, one of the lawyers working on the brief. Boies knew him because the young lawyer, who aspired to be a Supreme Court specialist, had worked for a short time at the D.C. office of Boies's law firm. Goldstein was helping Tribe when the word came down that Boies would be replacing him. Another lawyer working on the brief, Peter Rubin, was livid about this change in course. Rubin, a former assistant to Tribe, thought the slight was particularly painful because the press had already reported that Tribe would be representing Gore for the final argument. After Goldstein heard the news about the replacement, he called Boies at home in Armonk, suggesting that he call Tribe to make things easier. Boies was quite gracious on the phone to Tribe, telling him that he thought Tribe was the better person to make the argument. But now, on the plane, all of that was ancient history. Boies wanted to make some suggestions to Goldstein over the cell phone, before the plane took off, but they got cut off; Boies was still intent on separating the Miami-Dade recount from the statewide remedy that the Florida Supreme Court had ordered.

Boies arrived at the Watergate at around noon, where the marathon process of getting the brief out by the deadline was in full force. Once the brief was filed, Tribe and Goldstein prepped Boies with questions. Boies wanted to see the five or six leading Supreme Court precedents that he would have to worry about. The team had already printed those out for him, and he read them. After an hour or two, Tribe left the Watergate, boarding a plane for Florida, where he had a condominium. Goldstein stayed on, and Walter Dellinger joined them. Dellinger, himself a Supreme Court specialist, had advocated Boies over Tribe in counseling Gore on what to do. Boies trusted Dellinger, and listened to him on the equal protection theories and how he might persuade Justice Sandra Day O'Connor, the member of the Court the Gore team believed it needed to win over to turn the case around.

Mary Boies arrived, and they all ordered dinner from the Watergate. Aware of Boies's taste for plain meat, Goldstein ordered hamburgers, but Boies refused to eat, continually munching from the two boxes of sourdough pretzels he had brought with him. Boies and Dellinger went over the case until about ten o'clock, when Boies left for the Mayflower Hotel to turn in. At that point, he had prepared for the case for about five hours.

The next morning, the camera crew from *60 Minutes* trailed Boies, his wife, and his twin sons, Christopher and Jonathan, as they left the Mayflower and headed for the Supreme Court. At the Gore counsel table that morning, Boies was flanked by Goldstein, whom he had requested as his second chair, and Teresa Roseborough, who had argued Gore's case at the Eleventh Circuit, which, just hours before the Scalia-led majority of the Supreme Court ruled for a stay of the recount, had rejected the Bush team's federal claims. Boies had asked that Dellinger sit as his third chair at the arguments, and Goldstein had already offered Dellinger this post when he discovered that the spot was already taken by Roseborough—in miniature, another sign of the loose way in which the Democrats had proceeded throughout the fight. At the opposing counsel's table sat Theodore Olson. In the spirit of military efficiency with which the Republicans had approached the fight, Olson had delivered every federal court argument in the case. Olson, like Tribe and Dellinger, was one of a handful of constitutional lawyers who practiced the minuet dance that was about to begin. Goldstein chatted with the reporters in the press gallery, and they all had one question: What kind of shoes was Boies wearing? Goldstein confirmed for them that Boies was, in fact, wearing his standard black Reebok sneakers.

In the moments before the arguments began, Boies seemed not worried at all. He shook hands and greeted the lawyers on the opposing sides, the many dignitaries who had come for this historic occasion. The legal teams had started the day in the lawyers' lounge, for the traditional briefing that Supreme Court advocates receive before entering the red velvet–draped chamber. Then for the historical record, each advocate signed what is known as the day's call sheet. Boies handed his case files to Goldstein and told him that if, during the argument, Boies referred to a case, Goldstein should pull it out of the folder and lay it on the counsel table. Olson, as counsel for the appellant, went first. At one point during Olson's argument, Boies turned to Goldstein and asked whether a certain Florida state court case was in the files that they had brought to court. It wasn't. But Goldstein, versed in the smallest of details of Supreme Court procedure, knew that the Court's personnel were available to retrieve materials from the library during an argument. Goldstein wrote Boies a note, asking him if he knew the citation, and Boies closed his eyes and wrote the citation from the *Southern Reporter* from memory. "He looked into his mind and remembered it," recalled Goldstein in awe. The marshal's office brought the book, and sure enough, the case was there.

During Olson's argument, the dissenters to the stay decision pressed him about whether it would, in fact, be feasible to establish a uniform standard for the counting of ballots and send the case back to Florida to complete the recount without violating the equal protection clause. Olson did his best to dodge these questions. When Justice Stephen Breyer finally said, "I would still like to get your view as to what would be the fair standard," Olson hesitated. "I don't—I haven't crafted it entirely out. This is a job for a legislature." Pressed again, Olson said that at a minimum there should be a penetration of the ballot "because indentations are no standards at all." These were the dimpled chads that Gore was counting on to win Florida. Counting the dimples, he said, would be a "complete change" in Florida election law that would violate Article II of the Constitution. Olson was taking some ribbing about the duplicity of his argument from Justices Ruth Bader Ginsburg and David Souter—the intent of the voter standard was so vague and subjective that it violated equal protection, and anything more specific would violate Article II—when Justice Scalia stepped in to rescue him. Scalia reminded Olson that part of Bush's argument was that the undervotes were caused by voters who could not complete the simple act of punching through a chad. "The voters are instructed to detach the chads entirely, and the machine, as predicted, does not count those chads where those instructions are not followed, there isn't any wrong," Scalia pronounced. Olson could not have agreed more.

Boies was well into his allotted time when the inevitable question on standards came. Justice Anthony Kennedy demanded to know whether there should be a "uniform standard" for the counting of ballots, and Boies fell back on the line that the campaign had stuck to, citing the intent of the voter standard for Kennedy. Boies allowed that the application of the standard could vary from county to county, from individual to individual, even from counting table to counting table. Boies tried to cast the interpretation of intent as commonplace in the law, but Kennedy cut him off. "But here you have something objective," Kennedy said. "You are not just reading a person's mind. You are looking at a *piece of paper* and the Supreme Courts in the state of South Dakota and other states have told us that you will count those hanging by two corners or one corner, this is susceptible of a uniform standard, and yet you say it can vary from table to table within the same county." Boies countered that even the Texas statute, which listed more specific standards for ballot counting, had a catchall provision on the intent of the voter. This seemed like little more than a subtle dig at Bush's origins.

Then, Justice Souter came forward with some gentle questions. What was bothering Justice Kennedy, Souter said, and what was "bothering a lot of us here," was this: Why shouldn't there be a consistent, objective rule to determine that a hanging chad or a dimple on a ballot counted as a vote? "Why shouldn't there be one objective rule for all the counties, and if there isn't, why isn't it an equal protection violation?" Souter asked. Boies kept resisting. Interpretations of intent could vary "from jury to jury, from public official to public official," he said. The "jury to jury" analogy obviously glossed over the fact that ballot counters were confronted with an objective thing. "All we have are certain physical characteristics," Souter pointed out. Boies finally admitted that if, for instance, one county had counted indented ballots while another counted only the ballots with chads punched through, that might raise an equal protection problem.

"All right, we are going to assume we do have that," Souter told Boies.

"On that assumption, what would you tell them to do about it?" Here it was. Souter seemed to be building a back channel in the argument that would, if Boies could muster a satisfactory response, perhaps, deliver O'Connor or Kennedy from their place in the majority. There was a silence in the chamber, a yawning silence that lasted no more than a few seconds but seemed much longer. Finally, Boies offered only: "Well, I think that's a very hard question." Souter's lifeline slipped away in an instant. Taking advantage of Boies's fumble, Justice Scalia interjected with a snarky, "You would tell them to count every vote!" The courtroom erupted in laughter, and Scalia savored the moment. "You would tell them to count every vote, Mr. Boies, wouldn't you?" Boies agreed that, yes, "I would tell them to count every vote."

Justice Stevens had a question, but Boies cut Stevens off and used some precious remaining minutes to refer to the Texas statute again. If the justices were looking for some specifics in the standard, he said, the Texas statute gave them "a pretty good standard." Stevens, the oldest and most liberal of the justices on the Court, reminded Boies that uniformity could be achieved because one judge would ultimately review the counting under way in Florida. "That's what I was going to say, your honor," Boies responded. But Boies was not in the courtroom to deliver Justice Stevens for Gore. He needed an answer that would satisfy Souter, who was in turn trying to convert either Kennedy or O'Connor. (Souter suggested a possible remedy for the equal protection problems in the opinion he filed in the case: he would have remanded the case to the Florida Supreme Court with instructions to establish uniform standards for the treatment of physical characteristics such as hanging and dimpled chads.)

But Boies was intent on suggesting that the justices could cut back on the statewide remedy Gore had not asked for if they found problems with statewide recounts. Chief Justice Rehnquist nailed Boies on this point, reminding him that the Florida Supreme Court "thought that to do just what he [Gore] wanted would be unfair" and had ordered the broad count "out of fairness." Boies had to agree. "I think that's right. I think that's the way I would interpret it, Mr. Chief Justice."

In the last moments of the argument, Justice Souter returned to the solution suggested by Stevens. If a Florida judge, as Stevens had suggested, ultimately put his stamp of approval on the counting under the intent of the voter standard, would that be good enough, even if there were *different* standards? Boies had no more time left, but Rehnquist gave him another two minutes. Boies came up with another theory to deflect the equal protection concerns: the differing standards applied by the counters would have a lot less effect on the vote than the different voting machines used from county to county. Five times as many undervotes occurred in counties that used punch-card systems as opposed to optical ballot systems. It was a fair point, but, even then, it seemed not enough to persuade Justice Kennedy or Justice O'Connor to change their minds. Boies's time was up.

In the moments after the arguments ended, Neal Katyal, a Georgetown law school professor who was one of the many lawyers called to work on the Gore briefs, sighed as he got up from his seat on the couch in the marshal's office, where a few of us could hear but not see the arguments. Katyal shook his head in disappointment, and said, to no one in particular, "He let them down."

I did not speak with Boies until the next morning, when the *Wall Street Journal* ran a page-one story under the headline "For Some Justices, the Bush-Gore Case Has a Personal Angle." The *Journal* story detailed family attachments and personal reasons that might effect a decision from the Court. The article's biggest scoop concerned Justice O'Connor; three witnesses at an election-night party had heard O'Connor's husband say that his wife wanted to step down, but she would be reluctant to do so if a Democrat were in the White House to choose her replacement. "That's what you really need to look at," Boies told me. If O'Connor could rule for Bush in a way that would not embarrass her, Boies figured she would do it. "One of the things that I think is clear to the justices is that they have no principled ground on which to stand," he said. Boies saw part of his role at the argument as demonstrating that fact to them.

Boies and his wife had lunch with the vice president and his family on the afternoon of the arguments, where, surreally, Boies listened to the delayed audiotape of the proceedings as he finally got the chance to meet with his client since he had been hired by the campaign. Mrs. Gore gave Mary Boies a Christmas tree ornament as a momento. That night, Boies had dinner at his favorite spot in town, The Prime Rib. By the next morning, he was ready to go home, but this proved problematic. The airport could not accommodate a departure on the Lear, so Boies opted to take the Amtrak Metroliner to New York. It was difficult for Boies to remain at rest.

It was nightfall by the time Boies, Mary, and I arrived in New York.

Boies's son Jonathan was there to greet us. By then, the speculation about what the Supreme Court would do with the case had reached a fever pitch. "What do you think they're doing?" Boies asked Ron Klain as we were on our way in a car toward dinner. Boies and Klain laughed about the fact that twenty-five states—a huge number—had not gotten their electoral votes filed by December 12, the deadline that had seemed such a life-or-death matter in Florida.

We ate at Chin Chin, a posh Chinese restaurant in midtown and one of the few places where Boies varied his beef-and-potatoes diet, ordering mai tais, salt-and-pepper shrimp, and spare ribs. He was every bit the trial lawyer at dinner. Justice Scalia had taken up valuable minutes during the argument by professing a genuine confusion over the protest and contest phases of Florida's election law. The Gore team speculated that his questions were designed to disrupt the argument. But Boies crowed that Scalia just didn't want to take Boies on because he knew that he would "clobber" him. Mostly, Boies looked back on the extraordinary efforts of his Tallahassee team. He knew that every one of them had worked through many nights, slaving away on the briefs, never letting up for a moment. "I have gotten more sleep, I think, than any lawyer down there," he said. Like any general, he appreciated the efforts of the foot soldiers working the fields.

Mary told a story about her conversation with Norman Brokaw, the chairman of the William Morris talent agency. Brokaw had called and put Bill Cosby on the line, insisting that Boies could become a brand, of sorts. The next month, with Brokaw as his agent, Boies signed a book contract with Talk/Miramax Books to write his memoirs, a contract that made him a frequent guest at Tina Brown's soirees at her Sutton Place apartment. Brokaw, who happened to be a client of Boies's, had a leg up on the other literary agents chasing Boies. Esther Newberg, the legendary literary agent, had faxed Boies at the Governors Inn in Tallahassee on the night of the final Florida Supreme Court decision, encouraging him to write the story of his life.

When dinner was over, Boies and his family piled into a Lincoln Town Car and headed toward Armonk. The justices finally released their decision after ten o'clock that night. By then, Boies had arrived home, to be greeted by a group of television satellite trucks parked at the gate. Mary printed out the pages of the lengthy ruling from her computer, six opinions in all, and the Gore team tried to figure out what it all meant. The reporters on television were having just as difficult a time. At first, there seemed to be some hope for Gore; the majority opinion ended with a note that the case should "be remanded for proceedings not inconsistent with this opinion." On ABC News, Dan Abrams, the legal affairs correspondent and son of Floyd Abrams, the highly respected First Amendment lawyer, found a passage that sounded deadly: "Seven Justices of the Court agree that there are constitutional problems with the recount ordered by the Florida Supreme Court that demand a remedy," Abrams read from the opinion. "The only disagreement is as to the remedy."

And so, absurd as it seemed, this was the ruling in *Bush v. Gore:* a five-member majority of the Court led by Rehnquist—a Court that for years had supported "states' rights"—concluded that there were equal protection problems with the recount in Florida and that they had to step in to stop the problems created by a state court's rulings. The crucial line, the line that would establish Boies's belief that the justices could not arrive at a "principled" ruling, would only be focused on later. The most damning sentence in the opinion, it all but suggested that five justices were throwing the election for George W. Bush: "Our consideration is limited to the present circumstances, for the problem of equal protection in election processes generally presents many complexities." In other words, this decision set no precedent, no guiding principle on matters of equal protection in future elections. It was equal protection for Bush, and Bush alone.

After the decision, there were a couple of conference calls among the members of the Gore team, and the team refused to give up until one final conference call the next morning, when Gore finally decided to concede. Overnight, the Gore legal team in Tallahassee drafted one last brief, a remand brief, in the faintest hope that the Supreme Court majority meant anything other than what it had said. This brief told the Florida Supreme Court to "direct the counting of all ballots which contain a discernible indentation or other mark, at or near the ballot position for the candidate." The Gore team finally and clearly said every dimple should count, in the one legal document that they did not file with a court.

Boies paid little attention to this frantic scurrying. He realized it was over as soon as he took a quick look at the decision. After the final conference call, Boies didn't miss a beat and went back to business as usual, toward meetings in Albany on his ongoing cases. "I mean, they did what they did," Boies told me as we boarded one last plane on the morning of

December 13 and headed from Westchester to Albany. Time had simply run out on Gore, from Boies's perspective.

The most important thing to Boies about the final and fatal ruling was the 5–4 outcome. I discovered this the hard way when I asked a question about the majority, per curiam opinion. The four dissenters wrote separate opinions, each with their own reasons why the majority had the law wrong. Still, Justices Souter and Breyer, two members of the Court's solidly liberal block, agreed that there were equal protection problems with the lack of standards in the Florida recounts.

"Were you surprised by the fact that Breyer and Souter signed on to the per curiam opinion insofar as it dealt with standards?" I asked.

"*No*, they did *not* sign on to the per curium opinion!" he snapped. Boies was, of course, technically correct. And quite annoyed. "But they say there are equal protection problems—" I stammered. Boies cut me off. "Yeah, they say there are equal protection problems to be addressed but they do NOT sign on to the majority opinion!" I felt I had to justify myself, and began to repeat the sentence from the text: "I don't know who wrote this sentence," I said, repeating the line from the text, which read, "Seven justices agree that—" He cut me off again. "I mean they can write whatever they want!" he said with a tight laugh. "It isn't true. You can count them up!"

In the months that I had spent tracking Boies, he had never been rattled, had never projected anything but a casual coolness. But for a fleeting moment, a flash of anger passed over the face of the inscrutable Boies. My question had jarred a nerve, because the 5–4 outcome was all that mattered to Boies. The fact that two justices in the liberal block had found credence in the Republicans' equal protection claims—and therefore had not been persuaded by Boies's arguments to the contrary—was a matter he did not wish to discuss.

The moment passed.

And how would this decision from the Court be remembered? Boies, on this morning, was not in a talkative mood. "Not kindly," Boies simply said, icily.

Boies spent most of 2001 in a state of reflected glory. In the wake of the Supreme Court ruling in *Bush v. Gore*, he became a popular figure on the lecture circuit, and he was often asked if he would have done anything differently, especially in his argument at the high court. Boies's answer was always the same: he couldn't think of anything. "I think the only thing that would have made a difference is something that would have changed the minds of those five justices in the United States Supreme Court majority, and I haven't been able to think of what that is," Boies told a group of lawyers and law students gathered at the Cardozo School of Law in April 2001 for a conference organized by Paul Verkuil.

The places where Boies spoke—the law schools at NYU, Yale, and Berkeley—were all bastions of liberalism, and he was greeted with adoration. (One of his corporate clients—Sheldon Solow, a Manhattan real estate mogul who had dropped out of NYU as an undergraduate and now served on its board of trustees—even came to, quite literally, bow down to him, and present him with a napkin at his luncheon table, when Boies gave a speech to the alumni of New York University Law School in late January 2001. At NYU, Boies took pains not to criticize the five justices in the majority in *Bush v. Gore.* "We all believe in the rule of law, and one of the things that we said from the beginning is that once the United States Supreme Court made a decision, we would accept that decision and abide by it. We did that, and I think we did it without rancor, and I think we did it in a way that was respectful of the institution and of the justice system of the United States," Boies told the assembled crowd. Still, the room erupted in laughter when Boies said he thought the Court had "made a mistake." In talking about the decision, at NYU and elsewhere, Boies often invoked the names of the most infamous cases in the Court's history; the *Dred Scott* decision, upholding slavery, and *Plessy v. Ferguson,* the decision adopting the "separate but equal" doctrine.

Dred Scott? Plessy v. Ferguson? These cases had precipitated the Civil War and the civil rights movement. It was hard to find inspiration for such a fundamental revolution in *Bush v. Gore.* In the wake of the case, the future of the punch-card ballot seemed bleak, and there was talk of election reform. But long before the terrorist attacks rendered chads irrelevant, the idea that the justices in the majority could never again be seen in the same light seemed to fade. As Laurence Tribe explained it to me, "The decision is likely to be encased in a coffin of unreason. The coffin will open a crack, as it were, whenever there's a Supreme Court vacancy." As of this writing, Justice Stevens was still hanging in there. It was Stevens, the most eloquent of all the dissenters in *Bush v. Gore,* who wrote that we will never know "with complete certainty" the true winner of the election, but that the identity of the loser was perfectly clear; it was, as he said, "the Nation's confidence in the judge as the impartial guardian of the rule of law."

It was so easy, so very easy, in the days and weeks following the majority's decision in *Bush v. Gore*, to find fault with it. The halo remained above Boies's head. *Time* magazine stopped short of naming Boies its man of the year, once the Supreme Court made its ruling, but it came close. "He had been involved in three of the most interesting cases of the year—Microsoft, Napster, and the election cases," said Walter Isaacson, then editor-in-chief of *Time*. "He was sort of a symbol of the lawyering of America." That line would appear in the magazine, as part of the runner-up profile of Boies. "When he lost at the Supreme Court, it would have been kind of perverse to have made him person of the year," Isaacson told me. Of the ultimate outcome at the Supreme Court, *Time* said, "No lawyer in memory has ever won so much by losing."

In the wake of the election wars, *60 Minutes* devoted a segment to a glowing profile of Boies that ran in late February 2001. Several weeks later, there was a gala sixtieth birthday party for Boies in the Rainbow Room, atop Rockefeller Center. Among the guests were *Time* magazine's Isaacson, Steve Kroft, the *60 Minutes* correspondent who reported the Boies segment, Dan Rather, the anchor of *CBS Evening News*, and Tom Brokaw, anchor of *NBC Evening News*. (Guests joked that Peter Jennings of ABC must have been out of town.)

As the toasts began, Mike Wallace took a seat next to a large screen. Wallace believed that Boies had saved his life in the Westmoreland case, and he told the assembled guests this as he introduced the video that would become the talk of the party. It was a mock documentary, a spoof of a *60 Minutes* segment that purported to reveal the result of an investigation of the Supreme Court's ultimate vote on the 2000 election. The conclusion: it was *Boies* who had been elected president. The tape included a mock interview with Gore, who woodenly, but gamely, called into question Boies's addiction to gambling and his habit of wearing sneakers to court.

Many in the audience winced when the video cut images of Boies wrapping his arms around a couple of young women in a Las Vegas casino with outtakes from his actual interview with *60 Minutes*, with Boies making references to "tedious work" that was "ultimately satisfying." The video concluded with the image of Al Gore looking directly into the camera at the conclusion of his mock interview with Mike Wallace, a huge smile on his face. "Happy Birthday, David!" he cheered. Trevor Nelson of CBS was among the attendees at the birthday bash. Nelson produced the mock documentary; he also produced the 60 *Minutes* segment on Boies. Nobody, apparently, questioned the fact that Nelson had worked on both the segment that was broadcast and the roast of Boies by his good friend and client Wallace.

"Did you see the video?" Boies asked me, as I passed him briefly toward the end of the party. We had also viewed a montage of Boies en famille, set to Louis Armstrong singing "It's a Wonderful World," at the party, but I knew that he was referring not to that but to the Al Gore moment. Big Media ate him up, and Boies enjoyed the adoration. They ran in the same crowd. He and Mary were, after all, frequent players in the Sunday-afternoon softball game that Steve Brill held at his home, where the players often included people like Isaacson and Paula Zahn.

Sainted in defeat, Boies seemed to embrace the notion that there was honor in losing the "right" case. He spoke of it on a perfect day in May 2001, drenched in sun without a cloud in the San Francisco sky, as he addressed the new graduates of Boalt Hall, the law school at the University of California at Berkeley. The students sat on a stage in the Greek theater behind him, and Boies took the microphone off the podium, turned his back to the parents and the others in the amphitheater, and addressed the students directly. "Babe Ruth said you can't hit a home run unless you're prepared to strike out," Boies told them. "I would tell you that the best case is the case that you're on the right side of and you can win. The second-best case is the case that you're on the right side of, even if you lose." It was a strange turn of events for the man who, at the age of forty-five, had landed on the cover of the *New York Times Magazine,* hailed as the litigator all of Wall Street wanted, the man who had never lost a case (though, in the article, he admitted to having lost some motions).

Boies was now addressing a new generation, and, as his friend George Vradenburg liked to say, every new generation rediscovers David Boies. "You know, they discovered him in the IBM case," Vradenburg told me. "And they discovered him in the Westmoreland case. And now, it's sort of 'Who is this David Boies?' Well, David Boies has been around a long time, and he's made his mark in some rather extraordinary litigation. And if I retain him twelve years from now, at age seventy-two, he will come up with some fascinating new case and people will say, 'Now isn't this interesting. Who is this guy David Boies?' "

EIGHTEEN

The Jule Dice

At the end of my miracle year with Boies, I attended his law firm's annual retreat in December 2001, this time at Disney's Yacht & Beach Club, Disney's version of Cape Cod. Boies arrived at Disney World fresh from a whirlwind of ceremonies in his honor. The first was an award from the Lab School of Washington, a learning center for children with disabilities such as dyslexia. Ted Olson, his opponent at the Supreme Court, who became Bush's solicitor general, presented Boies with the award. "He is the best," Olson began, but was cut off by a round of applause. The ceremonies and awards were topped off at the Beverly Wilshire Hotel on Rodeo Drive, where Boies had once been feted by IBM after his win in the CalComp case, when the chief executive of IBM gave Boies General Patton's helmet. Now, in December 2001, Boies was being honored there by the Beverly Hills Bar Association. The event was hosted by his former client Garry Shandling.

Boies was introduced by Warren Beatty, and his fellow nominee was none other than Dick Wolfe, the creator of the TV series *Law and Order*. Boies and Beatty spent a long time after the ceremony in the Beverly Wilshire's cocktail lounge, hashing over the election yet again. It was official: David Boies had gone Hollywood. Then it was on to Orlando.

"Thank you all for what was, in the words of our hotel, a major year," Boies announced at the firm's breakfast meeting, where he selected a heaping plate of bacon. "On the other hand, we don't want to be one thousand lawyers, or even five hundred." The firm's rapid growth inevitably meant that it had become a more conventional place to work. Boies had yielded to some administrative structure. The firm distributed a blue binder to the partners that year laying out just exactly what all of the partners, excluding those whose names were on the firm, had billed out during the past twelve months, an accounting that drew embarrassment about the hours logged by some partners, and sheer disbelief about the hours logged by others. The accounting was part of the firm's bottom-line "formula compensation" system. Some partners dropped their jaws when they saw that Robert Silver had racked up more than four thousand hours that year. It was an astounding number, even more astounding considering that Silver suffered from numerous health problems that kept him working at home. One partner huffed that he expected Silver's prolific work to land in the *American Lawyer* or the *Wall Street Journal*.

Silver had managed to carve out a practice for himself, bringing in Echostar, the Denver-based satellite TV broadcaster, as a client to represent it in a lawsuit against its primary competitor, DirecTV. When Echostar changed course and made its controversial move to buy DirecTV, the antitrust work generated more than $5 million in billings for the firm. The retainer agreement between Echostar and Boies Schiller was an eye-popping document. It provided that the Boies Schiller lawyers would be paid 150 percent of their standard fees. The demand reflected the firm's philosophy that clients should pay a premium for access to David Boies. The contract spelled out that Boies himself would "be personally involved in providing direction and strategy," take the key depositions, and be the lead attorney at the trial. Silver wanted to press for even more of a premium—stock options in Echostar—as part of the retainer, but Boies rejected that. "David believes one shouldn't ask for *too* much, even if one can get it. I don't believe that at all," Silver told me, shortly after he had landed the client.

For the annual retreat, Silver had prepared an elaborate PowerPoint presentation on the antitrust issues. Most of what Silver said was so heady and complex that it flew over the heads of the lawyers in attendance. He didn't quite realize this, which was part of his wonky nature. "I met [Echostar] at a Patent Bar Meeting at the Waldorf. Ever been to one of those things?" Silver told the crowd, and they woke up and laughed. The Echostar case was Silver's show. Still, he paid homage to Boies, mentioning Charlie Ergen, Echostar's famously penny-pinching chief executive, a man worth $5 billion. "Ergen, he's a great admirer of David Boies, including the way he dresses."

Most of the lawyers at the firm were laborers in a plantation, working on corporate cases generated mainly by two lawyers: Boies and Flexner. Flexner's cases could be particularly drab. He represented the telephone company SBC in several cases, including a case alleging antitrust violations in the pay phone market that was pending in Oklahoma. Flexner's group had also made a successful pitch to DuPont, which has a singularly rigid selection process for choosing its legal counsel, to designate Boies Schiller as one of its forty primary law firms.

There were still oddities stemming from the fact that the firm revolved around David Boies. When Boies's son Christopher explained the work of the firm's corporate department at the December 2001 retreat, he admitted, "It's been a little lumpy this year." That the firm, essentially a litigation boutique, even *had* a corporate department for mergers and deals, which required armies of lawyers at firms like Cravath, was odd. The primary client of Christopher's four-lawyer group, which included his brother Jonathan, was an energy company called Caithness. The representation had sprung out of David Boies's pre-existing relationship as an attorney for Florida Power & Light and his close relationship with its general counsel, Edward Tancer. It was hard to see where the corporate practice could go; corporate work inevitably required the resources of a firm like Cravath. But the corporate department, such as it was, allowed Boies to work with his son, to have his "nice family practice."

By then, Boies's loose management style had also caused a mini crisis that threatened to put a chink in the halo. The firm was always putting fires out, but this particular crisis was bound to catch the attention of the news media: two disgruntled former employees were claiming that Boies discriminated against women.

Two female associates who had attended the Disney World retreat in

2000 were not in attendance the following year. They were Rachel Baird and Bonnie Porter. It didn't surprise me that Baird had left. During the Napster case, I remembered that Baird had been stuck with the administrative staff, appearing to be relegated to paralegal work, while a young Yale Law student, Brian Willen, worked alongside two other young associates, both of them men, researching legal questions for the briefs to the court. I did not know it at the time, but Baird herself was a 1992 Yale Law School graduate. At the 2000 retreat, she dared to ask a question of Boies, her voice shaking as she spoke. Baird left the firm in January 2001, at a time when three other female associates also quit. The situation made even some of the male associates within the firm uncomfortable. One school of thought held that neither Boies, Schiller, nor Flexner noticed who was actually doing the grunt work. The firm had no center of gravity—no office, no schmoozing, no face time required. It was simply a work machine. But the men were getting the better assignments. "Boies is a guy's guy," one associate told me.

Baird sued Boies, Schiller & Flexner in January 2002. Bonnie Porter, who also left the firm, joined her in the lawsuit. They claimed that the Armonk office of Boies Schiller maintained a discriminatory two-tiered system for hiring associates, placing all the male associates on the partnership track and relegating females to lower-paid positions.

"All the women were paid differently. The men were all paid the same," Porter told me. When Porter took the job at Boies Schiller, two men who had graduated the same year as she had, 1998, had base salaries of $145,000. The firm offered her the job at $114,000. At the time, there were two women making as little as $58,000 or $78,000 a year, according to the complaint filed in the lawsuit. "They would never have offered a male those salaries, never," Porter says.

At about ten o'clock the night before Porter's interview, Bob Silver called Porter to inform her that if the firm hired her, she would be on a non-partnership track position. Porter quizzed the firm's partners on whether this title would stigmatize her at the firm, and they assured her that it would make no difference in the quality of the assignments she received. Porter took the job; she wanted to move from the Manhattan law firm where she worked to one closer to her home in Westchester County.

Once there, Porter discovered that the Armonk office was not a social place. The lawyers were dispersed between two office buildings off the highway, miles apart from one another, and it was difficult to get to know the players in office politics. But after a while, she recognized there was widespread consternation among the women, especially about how the firm awarded the all-important bonuses at the end of each year.

Around the time that Porter left, she heard that Korologos, the Armonk office's "managing partner," along with Boies's son Christopher, were wondering why so many women were leaving the firm. Porter offered to meet with them to discuss it, and told them the two-tier system discriminated against women. Christopher told her that he had never really liked the system, which definitely looked bad, but that it made sense for the business. Korologos sat poker-faced. "He sat there silent, which is his specialty," Porter said. Before she left the firm, Porter had another meeting, in which she pressed the claims again, and also asked for an unpaid part of her bonus. Korologos called the meeting to an abrupt end, and Christopher phoned her moments later, accusing her of extortion.

When news of the suit broke, the headline was already written. The tabloids could not resist referring to the firm as "Boies' Club" or "the Boies Room." Boies Schiller had readied a thirty-six-page press release to counter the suit, claiming that Baird and Porter had demanded $1 million to make it go away. The dossier was filled with testimonials from other women lawyers at the firm, one of whom had started as a temporary receptionist. Schiller handled the press calls; David Boies was not available for comment.

Baird and Porter's legal complaint also tacked on personal claims for damages against Korologos, Silver, and Boies. The defense of these claims became a Boies family affair: Mary Boies was listed as counsel for Korologos and Silver. Boies chose to represent himself. The tactic allowed him to personally grill Rachel Baird at her deposition in April 2002, an all-day affair that was videotaped. Boies asked question after question to suggest that, despite Baird's Yale diploma, she did not have the skills to handle the complex litigation of the firm from her eight years of experience as a Connecticut prosecutor. In the legal jousting leading up to the deposition, Boies Schiller had described her work as "inconsistent and unreliable," and accused her of "inexcusably" failing to fill out time sheets in her last two months at the firm. Baird's lawyers had countered that she had not filled out time sheets because her last assignment was a pro bono matter for Amy Habie, "a woman who was rumored to be respondent Boies's girlfriend." During the deposition, Boies pressed Baird repeatedly about this last assignment, which she never completed, and Baird finally answered: "I was beaten down by that point. I was crushed. I just wanted it to end."

The lawsuit ended before the month was out. Acting as his own lawyer, Boies participated in the settlement negotiations, and did most of the talking for the defense team. Some on the plaintiffs' team believed that Boies had hijacked the settlement talks, and that the presiding judge, Denny Chin, took his side as he brokered a compromise between the parties. Boies Schiller agreed to pay $37,500 each to Baird and Porter. Mary Boies described it as a "nuisance settlement" in her interviews with the press. But the plaintiffs declared victory, because they claimed the firm had made changes, promoting several women to the partnership track.

Under the settlement, Hillary Richard, the lawyer for Baird and Porter, was entitled to seek an award of attorneys' fees. The fight over her request of more than $191,000 triggered the main courtroom battle of the short-lived lawsuit in June 2002. David Boies did not attend or argue the hearing, which Judge Chin selected as the case that he would invite law students to attend and discuss with them afterward. Mary Boies rose to make an additional argument on behalf of the defense, after the lead lawyer representing the firm had already made a full presentation. Judge Chin finally threw up his hands. "Enough! Enough! Enough! Enough!" he said, Afterward, Mary took the opportunity to chat with the law students in the gallery. "David loves women! He does," she told them. She cited one of the claims—Baird had complained that Boies had asked her to pay for cab fare. (On this, at least, Boies was an equal opportunity offender. He often seemed to forget to carry cash in his pocket.) There were tears in Mary Boies's eyes as she talked about the lawsuit.

Chin issued his fee opinion in September 2002. His ruling chopped Richard's fee request to $54,723, but his language was the most devastating aspect of the decision. "Plaintiffs' rights were not 'vindicated' in any meaningful way, and the public interest in civil rights enforcement was not significantly advanced," he wrote. Chin found that Baird and Porter accepted the settlement because "they had little hope of success on the merits." He also rejected out of hand the claim that the lawsuit had forced Boies Schiller to make changes on behalf of women. Boies Schiller sent a letter under David Boies's signature to its clients, among them Philip Morris, quoting from Chin's decision, and emphasizing the firm's commitment to equal opportunity.

Boies's firm may not yet be cleared of the sex discrimination claims: on August 7, 2003, the Equal Employment Opportunity Commission issued a determination that it had found "reasonable cause to believe" that Boies's firm had discriminated against female associates. That determination triggered the EEOC's "conciliation" process. The agency proposed remedies that would have required the firm to have its partners and managers undergo a training program in the federal laws prohibiting discrimination, and to codify its two-tiered attorney track and the pay and bonus structures for attorneys. It would have also required Boies's firm to pay back pay and compensatory damages of up to $300,000 to Baird, Porter, and other members of the class, and would have required the EEOC to monitor the firm's compliance for three years. In late August, just two weeks after the determination, the EEOC determined that effort to conciliate the charges had failed, and Spencer H. Lewis Jr., director of the New York district office, referred the case to its legal department for review. In a letter to the firm stamped November 3, 2003, the EEOC indicated that it had decided "not to pursue this litigation" and that "no further action will be taken by the EEOC with respect to these changes." The letter also indicated that Baird and Porter would receive notices of their right to sue—which was by then a moot point.

At the December 2001 annual retreat, the firm had set up an executive committee, and, more ominously, a committee to review the "formula compensation" system. The hard-toiling associates could not have been encouraged by the partnerships awarded that year: five of the seven lawyers elected partner were lateral moves by older lawyers, and two of those lawyers, Ann Galvani and Robert Dwyer, had been associates for Boies at Cravath.

Boies called Mary from the Saturday-evening holiday party at Disney World, marveling that there must have been three hundred people in the room. The person who brought them together, undeniably, was Boies.

I could not help remembering what his second wife, Judith, told me about why their marriage fell apart. Boies was not only a star in the sense that he was a rising associate at Cravath. "He was a star in another sense," she told me. "He had a great and overwhelming need and determination to be the center of his universe, and literally everything else had to fall into the center of his universe." That was the essential deal that everyone around him was required to make. I have a lasting image of Boies, seated in the lobby of the Disney World Yacht & Beach Club after the 2001 retreat. He and I were talking about his world-watched cases, but I was too focused on the past for his tastes. He didn't care to relive the Bush administration's recent settlement of the Microsoft case or the newspaper recounts of the election. Then it was time for Boies to go. A car was waiting to take him to Palm Beach, to attend a hearing on behalf of his longtime client Florida Power & Light.

As Boies was about to check out, he decided he would bring his son Jonathan to the FPL hearing. There was no question that Jonathan would go—no one denied Boies. But Jonathan's clothes had already been sent back to New York. He reminded his father that he didn't have a dress shirt appropriate for the hearing the next morning. Boies ordered Riccardo, his assistant, to dig a shirt out of his duffel bag for his son. Then Boies piled into a white car with Jonathan and Amy Habie, his erstwhile client, long-time friend, and part-time employee. They headed south.

He was a streak of blue, in his cheap suit, light on his feet and in a hurry. He didn't need to pause, to look around, to check what was in his bags, like the rest of us.

David Boies has become the most sought-after lawyer in America. In the time since I stopped trailing him—the time since his miracle year—he has been hired, always with great fanfare, in many high-profile cases. This is a testament to his reputation, but also further evidence of his almost unquenchable thirst to be at the center of things.

Corporate scandals dominated the headlines in 2002. As corporate boards scrambled to contain meltdowns amid allegations of widespread accounting fraud—self-dealing by corporate executives lining their pockets at the expense of shareholders—they turned to law firms to conduct what is known in the legal business as an "internal investigation." These inquiries are billed as an attempt to get to the root of the problem, assess blame, and in the process restore a company's credibility with its investors while showing good faith with the government regulators mulling charges. Companies usually turned to law firms known for their expertise in the securities laws. Boies's firm, essentially a litigation boutique, albeit the fastest growing one in the country, didn't have such an expertise, but he was hired by the board of directors at companies embroiled in two of the most notorious scandals—Adelphia and Tyco. In the wake of cable giant Adelphia Communications disclosure in March 2002 that it had guaranteed more than $2 billion in loans to members of the Rigas family, its founders, that were kept off the company's balance sheet—loans they used to purchase company stock, build a golf course, pay off family debts, and buy luxury condominiums—Adelphia's independent directors turned to Boies. Several months later, John Rigas, the seventy-eight-year-old founder of the company, and his two sons became the latest corporate executives to do the perp walk before television cameras. They were arrested at six o'clock in the morning at their Manhattan apartment, on charges that they had stolen more than a billion dollars from Adelphia and used the company as their "personal piggy bank."

More spectacular still was the collapse of Tyco International, one of the world's largest conglomerates—the product of thousands of acquisitions made in the 1990s by its chief executive, L. Dennis Kozlowski, one of the most high-flying and celebrated CEOs of the decade. In 2002, Tyco lost 65 percent of its value—$76 billion—as questions mounted about its accounting practices and investors lost confidence in management. Boies was hired by Tyco's independent directors in late April to conduct an internal investigation into self-dealing by management, as well as to pursue any litigation against the company's officers and directors based on their probe. The situation unraveled rapidly for Kozlowski, who was forced to resign on June 3, the day before he was indicted by the Manhattan district attorney's office on charges of evading $1 million in taxes on the purchase of six paintings, including a Monet and a Renoir.

The tax fraud charge was just the tip of the iceberg, and as prosecutors expanded their probe and Boies's firm continued its inquiry, evidence began to emerge to indicate that Kozlowski and his closest advisors had looted the company of tens of millions of dollars to finance a lavish lifestyle. Just one week after Kozlowski's indictment, Boies had a very public dust-up with Tyco's general counsel, Mark Belnick. Belnick had taken the top legal job at Tyco in 1998, after a long and distinguished career at the New York law firm of Paul, Weiss, Rifkind, Wharton & Garrison, where he had been the protégé of the great Arthur Liman, working with Liman at the U.S. Senate's Iran-Contra hearings, and in defending junk bond king Michael Milken. Belnick's fall from grace came as an enormous surprise to those in the legal community who knew him, including Boies. Belnick was dismissed after a clash with Boies, when Boies accused him of receiving $20 million in undisclosed compensation and refusing to cooperate with his internal investigation. Prosecutors later charged Belnick with, among other things, grand larceny for improperly receiving $17 million in cash and bonuses. Belnick was escorted from the company's Manhattan headquarters on West Fifty-seventh Street, but rather than remain silent—which anyone in that position would and should have done—Belnick fired back. His defense lawyer issued press releases portraying Belnick's firing as the result of a boardroom turf battle, with Boies taking the opportunity to "take control" of Tyco's legal business. The vignette was worthy of a tabloid, and the *New York Post* ran a "tale of the tape" the next day, pitting pictures of Boies and Belnick against each other. "Tyco's Top Dog: Boies Wins Legal Shootout, Ousts Belnick," ran the *Post's* headline. (In the summer of 2004, after a long trial, a jury acquitted Belnick of all charges.)

In mid-September of 2002, Boies and his firm issued a report that detailed a raft of undisclosed bonuses and secret loans issued to Kozlowski and his associates—without board approval and at the expense of investors. The Boies report, filed with the Securities and Exchange Commission, found $56 million in bonuses to fifty-one Tyco employees and $39 million more to pay the taxes on bonuses. More outlandish, at least in the details, were the extravagances that Kozlowski, perhaps the best-paid chief executive in America, charged to the company, which paid for his $16.8 million apartment on Fifth Avenue, $3 million in renovations, and $11 million in furnishings. The company also paid for a $7 million Park Avenue apartment for his ex-wife. Among other purchases were a $6,000 shower curtain, a $15,000 dog umbrella stand, a $17,100 traveling toilette box, and two sets of sheets for $5,960. The report also noted that the company spent more than $1 million for a birthday party in Sardinia for Kozlowski's wife. The Boies firm filed its report days after the indictment against Kozlowski was expanded to include charges that he had his chief financial officer, Mark Schwartz, engaged in a racketeering scheme to loot the company of $600 million. (Kozlowski and Schwartz's trial ended in a mistrial. At the time this book went to press, prosecutors were preparing to retry the case.)

Tyco remained a viable business, and new management was eager to restore investor confidence. It remained for Boies and his team to examine the accounting practices that Tyco employed in the years leading up to the disaster. At the end of December, Boies issued a thirty-three-page report of his findings, which was called "Phase 2" of the Boies firm's work. The report, which was filed with the SEC, touted the fact that about twenty-five lawyers and one hundred accountants were engaged in the Phase 2 investigation, spending more than fifteen thousand lawyer hours and about fifty thousand accountant hours on their review. The report that Boies issued could only cheer investors. It found a "pattern of aggressive accounting" that, even when in accordance with the prevailing standard, was "intended to increase reported earnings above what they would have been had more conservative accounting been employed." To correct errors, Tyco said it would take charges of $383.3 million for fiscal year 2002. Still, the Boies report noted, "Aggressive accounting is not necessarily improper accounting." It took pains to say that, in those instances of "questionable" accounting, there was no "credible evidence of intentional fraud." In the end, the Boies inquiry concluded: "There was no significant or systematic fraud affecting the Company's prior financial statements."

Serious questions about Boies's report arose in the following months, when Tyco announced new accounting problems totaling $1.6 billion. The company made a new filing with the SEC, alerting the agency that the Boies inquiry was "not an exhaustive review." The financial press reacted with fury: Tyco, in the days after Boies's bill of clean health, had floated a bond offering that was a huge success, growing to $4.5 billion from the $3.25 billion that had been announced initially. Edward Breen, Tyco's new chief executive, explained that the Boies report "clearly didn't look at everything." At the time, the report was rumored to have cost $40 million, and an editorial in the *Wall Street Journal* carped, "Maybe shareholders should ask Mr. Boies, or Mr. Breen, for a refund." (When Boies was called by prosecutors to testify at the trial of Kozlowski and Schwartz in March 2004, Boies said that his firm's legal fees amounted to $30 million by the end of 2002.)

When filed, the report had touted the extent of the effort, saying that "Few, if any, major companies have ever been subjected to the corporate governance and accounting review entailed in Phase 2." But the Boies report was also careful to hedge its bets, noting that the company had not sought to examine "every accounting decision," and pointing out that the top corporate officers were not available to them, as they were under indictment. Boies eventually told the *Wall Street Journal* that his probe was not an "archaeological expedition."

Boies's firm continues to represent Tyco in lawsuits against Kozlowski and other officers and directors. I saw the questions raised about the thoroughness of Boies's probe as further evidence that Boies, as a result of having built his firm so rapidly, sometimes fell short. In the Tyco case, Boies's firm edged out Wilmer, Cutler & Pickering, a Washington-based firm that is home to many ex-officials from the SEC, including Bill McLucas, who led the SEC's enforcement division for twenty years. Boies's firm did not have that depth of experience. Still, Boies could not pass up Tyco, or, for that matter, most cases in the spotlight. Boies's representation of Tyco spawned a new crop of Boies headlines, like the one that appeared in a profile of him in the Sunday edition of the *New York Times* in June 2002, under the headline "Company in Trouble? Just Let Him Loose."

Boies's hunger to be at the center of things inevitably meant that his attentions were constantly divided: his dizzying schedule, kept so religiously by Linda Carlsen and prized as a method of keeping track of him by his colleagues, was just one window into his method of practicing law. One of his former adversaries, in a case that Boies's firm lost miserably, noted, "He's kind of like a hummingbird, who settles down for a moment, and then disappears." Boies enjoys nothing so much as parachuting in at the eleventh hour, to prepare like a dynamo and then take the stage. During the Microsoft trial, when Boies's performance was receiving daily accolades in the press, one of his former Cravath partners commented to me, "David was up there, doing his usual high-wire act."

This takes unvarnished confidence, which Boies has in reserve. He is the most confident man I know. But Boies also demanded the sweat labor and extensive preparation of his legal team for the high-wire act to succeed. The Justice Department's solid case against Microsoft gave him that, and he had that kind of success at his own firm as well in the time that I spent trailing him. Boies's biggest client in the years 2000 and 2001 was Big Tobacco. Coverage of the Microsoft trial had left the impression that as a trial lawyer, David Boies wore a white hat. But a lot of the business that came pouring in as a result of the firm's raised profile were corporate cases very similar to the ones that Boies left behind at Cravath. Tobacco giant Philip Morris accounted for more than $6.8 million in billings—14 percent of Boies Schiller's $48 million revenue in the year 2000, and about $12 million—22 percent of its $54 million in fees billed—in the first three quarters of 2001.

Boies got the business in the way that he savors most: Philip Morris contacted him in mid-1999 after it had suffered a defeat—while represented by another law firm. By then, the three other leading tobacco companies had been successful in the early rounds of a lawsuit claiming that Philip Morris had abused its power as the industry's leader and violated the antitrust laws, by cutting deals with retailers that gave prominent display only to Philip Morris brands, exiling its competitors to the lower shelves.

The other cigarette companies had managed to get a preliminary injunction against Philip Morris, blocking the company from following through with its marketing plan.

Boies referred to the litigation with the same ironic detachment that he applied to all of his other cases. "My initial reaction was that the tobacco companies surely had enough litigation without suing each other, but that does not seem to have penetrated," Boies told the assembled staff at the firm's annual retreat in December 2000. Boies's partners handled most of the daily work in the case, but Philip Morris demanded that Boies appear for the crucial hearings. One of them occurred in May 2001, when the other tobacco companies were accusing Philip Morris of violating the terms of the preliminary injunction. Philip Morris was willing to move heaven and earth to get Boies to appear at the hearing in Greensboro, North Carolina—and it nearly took that, given that Boies was scheduled to travel to Stresa, Italy, for a conference that afternoon. In the end, Philip Morris arranged for a private jet. The arrangements were made, rather frantically by his partners, as Boies was headed to give a speech at the Yale Law School. Boies was on his cell phone, in the back of a Lincoln Town Car, quite at the center of a storm, as usual. When he got off the phone, he told me that he really didn't think his presence was necessary at the hearing, but he was happy to comply. "It's sort of the security blanket syndrome," he said, shrugging it off.

When Boies appeared at the hearing, the judge made it clear, by his comments from the bench, that he was going to rule against the other tobacco companies. When Boies rose to give his presentation for the defense, he reveled in a classic move: pulling out one of the pictures that the plaintiff tobacco companies had offered in evidence, a snapshot of shelving at a convenience store taken just days earlier. The plaintiffs had offered the photo to show that their brands were ostracized, but Boies pointed out to the judge that there was a package of Newports—the brand of competitor Lorillard—in the shot. "The person who was doing the photograph maybe didn't crop it in the way they intended," he remarked casually. The team of men in dark suits from the plaintiffs' table dropped their shoulders, and there was a collective snicker from the Philip Morris table. After a short recess, the judge announced that the plaintiff tobacco companies should file for a new injunction if they wanted relief. Boies had won.

Boies had landed his "Gotcha" punch with the photograph—and

delighted in it after the hearing. "Can you believe that photograph??" he asked, a deliciously devilish grin on his face. Nothing pleased Boies more than to turn the other side's exhibits against them. The pyrotechnics of the courtroom were irresistible to him. "Never give me anything!" he announced. "It's dangerous!" With that, he was off to Italy with Mary, who was looking on, beaming. "We regard plane rides as dates," Mary told me as they got into the car.

The Boies firm, by the end of 2001, had turned the Philip Morris case around. Boies presided over a three-day evidentiary hearing in October, and at its end, he argued on Philip Morris's behalf: "Marlboro is one of the great success stories in marketing. And does that brand give Philip Morris an advantage in the marketplace? Yes, it does. Is that what competition is designed to do? Yes, it is. Is that one of the fruits, one of the incentives that our free society and our free economy gives companies to compete success-fully? Exactly. . . . The antitrust laws do not permit them to be used to hob-ble the successful competitor in order to prop up the competitor that has not done well." It was an argument that Microsoft could well have made. The Philip Morris case played to Boies's strength and experience with the antitrust laws—and his team, among them the brainy Bob Silver, hired the best experts. Boies and his firm won a summary judgment for Philip Morris in May, 2002, when the judge found no basis for antitrust claims in the Philip Morris marketing program.

Boies continued to represent Big Tobacco in other lawsuits—antitrust cases that tended not to make the headlines, but complicated cases that generated substantial legal work for his firm. That Big Tobacco was a light-ning rod for criticism, and an industry that wore a black hat in the public eye, simply did not register with Boies. It made sense, for he remained agnostic in most every battle. At the time of the Westmoreland trial, Boies had offered that he would have gladly represented the general, had he con-tacted him first. And he said that he would have taken up the defense of Microsoft had they chosen to hire him. It reminded me of the bloodless detachment he had displayed early in life, when in the essay for his applica-tion to transfer to Yale Law School in 1964, he wrote, "More than ever rules of law delimit and direct the actions of individuals, businesses, and even nations. Without passing a value judgment on this expansion of the rule of law, it seems sufficient to note that such expansion continues apace and that increasingly the role of the lawyer can not help but be filled with opportunities for personal and public service." He simply wanted to be at the center of the action—and chose Cravath because it was the best that the legal profession had to offer. And at Cravath, the IBM case was the center of the action.

But Boies had private causes, taken up for personal reasons. Chief among them was litigation involving Amy Habie, whom Boies began representing in 1992, while still a Cravath partner, at the request of his friend and greatest admirer, Jimmy Miller. "I don't think he would ever say no to me," Miller told me, with awe. Habie's divorce from her husband, José Habie, a Guatemalan textile tycoon, evolved into a fantastic legal odyssey after José kidnapped the couple's twin children and flew them to Guatemala on his private jet. After that, the Habies, who had run a business together, began to sue each other. As the lawsuits piled up, Cravath continued to offer pro bono representation to Amy. The case was a boon to Boies's Cravath associates, among them Philip Korologos, because the case gave them a chance to appear in court long before the Cravath system would allow. But the Habie litigation was never popular among Cravath's partners, as they watched about $4 million in pro bono legal fees get billed to the Habie cases. These cases included Amy's battle with Scott Lewis, the West Palm Beach gardener from whom she had purchased a landscaping business in 1996—a business in which Boies had invested $100,000.

Amy and Scott Lewis settled their dispute over the business in 1996—and have been fighting over the terms of that settlement ever since. Scott Lewis, a born-again Christian with a southern accent, conducts himself like a lawyer manqué and seems to revel in the notion that he is beating David Boies. Lewis has sent out press releases touting his victories against Boies, one of which read, "Lawyer Who Beat Microsoft No Match for Local Gardeners in Real David and Goliath Story." The dispute between Amy and Lewis continues: in the latest round, Lewis appeared, at least initially, to have piqued the interest of the Florida bar, where he has filed several charges against Boies over the years, accusing him of violating the ethical rules that apply to lawyers. Ironically enough, Boies found himself in potential trouble for having stayed away from the gardening mess. It came out that Boies had spent more than $400,000 to hire lawyers from *other* law firms to represent Amy—who by then had assumed the position of chief financial officer at Boies's firm—in the fracas with Lewis. A Florida judge who presided over one of the many hearings in which Amy was accused of being in contempt of the provisions of the 1996 gardening dispute settlement was alarmed at the amount of money Boies had fronted for her representation, and referred the matter to the Florida bar to investigate possible ethical violations. In December 2003, the Florida bar found probable cause to pursue a disciplinary violation against Boies, on the ground that he had advanced hundreds of thousands of dollars to a client who was not indigent. But a Florida judge dismissed the ethical charges against Boies in April 2004.

In my mind, the most troubling aspect of Boies's representation of Amy concerned the ultimate result of her custody dispute with José. The fight came to a head in September 2000, just as Boies was about to head to San Francisco for an argument in the Napster case. Boies stopped off in Florida, where José had been arrested, and where the final details of José and Amy's settlement would be worked out. José had agreed to travel to the United States as a test of his commitment to a final settlement, under which Amy was to be paid $1.5 million in a trust for her children and another $1.5 million in legal fees and expenses.

But José was flabbergasted to find himself arrested by FBI agents when his Learjet arrived at the Florida Executive Airport. Boies, at Amy's request, rushed to the courthouse from Dallas, where he was attending a meeting. José spent a night in the cell, visited by Boies and his own attorney, Barry Levine, a Washington, D.C., lawyer best known for representing John Hinckley, the man who attempted to assassinate President Reagan. By morning, José had agreed to settle the custody case and allow his wife joint custody of the twins. When I caught up with Boies about the Habie case after the Napster hearing in San Francisco, he sat back in his chair at the airport, munching on crusts of sourdough bread, and announced, "Well, we had him arrested." I responded, "You mean, like a sting operation?" Boies agreed, and Bob Silver interjected that José had even thanked Boies. "That's exactly the point of the sting!" Boies burst out. "Remember? In the movie?" None of us at the table could quite recall that scene in the Redford-Newman movie, but it was obviously still vivid in Boies's mind.

Months later, when I called Barry Levine for an interview, he had a nagging question for me: "Did David tell you that he was surprised that José was arrested? That's a real issue here. The settlement was supposed to decriminalize the process." It struck me that Levine, like others who had dealt with Boies, had questions about whether or not he could trust him. In any case, José's arrest finally brought the saga to a close. José was facing a maximum prison sentence of three years, but Amy made the decision that it would be best for her children if he were allowed to go free on probation and for them to share custody. Boies described it as "one of the most extraordinary things" he had witnessed in practicing law, "one of the sacrifices that only mothers make." In Levine's view, it was Amy who lost: the twins, then eleven years old, held her accountable for their father's arrest, and returned to Guatemala with him. Amy was to see the twins on vacations and holidays, according to the agreement. "José's not suffering, not in the slightest," Levine told me.

Boies spoke often, and quite eloquently, about how a lawyer's most valuable asset was his credibility—with a judge, the jury, and the public. But there were times when Boies seemed to be playing by his own set of rules. The Habie case was one of them. His representation of diamond heir Bruce Winston was another. Boies took the case in 1995, while still at Cravath, and it was among the cases that his partners frowned upon. Bruce and his brother Ronald had been at each other's throats for years in the courts fighting over the diamond dynasty that had been built by their legendary father, Harry. The case was settled in late 2000, when Ronald and an investment bank agreed to buy out Bruce for $54.1 million. The case seemed to be an outstanding success for Boies, but along the way he had negotiated a contract with one of the witnesses in the case that pushed the limits of legal ethics. The contract, with Kathleen Kerr, one of Ronald's former personal assistants, offered Kerr a $25,000 payment and a "bonus" between $100,000 and $1 million, depending on the successful conclusion of the case. Ronald's lawyer told me he was "incensed" when they discovered the agreement—it seemed to clearly run afoul of the ethical rules that forbid the payment of fact witnesses—and brought a lawsuit in New York in which a federal judge issued an opinion that called the contract "troublesome indeed irrespective of whether it constituted a crime." Lawyer Edward Wohl faced disciplinary charges in Florida based on the contract. In his testimony, Wohl suggested that he had relied on the expertise of Boies and Bob Silver. "The litigators for Bruce called the shots," Wohl testified. In March 2003, the Florida Supreme Court ruled that the offering of "financial inducements to a fact witness is extremely serious misconduct," and suspended Wohl for ninety days. Ronald also pursued disciplinary complaints against Boies in New York, but Boies's lawyer maintains that the contract passes muster under New York's ethical rules.

The Departmental Disciplinary Committee, an arm of New York's judicial system charged with oversight of attorney conduct, later sought "reciprocal discipline" against Wohl based on the Florida Supreme Court's finding of misconduct against him. On June 25, 2004, a five-judge New York appellate panel issued an unpublished order denying the Departmental Disciplinary Committee's petition against Wohl. On June 29, 2004, the Departmental Disciplinary Committee issued a letter to Boies stating that it had "administratively closed" the file in connection with Winston's complaint against him. No action was taken against Boies.

Mostly, Boies seemed drawn to clients with outsize personalities; he identified with those willing to take the ultimate risk. Often, these men or women were moguls who ran their businesses with an iron fist and had a penchant for bringing lawsuits. George Steinbrenner, the Yankees' owner, was one. Boies thrilled in his box seat at Yankee Stadium, and, according to his Boies Schiller partners, Steinbrenner cooed over his lawyer. But Steinbrenner's suit challenging all of Major League Baseball, the ostensible reason why Boies left Cravath, had ended with a whimper: in May 1998, the Yankees agreed to drop their lawsuit, and MLB signed a licensing and advertising deal with Adidas. The Yankees got to keep their $95 million deal. As part of the agreement, the league agreed to reinstate Steinbrenner, who had been suspended after filing the suit, to its executive council. But Steinbrenner paid a steep price for his audacious move: as part of the deal, the Yankees paid the legal fees of the baseball commissioner's office, which totaled about $500,000. (Steinbrenner later retained Boies again, in a fight with the cable operator Cablevision, over carriage of a new cable network that featured Yankees games.)

Boies took on the case of another mogul, Howard Milstein, at the height of the Microsoft trial. Milstein, a New York real estate magnate, had made a record bid of $800 million to purchase the Washington Redskins football franchise, but ran into trouble when the National Football League's commissioners began to question his financing. He walked away from the approval process and hired Boies to pursue a lawsuit. A column in the *Washington Post* piled on the superlatives about Boies's hiring: "When you hire David Boies as your lawyer, that's not a threat. That's a promise. Retaining Boies is to lawsuits what nuclear bombs are to warfare. It's the option that you choose when you are really, really serious." But, in this case, the bombs never detonated. The outcome of the litigation, in which Boies ultimately had little involvement, was a complete fiasco. Not only did the firm fail miserably on the claims that it alleged for Milstein, but it managed to lose him another $20 million, the amount of Milstein's deposit toward his bid to buy the Redskins, which the sellers offered to pay back if Milstein would stop suing everyone in sight.

Boies's latest client with audacious litigation goals is Darl McBride, the chief executive of a Utah-based software company called SCO Group. McBride has earned the wrath of the entire software industry by claiming that his company owns code in Linux, the free software that is the pioneer of the open-software movement. Linux is considered the best hope of freeing the software industry from the stranglehold dominance of the Microsoft Windows operating system—a fact mentioned frequently during the Microsoft antitrust trial. McBride believes that any user of Linux owes him a fee for the licensing of his intellectual property, and he hired Boies to step up the attack. Boies's first shot across the bow was a $3 billion lawsuit against IBM, one of Linux's largest corporate supporters, which is represented by Evan Chesler, Boies's former Cravath partner.

SCO gave Boies's law firm $1 million in cash and 400,000 shares of stock as part of an unusual contingency agreement to pursue the litigation. Boies's firm would receive 20 percent of judgments or settlements in the litigation—and 20 percent of SCO's sale price in the event that the company is sold. SCO has sent letters to fifteen hundred companies demanding licensing fees of about $700 for every server computer running the Linux operating system. To the growing and loyal Linux community, these threats amount to extortion. On SCO's side is none other than Microsoft, which is SCO's biggest licensee, and has paid SCO more than $10 million.

To the journalists following the SCO case, Boies's representation of McBride presented obvious ironies. But after Boies ended his representation of the Justice Department in the Microsoft suit, he didn't look back. For instance, he didn't seem to care that the Bush administration had swept into office and made a settlement with Microsoft that many believed to be a sweetheart deal. An elderly man approached Boies at a function in New York in November 2001, where Boies received an award from LD Access, a charity dedicated to the needs of those with learning disabilities such as dyslexia, eager to commiserate over the fate of the case. But Boies shrugged off the Republican settlement, as the old man just stared at him in awe. "Administrations change; policies change," Boies said simply, shrugging his shoulders.

Boies was equally uninterested in the recounts that the media pursued in the wake of the Supreme Court's ruling for Bush. In November 2001, a consortium of media outlets, including the *New York Times,* the *Washington Post,* and the *Wall Street Journal,* released the results of recounts that their collective auditors had been at work on for months. The media found that if Gore's four-county recount had gone forward according to his original plan—to recount the four counties of Broward, Miami-Dade, Palm Beach, and Volusia—Bush would have won the election by 225 votes. This scenario included the Palm Beach County recount, and therefore ignored the 3,300 ballots that, according to the Democrats, ought to have been looked at again. If, on the other hand, the statewide recount had occurred, as the Florida Supreme Court had ordered, using as the standard fully punched chads—the standard the Republicans demanded and the Gore team railed against—Gore would have won by 115 votes. If each county had used its own standard, Gore would have won by 171 votes, and if dimples were allowed on all the ballots, Gore would have won by 107 votes.

For a person of such fierce intelligence, Boies is one of the least reflective people I have known. I came to believe that it was part of his strength: in his own mind, he was always winning or about to win in any decision he made. Mary Boies put it best, when she described the process that led to his departure from Cravath: "He thought about it, but I don't think he thought about it for very long. He does not agonize over decisions. David will never be confused for Hamlet."

That Boies had taken the SCO case was not surprising to me. It was a high-stakes gamble, and Boies loves nothing more than that. He loves to play with the Jule dice.

The first time I heard the term was at lunch one day, with Boies and his law partner Paul Verkuil, at Sparks, the dark-paneled midtown Manhattan steakhouse that caters to men who crave red meat and martinis at lunch. (We were enjoying a 1996 Latour Reserve from the Beaulieu Vineyard.) Verkuil was playing with his food. He rolled up two little balls from the heart of a dinner roll and tossed them across the table. "The Jule dice!" Boies said, picking them up. I tried to play along, but when it became clear to Boies that I didn't know what he was talking about—a circumstance that he seemed to relish—Boies offered the explanation. He was referring to Big Jule, a character in the musical *Guys and Dolls.* Later, I rented a video of the 1965 movie, starring Frank Sinatra, and discovered why Boies, who didn't seem at all to be a fan of musicals, liked this one. It revolves around Boies's passion—gambling. At the beginning, Nathan Detroit, a small-time New York City hood, sets up the craps game of his life, and Big Jule, a gangster from Chicago, turns up as the most forbidding of the invitees. Down $25,000, Big Jule still wants to play, and offers his "marker"—a signed card that is the gambler's code of honor—for one more roll of the dice at craps. For the turn, he brings out his own dice, which have no spots on them. Big Jule tells Nathan Detroit that he had the spots removed for luck. "But I remember where the spots formerly were," Big Jule announces.

I had watched Boies roll the dice on a couple of occasions. The first was an icy weekend in Atlantic City, when Boies, his children Caryl and David III, and the Millers got together for Super Bowl Sunday in January 2001. Boies and Miller had terrible luck that weekend at the craps tables. Over the course of several hours, Boies had taken out more than $25,000 in markers. At one point, Miller turned to Boies to suggest that they continue. Boies looked at him coolly and said, "What are we going to do, stand around and lose all day?" Caryl, who had come to Atlantic City with $300 to gamble, was down $600 in the wee hours of Sunday morning, when her luck changed. She cashed out at about four-thirty on Sunday morning, taking home winnings of $900. At the cashier's booth, Caryl looked at her brother David and laughed, "What does Dad say? It's better to be lucky than smart?"

Boies had a better outing in Las Vegas that November, where he squeezed in an afternoon of craps to combine business with pleasure, quite literally. Boies had come to Vegas to argue a motion in a class action against the nation's casinos, alleging that video poker machines and electronic slot machines on the casino floors misrepresented the way they worked. Many members of the Boies tribe had worked on the lawsuit, among them Mary, who was along for the trip, and Caryl. Caryl was much more familiar with the lawsuit than her father, but he still insisted that she was wrong about the way the video poker machines worked when the topic came up as they were traveling together for Thanksgiving during the 2000 election. Caryl said she was willing to bet him even odds that she was right, but Boies suggested stakes of $60,000. If Caryl lost the bet, she could pay the debt with what Boies called "slave time." He wanted sixty hours of free labor. "Sixty

thousand dollars?" Caryl sputtered. "Who do you think I am? I'm a working girl! Sixty thousand dollars?" Cary was dumbfounded, but her father
was nonplussed. "But I'm not asking for sixty thousand dollars," he ventured, and Cary shot back, "Yes, you are!" The bet settled somehow—perhaps—on the figure of $30,000 or that equivalent in slave labor. But it
never went anywhere. On the eve of the casinos hearing, when I asked Cary
about it, she laughed, but couldn't quite remember the final figure. "He
always wants to bet an amount of money that the other person would be
uncomfortable with," she told me.

The hearing in Vegas, on whether a nationwide class could be certified,
suggested that the nation's video poker players might have a difficult time
getting their quarters back through this class action. Boies tried to focus on
the uniform alleged fraud in video poker, but the judge kept coming back to
the diverse millions who passed their time feeding quarters into the
machines. They ranged, the judge pointed out, from the woman who
throws a quarter into a machine at a gas station while waiting for her husband to fill the tank, to the inveterate gambler who spends thousands at the
casino slots. The victims were too diverse a lot under the class action rules.
"Do you have 100,000 different trials? This is what I'm struggling with,"
U.S. District Judge David Ezra remarked toward the end of Boies's argument. With the hearing over, Boies piled into a car and headed back to his
suite at the Golden Nugget, shaking hands with the card-counting gambler—a potential class member—who sat in on the hearing. "They won't let
me in there!" the man said, laughing, as Boies said his good-byes on his
way into the hotel.

Boies asked Mary where she would like to go, and they settled on the
Venetian. Boies opened a credit line of $250,000 within a couple of min-
utes. In the gambling trip to Atlantic City, I had had none of the luck that a
"craps virgin" is supposed to bring to the table. I fared much better in
Vegas, and, with every throw of the dice, my friends at the table cheered me
on, including the Boieses. For every time the shooter wins, the rest of the
gamblers at the table also collect. That is the thing about craps; it is a com-
munal game. The croupier, who moves the dice toward you when it is your
turn to play, shouts "Shooter, shooter!" The whole table is on your side,
especially if you are on a roll. I had never gambled in a casino before I met
Boies. And as I watched the scene, as I heard the cry for "Shooter, shooter,"
it was clear to me why he loved it so. To be the shooter is to be at center

stage. Everyone at the table cheers a shooter on a roll, though the streak is bound to end. It is inevitable, mathematically; eventually, a seven or eleven—deadly numbers once the game of craps is in play—will turn up if the shooter continues to roll. But Boies had no such worries. He was concerned with neither the past nor the future, but the present moment. And in that moment, he had the Jule dice in his pocket. He knew they would always be there for him, unspotted and perfect.

Acknowledgments

The inspiration for this book came during my coverage of the Microsoft trial, which turned into the assignment of my career. It was a great story and drew some of the biggest talents in the journalism business. One night, as the scrum of reporters bonded at our ritual drinks session, I mentioned that I thought there was a book in the role that Boies played as the government's chief prosecutor, all the while building his own nascent law firm. The enthusiastic response of my colleagues, among them Joseph Nocera of *Fortune* magazine, whose work I had long admired, encouraged me to pursue this project. Their support throughout my work on this book—a process that took longer than anyone, especially myself, thought it would—has been invaluable.

I am forever grateful to Mark Gitenstein, one of the sharpest lawyers on Capitol Hill, who put me in touch with his agent, the indomitable Flip Brophy. Flip was enthusiastic, and she and Jim Silberman, a veteran and sage book editor down to his suspenders, agreed to take on the project. I could not have been luckier. There were many days when I did not believe that I could finish this book, but their confidence in me never wavered. Jim steered me toward the right structure for the narrative when my year-in-the-life-of-Boies wasn't quite working and lent his keen eye through several drafts. Dan Frank, the editorial director at Pantheon, took a chance on a first-time author and was patient while I was writing and rewriting. His deft sense of pace in the final edits rescued the book from my impulse to cover all aspects of Boies's work in minute detail. His assistant, Rahel Lerner, could not have been more gracious or supportive.

To write the book, I left my job and home at the *National Law Journal*, where I had been a reporter and editor for almost ten years. The book sprang out of my coverage of the Microsoft case, which was only possible because my editors at American Lawyer Media, led by Aric Press, its editorial director, chose to devote the resources to provide gavel-to-gavel coverage of the trial. My editor at the *NLJ*, Patrick Oster, was patient when my daily coverage of the trial for other *Am Law* publications led to pressing deadlines on my weekly analysis of it for the paper where I worked.

David Boies offered to cooperate in this book before I had a contract, before I had anything other than the notion that his work on the Microsoft trial could be a book, and for that I am truly grateful. The book transmogrified into much more than that. My trailing of Boies inevitably meant that he and his wife, Mary, traveled with a reporter in tow and they were always in good humor about it, especially during a long stay in Tallahassee. Many people at Boies's law firm took time for me despite their chaotic schedules. I was particularly blessed by help from Boies's personal assistant, Patrick Dennis, who kept me apprised of Boies's hairpin schedule and helped me out in many uncountable ways, and by Boies's law partners Jonathan Schiller and Bob Silver, and Silver's hard-toiling assistant, Mary Ford. I am also grateful to the young lawyers at Boies's firm, both named and unnamed, who put up with a reporter in their midst and were candid with me about their experiences at the firm. Three of Boies's children work at his firm, and they gave me much of their time. I am particularly thankful to Boies's first wife, Caryl, and his second wife, Judith, for agreeing to speak with me.

My main focus was the man and his cases, and in reporting on them I got help from all quarters. Both during and after the Microsoft trial, members of Boies's legal team were generous with their time, among them Phil Malone, Steve Holtzman, and Karma Giulianelli, as well as Joel Klein, the Justice Department's antitrust chief, and Gina Talamona, his public affairs officer. I am also thankful to Microsoft's defense lawyers, John Warden and the ever-brave Michael Lacovara, and to the hard-pressed members of Microsoft's public relations team, among them Vivek Varma and Jim Cullinan. Judge Pierre Leval unearthed the ten-thousand-page transcript from the Westmoreland case from his files and allowed me access to his chambers to pore over it for my research. Hank Barry, Napster's chief executive, was true to the company's revolutionary bent and relaxed the attorney-client privilege so that I could witness Boies and his team as they prepared Napster's case—access that gave me an extraordinary window into how Boies worked. Ron Klain, Walter Dellinger, Jeremy Bash, Tom Goldstein, Mark Steinberg, Kendall Coffey, Mitchell Berger, and Dennis Newman were invaluable in helping me piece together the battle over the 2000 election, both in Tallahassee and afterward. Scores of partners and adversaries, some unnamed, helped me.

Boies is a steely character, and I was blessed by some candid revelations by the few who know him well, among them George Vradenburg III, Paul Verkuil, and Steve Brill. Boies's former Cravath partners, both named and unnamed, helped me enormously. Frank Barron even lent me his copy of the three-volume history of the Cravath firm.

Last, and most importantly, I owe my deepest thanks to the family and friends who have sustained me through the long and often lonely process of writing a book. This book is dedicated to my parents, who have always supported me. My cousin Frances prodded me to finish the book, my aunt Emma believed I could do it, and my brother Paul, thankfully, had a light touch in asking about how it was going. But I am also blessed by a wide family of friends. Julia Montgomery and her family, who have, quite literally, given me a home away from home since I moved to New York from Boston, lived through the ups and downs of this book from nearby Brooklyn, and celebrated each time that I thought I was finished. (There were several!) My oldest friends, Linda Waterman, Deborah Homer-O'Leary, and Karen Colucci, were so true in their faith in me. They listened over long hours of telephone conversations and visits to New England and Linda provided me with bed and board. I am also lucky to have a circle of reporter friends who gave me great advice throughout the project, among them Mike France of *Business Week*, and his wife, Shirim Nothenberg, a lawyer with Children's Rights. Mike, like me, is a former lawyer, and he gave me confidence that a book about Boies would work. I am indebted to the support of my former colleagues from the *NLJ*, Anthony Paonita, Douglas Hunt, Marianne Lavelle, Harvey Berkman, Marcia Coyle, Cynthia Cotts, and Fred Strasser. Fred taught me so much as my editor. John Wilke of the *Wall Street Journal*, Jim Rowley of Bloomberg, David Lawsky of Reuters, and Ken Auletta of the *New Yorker*, Microsoft trial buddies, all cheered me on. (When Ken signed his Microsoft book for me, he advised me to "write your book quick" and, alas, I was unable to follow that advice.) After my book was nearly done, I entered the Knight-Bagehot fellowship program for business journalists at Columbia, along with nine other journalists, and each of them was enthusiastic and excited for me.

All of them made this book possible, and I am grateful to them all.

Index

Printed in the United States
by Baker & Taylor Publisher Services